NEXUS OF GLOBAL JIHAD

COLUMBIA STUDIES IN TERRORISM
AND IRREGULAR WARFARE

COLUMBIA STUDIES IN TERRORISM AND IRREGULAR WARFARE

Bruce Hoffman, Series Editor

This series seeks to fill a conspicuous gap in the burgeoning literature on terrorism, guerrilla warfare, and insurgency. The series adheres to the highest standards of scholarship and discourse and publishes books that elucidate the strategy, operations, means, motivations, and effects posed by terrorist, guerrilla, and insurgent organizations and movements. It thereby provides a solid and increasingly expanding foundation of knowledge on these subjects for students, established scholars, and informed reading audiences alike.

Ami Pedahzur, *The Israeli Secret Services and the Struggle Against Terrorism*

Ami Pedahzur and Arie Perliger, *Jewish Terrorism in Israel*

Lorenzo Vidino, *The New Muslim Brotherhood in the West*

Erica Chenoweth and Maria J. Stephan, *Why Civil Resistance Works: The Strategic Logic of Nonviolent Resistance*

William C. Banks, *New Battlefields/Old Laws: Critical Debates on Asymmetric Warfare*

Blake W. Mobley, *Terrorism and Counterintelligence: How Terrorist Groups Elude Detection*

Jennifer Morrison Taw, *Mission Revolution: The U.S. Military and Stability Operations*

Guido W. Steinberg, *German Jihad: On the Internationalization of Islamist Terrorism*

Michael W. S. Ryan, *Decoding Al-Qaeda's Strategy: The Deep Battle Against America*

David H. Ucko and Robert Egnell, *Counterinsurgency in Crisis: Britain and the Challenges of Modern Warfare*

Bruce Hoffman and Fernando Reinares, editors, *The Evolution of the Global Terrorist Threat: From 9/11 to Osama bin Laden's Death*

Boaz Ganor, *Global Alert: The Rationality of Modern Islamist Terrorism and the Challenge to the Liberal Democratic World*

M. L. R. Smith and David Martin Jones, *The Political Impossibility of Modern Counterinsurgency: Strategic Problems, Puzzles, and Paradoxes*

Elizabeth Grimm Arsenault, *How the Gloves Came Off: Lawyers, Policy Makers, and Norms in the Debate on Torture*

ASSAF MOGHADAM

NEXUS OF GLOBAL JIHAD

Understanding Cooperation Among Terrorist Actors

Columbia University Press / New York

Columbia University Press
Publishers Since 1893
New York   Chichester, West Sussex
cup.columbia.edu
Copyright © 2017 Assaf Moghadam
Paperback edition, 2019

Library of Congress Cataloging-in-Publication Data
Names: Moghadam, Assaf, 1974– author.
Title: Nexus of global Jihad : understanding cooperation among
terrorist actors / Assaf Moghadam.
Description: New York : Columbia University Press, [2017] |
Series: Columbia studies in terrorism and irregular warfare |
Includes bibliographical references and index.
Identifiers: LCCN 2016056245 (print) | LCCN 2017014117 (ebook) |
ISBN 9780231538152 (e-book) | ISBN 9780231165372 (cloth) |
ISBN 9780231165365 (pbk.)
Subjects: LCSH: Terrorism. | Terrorism—Religious aspects—Islam. |
Cooperation—Poliitcal aspects. | Strategy. | Alliances.
Classification: LCC HV6431 (ebook) | LCC HV6431 .M634 2017 (print) |
DDC 363.325—dc23
LC record available at https://lccn.loc.gov/2016056245

Cover design: Martin N. Hinze

For N. E. and J., with love

CONTENTS

Acknowledgments ix
List of Abbreviations xiii

INTRODUCTION

1

PART I
UNDERSTANDING CONTEMPORARY
TERRORIST COOPERATION

1. THE PUZZLE OF TERRORIST COOPERATION

17

2. ACTOR SPECTRUM:
Organizations, Networks, and Entrepreneurs

42

3. SHIFTING ENVIRONMENT:
Ideology, Social Media, and Armed Conflicts

68

4. CONTEMPORARY TERRORIST COOPERATION:
A Holistic Typology

97

PART II
TERRORIST COOPERATION
IN THE GLOBAL JIHAD

5. PRE-9/11 COOPERATION IN THE GLOBAL JIHAD

123

6. POST-9/11 COOPERATION IN THE GLOBAL JIHAD

144

7. HIGH-END COOPERATION:
Al Qaeda and Al Qaeda in the Arabian Peninsula (AQAP)

170

8. LOW-END COOPERATION:
Al Qaeda, Iran, and Hizballah

195

9. NETWORKED COOPERATION:
From Bojinka to the Sharia4 Movement

222

CONCLUSION

261

Notes 279
Bibliography 335
Index 365

ACKNOWLEDGMENTS

THIS BOOK has been several years in the making and would not have seen the light of day were it not for the support I received along the way from my family, friends, colleagues, research assistants, and students.

My first thanks goes to the administration and faculty at the Interdisciplinary Center Herzliya (IDC), which welcomed me with open arms when it became my new academic home in February 2011. I would like to thank Uriel Reichman, the IDC's president, for continuing to steer this uniquely vibrant institution with inspiring leadership and vision. I would also like to extend my gratitude to the IDC's provost, Mario Mikulincer, and to its vice president, Jonathan Davis, for their contributions to making the IDC the success story that it has become.

The Lauder School of Government, Diplomacy, and Strategy at IDC has served as an intellectually stimulating environment for me to pursue my research. I would like to thank Boaz Ganor, the Lauder School's dean, for his leadership and friendship. For their helpful comments, suggestions, and encouragement, I would also like to thank my Lauder School colleagues Dima Adamsky, Amnon Cavari, Asif Efrat, Sivan Hirsch-Hoefler, Amichai Magen, Shavit Matias, Alex Mintz, Shaul Mishal, Daphne Richemond-Barak, Liza Saban, and Lesley Terris. Special thanks go to Maoz Rosenthal, who has been especially generous with his time and who provided sage advice throughout the life of the project.

I am also grateful to my colleagues and the capable support staff at the International Institute for Counter-Terrorism (ICT), a home within a home at IDC, led by Boaz Ganor and Deputy Director Eitan Azani. I have benefited in particular from discussions with Yoni Fighel. My valued colleague Ely Karmon shared with me some of his immense knowledge of terrorism, read the entire manuscript, and provided many helpful comments. Stevie Weinberg, ICT's indispensable director of operations, deserves special thanks for sharing his insights on jihadism in Belgium.

I have been fortunate to be able to count on a small army of capable and dedicated research assistants. The fruits of their labor are found on every page of this book. They include Amber Atteridge, Ria Barber, Kasey Barr, Eli Cornblit, Robby Dunn-Bernstein, Nirran Hebron, David Hoffman, Tali Jona, Hannah Katz, Eve Mamane, Gilad Mayer, Kajsa Mayo, Robert Pulwer, Gideon Scher, Nicolas Seidman, Tal Shaanan, Yael Shuval, Liat Studnik, and Ranan Tannenbaum. I would like to highlight in particular the outstanding contributions of five research assistants. Zachary Schenk has done a phenomenal job gathering information on AQAP and terrorist entrepreneurs. Danit Gal has contributed substantial portions to the discussion on the use of the Internet for terrorist cooperation. Michel Wyss, an expert on jihadism in his own right, provided many insightful comments, while correcting a few mistakes along the way. Polina Beliakova deserves my gratitude for her careful reading of the text and her outstanding comments throughout, especially on the theoretical sections of the book. Finally, Ronit Berger has played multiple critical roles in this book from the very outset, which included not only coordinating the entire project but also serving as a sounding board for my half-baked ideas. She too provided many useful comments that strengthened the final product significantly.

I have also benefited from comments I received from IDC students, especially those in the MA Program in Counter-Terrorism and Homeland Security between the years 2012 and 2016.

In addition, I am indebted to a large number of colleagues who have contributed to this book by offering words of encouragement, advice, and guidance or by inspiring me through their own work on terrorism. I owe a particular debt to Bruce Hoffman, a dear friend, colleague, and mentor who never hid his enthusiasm for this research project and supported it from day one. I am also grateful to Martha Crenshaw, a valued friend and colleague who personifies intellectual excellence and curiosity and serves as an inspiration to me and countless other students of terrorism. For their valuable advice on this project I would like to thank in particular Max Abrahms, Gary Ackerman, Benjamin Acosta, Rogelio Alonso, Aymenn Jawad al-Tamimi, Peter Bergen, J. M. Berger, Michael Boyle, Bill Braniff, Alexander Evans, Brian Fishman, James Forest, Daveed Gartenstein-Ross, Ogen Goldman, Thomas Hegghammer, Matthew Levitt, Shiraz Maher, Alexander Meleagrou-Hitchens, Barak Mendelsohn, Yassin Musharbash, Ami Pedahzur, Arie Perliger, Brian Philipps, Bryan Price, Paul Quinn, Don Rassler, Fernando Reinares, Alex Schmid, Yoram Schweitzer, Richard Shultz, Guido Steinberg, Jessica Stern, Clint Watts, Florian Wätzel, and Aaron Zelin.

I would also like to acknowledge the insightful comments I have received from two anonymous reviewers, which significantly improved the manuscript.

Tricia Bacon deserves my special thanks for sharing with me her deep insights on terrorist cooperation, which have informed many parts of this book. She has been a true partner in crime while we were both pursuing research along very similar lines.

I am also especially grateful to Dan Byman for kindly and readily agreeing to review the chapter on Al Qaeda's cooperation with Iran and providing thoughtful comments. I have also benefited tremendously from discussions with Ron Hassner, who gave me much needed advice on the theoretical sections of the book. Special thanks also go to Lorenzo Vidino, who generously provided me with the English language versions of his edited volume on the Sharia4 movement, currently available only in Arabic.

I would also like to thank the Cluster of Excellence "Normative Orders" at Goethe-Universität Frankfurt for inviting me to give a talk on terrorist cooperation, after which the audience offered many helpful suggestions. I thank especially Christopher Daase, Nicole Deitelhoff, and Janusz Biene for arranging the talk and for providing useful feedback. I would also like to thank Peter Neumann and the International Centre for the Study of Radicalization at Kings College London (ICSR) for co-organizing (together with ICT and the Norwegian Defence Research Establishment) an event on the future of jihadism held in the memory of the late Reuven Paz and giving me an opportunity to present my work in progress and receive several useful comments.

I am immensely grateful to the Smith Richardson Foundation, which provided a generous grant through its Strategy Fellows Program without which this book could not have been written. My thanks go in particular to the foundation's senior program officer, Allan Song, and to its friendly and competent administrative staff, Paula Landesberg, Dale Stewart, and Kathy Lavery.

At Columbia University Press, my thanks go to Senior Editor Anne Routon for being a staunch supporter of this book from the outset and overseeing the publication process with such competence. I would also like to thank Erin Davis and Michael Haskell for coordinating the production of the book, and especially Tatiana Holway for her outstanding copyediting of the manuscript.

I would be remiss not to mention my dear friends and colleagues Reuven Paz and Jonathan Fine, from whom I learned so much. Their untimely and sudden passing has left a deep void. May their memory be blessed.

Last, but not least, I would like to express my deepest gratitude to the most important people in my life: my parents for their unconditional love and selfless support, and my wife for her love, encouragement, and patience. I dedicate this book to our children, who keep reminding us every day of the goodness in this world.

ABBREVIATIONS

ABM	Ansar Bayt al-Maqdis
AD	Action Directe (Direct Action)
AIAI	Ittihad al-Islami
AM	Al-Muhajiroun
AMEF	Ansar al-Mujahideen English Forum
ANO	Abu Nidal Organization (a.k.a. Fatah–Revolutionary Council)
AQAP	Al Qaeda in the Arabian Peninsula (based in Yemen)
AQAP-SBY	Al Qaeda in the Arabian Peninsula–Soldiers Brigade of Yemen
AQC	Al Qaeda Central
AQI	Al Qaeda in Iraq
AQIM	Al Qaeda in the Islamic Maghreb
AQSAP	Al Qaeda in the Southern Arabian Peninsula
ASG	Abu Sayyaf Group
BIF	Benevolence International Foundation
CNG	Clan Na Gael
CTC	Combating Terrorism Center at West Point
DFLP	Democratic Front for the Liberation of Palestine

DNI	Director of National Intelligence
EIG	Egyptian Islamic Group (Gamaah Islamiya)
EIJ	Egyptian Islamic Jihad
EOKA	National Organization of Cypriot Fighters
ETA	Euskadi Ta Askatasuna (Basque Country and Freedom)
FARC	Fuerzas Armadas Revolucionarias de Colombia (Revolutionary Armed Forces of Colombia)
GAM	Free Aceh Movement
GIA	Armed Islamic Group
GICM	Moroccan Islamist Combatant Group
GSPC	Groupe Salafist pour la Prédication et le Combat (Salafist Group for Call and Combat)
HM	Hizb-ul Mujahideen
HQN	Haqqani Network
HT	Hizb ut-Tahrir
HUJI	Harkat-ul-Jihad al-Islami
ICU	Islamic Courts Union
IJU	Islamic Jihad Union
IMU	Islamic Movement of Uzbekistan
IRA	(Provisional) Irish Republican Army
IRB	Irish Republican Brotherhood
IRGC	Iranian Revolutionary Guard Corps
IS	Islamic State
ISI	Islamic State in Iraq
ISIS	Islamic State in Iraq and Greater Syria
JEM	Jaish-e Muhammad
JFS	Jabhat Fath al-Sham
JI	Jemaah Islamiya
JN	Jabhat al-Nusra
JRA	Japanese Red Army
LEJ	Lashkar-e Jhangvi
LET	Lashkar-e Taiba
LIFG	Libyan Islamic Fighting Group

LTTE	Liberation Tigers of Tamil Eelam
MAC	Muslims Against Crusades
MAK	Maktab al-Khidamat (Services Bureau)
MAP	Mujahidun on the Arabian Peninsula
MILF	Moro Islamic Liberation Front
MOIS	Ministry of Intelligence and Security (Iran)
MSM	Majlis Shura al-Mujahideen
MUJAO	Movement for Oneness and Jihad in Africa
PFLP	Popular Front for the Liberation of Palestine
PFLP-EO	Popular Front for the Liberation of Palestine–External Operations (a.k.a. Wadie Haddad Faction)
PFLP-GC	Popular Front for the Liberation of Palestine–General Command
PIJ	Palestinian Islamic Jihad
PKK	Kurdistan Workers Party
PLO	Palestine Liberation Organization
PULO	Patani United Liberation Organization
QAP	Al Qaeda in the Arabian Peninsula (based in Saudi Arabia)
RAF	Rote Armee Fraktion (Red Army Faction)
RB	Brigate Rosse (Red Brigades)
RUF	Revolutionary United Front
RZ	Revolutionäre Zellen (Revolutionary Cells)
TIKKO	Liberation Army of the Workers and Peasants of Turkey
TTP	Tehrik-e Taliban Pakistan
UVF	Ulster Volunteer Force

NEXUS OF GLOBAL JIHAD

INTRODUCTION

WHO PLANNED the attacks of September 11, 2001? The answer is not as obvious as it may seem. Conspiracy theories aside, Al Qaeda is typically considered the perpetrator, although the fact is that the jihadist group did not act alone. Instead, the most devastating attacks on the United States since Pearl Harbor were the fruits of cooperation between two different types of terrorist actors: on the one hand, Al Qaeda, the organization founded by Osama bin Laden in 1988; on the other, an independent Kuwaiti jihadist who approached the group's leader in 1996 with an idea that would make history.

As the *9/11 Commission Report* states, the 9/11 plots were originally devised by Khaled Sheikh Muhammad, an ingenious and highly motivated individual with prior involvement in terrorism. KSM, as Western intelligence services came to refer to him, was not a member of Al Qaeda when he first approached bin Laden with a grandiose proposal to hijack ten U.S. aircraft, crash nine of them into targets on both U.S. coasts, steer and land the tenth plane himself, kill all adult male passengers on board, and then hold a press conference denouncing the United States, Israel, and other enemies of jihad.[1] Nor did KSM agree to swear allegiance to bin Laden two years later, when the Al Qaeda leader accepted a scaled down version of KSM's original proposal.[2] According to bin Laden's new plan, which involved reducing the number of airliners to be hijacked and limiting the attacks to strategic targets on the East Coast, KSM would not fly a plane himself. He would, however, receive all the necessary manpower and material support to turn his plan into reality.[3]

It may not be an explicit conclusion of the *9/11 Commission Report*, but it is an inescapable one nevertheless: Cooperation between different terrorist actors played a critical role in the success of the most consequential terrorist attack in modern history. While this role is not entirely unknown, it is, like terrorist cooperation in general, largely overlooked. "Scholars of terrorism," Barak Mendelsohn noted as recently as 2015, are "only beginning to explore the dynamics of inter-organizational relations."[4]

Cooperation between terrorist organizations has indeed received scant attention to date, and in the case of 9/11 our knowledge gap is even deeper. For the 9/11 attacks were not a product of interorganizational terrorist cooperation, but of collaboration between altogether distinct types of actors: a formal organization and what the *9/11 Commission Report* refers to as a "terrorist entrepreneur."

The collaboration between different types of terrorist actors is not unique to the 9/11 attacks. Rather, it is representative of a growing trend in which activities directly and indirectly related to terrorism increasingly involve some level of interplay among a diverse array of militant actors. Besides formal terrorist and insurgent organizations and individual terrorist "entrepreneurs" like KSM, terrorist actors also come in the form of states and, increasingly, informal networks. Note, for example, the growing influence of informal Salafist and jihadist networks in Europe. Some of the most militant of these networks, such as Sharia4Belgium, have facilitated the travel of foreign fighters to conflict areas in Syria, Iraq, and elsewhere, where their members have trained and fought with groups such as Jabhat al-Nusra and the Islamic State.[5] In other cases, informal networks of foreign fighters have functioned as intermediaries between cooperating organizations, such as the Islamic State and some of its local partners.[6] As is the case with 9/11, these and similar activities are not generally seen in terms of terrorist cooperation. This book, however, not only argues that they should be, but also constructs a novel framework precisely for understanding how contemporary terrorist actors cooperate.

There is a growing assortment of terrorist and jihadist actors who are both motivated to and capable of working together, sometimes with painful consequences for their enemies. These collaborations, in turn, are facilitated by several environmental factors, including jihadist ideology, which has proven remarkably resilient and provides a key motivation for jihadist actors to seek innovative ways to cooperate in order to advance their goals. Today's enabling environment also features numerous insurgencies and civil wars in places such as Syria, Iraq, Yemen, and Libya, which offer insurgent and terrorist actors ample opportunities to join forces. Moreover, the Internet further facilitates terrorist cooperation, especially through social media platforms such as Facebook or Twitter, which enable terrorists to communicate with each other at the push of a few buttons and even to plan attacks. In August 2013, for example, U.S. authorities intercepted electronic communications between Al Qaeda leader Ayman and the leaders of some associated groups, including Al Qaeda in the Arabian Peninsula (AQAP), in which al-Zawahiri called upon his allies to conduct terrorist attacks.[7]

In addition to the growing diversity of actors and a highly enabling environment, contemporary terrorist cooperation can take a multitude of forms, whether ideological, logistical, operational, or any combination of these. Moreover, actors can engage in different types of relationships with each other, agreeing to a noncommittal relationship involving a limited number of transactions, for example, or creating a short-term tactical partnership. Relationships can also take the form of longer term strategic alliances. In extreme cases, terrorist actors may pool all of their members and resources together permanently to establish full-blown mergers. Some terrorist collaborations exist despite differences in the ideological orientations of these entities. Indeed, while some of them are ideologically aligned and others have incompatible world views, ideological alignment is no guarantee of ongoing cooperation, as is illustrated by the rift between Al Qaeda and the Islamic State.

One and the same terrorist entity can establish multiple forms of cooperation with a variety of partners, sometimes creating the strangest of bedfellows. Al Qaeda, for example, has struck a range of partnerships since its founding, and in 2001, it concluded a full-scale merger with another organization, the Egyptian Islamic Jihad, renaming the newly enlarged entity Qaedat al-Jihad. Al Qaeda has also struck formal alliances with other partners in places like Iraq, Yemen, Somalia, Algeria, and Syria, as well as engaging in less formal associations with entities such as the Afghan and Pakistani Taliban and the Haqqani Network. In still other cases, Al Qaeda has cooperated with groups it opposes. For example, Al Qaeda's Syrian affiliate, Jabhat al-Nusra (now known as Jabhat Fath al-Sham), has engaged in limited cooperation with the Islamic State, in spite of the official rupture between Al Qaeda and the Islamic State that occurred in 2014.[8] In a more extreme case, militant Sunni Al Qaeda is known to have cooperated with Shiite Iran—a collaboration that defies the notion that cooperation is conditional upon ideological affinity.

In sum, with increasingly diverse terrorist actors benefiting from a highly enabling environment in order to engage in a broad range of cooperative relationships, the terrorist landscape has become extremely complex. In exploring the interwoven and multifaceted dynamics that make up this landscape, this book examines the following research question: How do contemporary terrorist actors cooperate? As I will demonstrate, these developments are of major policy importance because, far from being a marginal phenomenon within terrorism, terrorist cooperation permeates and defines much of the threat that terrorism poses today.

My main argument is that contemporary terrorist cooperation combines established forms of organizational cooperation with novel forms of what I call *networked cooperation*. In contrast to *organizational cooperation*, which refers to collaboration between formal terrorist organizations, networked cooperation involves at least one informal terrorist actor—that is, an informal network or a terrorist entrepreneur. I further argue that both organizational and networked forms of cooperation can feature relationships of varying qualitative strengths. To that end, I offer a new conceptual distinction between "high-end" cooperation and "low-end" cooperation.

To examine the book's main question and formulate the main argument, I establish a comprehensive and dynamic typology of terrorist cooperation, which several case studies illustrate and validate. This typology consists of two stages that together form a "holistic" model. These two stages represent two important insights: first, that contemporary terrorist cooperation can occur between different types of terrorist actors (stage 1); and second, that these relationships can also differ in terms of their strength, or quality (stage 2). Thus, in describing the first stage, I present six types of cooperation that differ from each other in terms of the types of actors who collaborate. The first of these six types is the classic form of organizational cooperation, while the remaining five represent variants of networked cooperation. These variants reflect the fact that several informal actors—including informal networks and terrorist entrepreneurs—can cooperate among themselves, as well as with formal terrorist organizations. In the second stage of the typology, I distinguish varying types of relationships in terms of their quality. To that end, I distinguish "high-end" cooperative relationships, which include mergers and strategic alliances, from "low-end" cooperative relationships, which include tactical and transactional collaborations. Table I.1 illustrates the combination of these stages in a holistic model. It also shows that each of the six types of cooperation identified in stage 1 can be further broken down in terms of the nature of the relationship between the relevant actors, resulting in a total of twenty-four ideal types of cooperation. Thus, for example, organizational cooperation between two formal organizations, as represented by the center box in table I.1, can be further classified in one of four ways: as a transactional cooperation, a tactical cooperation, a strategic alliance, or a merger. The same applies for each of the five variants of networked cooperation.

"Explanatory typologies," Colin Elman has noted, are "powerful tools in the qualitative study of international politics."[9] As I will show, my typology can be particularly valuable for scholars and policy analysts alike for several reasons. First, it accounts for both actor-based and qualitative differences in terrorist cooperation. Second, it is highly dynamic. As will be seen in chapter 4, where the typology is discussed in detail, it can account

TABLE I.1 A HOLISTIC TYPOLOGY OF TERRORIST COOPERATION

	Terrorist Entrepreneurs		Terrorist/Insurgent Organizations		Informal Networks	
Terrorist Entre-preneurs	Networked Coop. (Variant 1)	Mergers*	Networked Coop. (Variant 2)	Mergers**	Networked Coop. (Variant 3)	Mergers
		Strat. Alliances		Strat. Alliances		Strat. Alliances
		Tactical Coop.		Tactical Coop.		Tactical Coop.
		Transact. Coop.		Transact. Coop.		Transact. Coop.
Terrorist/ Insurgent Organi-zations			Organizational Cooperation	Mergers	Networked Coop. (Variant 4)	Mergers
				Strat. Alliances		Strat. Alliances
				Tactical Coop.		Tactical Coop.
				Transact. Coop.		Transact. Coop.
Informal Networks					Networked Coop. (Variant 5)	Mergers
						Strat. Alliances
						Tactical Coop.
						Transact. Coop.

*A merger between two terrorist entrepreneurs amounts to the establishment of an informal network.

**A merger between a terrorist entrepreneur and a formal organization entails the incorporation of the entrepreneur into the organization.

for changes in the identity of actors over time; it assumes that the boundaries between different qualities of cooperative relationships are soft, meaning that a given relationship can lie "in between" two ideal types; and it acknowledges that relationships of cooperation may change over time. Third, it can be extended to include additional terrorist actors not dealt with at length, such as states.

The typology is empirically grounded in qualitative data on terrorist cooperation, compiled from a multitude of historical and contemporary sources, including terrorism and jihadism studies.[10] It is also based on analysis of primary sources, such as original documents attributed to Al Qaeda and released by the Combating Terrorism Center at West Point (CTC) and the Office of the Director of National Intelligence (DNI).[11]

Theoretically, my typology is informed by the agent-structure debate—a debate devoted to the timeless question about whether social change is brought about by humans and their organizations (i.e., agency) or by broader environmental processes (i.e., structure).[12] The value of the agent-structure framework is that it is able to capture the two fundamental processes that affect how contemporary terrorist actors cooperate—namely, the changing nature of actors (agents) and their enabling environments (structure). To date, few scholars have operationalized the agent-structure problem to explain contemporary social problems.[13] The application of this conceptual framework to nonstate actors, and especially to the problem of terrorism, is particularly rare and represents an important theoretical contribution of the book apart from its policy relevance.[14]

In addition to developing this typology, I also devote several chapters to a chronological overview of terrorist cooperation in the global jihad movement from the origins of Al Qaeda to the rise of the Islamic State to case studies that illustrate the validity of the typology and, more generally, the book's main argument.

As space limitations do not permit the illustration of all twenty-four types of cooperation reflected in table I.1, I selected case studies based on their ability to showcase the differences between high-end and low-end cooperation and between organizational and networked cooperation, which are the main dimensions of the holistic typology. In addition, one case study illustrates the convergence of these dimensions.

DEFINITIONS AND SCOPE OF THE BOOK

For the purpose of this book, I define *cooperation* as consisting of formal or informal collaborative arrangements made in the pursuit of joint interests. *Formal arrangements* involve explicit agreements between the parties, while *informal arrangements* involve tacit agreements between the parties.[15] Both kinds of arrangements can govern a range of activities, including resource-sharing, strategic coordination, tactical collaboration, and transactional exchanges.[16] They also include ideological statements of support insofar as such statements are made explicitly, are expressed through public and formal channels, and are mutual.

As Tricia Bacon observes, such formal or informal arrangements involve a "conscious effort to work together."[17] This excludes from the definition uncoordinated behavior that may happen to be mutually beneficial, but was not originally designed to that end. For example, Al Qaeda's successful use of multiple suicide attacks on September 11, 2001, served as an inspiration to other jihadist groups, some of whom adopted suicide attacks as a result.[18] This served the ideological goals of all parties concerned, but since inspiration is not a coordinated behavior, post-9/11 suicide attacks would not be considered an example of terrorist cooperation.

Or take the example of the Weather Underground, a Marxist group active in the United States between 1969 and 1973, whose leader, Bernardine Dohrn, declared, "Now we are adapting the classic guerrilla strategy of the Viet Cong and the urban guerrilla strategy of the Tupamaros to our own situation here in the most technically advanced country in the world."[19] Short of evidence that the Viet Cong and the Tupamaros were similarly inspired by the Weather Underground, such unilateral declarations do not amount to terrorist cooperation as defined here.

In accordance with the above definition of cooperation, I define *terrorist cooperation* per se as involving formal or informal collaborative arrangements between two or more actors who employ terrorist tactics in the pursuit of joint interests. Here, *terrorism* itself refers to premeditated, extra-normal violence against civilian or noncombatant targets, which is aimed at influencing a wider audience and achieving political ends through the deliberate creation of fear.[20]

Terrorist actors, for present purposes, include states, formal terrorist and/or insurgent organizations, informal networks, and so-called terrorist entrepreneurs. The book's main theoretical and empirical focus, however, is on cooperation between sub-state terrorist actors. The role of states is largely excluded from the present analysis partly because of space limitations and partly because cooperation between states and substate terrorist actors has received greater attention in the academic literature to date.[21] At the same time, because I recognize the important role that states continue to play in terrorism, I do refer to the role of states in terrorist cooperation in the first part of the book. I also examine the case of cooperation between Al Qaeda and the Islamic Republic of Iran in the second part, where I also suggest how the typology can be extended to account for state actors in the conclusion.

I also exclude from my analysis cooperation between terrorist actors and criminal groups. Although some criminal groups may employ terrorist tactics, they pursue primarily financial, rather than political goals, and I therefore do not consider them terrorist actors for present purposes. Furthermore, there is an established literature already available on the nexus between terrorist and criminal organizations.[22]

WHY TERRORIST COOPERATION MATTERS

Terrorist cooperation matters for several reasons. The first is that cooperation among terrorist actors demonstrably boosts the capacity and performance of terrorist groups. Existing research has shown that embeddedness in alliances with other militant groups increases a terrorist group's longevity, level of violence, and lethality.[23] Highly embedded groups are also more prone to adopt or seek access to innovative tactics such as suicide bombings or chemical, biological, radiological, or nuclear (CBRN) weapons.[24] As Kanisha Bond points out, such enhanced performance of militant groups also raises the bargaining leverage that these groups enjoy.[25]

Contemporary examples from two of the most formidable jihadist organizations today, Jabhat al-Nusra (renamed to Jabhat Fath al-Sham in July 2016) and the Islamic State, confirm these scholarly findings. For Jabhat al-Nusra, Al Qaeda's formal affiliate in Syria, for example, entering into coalitions with other rebel groups has been a core element of its strategy to gain a firm foothold in Syria. Such alliances have helped the group win broad acceptance among Syrian opposition movements and paved the way for Jabhat al-Nusra to adopt a more assertive ideological stance later on.[26]

The Islamic State has also engaged in valuable cooperative arrangements with other groups. By early 2016, the group boasted partners in Afghanistan, Algeria, the Caucasus, Egypt, Libya, Nigeria, Pakistan, Saudi Arabia, and Yemen, among other places, where it declared so-called *wilayat* (provinces). In Libya, for example, the Islamic State crafted alliances with local jihadists to prepare its takeover of the city of Sirte.[27] In most regions where the group has established a foothold, its local partners have been able to boost their propaganda capabilities, obtain money, receive technical assistance, and gain access to foreign fighters. In return, cooperation has brought dividends to the Islamic State. Overseeing a growing network of associates, the Islamic State can more easily spread its jihadist ideology. By extending its brand to other groups, it also maintains a semblance of "momentum" that portrays the group as more powerful than is actually the case, which, in turn, helps it attract more recruits. As Daniel Byman notes, newly associated groups provide the Islamic State both strategic reach, by enabling the Islamic State to establish bases from which to attack nearby countries, and "fallback options, creating potential refuges for its leaders" if the group suffers military losses in its core region of Iraq and Syria.[28]

Terrorist cooperation also matters because it defines and underlies much of the contemporary threat posed by terrorism. As one important study notes, "Terrorist interactions are a key aspect of understanding terrorist threats."[29] As mentioned, this observation applies in particular to the global jihadist movement, which continues to pose the most urgent terrorist challenge today, and which is the focus of the empirical discussion in this book.[30] To illustrate the importance of global jihadist actors in contemporary terrorism, as well as the key role that cooperation plays in the global jihad, we can look to data from the Global Terrorism Database (GTD) for 2012. In that year, the six most lethal groups were all associated in some form with Al Qaeda and the global jihad movement. Together, the Taliban, Boko Haram, the Islamic State in Iraq, Tehrik-e Taliban

Pakistan, Al Qaeda in the Arabian Peninsula (AQAP), and al-Shabaab were responsible for at least five thousand fatalities.[31] In his presentation of the data during testimony to the House Armed Services Committee in 2014, Consortium for the Study of Terrorism and Responses to Terrorism (START) Executive Director Bill Braniff argued that these figures "reinforce the hypothesis that groups generally associated with Al Qaeda remain the most lethal groups in the world."[32] It stands to reason, then, that their cooperative relationship with Al Qaeda at least partly explains the high fatality rate they are able to effect.

In a more recent congressional statement on the *Worldwide Threat Assessment of the U.S. Intelligence Community*, U.S. director of National Intelligence James Clapper confirmed the ongoing relevance of global jihadist groups as a threat to the international order. The statement, delivered to the Senate in February 2016, highlighted in particular the "preeminent terrorist threat" posed by the Islamic State. Clapper's remarks are particularly revealing of the great extent to which the threats ascribed to the Islamic State and other jihadist actors derive from their ability to cooperate with other militant actors, while leveraging that cooperation to further their objectives. According to Clapper, the Islamic State (also known as ISIS or ISIL) derives its power in part from "its branches and emerging branches in other countries, and its increasing ability to direct and inspire attacks against a wide range of targets around the world. The group's narrative," Clapper added, "supports jihadist recruiting, attracts others to travel to Iraq and Syria, draws individuals and groups to declare allegiance to ISIL, and justifies attacks across the globe."[33] He also noted that dozens of individuals were arrested in 2015 in the United States alone, most "for attempting to provide material support to ISIL."

According to his assessment, the Islamic State's branches "continue to build a strong global network that aims to advance the group's goals."[34] The group also continues to inspire potential adherents due to its use of "highly sophisticated media."[35] It has managed to attract thousands of foreign fighters who "might potentially leverage skills and experience to plan and execute attacks in the West."[36] Lastly, Clapper predicts that "ISIL will seek to influence previously established groups, such as Boko Haram in

Nigeria, to emphasize the group's ISIL identity and fulfill its religious obligations to the ISIL 'caliphate.'"[37]

DNI Clapper's February 2016 assessment of terrorism also addressed threats posed by other terrorist actors, as well as emphasizing trends and patterns that relate to cooperation among them. Observing that Sunni violent militant groups are "increasingly joining or initiating insurgencies," he added that while some have instigated insurgencies single-handedly, others, including the Islamic State and Al Qaeda in the Islamic Maghreb, "have worked with local militants to incite insurgencies."[38] Still others, including Al Qaeda Central, "have taken advantage of the relative safe haven in areas controlled by insurgent groups to build capabilities and alliances without taking on a primary leadership role in the local conflict."[39]

DNI Clapper's statement also highlights some of the environmental factors that help enable contemporary terrorist cooperation. "Some terrorists," he says, adopt new technologies "to increase the speed of their communications, the availability of their propaganda, and ability to collaborate with new partners. They will easily take advantage of widely available, free encryption technology, mobile-messaging applications, the dark web, and virtual environments to pursue their objectives."[40]

In sum, the above paragraphs indicate a clear and growing relevance of terrorist cooperation. They also indicate a chaotic terrorist environment in which an increasingly diverse set of terrorist actors, oftentimes active in areas of conflict where they enjoy a safe haven, exploit new technologies and other opportunities to collaborate with like-minded actors in multiple ways.

PLAN OF THE BOOK

The book is divided into two parts. Part 1 offers a theoretical and conceptual analysis of terrorist cooperation, while part 2 focuses on examples and analysis of cooperation within the global jihad movement.

While the first chapter of the book presents the main insights gained to date into the question of why and how terrorists cooperate, the next two chapters introduce the theoretical framework of the book, take up the agent-structure debate, and justify its application to the problem of terrorist cooperation. More specifically, chapter 2 describes today's diverse terrorist actors (or terrorist "agents," in the parlance of the framework) and examines the extent to which cooperation among them extends beyond formal terrorist organizations to include informal networks and terrorist entrepreneurs. Chapter 3 then applies the agent-structure framework to explore the contemporary environment (the "structure") that enables these terrorist agents to flourish and to cooperate and highlights three factors of special importance: jihadist ideology as a motive for cooperation; the use of the Internet and social media as the main medium of cooperation; and the prevalence of armed conflicts, which provide ample opportunities for collaboration. Drawing on the preceding chapters, chapter 4 argues that contemporary cooperation is best understood as combining traditional organizational cooperation with novel forms of networked cooperation; introduces the distinction between "high-end" and "low-end" cooperation as a means for gauging qualitative differences in various cooperative relationships; and then offers a holistic and dynamic typology based on these insights and concepts.

Part 2 begins with a historical overview of terrorist cooperation in the global jihad movement. Thus, chapter 5 provides an overview of terrorist cooperation from the founding period of Al Qaeda up to the attacks of September 11, 2001, while chapter 6 covers the post-9/11 period up through the end of 2015. Given these broader historical contexts, chapters 7 through 9 go on to focus on specific case studies, which both validate the typology introduced in chapter 4 and illustrate the differences between high-end and low-end cooperation. Thus, while chapter 7 explores the high-end cooperative relationship between Al Qaeda Central and its Yemen-based affiliate, AQAP, chapter 8 considers low-end cooperation in terms of the relationship between Al Qaeda Central, on the one hand, and Hizballah and Iran, on the other. Subsequently, chapter 9 goes on to illustrate the concept of networked cooperation, through five shorter case studies, each of which demonstrates one of the five variants of networked cooperation first introduced in chapter 4. The discussion of 9/11, which forms one of the case studies, also goes further in that it demonstrates the changing quality of the cooperative relationship between KSM and Al Qaeda over time. The 9/11 case study discussion thus exemplifies the holistic, dynamic nature of the typology introduced in chapter 4.

PART ONE

UNDERSTANDING CONTEMPORARY TERRORIST COOPERATION

1

THE PUZZLE OF TERRORIST
COOPERATION

F OR TERRORISTS, cooperation with their peers is hardly a matter of course. It involves a tradeoff: on the one hand, it can bestow many benefits on the cooperating organizations; on the other, it carries risks that may bring harm upon these groups, and these are considerable. Terrorist groups operate under an unusual set of constraints because even minor mistakes can jeopardize their survival. Operational failure or oversight carries great potential risk because the interception of terrorist communications or the capture and interrogation of operatives can compromise the group's security and survival. Terrorist organizations therefore try to avoid government attention while exercising strict control over their own violent and political activities.[1]

If the terrorist's dilemma is maintaining organizational control while staying covert, as Princeton scholar Jacob Shapiro argues, cooperation between terrorist groups would seem counterproductive.[2] Cooperation entails a certain level of communication and knowledge-sharing and often involves face-to-face encounters between operatives, and thus it undermines both the imperative to maintain organizational control and the need to maintain secrecy. The characteristic features of most terrorist actors also render cooperation cumbersome and difficult to arrange and to maintain. The secretive nature of these organizations hampers their ability to meet and interact openly and regularly. Lack of regular interaction between any cooperating entities heightens the risk of the parties misinterpreting each other's signals and intentions and can lead to greater mutual suspicion, thereby undermining the rationale that led to cooperation in the first place.[3] Moreover, the nature of terrorist groups and the hostile environment in which they operate also place a strain on their ability to reach agreements, implement them, and maintain their spirit. Of course, this problem also applies to cooperation among nonmilitant actors, but in the case of terrorist groups even fewer recourses are available to punish those who fail to meet their commitment.[4] For them, a more serious problem is that the interactions inherent in cooperative engagement provide governments opportunities to foil attacks, intercept messages, or apprehend operatives. These interceptions can have second order effects that can compromise these terrorist organizations more severely, even resulting in their demise.[5]

Cooperation between terrorist groups can also create divisions over tactical and strategic questions, especially in uneven relationships between senior and junior partners. The alliance between Al Qaeda and Jamaat al-Tawhid w'al Jihad (later to become Al Qaeda in Iraq, or AQI) is a case in point. While the alliance was initially expected to serve the mutual interests of the two groups, Al Qaeda in Iraq's growing use of indiscriminate violence, including violence against Muslims, created a backlash against Al Qaeda among Muslims and therefore became costly to Al Qaeda. Its deputy leader at the time, Ayman al-Zawahiri, was compelled to reprimand AQI leader Zarqawi in a letter that was later intercepted and published by the U.S. Director of National Intelligence. According to Shapiro, such "principal-agent problems" occur when the preferences of the principal—in this case the senior partner, Al Qaeda, which was responsible for offering strategic guidance in the alliance—increasingly diverge from those of the agent—here the junior partner Al Qaeda in Iraq, which embarked on a path that hurt Al Qaeda's reputation.[6]

For their part, junior partners in collaborative relationships with more powerful groups may fear that their autonomy could be eroded and that they could be made overly dependent on their alliance partner. The case of the former left-wing German group Revolutionäre Zellen (Revolutionary Cells, RZ), some of whose members participated in the 1976 hijacking of an Air France aircraft to Entebbe, Uganda, exemplifies this case. According to one member of the group, Hans-Joachim Klein, it was the group's dependence on the Popular Front for the Liberation of Palestine–External Organization (PFLP-EO), also known as the Wadie Haddad Faction after its charismatic and innovative leader, that compelled the RZ to participate in hijacking. The RZ, Klein explained years later, "are dependent on others because they need countries where they can seek refuge. They depend on others for their money and weapons. All that has a price: the participation of German guerrilla members in other actions. Since Haddad needs people who aren't Arabs for his operations, that's exactly what happened at Entebbe."[7]

Cooperation with other groups can also generate new enemies and lead to new counterterrorism pressures. Especially when smaller groups seek collaboration with better known terrorist groups, the junior partner may find that along with more international recognition comes added pressure from a new set of foes. Groups such as the Salafist Group for Call and Combat (GSPC) in Algeria, Jabhat al-Nusra in Syria, or Boko Haram in Nigeria, for example, largely escaped international attention until they pledged allegiance to or expressed open support for Al Qaeda.

Cooperation can therefore significantly affect the operational, strategic, and ideological environment of a group and have detrimental effects on group cohesion. The period before the merger of the Egyptian Islamic Jihad (EIJ) and Al Qaeda in 2001, for example, shows the deep divisions that the mere idea of cooperation can create within groups. When Ayman al-Zawahiri, who reassumed leadership of the EIJ in the spring of 2001 after a nearly two-year hiatus, recommended that his group merge with Al Qaeda in order to solve its financial problems, he encountered stiff resistance from some EIJ operatives. Concerns over compromising the group's extant ideology and strategy featured prominently among the objections, while the question of where jihad would be waged next became a significant issue in the heated debate of the future direction of the EIJ. Those who objected to Zawahiri's close ties with bin Laden stated their preference to keep their jihad focused on the liberation of Egypt, as opposed to waging the global jihad that bin Laden advocated. But some members of the EIJ also objected to bin Laden on personal grounds—they viewed him as a "publicity hound."[8]

The example of the EIJ's objections to Zawahiri's decision to merge his group with Al Qaeda demonstrates that groups heavily reliant on terrorism have a natural tendency to jealously guard their independence and ideological stance, and it is precisely these tendencies that, on the face of it, would render terrorist groups less likely to seek cooperation. And yet, cooperation between militant groups does occur. This raises an important question: What factors explain why cooperation between terrorist actors occurs despite the obvious risks involved?

WHY TERRORIST GROUPS COOPERATE

Terrorist groups cooperate in spite of the risks involved because they have other important objectives that they need to weigh against their tendency to ensure organizational control and self-maintenance. These objectives include their long-term survival, the build-up of organizational capacity, and the ability to achieve political and ideological objectives. Cooperation, as will be seen, can serve these objectives.

Cooperation between militant actors can also occur when interests between two or more groups converge. Regardless of whether cooperation is limited or encompasses a broader set of issues, mutual benefit is its main underlying cause—it is the "bedrock of cooperation," in Phil Williams's words.[9] Militant groups expect the benefits of cooperation with other militant groups to promote one of two types of group objectives, and preferably both: namely, process goals and outcome goals.[10] Process goals are those objectives that help sustain militant organizations, such as recruitment of personnel, media attention, or the acquisition of materiel. They are what help groups to "survive and thrive." Process goals include attempts by the group to overcome the weaknesses and vulnerabilities that jeopardize its existence, as well as efforts to expand the group's resources and capabilities in order to ensure its continued well-being. Much of the "survive and thrive" imperative revolves around an effort to amass resources and thereby build up the group's physical capacity, although process goals also include efforts on the part of militant actors to gain international attention and recognition.

Outcome goals are the group's stated political and ideological objectives. These goals are designed to boost these groups' ability to "influence and succeed"—that is, to promote their ideological influence and successfully pursue their stated objectives. Of course, process goals and outcome goals are related to one another because a group's physical capacity affects its ability to expand influence and accomplish its political and ideological objectives.

When militant groups engage in cooperation with each other, they prefer that collaborative action will support both process and outcome goals simultaneously, but cooperation can occur if only one of these goals are served.[11]

"SURVIVE AND THRIVE": COOPERATION IN SUPPORT OF PROCESS GOALS

Starting in the 1980s, terrorism scholars began incorporating concepts and theories from organizational behavior into the analysis of terrorism. Since that time, modern terrorist organizations have been seen as largely rational entities that, like all political organizations, are concerned about their own survival and well-being.[12] Scholars of terrorist cooperation largely agree that the imperative to persist and flourish—"survive and thrive"— also explains why terrorist groups seek cooperative engagement with one another.

The fundamental need to survive implies that if survival is perceived to be endangered, terrorist groups will act in ways they believe will promote their continued existence. In his classic work *Coalitions Between Terrorist Organizations*, for example, Ely Karmon argued that the perception of a threat to the group's well-being best explains why groups seek to engage in

alliances with other groups.[13] He supported his argument by means of a series of comparative case studies, focusing mainly on the links between Palestinian and European militant organizations during the 1970s and 1980s.[14]
Fatah's support of the Red Army Faction (RAF), for instance, came at a
time when the Palestinian group was weak and eager to gain international
recognition, while the formal alliance between the RAF and the French
Action Directe (AD) was preceded by an unsuccessful campaign against
Jewish targets by the AD as well as the internally weak state of the RAF.
More recent examples further bolster Karmon's thesis. The anti-Shiite
Pakistani Deobandi group Lashkar-e Jhangvi (LeJ), for example, became
associated with Al Qaeda under circumstances of duress, when the former
lost its safe haven in Afghanistan after the fall of the Taliban. Subsequently, Al Qaeda agreed to establish ties with LeJ and used some LeJ
members in terrorist attacks and for recruiting suicide bombers.[15]

Threats to the group's survival can have various origins. They can result
from internal organizational or movement divisions;[16] from difficulties to
mobilize supporters for the organization or for its larger cause; from pressures placed on the group by the enemy state; from broader international
factors; or from any combination of the above.[17] Even tensions with competing organizations can drive terrorist groups to seek cooperation with
new groups. When competing with Amal for power in Lebanon in the late
1980s, for example, Hizballah decided to collaborate with the Abu Nidal
Organization (ANO).[18] The current competition between Al Qaeda and
the Islamic State also illustrates this point, as it involves in part a race to
seek new allies. To that end, the Islamic State has even appealed to Al
Qaeda's partners to switch allegiance to the Islamic State.[19]

Cooperation can also help assure organizational endurance for psychological reasons. For small groups in particular, cooperation may fill
psychological needs for reassurance.[20] Transnational cooperation, in particular, can provide a sense of empowerment—a feeling that the group is
stronger than is actually the case. The Popular Front for the Liberation of
Palestine (PFLP), for example, trained foreign militants in part to build
"transnational revolutionary bridges," as Bruce Hoffman observed, a goal
that can serve physical and psychological goals alike.[21] These psychological

needs may become even more important when a group is under intense pursuit by government forces.

Even though the benefits of cooperation may be perceived by militant groups instinctively, recent research has offered empirical evidence in support of the benefits of intergroup cooperation on group longevity. Brian Phillips, for example, has shown that the more relationships a terrorist group has with other groups, the longer the group tends to exist.[22] The underlying reason is that cooperation facilitates resource aggregation. When groups share resources with each other—men, materiel, know-how—there is reduced pressure to generate these resources on their own. Cooperation, in Phillips's terms, therefore helps these groups mitigate challenges to their mobilization efforts.[23] The case of al-Shabaab illustrates this point. Once the East African group pledged allegiance to Al Qaeda in 2009, it was able to recruit more foreign fighters.[24]

While the likelihood of a group seeking cooperation with another militant group increases if survival is deemed to be endangered, groups may seek cooperation even when their existence is not immediately at stake. The desire to thrive—that is, the wish to expand their existing capacity—may be as important to a group's decision to seek cooperation as the imperative to survive.[25] At the same time, while limitations in resources and know-how underlie terrorist, rebel, and other militant groups' attempts to bolster their capacities,[26] the constant quest for attention and recognition is another critical process goal that cooperation between like-minded groups can support. As Japanese Red Army (JRA) leader Kozo Okamoto stated during the trial that followed the 1972 Lod Airport Massacre carried out by his group on behalf of the PFLP, the decision to establish a relationship with the PFLP was "a means of propelling ourselves onto the world stage."[27]

The more obvious reason for cooperation lies in resource limitations, which can negatively affect these groups' ability to mobilize manpower and materiel; to plan and execute attacks successfully; to adapt to changing operational environments; to extend their reach into new theaters; to improve existing skills and adopt innovations; to collect and use intelligence information; to overcome the defenses erected by governments; and to withstand government efforts to weaken or destroy these groups.[28]

The desire to overcome weaknesses and vulnerabilities involves a process of learning, which can be defined as "change aimed at improving a group's performance."[29] Although militant groups initially utilize the expertise of their members to generate knowledge, the knowledge acquisition process often involves relying on external sources. This applies especially to small groups, whose ability to generate knowledge in-house is limited due to small membership size.[30] Groups can learn from other groups through remote observation, but a more valuable and reliable pathway toward knowledge acquisition involves cooperation with other groups.[31] According to an influential study on terrorist learning, cooperation is particularly likely to occur when the knowledge sought by groups is tacit as opposed to explicit. Tacit knowledge, such as expertise in handling explosives or battlefield intuition, is harder to transfer between groups than explicit knowledge such as actual weapons or attack plans. The people-to-people contacts that are typical of cooperation are therefore crucial for transferring tacit knowledge.[32] One example of the transfer of tacit knowledge are Hizballah's collaboration with the Irish Republican Army, which included information exchanges related to specialized units tasked with intelligence gathering. More recently, the collaboration between Islamist and Baathist insurgents in the early period following the U.S.-led invasion of Iraq in March 2003 involved deposed Baathist officers training Islamist fighters in critical counter-surveillance and counter-detection techniques.[33]

Establishing links to other terrorist groups can help militant actors overcome at least some of the challenges posed by resource scarcity and other limitations, even if such cooperation may not be decisive in strategic terms.[34] Cooperation can result in the expansion of operations to broader regional and international operations by militant groups with a traditionally local focus. This was one of the consequences of the support given by Palestinian groups to their European counterparts.[35]

Cooperation can help groups raise funds, as the Palestinian Liberation Organization did by charging militant groups up to $10,000 for six-week long training programs.[36] The Irish Republican Army (IRA) reportedly received $2 million in return for training the Revolutionary Armed Forces of Columbia (FARC) in the use of mortars.[37]

Cooperation can support the acquisition of new weapons and technologies and provide opportunities to conduct joint training exercises or develop specialized skills, all of which can boost group performance. Recent research has shown, for example, that terrorist intergroup cooperation can increase the lethality of group operations. Examining the number of linkages of groups to other groups, Victor Asal and R. Karl Rethemeyer found that those with more links to other groups tended to be more lethal than those with fewer links.[38]

Cooperation between terrorist groups can also lead to an overall expansion of access to knowledge useful not only for bolstering capacities, but also for addressing enemy strengths. In preparation for the beginning of Israeli military operations in 2002, for example, fighters from Hamas, Palestinian Islamic Jihad (PIJ), and Fatah worked together in identifying potential points from which the Israel Defense Forces (IDF) would enter the Gaza Strip, with the aim of maximizing IDF casualties in the process.[39]

Links with other groups can also promote the adoption of certain innovations. As Michael Horowitz has argued, groups are more likely to adopt the innovation of suicide attacks, for example, if they have links to groups that already employ this tactic.[40] Thus, when Al Qaeda decided to adopt suicide terrorism, it sent group members to learn the necessarily skills from Hizballah. In Lebanon, Al Qaeda then "pick[ed] up the tacit knowledge necessary to conduct its own operations."[41] Since Al Qaeda subsequently became a key exporter of this tactic, Horowitz continues, the Al Qaeda–Hizballah connection had second-order effects on the global proliferation of suicide missions, and this, in turn, underscores the potential importance of how terrorist groups learn from one another and emulate each other's tactics.[42]

Somewhat counterintuitively, however, the information-sharing inherent in terrorist cooperation is not always designed to bolster the capacity to inflict violence. At times, cooperation between militant actors can be geared for more peaceful ends, such as the exchange of views and best practices on how to disengage from terrorism or embark on a path of dialogue with former enemies. Members of the Ulster Volunteer Force (UVF), for example, exchanged views with members of the Basque group

Euskadi Ta Askatasuna (ETA) about how best to move away from a strategy focused on violence. According to one UVF commander, ETA members asked the UVF leadership "for a meeting and we went and talked to them and they asked for our help on how do we get out of the situation we are in. . . . So what we said to them was one of you should call a ceasefire, but have a condition within the ceasefire that after the ceasefire is held for so long that there is a repatriation of your prisoners into the one place, and then you start to debate and the discussion on how you move forward."[43]

According to Neil Ferguson, similar discussions between militant groups focused on reassessing the merits of the use of violence were held between the IRA and the African National Congress (ANC), as well as between the ETA and the IRA. Moreover, former associates of these groups have been involved in similar discussions with Palestinian and Colombian groups at least since 1998.[44]

"INFLUENCE AND SUCCEED": COOPERATION IN SUPPORT OF OUTCOME GOALS

Apart from militant groups cooperating in order to increase their capacity, they also collaborate in order to promote their stated political and ideological objectives—in other words, their outcome goals. Such goals include the attainment of a national homeland, the struggle to end an occupation, or the establishment of an Islamic caliphate. Groups that cooperate to these ends often, although not always, share an ideological affinity, a common goal, or a common enemy.[45]

Ideological affinity is frequently raised as one of the key factors underlying terrorist intergroup cooperation.[46] At times, groups cooperate almost exclusively in the ideological realm, which, according to Karmon, involves merely "verbal commitment and expressions of solidarity" through joint declarations or leaflets signed by the cooperating groups. Such ideological cooperation can, however, lead to more concrete cooperative engagements in the future.[47]

Groups may at times present ideological and strategic alignment as a precondition for cooperation. The Red Brigades (RB), for example, made cooperation with another group contingent upon the other group accepting the RB's political-military program.[48] Ideological affinity can help explain the cooperative interactions between various actors in the global jihad movement, such as Al Qaeda Central and its affiliates, and this trend applies to non-jihadi groups in equal measure. In 1997, for example, the Earth Liberation Front formalized an alliance with the Animal Liberation Front. In the aftermath, the groups stepped up joint attacks, established branches in various countries, and even shared best practices on operational security.[49] Revolutionary left-wing groups in Western Europe, which frequently cooperated during the 1970s and 1980s, often stressed their common ideological goals in joint statements.[50]

Shared ideologies, however, are not sufficient in and of themselves to explain why groups cooperate, much less why they establish formal alliances. First of all, not all groups that share similar ideologies necessarily cooperate. The Lebanese jihadist group Fatah al-Islam sought a formal affiliation with Al Qaeda, an ideologically like-minded group, only to be rejected by the latter for fear that its brand would be diluted as a result.[51] Moreover, splits do occur between ideologically like-minded groups, as demonstrated by Al Qaeda Central's breakup of ties with the Islamic State in Iraq and Greater Syria (ISIS) in 2013. Meanwhile, as shown in chapter 8, sporadic tactical cooperation between Shiite Hizballah and Sunni jihadi Al Qaeda, two ideologically incompatible groups, shows that terrorist cooperation can overcome ideological divides. Operational expediency often trumps the pursuit of common ideological goals.

Still, militant groups that are cooperating frequently share similar outlooks. As Michael Barnett argues, identity "makes some partners more attractive than others."[52] The goals of the ETA and the IRA, for example, are not congruent, but their overall approach and ideology—both are ethno-nationalist/separatist groups with leftist leanings—are similar, as are their cultural backgrounds. Both are European groups contending with a perceived foreign occupation by powerful European countries. As one ETA leader put it when describing the group's ties with the IRA: "For me it is normal that the movements of national liberation, wherever they are, in Ireland, Colombia or Corsica, should work together, put their experience in common and help each other work—why not?"[53] A similar perception of shared grievances and ideological affinity—including a common ideological revulsion against perceived imperialism—also explains the IRA's warm relations with various Palestinian militant groups, including Fatah and the PFLP.[54]

Closely related to the discussion on the role of ideology in terrorist cooperation is the assumption that coalitions rest on the identification of a common opponent—an idea prevalent among Realist international relations scholars concerned with the cooperative engagement between states.[55] In the context of militant groups, the notion that cooperation is designed to thwart common enemies is often used to explain cooperation between ideologically divergent groups, such as Hizballah and Al Qaeda, or coordinated attacks against Israel by Hizballah and Hamas.[56] Such groups often willingly admit that their cooperation is based on a common enemy. In September 1979, the leader of the ETA stated, "We see ourselves as an integral part of the Palestinian struggle. We have a common enemy."[57] In July 2014, at the height of a round of conflict between Hamas and Israel, which the Israel Defense Forces termed "Operation Protective Edge," the head of Hamas's external relations department, Osama Hamdan, was quoted as saying about his group's cooperation with the Lebanese Hizballah that "the enemy is the same and our tactics are the same. Therefore, we put in efforts to exchange expertise. There is constant field cooperation and coordination." "These ties," Hamdan continued, "are based on confronting the Zionist and working on liberating Palestine. Everyone is keen on preserving such a relationship regardless of how much the circumstances change and opinions differ."[58] Hamdan's interview speaks to the supremacy of tactical benefits over ideological differences in the decision of militant groups to cooperate.

The assumption that a common enemy is a sufficient factor to explain the onset of terrorist cooperation is, however, off the mark, given that many groups that do share the same enemy do not cooperate. Nor can it account for the fact that groups that have cooperated against a shared enemy oftentimes change their alliances or become rivals.[59] Hence, as Tricia Bacon explains, even when terrorist groups do collaborate in an effort to confront a common enemy, "The actual mechanisms operating to produce such an outcome [remain] under-specified."[60]

FACILITATING FACTORS

Apart from the underlying reasons for terrorist cooperation, empirical evidence suggests that a number of conditions can facilitate the emergence of mutual links between militant groups. These conditions, though not necessary, are conducive to the development, as well as the endurance, of cooperative relations. The discussion below draws on historical cases to highlight some of the most prominent conditions that contribute to terrorist cooperation. In chapter 3, I will discuss environmental factors in contemporary contexts.

Safe Havens and Conflict Zones

Safe havens where militant groups can operate relatively freely are hotbeds for terrorist cooperation. These safe havens often emerge in areas where the central state has limited access and the government has lost its monopoly on the use of force.[61] Safe havens and poorly governed territories have multiple benefits for such groups. They provide opportunities for establishing training camps, weapons depots, and networking facilities. They also enable recruitment and can serve as transshipment points that facilitate illicit trafficking in drugs, weapons, and contraband.

Safe havens afford physical security to groups under constant threat. The Indonesian Islamist group Jemaah Islamiyah (JI), for example, conducted training in the Philippines using bases of the Moro Islamic Liberation Front (MILF) because they were safer than those in their home country.[62] Similarly, in 2001, Abu Musab al-Zarqawi moved members of his network to Northern Iraq, where they could enjoy the protection of Mullah Krekar, the leader of the Kurdish Islamist faction Ansar al-Islam.[63]

Safe havens tend to emerge in countries ravaged by civil wars. Civil wars, in turn, promote the rise of insurgent groups that may collaborate in their efforts to undermine the incumbent regime.[64] As chapter 5 will show,

Al Qaeda's safe haven in Afghanistan, especially between the years of 1996 and 2001, helped the group train thousands of fighters and paved the way for the future inter-linkages among dozens of jihadi groups. In Southeast Anatolia, the Kurdistan Workers Party (PKK) provided a safe haven for the Revolutionary People's Liberation Party/Front (DHKP/C). Here, the role that external events can play in fostering cooperation among terrorists can be important. Numerous researchers, for instance, have pointed to the 1979 Soviet invasion of Afghanistan as a catalyst that encouraged subsequent collaboration among a host of jihadi actors, as well as the formation of the Al Qaeda network of jihadi groups.[65]

In addition, the so-called Arc of Instability that spans from Mali in West Africa all the way to Somalia in the Horn of Africa has also been a site for the formation of collaborative ties between Al Qaeda in the Islamic Maghreb, the Movement for Oneness and Jihad in Africa (MUJAO), Boko Haram, al-Shabaab, al-Murabitun, and several other jihadi groups based on the African continent.[66]

State Sponsorship

A number of terrorist safe havens have been set up by states, whose sponsorship is another facilitating factor for terrorist cooperation. Pakistan, for example, has set up training camps for a "bewildering array" of militant groups in Kashmir, whose members are prone to "considerable intermixing."[67] Former Libyan dictator Muammar Qaddhafi opened his country to a host of terrorist actors, running the gamut from Palestinian groups such as the PFLP, the Democratic Front for the Liberation of Palestine (DFLP), and the Popular Front for the Liberation of Palestine–General Command (PFLP-GC), to European ethno-nationalist groups such as the IRA and ETA, and to left-wing revolutionary groups such as the RAF, the JRA, and the Red Brigades, among others. Cuban leader Fidel Castro, who first opened terrorist training camps in 1961, hosted Palestinian, European, and even American terrorists such as members of the Weather Underground, while offering safe haven to members of the ETA and

FARC. Syria is known to have offered a safe haven to the PFLP-GC, Hamas, the PIJ, and the JRA, while Sudan was placed on the U.S. State Department's list of states sponsoring terrorism in 1993. In that year's report on *Patterns of Global Terrorism*, the State Department described Sudan's "disturbing relationship with a wide range of Islamic extremists," especially those backed by Iran.[68] Bruce Riedel described the Sudan of the early 1990s as host to a "potpourri of Islamic and Arab radicals"[69] who included Osama bin Laden, Carlos the Jackal, Abu Nidal, and Hizballah's Imad Mughniyeh, among others. Meetings hosted by Sudanese leader Hassan al-Turabi, such as the 1991 Arab and Islamic Conference, brought militants and terrorists from various stripes together and enabled future cooperation among some of these groups.[70]

Common Experience

Having a shared experience also supports terrorist cooperation. During the 1980s, for example, Afghan mujahideen and a plethora of other militant outfits fought together to rout the Soviet Union from Afghanistan. The common bonds that were created in the process led to some lasting ties.[71] The importance of these ties is evident in the case of Algerian jihadists who fought in Afghanistan during the 1980s and then used their network ties again in the early 1990s in order to sustain their insurgency against the military regime in their home country. In addition, the Armed Islamic Group (GIA), which later became notorious for its liberal employment of takfir (the process of labeling other Muslim groups as infidels), for instance, was founded with the help of Algerian veterans of the Afghan jihad, who managed to acquire financing, communications equipment, and weapons through linkages with other so-called "Afghan Arabs."

A common experience can also occur in other settings, such as prison. In the 1950s, for example, future members of the Provisional Irish Republican Army (PIRA) spent time in prison together with members of the Greek Cypriot terrorist group known as the National Organization of Cypriot Fighters (EOKA). According to some reports, these contacts resulted in learning and strategic adaptation.[72] In another case, an encounter in prison between members of the left-wing Kurdish Liberation Army of the Workers and Peasants of Turkey (TIKKO) and members of the PKK resulted in TIKKO members joining PKK forces in Syria and Lebanon after their release.[73]

Geography

Geographic proximity has also been a major factor facilitating cooperation among militant groups, whose members can travel shorter distances to conduct face-to-face meetings or seek sanctuary and thereby run fewer risks of being apprehended.[74] The relative ease of travel throughout the littoral countries of Southeast Asia and in the triborder area of Latin America is known to have facilitated transnational trade in contraband and can facilitate terrorist cooperation as well. Moreover, in the case of the Indonesian jihadi group Jemaah Islamiya and militant Filipino groups, cooperation between them was not only based on historical interaction and a common experience among some members fighting in the Afghan jihad, but also abetted by porous borders between these countries.[75] In the case of the People's Liberation Army of Turkey (THKO), to cite another example, geographic proximity meant that members could reach the PFLP's training camps in the Levant by boat.[76]

Technology

Over and above geographical proximity, the information revolution has significantly enhanced opportunities for cooperation. Internet chat rooms and the social media have enabled individuals to connect with each other more quickly and more easily. Indeed, the role of the Internet and social media is hard to exaggerate. Not only does it enable communication among terrorist actors; it also functions as a medium for propagating ideology and mobilizing new adherents. Its influence on terrorist cooperation will be discussed in chapter 3.

HOW TERRORIST GROUPS COOPERATE

While some of the above-cited examples do speak to the ways that terrorist groups can cooperate, the question of *how* these actors cooperate—the main focus of this book—has garnered far less scholarly attention to date. Two existing studies, however, by Ely Karmon and Tricia Bacon, do address this question at greater length. They also make important contributions to the typology I introduce in chapter 4.

EXISTING TYPOLOGIES OF TERRORIST COOPERATION

Ely Karmon offered an early typology that distinguishes among ideological, logistical, and operational cooperation. I will discuss Karmon's contribution at greater length because it provides a useful framework for describing the main activities that cooperating terrorist groups can pursue jointly. Hence, Karmon's typology examines an important aspect of the question of how terrorist actors cooperate. Even so, I will argue later in this chapter that Karmon's classification does not amount to a comprehensive typology of terrorist cooperation because it fails to examine two other critical aspects of this problem: first, the nature of the terrorist actors engaged in cooperation; and second, the nature of their relationship.

Ideological Cooperation

Ideological cooperation can take the form of verbal or written expressions of solidarity as well as formal manifestos declaring ideological affinity or the joint pursuit of a common objective between two partners.[77] Examples of ideological cooperation include the first manifesto released by the West German RAF and the French AD following their decision to forge a strategic alliance. Titled "For the Unity of West European Revolutionaries," the document laid out the need for a new revolutionary strategy focused on striking the allegedly unified Western imperialist enemy. Such a strategy required the consolidation of the West European guerrilla organizations that claimed to be the true representatives of the proletariat.[78] A more recent and better known example of ideological cooperation is a statement published on February 23, 1998, under the name "World Islamic Front against the Crusaders and the Jews." The statement, which Marc Sageman termed the "manifesto of the full-fledged global Salafi Jihad," was an attempt by Al Qaeda to broaden the group's platform by including as signatories a number of leaders of other militant Islamic groups.[79]

Logistical Cooperation

Logistical cooperation includes a broad variety of activities, ranging from the exchange of propaganda material on the lower end of the spectrum to knowledge- and information-sharing, funding, material support, and weapons transfers on the higher end. Logistical cooperation probably accounts for the bulk of concrete activities associated with terrorist cooperation.

Information and knowledge-sharing can be related to the group's political experience, as exemplified by the ETA's and the IRA's ongoing political consultations throughout the 1990s.[80] Other activities that fall within the range of logistical cooperation include collaboration in the preparation of forged documents. Palestinian militant groups such as Fatah and the PFLP had an efficient infrastructure in place, which allowed them to forge documents and assist other groups in doing so as well. So, too, did the terrorist network of Carlos the Jackal.[81]

Material support is a prominent example of terrorist cooperation. Ties between the Liberation Tigers of Tamil Eelam (LTTE) and Palestinian groups, for example, grew especially close as the LTTE made a name for itself as an international logistics hub for arms sales.[82] In 1995, an LTTE shipping fleet gave logistical support to the Harakat al-Mujahideen by handling the transportation of weapons on its behalf to Abu Sayyaf.[83] In addition, the LTTE also acquired weapons from other groups. As reported in *Jane's Intelligence Review*, the LTTE received eleven surface-to-air missiles of Greek origin from the Kurdistan Workers Party (PKK).[84]

Terrorist cooperation can also enable groups to test certain weapons in more hospitable environments. The cooperation between the IRA and

FARC illustrates this point. According to a congressional investigation, IRA members "have been training in the FARC safe haven in explosives management, including mortar and possibly car-bomb urban terrorist techniques, and possibly using the rural jungles of the safe haven as a location to test and improve the IRA's own terrorist weapons and techniques."[85]

Funding is another prominent logistical activity associated with terrorist cooperation. Al Qaeda, for example, is known to have provided general funding to organizations, as it did to the Egyptian Islamic Jihad prior to its merger with Al Qaeda. While Al Qaeda has also given seed money for specific terrorist projects, such as the November 2003 attacks by a Turkish jihadist network against two synagogues, the British Consulate, and a branch of HSBC Bank in Istanbul,[86] it has provided partial or full funding for many other terrorist acts, including the 2002 Bali bombings, the attacks on the Marriott Hotel in Jakarta, Indonesia, in August 2003, and the bombing of the Australian embassy in Jakarta in 2004, to name but a few.

Logistical cooperation can also take the form of physical protection or the provision of safe havens to members of other groups.[87] For instance, in the 1970s and 1980s members of Western and Latin American organizations frequently found refuge in Palestinian terrorist camps in the Middle East, especially after carrying out their attacks.[88] FARC, to cite another example, offered refuge to members of ETA (in return for received medical assistance and other services), while Lashkar-e Taibeh famously offered bin Laden's associate Abu Zubaydah a place in a safe house in Faisalabad, Pakistan, where he was arrested in March 2002.[89] States sponsoring terrorism are also known to harbor terrorists, including those seeking refuge following terrorist attacks. Thus, five Japanese terrorists who attacked the U.S. embassy in Malaysia in 1975 found refuge in Libya, and members of the JRA who hijacked a Japanese plane in 1977 found refuge in Algeria.[90]

A quintessential form of terrorist cooperation is training, which can take a number of forms. For one thing, groups can decide to send some or most of their members to receive training at camps run by other groups. Operatives from several outfits such as Jemaah Islamiya and the Free Aceh Movement (GAM) reportedly received training in various areas of specialization, including the manufacturing of explosive devices, weapons handling, surveillance and communication, and cell formation in camps run by the MILF.[91] Hizballah has provided training to Hamas and Palestinian Islamic Jihad, in explosives and strategy, including how to exploit suicide attacks in order to achieve the maximum shock effect.[92] As Jeffrey William Lewis writes, "Hizballah members seem to have impressed upon the Palestinians the importance of video-taped testimonies for ensuring the reliability of their recruits prior to the mission and for exploiting the media value of the attacks after the fact."[93]

Militant groups have also been known to send their trainers elsewhere. For example, the Turkish government cracked down on Turkish insurgents in the early 1970s, which meant that they were unable to travel to the Palestinian camps and had to receive training locally instead. As the Turkish daily *Hürriyet* reported in May 1971, the "PFLP sent instructors to Turkey in order to train Turkish youth in urban guerilla fighting, kidnappings, plane hijackings and other matters."[94] More recently, members of Hizballah have trained Houthi rebels in Yemen, most likely at the behest of Iran.[95]

Operational Cooperation

The third category of terrorist cooperation identified by Karmon is operational cooperation. While Karmon does not provide a precise definition, for present purposes we can define operational cooperation as the joint planning or execution of terrorist attacks; the planning and/or execution of attacks on behalf of other groups; or other cooperative activities in direct support of acts of terrorism.[96] Operational cooperation, for example, can involve the collection and sharing of intelligence in direct support of terrorist attacks. Cases of operational cooperation between militant groups can be found as early as the 1880s, when Irish Republican groups Clan na Gael (CNG) and the Irish Republican Brotherhood (IRB) cooperated and conducted joint attacks over a period of at least five years.[97] In 1975, when the PFLP attacked an EL Al plane at Orly airport outside of Paris, it was a German left-wing terrorist, Johannes Weinrich, who rented the car used in the attack. In September 1974, when three members of the JRA stormed the French embassy in The Hague, Netherlands, they had assistance from the PFLP, which helped with preparations for the attack.[98]

Operational cooperation between terrorist groups skyrocketed in the early 1970s. Algerian operatives in France, for example, provided support to Fatah members in Europe in planning and carrying out attacks on oil and gas installations in the Netherlands in 1971 and 1972.[99] German militants also reportedly provided logistical assistance to members of the Black September group, who were responsible for the 1972 massacre at the Munich Olympics.[100] More recent examples of cooperation in the planning of terrorist attacks include the support provided by the Patani United Liberation Organization (PULO), a southern Thai separatist organization, to Hizballah in the 1994 attempt to bomb the Israeli embassy in Bangkok. In exchange, PULO reportedly received arms and financing from the Lebanese group.[101]

Perhaps the ultimate form of terrorist cooperation occurs when groups conduct joint terrorist attacks, or alternatively, carry out such attacks on behalf of the other party. Such joint execution provides two distinct benefits: First, it creates a shared operational experience; and second, it enables the expression of a united political and ideological front. Among the most prominent partnerships were those between Palestinian and German terrorists, which resulted in a number of joint attacks such as the kidnapping of oil ministers at the Organization of Petroleum Exporting Countries (OPEC) conference in Vienna in 1975; the hijacking of an Air France flight to Entebbe, Uganda, in 1976; and the hijacking of the Lufthansa airliner "Landshut" to Somalia in 1977, which turned out to be an unsuccessful attempt to force the release of members of the RAF from prison.

In late 2001, a sophisticated series of attacks intended to take place in Singapore was thwarted. The planned attacks included the use of multiple suicide bombers to target a bus transporting U.S. soldiers; U.S. vessels; the U.S., British, Israeli, and Australian consulates and embassies; and U.S. companies and financial organizations. Members of the Indonesian jihadist group Jemaah Islamiya (JI) were instructed by Al Qaeda members to prepare the logistical and operational infrastructure, while Al Qaeda agreed to provide the suicide bombers, which it was supposed to send to Singapore shortly before the attack. To that end, two Al Qaeda operatives were dispatched by 9/11 mastermind Khaled Sheikh Mohammed to liaise with the local JI group in Singapore, which was formed and managed by Hambali, who also served as an operational coordinator between JI and Al Qaeda. Luckily, the Singapore plot was foiled before it came to fruition.[102]

Joint operations between terrorist groups persist, sometimes with great effect. In 2009, for example, a suicide bomber attacked the CIA station in Khost, Afghanistan, killing nine people and wounded six others. The attack, which was a joint operation carried out by Al Qaeda, the Tehreek e-Taliban Pakistan (TTP), and the Haqqani network, was the most lethal assault on the CIA in a quarter century.[103]

ACCOUNTING FOR THE QUALITATIVE STRENGTH OF COOPERATION

Karmon's distinctions among ideological, logistical, and operational cooperation demonstrate different types of activities that terrorist groups can pursue in collaboration. While this classification is valuable, however, it stops short of examining in depth the varying qualitative strengths of different cooperative relationships. Historically, such collaborative partnerships have run the gamut from short-term, less committed relationships to strong alliances, and even mergers. Tricia Bacon, a former State Department counterterrorism analyst, recognized this lacuna and developed an alternative typology that fills this gap. Her typology is concerned with terrorist alliances, not terrorist cooperation more generally, but nevertheless produces important insights that inform the development of the holistic typology I present in chapter 4. Terrorist alliances, according to Bacon, are "formal or informal relationships of security cooperation among two or more terrorist groups involving some degree of ongoing coordination or consultation in the future."[104]

Bacon distinguishes four types of relationships between terrorist groups that meet her criteria of alliances: namely, pooled, integrated, subordinate, and reciprocal relationships.[105] These types of alliances differ based on a number of factors: the treatment of organizational resources such as money, weapons, skill, and knowledge; the cooperating parties' time horizon for the relationship; the degrees of autonomy, equality, and independence of the partners; and the breadth and parameters of cooperation.

Pooled relationships involve fully codependent alliance partners bound in a relationship that the alliance partners believe has an infinite time horizon. They cooperate in an unlimited number of ways, while retaining none of their independence in the process. The merger between the EIJ and Al Qaeda after 2001 exemplifies this relationship.

Integrated relationships feature extensive interdependence between the partners. The time horizon in an integrated relationship is extended (although not infinite). Partners in an integrated relationship retain some of their organizational independence, and possible areas of their cooperation are more dynamic. Bacon cites the relationship between Al Qaeda and the GSPC after 2006 as an example of this type of relationship.

Subordinate types of relationships, according to Bacon, are relationships where one side is more dependent on its partner than the other. Such relationships are also meant to have an extensive time horizon. In such relationships, one partner relinquishes its autonomy. According to Bacon, the alliance between the EIJ and Al Qaeda in the five years preceding the official merger in 2001 qualifies as a subordinate relationship.

As their name suggests, reciprocal relationships are more equal partnerships where both sides retain their autonomy, and hence establish only limited dependence on one another. The envisaged time horizon for such alliances is short, while cooperation is more defined than in stronger relationships. The PFLP-EO, according to Bacon, entertained reciprocal relations with the RAF and the JRA during certain periods.

Bacon's typology offers a useful model that addresses the varying qualitative strengths of cooperative relationships, and is hence an important complement to Karmon's focus on the activities, or domains, that terrorist cooperation can encompass. In fact, both Bacon and Karmon individually address critical aspects of terrorist cooperation. Neither model, however, incorporates the insights from the other model to establish a more comprehensive, integrated typology. Moreover, both models fail to address an additional crucial aspect: the fact that cooperation can also differ based on the nature of the collaborating terrorist actors.

The typology that I develop in the remainder of the first part of this book builds upon and integrates the important contributions of Karmon and Bacon while also accounting for a third critical variable of terrorist cooperation ignored in previous typologies, namely the variegated nature of the cooperating actors. While Karmon and Bacon focus exclusively on formal terrorist organizations, I argue that contemporary terrorist cooperation must also account for other types of terrorist actors, including informal networks and terrorist entrepreneurs. The resulting typology I introduce in chapter 4 offers a holistic, comprehensive, up-to-date, and dynamic classification of the way in which contemporary terrorist actors of varying stripes collaborate in pursuit of their objectives.

* * *

In this chapter, I have reviewed the existing body of work on terrorist cooperation. The discussion has highlighted several shortcomings. First, the vast majority of the existing studies are primarily concerned with the question of *why* terrorist groups cooperate, not *how*. The few studies that do tackle the question of how terrorists collaborate are limited in scope.[106] Second, all above mentioned studies examine the problem set of terrorist cooperation through the lens of formal terrorist organizations, while largely overlooking the growing importance of a broader array of terrorist actors such as informal networks and terrorist entrepreneurs. Finally, few, if any, of the main studies consider changing environmental conditions and their impact on terrorist cooperation. No major study, for example, has been devoted to the question of how the rise of the new social media affects the ways in which terrorist actors collaborate.

This book seeks to fill the gaps outlined above. First, it is devoted entirely to examining *how*, rather than *why*, contemporary terrorists cooperate. Second, to that end, it develops a more comprehensive classification that builds upon existing approaches of terrorist collaboration while also accounting for a critical, yet largely overlooked, variable: namely, the nature of the cooperating terrorist actors. Third, in developing the holistic typology, the study adopts a sophisticated theoretical framework to address the changing nature of terrorist cooperation over time, namely the agent-structure model. This framework provides an analytical tool to gauge the increasing diversity of terrorist actors, as well as examining the broader contextual factors that shape the way in which these contemporary actors collaborate.

2

ACTOR SPECTRUM

Organizations, Networks, and Entrepreneurs

H OW DO CONTEMPORARY terrorist actors cooperate? Examining this
question conceptually and theoretically, I will demonstrate that
terrorist cooperation has evolved significantly since the 1990s
due to changes among the perpetrators of terrorism, which are discussed
in this chapter, and to the environment in which they operate, which are
discussed in the next one. Here, I argue that from the 1990s onward, established forms of organizational cooperation have come to be accompanied
by what I call "networked cooperation," that is, cooperation that involves
at least one informal terrorist actor, whether this be an informal network
or a terrorist entrepreneur. Moreover, the strength and quality of both organizational and networked cooperative relationships can differ significantly,
ranging from high-end forms of cooperation (such as mergers or strategic
alliances) to low-end forms of cooperation (such as tactical or transactional
collaborations). As the review of existing studies of terrorist cooperation
in the previous chapter reveals, explanations and conceptualizations have
up till now been focused almost exclusively on terrorist organizations,
which can be considered formal actors of terrorism and have served as
the standard unit of analysis in existing studies of terrorist cooperation.
Empirically, however, there are growing indications that informal terrorist
actors are playing increasingly prominent roles in terrorism in general and

therefore in terrorist cooperation in particular. In addition to largely ig-noring these informal actors as potential agents of terrorism, existing stud-ies have also presented a static image of cooperation between terrorist actors, distinguishing among different types of terrorist cooperation, but without sufficiently addressing new trends, such as the growing importance of the Internet and social media, which have become crucial platforms for terrorist cooperation in recent years. Even when the role of the social media is acknowledged, few conceptual models adequately account for its impact on terrorist cooperation; nor do they incorporate broader structural factors in their analysis.

This book offers a new approach to the analysis of terrorist cooperation by looking beyond terrorist organizations as the sole units of analysis to include various informal terrorist actors. It also examines in detail a number of key structural, or environmental, factors that have affected the ways in which terrorists cooperate and contributed to the advent of networked co-operation. The resulting holistic typology I develop in chapter 4 presents a more nuanced conceptual model to understand the complex and dynamic terrorist universe, with important policy implications. Networked co-operation between contemporary terrorist actors poses several challenges for counterterrorism because it raises the quantity and efficiency of coop-erative endeavors between terrorist actors, and therefore heightens the over-all threat posed by terrorist cooperation.

The emerging trend of networked cooperation does not imply that tra-ditional, interorganizational forms of cooperation are irrelevant or about to disappear. On the contrary, partnerships between formal militant groups continue to be an important facet of terrorist cooperation, as is illustrated throughout the book, and especially in the case study in chapter 7. That said, the relative importance of networked cooperation is growing, paint-ing a complex picture of terrorist cooperation in which networked forms of collaboration coexist alongside formal organizational ties.

Two broad trends account for the rise of networked cooperation: the growing diversity of actors employing terrorism today, and the changing environment within which these actors operate and cooperate. Under-lying the growing diversity of terrorist actors today is the "privatization of terrorism"—a process in which the role of formal organizations in terrorist cooperation is diminishing, whereas that of informal terrorist actors is expanding. Informal terrorist actors include private individuals or informal networks. The present chapter is devoted to describing the growing diversity of terrorist actors in greater detail and to examining the various ways they operate and cooperate. In the process, it focuses on the "agent" side of the agent-structure debate, which offers a particularly useful conceptual framework for understanding the changing dynamics of terrorist cooperation.

AGENTS, STRUCTURE, AND THE EVOLUTION OF TERRORIST COOPERATION

THE AGENT-STRUCTURE MODEL

The agent-structure model is the most recent iteration of a discussion that dates back to at least the Middle Ages concerning the relationship between individuals and society.[1] In its present form, it involves both an ontological question related to the "character of social reality"[2] and an epistemological question about the best ways to trace transformative processes in the international system.[3] It also reflects the interplay of two axioms of social life— the idea that human agency is a driving force of social change; and the notion that the possibilities for action driven by human agency are conditioned by broader circumstances, or structure[4]—and in the process, it seeks to develop guidelines for developing empirical research that accounts for these dual social forces.[5]

Among the core insights of the agent-structure debate is the recognition that human agents and social structures are "in a fundamental sense inter-related entities, and hence that we cannot account fully for the one without invoking the other."[6] According to Alexander Wendt, "Agents are inseparable from social structures in the sense that their action is possible only in virtue of those structures, and social structures cannot have causal significance except insofar as they are instantiated by agents."[7] Social action, he concludes, is "co-determined," or mutually constituted, by the properties of both agents and social structures.[8] Importantly, the agent-structure framework considers social phenomena as an outcome of a simultaneous involvement of agents and structures.[9] This mutual involvement "creates new possibilities for collective action by changing norms and institutions, as well as the evolution of existing and emergent actors (and their interactions)."[10] The resulting process can enable, as well as constrain, said actors as they pursue their goals.

Despite its prominence, the agent structure framework has been underutilized as a heuristic device for empirical research, for two main reasons: discussions of the agent-structure problem tend to be abstract; and efforts to operationalize the concepts of agent and structure, as well as their interdependence, have proven challenging.[11] The adoption of this conceptual framework for analyzing terrorist actors and the broader environment in which they operate are particularly rare, because international relations scholars have traditionally applied the notion of agency mainly to state actors.[12] But as I will argue, applying the concept of agency and structure to terrorist actors and their environment is not only justified, but can significantly advance our theoretical and empirical understanding of the social phenomenon under investigation: terrorist cooperation.

TERRORIST ACTORS AS AGENTS

Although the international relations literature has not offered a systematic definition of agency, a general consensus as to the general traits of agents has emerged over the years.[13] As Colin Wight summarizes, agency is "generally theorized as the exercise of power" by human beings and their organizations.[14] Wendt ascribes to an "agent" three capacities: "1) a theoretical understanding (however inaccurate) of its activities, in the sense that it could supply reasons for its behavior; 2) to reflexively monitor and potentially adapt its behavior; and 3) to make decisions."[15] Sharon Hays adds that agency involves the ability to choose "among the alternatives made available by the enabling features of social structure. . . . The central point that is implied in all definitions of agency [is that] alternative courses of action are available, and [that] the agent therefore could have acted otherwise."[16]

Agents make their choices consciously or unconsciously, and these choices are transformative—i.e., they can effect change in the agents themselves and in their environments.[17] That is, not only do agents have the capacity to use their reflexive knowledge to transform social realities; in the process, their choices can also lead to changes in their thinking and themselves.

Theoretically, any actor can potentially exercise agency, but only those that exert transformative power actually do.[18] Throughout much of the second half of the twentieth century, the predominant realist paradigm of international relations has considered states to be the most important units in those relations, and thus the transformative power and goal-directed nature of agents were mostly ascribed and applied to states.[19] To be sure, international security scholars of the post–Cold War period have written extensively about the rise of nonstate actors, and some have argued that the growing role of nonstate actors accompanies a gradual erosion of the traditional state.[20] However, few scholars have employed the agency-structure framework to argue that nonstate actors, including terrorists, are also agents. Kate O'Neill, Jörg Balsiger, and Stacy VanDeveer are an exception to this rule by arguing that nonstate actors that have transformative capacity represent a contemporary form of agents. They lay out an "agency diffusion hypothesis" according to which agency in international politics is shifting away from state actors toward nonstate actors, who are

> increasingly acquiring the ability to influence and transform international politics. This shift is not merely a result of a relative change in who shapes outcomes of international politics. It also responds to the changing conceptualization of international politics more broadly, to include important normative, in addition to material, dimensions. These changes in who acts and how international politics is conceptualized empower actors who traditionally have not been considered influential but who now wield normative/ideational power."[21]

If the concept of agency can be applied to nonstate actors, provided that they possess the capacity to exert transformative power, it does not seem far-fetched to extend this application to contemporary terrorist actors. Terrorist actors fall within the traditional understanding of agents for several reasons. First, they clearly possess a theoretical understanding of their activities. This theoretical understanding is provided in the form of a guiding ideology such as nationalism, Marxism, or jihadism. More than merely providing a cognitive map with which to view the world, ideologies can also guide militant actors' tactics and target selection.[22] Second, terrorism scholars have shown that terrorist groups, like all agents, monitor and adapt their behavior. Because terrorism is dependent on a broad range of knowledge "that incorporates skills, competency, creative thinking, some understanding of engineering, [and] coded communications," among other things, terrorist groups must regularly update their knowledge to ensure success.[23] In an abundance of case studies spanning such diverse organizations as Aum Shinrikyo, the IRA, Hizballah, JI, Hamas, FARC, and Al Qaeda, researchers have shown that the most notorious and innovative organizations are those that have proven to be able to learn and adapt.[24] Third, terrorism scholars have argued for decades that terrorist groups, like other agents, can be conceived as reaching decisions as a result of rational calculations that take into account the value of an action, the cost of the attempt and the potential cost of failure, the probability of success, and other variables.[25] Terrorist groups employ "reasonably regularized decision-making procedures," writes Martha Crenshaw, "in conscious anticipation of the consequences of various courses of action or inaction."[26]

The clearest sign, however, that terrorist actors are agents is their ability to effect change. This is due to the fact that terrorist groups possess transformative power, even though the source of that power differs from state agents. Unlike that of states, the transformative power of terrorist actors does not derive from an abundance of resources or territory (although the capacity of some actors, such as the Islamic State, may be immense). Instead, their power derives from their tendency to target civilians, strike at symbolic targets, or otherwise employ extra-normal violence that often provokes a harsh response from the target.[27] Moreover, not only is the response disproportionate relative to the number of people killed, but it can also fundamentally affect, even transform, regional and global political, military, and economic affairs.[28] This transformative power of terrorist actors is perhaps best reflected in Al Qaeda's attacks on the U.S. homeland on September 11, 2001, as measured by its far-reaching consequences to this very day. More recently, the Islamic State's campaign of gruesome beheadings has had perhaps no less serious ramifications for international security. It is precisely due to their willingness to use tactics that are provocative by nature that terrorist actors manage to wield transformative power regardless of their ability to achieve their ultimate goals.[29]

THE GROWING DIVERSITY OF TERRORIST AGENTS

The preceding discussion has demonstrated that terrorist actors can be considered agents, but what kinds of terrorist agents can we distinguish? One of the main weaknesses of existing approaches to understanding terrorist cooperation is the narrow focus on terrorist organizations as the main unit of analysis. Put simply, there is a strong tendency in existing scholarly treatments to present terrorism-related cooperative engagements as occurring primarily, or even exclusively, between two or more terrorist organizations. Insofar as these relations are often referred to as "coalitions" or "alliances" in the literature, the terms themselves are strongly indicative of a bias in favor of viewing organizations as the sole, or main, terrorist actors engaged in cooperation.[30]

The dominant approach is misguided in two respects. First, in the age of globalization, individuals and informal networks with terrorist aspirations are highly empowered for reasons that include easy access to information, the proliferation and miniaturization of weaponry, and the ability to connect and communicate easily and speedily with like-minded actors. As a result, formal terrorist organizations no longer have a monopoly as agents of terrorism—if ever they had, which is doubtful—and are joined today by a growing number of alternative terrorist agents that frequently adopt less formal structures.

Second, limiting our analysis of terrorist cooperation to relationships between formal terrorist organizations narrows our ability to properly identify new ends, ways, and means by which contemporary terrorist actors cooperate. More than simply evidence of a conceptual gap, the failure to identify a broader variety of terrorist actors as agents of terrorist cooperation also paints a misleading picture of terrorist cooperation as a phenomenon and can therefore hamper counterterrorism efforts to undercut links between terrorist actors. Today's landscape of actors involved in terrorist or jihadist cooperation extends beyond outdated notions of the "terrorist group" to include such nontraditional actors such as jihadist preachers, Internet activists, and foreign fighters. These new actors are difficult to conceptualize not only because they may be relatively new, but also because their involvement in, or with, terrorism, is at times indirect, as will be seen in chapter 9. Our own intellectual difficulties in grasping their nature and activities should not obscure their significance for international security. Moreover, the fact that these novel terrorist actors draw much of their transformative power from their ability to connect with like-minded actors makes their role all the more relevant to discussions of terrorist cooperation.

Alongside the fact that terrorism is no longer the preserve of formal terrorist organizations is a broader trend in recent decades of security becoming increasingly privatized. Whereas the safeguarding of the public and the ability to use force in a consequential manner have previously been reserved to the state, a variety of armed nonstate actors, ranging from private security firms and militias to rebels and insurgent groups, mercenary forces, tribal groups, warlords, and others, have proliferated.[31] The rise of new types of terrorist actors must be viewed in this context.

Since the appearance of modern international terrorism in the 1960s and 1970s, agents of terrorism have come in various forms that defy a simple, single classification and are better viewed as being situated on a spectrum, with informal terrorist actors on one end and formal terrorist actors on the other. Informal actors include terrorist entrepreneurs and informal networks, while formal terrorist actors include terrorist and/or

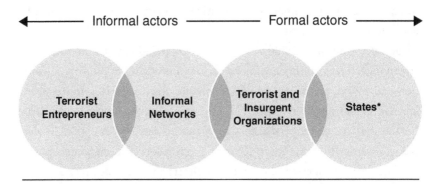

FIGURE 2.1 Spectrum of Contemporary Terrorist Actors

* Excluded from theoretical analysis in this chapter

insurgent organizations as well as states sponsoring terrorism or otherwise involved in its exercise (figure 2.1). Because this book is concerned mostly with cooperation among substate actors employing terrorism, and because the roles of states in sponsoring terrorism has been researched extensively, state actors are excluded from formal theoretical analysis in this chapter.[32] Chapter 8 will, however, examine cooperation involving two formal organizations, Al Qaeda and Hizballah, as well as a state actor, Iran.

While figure 2.1 presents the full spectrum of terrorist agents, the remainder of this chapter will focus on the substate terrorist actors: formal terrorist and insurgent organizations; informal networks; and terrorist entrepreneurs.[33]

TERRORIST AND INSURGENT ORGANIZATIONS

Formal terrorist organizations are the classic agents of terrorism and the focus of the existing literature on terrorist cooperation. Formal organizations, according to Crenshaw, have four main characteristics:

(1) The group has a defined structure and processes by which collective decisions are made; (2) members of the organization occupy roles that

are functionally differentiated; (3) there are recognized leaders in positions of formal authority; and (4) the organization has collective goals that it pursues as a unit, with collective responsibility claimed for its actions. Specific groups tend to have identifiable modus operandi or standard operating procedures.[34]

The Islamic State, for instance, met all the above criteria as of 2015. First, it is known to have a defined structure, with an identifiable leader, Abu Bakr al-Baghdadi, on top; two deputies, one in charge of Syria and the other of Iraq; and other leadership responsibilities distributed through a military, judicial, and media councils, among others.[35] Second, the Islamic State's membership is clearly identifiable in that each member swears *bayah*, an oath of loyalty, to the group's leader.[36] Furthermore, these members assume a variety of functionally distinct roles, such as heading the group's various ministries (*diwan*).[37] Third, in terms of leadership, Abu Bakr al-Baghdadi's authority is both evident and formal. It is so formal, in fact, that the Islamic State's leader has publicly declared himself a caliph. This form of authority derives from religious justifications and extends beyond the Islamic State organization in that it seeks to apply itself to the entire *umma*, or Islamic community of believers.[38] Finally, the Islamic State clearly pursues collective goals. These goals are conveyed in propaganda messages authorized by the group's centralized media council and distributed through a host of media outlets, such as its English-language news magazine *Dabiq*.

As the traditional unit of analysis described in the terrorism studies literature, the terrorist organization requires little further explanation. In the present study, however, I will refer to these formal organizational actors as terrorist *and/or insurgent* organizations, which does require a brief explanation.[39]

The existing scholarship on terrorism and its perpetrators suggests that terrorist groups differ from other militant actors such as guerrilla organizations in terms of their target selection, among other things. As Alex Schmid notes in his magisterial volume on terrorism research, "In the dominant understanding among experts, the victims [of terrorism] are predominantly not members of an armed force."[40] Moreover, terrorist groups are generally considered to be smaller in size, while employing uncompromising violence. Conventional wisdom holds that the secret nature and small size of terrorist organizations generally prevents them from holding territory, while their focus on extreme violence prevents them from enjoying popular support.[41] Bruce Hoffman, for example, writes that terrorists "do not function in the open as armed units, generally do not attempt to seize or hold territory, deliberately avoid engaging enemy military forces in combat, are constrained both numerically and logistically from undertaking concerted mass political mobilization efforts, and exercise no direct control or governance over a populace at either the local or the national level."[42] Terrorist groups, in other words, are generally considered to have a modus operandi that differs from those of guerrilla groups.

A cursory look at contemporary terrorist groups, however, suggests that these groups regularly carry out guerrilla operations as well. In the existing literature, those operations typically involve extended assassination campaigns, sabotage, and hit-and-run attacks carried out by small and highly mobile paramilitary units. Like terrorism, guerrilla warfare is described as a weapon of the weak designed to harass the enemy and gradually erode its will. Yet where terrorism is in essence an act of psychological warfare—it hopes to turn the targeted population against its own government—guerrilla operations primarily target their enemy's capabilities.[43] Functioning as small armies, potent guerrilla forces are large and strong enough to seize and hold territory. Moreover, guerrilla tactics differ from terrorist tactics in terms of their main targets. While the prime targets of guerrilla fighters are the enemy's armed forces, police or support units, and general governmental and economic concerns, the targets of terrorist groups are usually civilians, or at most, noncombatants.[44]

Whereas terrorist groups have traditionally been treated as distinct from guerrilla organizations, many contemporary militant groups apply both terrorist and guerrilla tactics. As Robert Scales and Douglas Ollivant argue, a growing array of Islamist "terrorists" have turned into "skilled soldiers" who increasingly use a blend of traditional terrorist tactics and modern war-fighting techniques.[45] Contemporary militants continue to use terrorist tactics to intimidate potential supporters and enemies alike, but their modus operandi has come to include skills that can pose considerable challenges to states and their populations. They now "maneuver in reasonably disciplined formations . . . and employ mortars and rockets in deadly barrages."[46] They rely on ambushes, roadside bombings, sniper fire, and other means, which, in places such as Iraq and Afghanistan, have imposed considerable challenges and losses to U.S. forces. Groups such as the Islamic State, Hizballah and Hamas are able to handle second-generation weapons such as Russian RPG-29s and possibly wire-guided anti-tank missiles, and they can build sophisticated underground tunnel systems.[47]

In a separate study, Assaf Moghadam, Ronit Berger, and Polina Beliakova have offered empirical evidence in support of the conclusion that the vast majority of contemporary groups commonly labeled as "terrorist groups"[48] carry out attacks against targets that are commonly associated with guerrilla warfare—namely, military, police, and government targets.[49] Most groups employing terrorism, therefore, appear to use guerrilla tactics as well. The label *insurgent organization* can be useful in this regard because theorists of insurgency have long argued that insurgents typically rely on several modes of warfare at once. Although theoretically these modes of warfare do not have to include acts of terrorism—insurgents can rely, for example, on a combination of conventional and guerrilla tactics—in practice they almost always do. Ariel Merari, for instance, observed that "whenever possible, insurgents use concurrently a variety of strategies of struggle. Terrorism, which is the easiest form of insurgency, is practically always one of these modes."[50]

That terrorist and insurgent organizations increasingly overlap has also been recognized by the U.S. intelligence community. In its annual Worldwide Threat Assessment, U.S. Director of National Intelligence James Clapper told the Senate Select Committee on Intelligence that

Sunni violent extremist groups are increasingly joining or initiating insurgencies to advance their local and transnational objectives. Many of these groups are increasingly capable of conducting effective insurgent campaigns, given their membership growth and accumulation of large financial and materiel caches. This trend increasingly blurs the lines between insurgent and terrorist groups as both aid local fighters, leverage safe havens, and pursue attacks against US and other Western interests.[51]

For all of the above reasons, the present study refers to formal organizations employing terrorism as terrorist and/or insurgent organizations. Adopting the insurgency label for these groups should not be seen as an attempt to play down the fact that these groups tend to commit heinous acts of violence. Yet it does help place these acts in a broader context of a more complex reality. According to this understanding, even the most violent groups using the most despicable tactics are likely to spend most of their time and energy doing something other than killing civilians: fighting regular troops and government forces and subverting their enemies by use of propaganda and other political means.

Formal terrorist and insurgent organizations continue to play a key role in terrorist cooperation, but they are hardly the only terrorist actors engaged in collaboration. Informal networks and individual terrorist entrepreneurs play critical roles in terrorist cooperation as well, as the remainder of the chapter will argue.

INFORMAL NETWORKS

Terrorist networks are hardly a new phenomenon, but their importance has grown in recent decades. Underlying their growing prominence in terrorism studies is a broader impact that the concept of "networks" has had on global societies and discourse. Networks, in Miles Kahler's words, have become the "intellectual centerpiece for a new era," replacing markets and state hierarchies as the "dominant social and economic metaphor."[52] Scholars from a broad range of disciplines, ranging from business to organized crime to the scholarship on social movements and collective action, have argued that networked organizations, despite some inherent weaknesses,[53] are by and large superior to more traditional bureaucratic forms of organization in promoting tactical and strategic goals through their ability to disseminate ideas and information, mobilize personnel and resources, coordinate action, and build alliances, among other things. The adaptability, flexibility, and resilience of networks also contribute to their effectiveness.[54]

Scholars have argued since at least the 1990s that networks play an important role in social protest, political conflict, and crime.[55] After September 11, 2001, analysts increasingly highlighted the impact of networks on terrorism and stressed the importance of network analysis as a fruitful methodology for studying terrorism.[56] Some scholars even hold that the threat emanating from terrorist networks is the most acute danger we face today. "Networks and relationships," Matt Levitt argued, "best describe the current state of international terrorism. . . . Too often people insist on pigeonholing terrorists as members of one group or another, as if such operatives carry membership cards in their wallets. In reality, much of the 'network of networks' that characterizes today's terrorist threat is informal and unstructured."[57] In a similar vein, Marc Sageman writes that "the individuals we should fear most form fluid, informal networks that are self-financed and self-trained. They have no physical headquarters or sanctuary, but the tolerant, virtual environment of the Internet offers them a semblance of unity and purpose. Theirs is a scattered, decentralized social structure—a leaderless jihad."[58] Even scholars such as Bruce Hoffman, who have challenged Sageman's emphasis on "leaderless jihad" as the preeminent threat, agree that the role of informal actors is "a critical part of the global terrorist network."[59]

Networks can be defined as any set of at least two interconnected nodes. The nodes can consist of individuals, cells, groups, organizations, or states. The connections between and among these nodes can assume forms of friendship, kinship or ethnic ties.[60] Generally speaking, the concept of networks spans a very broad spectrum of arrangements that can be both physical and virtual. In the words of Phil Williams:

They are simultaneously pervasive and intangible, ubiquitous and invisible, everywhere and nowhere. . . . Networks vary in size, shape membership, cohesion, and purpose. Networks can be large or small, local or global, domestic or transnational, cohesive or diffuse, centrally directed or highly decentralized, purposeful or directionless. A specific network can be narrowly and tightly focused on one goal or broadly oriented toward many goals, and it can be either exclusive or encompassing in its membership.[61]

The number and variety of arrangements covered by the concept of networks makes it all the more important to limit the scope of networks under consideration in this book and to call attention to some specific qualifications.

First, this book treats networks as types of agents, even though networks also have structural properties.[62] Put differently, networks are examined here as a form of organization—one that is distinct from formal terrorist organizations as described in the previous section. For that reason, I generally include the adjective "informal" to describe networks.[63]

Second, despite the distinction between informal networks and formal organizations, it is important to acknowledge that in real life, the boundaries between networks and organizations are murky. The vast, multidisciplinary literature on networks oftentimes describes networks as decentralized and flat and organizations as centralized and hierarchical. Upon closer inspection, however, the characteristics of networks and organizations often overlap.[64]

To complicate matters even further, each of these two forms of organization can exist as a subset of the other. Ami Pedahzur and Arie Perliger, for example, have demonstrated that Hamas and Fatah—formal Palestinian organizations—are better understood as "products of local, independent, horizontal networks rather than of a hierarchical organizational process."[65] As a veteran Israeli Army general put it, "The terrorist networks in the cities and villages operate almost independently; we are not facing Hamas or Fatah but a Balata terrorist network and a Dheisheh terrorist network."[66] Conversely, organizations can also be part of networks. In the years following the 9/11 attacks, for example, it was fashionable to describe Al Qaeda as a "network of networks," in the sense that it subsumed a broad variety of organizations and networks within its purview.

To avoid additional complexity, the discussion of informal networks in this book extends only to those networks that are mostly autonomous—that is, they are not subordinated to a formal organization and do not subsume formal organizations within them. In other words, they cannot be considered a "network of networks."

Third, some of the informal networks discussed in this book are not recognized "terrorist" networks in the legal sense that they have been declared as such in a court of law or by governmental offices such as the U.S. Department of State. On the contrary, many of the informal networks that will be described in several case studies in chapter 9 are purposefully walking a tightrope between legal activities and acts of terrorism. Those informal networks that have been involved in some terrorist-related activity, but have not been declared a terrorist entity by a court of law or the government will be referred to as *jihadist networks*, as opposed to *terrorist networks*.

Given the above reservations, the informal networks covered in the theoretical discussion and case studies of this book typically share the following characteristics: (1) lack of a formal organizational structure; (2) flexible membership; and (3) decentralization.

Lack of Formal Organizational Structure

Informal networks typically lack the formal structures of bureaucracy and processes of decision-making that characterize classic terrorist organizations. This is evident already from the spontaneous way in which many informal networks arise. Informal networks can spring up virtually anywhere and anytime, in prisons, in schools, in religious institutions, and increasingly through the Internet.[67]

Behind Bars, for instance, a Dutch jihadist and Salafist network, emerged rather spontaneously from disillusioned worshippers of the As Soennah mosque in The Hague and out of protests against the arrest of a Dutch jihadist in Morocco whose residence permit had been rescinded by Dutch authorities.[68] The birth of Street Dawah, another Dutch militant Salafist network, was connected to protests by Dutch Muslims against the burka ban that started in The Hague, but eventually spread to other Dutch cities with the goal of "hitting the streets every week to spread the message of Islam."[69]

Contrast this with the establishment of Al Qaeda, a formal organization. As will be described in more detail in chapter 5, Al Qaeda developed over the course of several years in the midst of the Afghan-Soviet war. Before founding Al Qaeda, Bin Laden honed his leadership skills through his involvement in the Maktab al-Khidamat organization and by establishing his own training camp, the Lion's Den. In addition, Al Qaeda's official founding was deliberated, codified, and eventually announced over the course of several formal meetings in Afghanistan during August 1988—hardly a spontaneous process.[70] The former Jabhat al-Nusra, Al Qaeda's formal affiliate in Syria until the summer of 2016, was similarly founded as a result of several secret meetings in Homs and Damascus over the course of October 2011.[71]

Informal networks usually lack the hierarchical bureaucratic structures of formal organizations. Relatively unencumbered by administrative red tape, these groups are particularly agile and adaptive, rendering government efforts to check these groups' activities more difficult. Their agility and adaptiveness enables streamlined operations within the network, which in turn affects a variety of important activities, from attracting new members to establishing new ties to other actors, and from overcoming counterterrorism hurdles all the way to planning attacks.[72]

Moreover, their informal structure renders these networks less visible, should they choose to keep a low profile (which, as chapter 9 shows, not all networks do). Network participants, for example, can "hide behind various licit activities . . . and maintain a profile that does not bring them to the attention of law enforcement."[73] Even if network participants do engage in some illegal activity, the network may not be outlawed because, as a Spanish investigator noted, "some European legal codes require proof of structure or organization before designating a group as a terrorist organization."[74]

Despite the informal structure of most of these networks, one should not conclude that these networks are devoid of any structure altogether.

As a Dutch intelligence report points out, "There is always a pattern of connections between individuals who communicate with one another with a view to achieving a common goal. In some cases these communication lines converge in one or more core groups, which thus play a coordinating and controlling role. In other cases there are random communication patterns between all members while the network functions practically without any leadership or central control."[75]

Flexible Membership and Fluid Organizational Boundaries

The relative lack of formal structures typical of these networks is usually accompanied by a high degree of flexibility and fluidity in their membership. This is illustrated, for example, by the way in which participants may enter or exit these networks, which are usually formed on a voluntary basis in the sense that participation is not imposed from above.[76] While formal terrorist and insurgent organizations may also receive volunteers, they are also known to forcibly recruit members, including children. Such is the case with the Sri Lankan Liberation Tigers of Tamil Eelam (LTTE), Sierra Leone's Revolutionary United Front (RUF), and the Islamic State.[77] Similarly, departure from informal networks is far easier than is abandonment of formal terrorist organizations. Members of informal networks can cease participating usually at little cost. Abandonment of a formal terrorist group, on the other hand, can result in serious consequences, including harsh forms of punishment or death.[78]

Flexibility and fluidity also characterize the relationship among network members. The interactions between core participants of the network are often based on trust and on shared beliefs and values. Members of the same networks frequently have a prior acquaintance in the form of friendship or kinship ties.[79] Relationships can also be based on shared political or religious ideologies, shared origins or ethnicities, or shared experiences in prison, training camps, or combat theaters.[80]

Where preexisting identity ties do not exist, participation in these informal networks helps establish these identities through social bonding and time spent together.[81] These social interactions also help establish social obligations.[82] These networks are often composed, either in part or entirely, of cliques—small, dense networks in which every node is connected to another node—which further contributes to group cohesion and the building of a collective identity.[83] As I will argue in the next chapter, jihadi ideology, broadly understood, forms the most important basis for these shared values and beliefs and for the formation of a common identity both within contemporary informal networks and among different terrorist actors in the broader global jihadi movement.

One of the most striking indications of the flexible nature of membership in these networks is that members sometimes have multiple affiliations. Perliger and Pedahzur, for instance, found that members of Palestinian suicide attack networks can also be members of other groups.[84] Similarly, the cell responsible for the Madrid train bombings of March 11, 2004, has been described as a "complicated confluence of groups inside and outside Spain, with links to the Casablanca bombing through the Moroccan Islamist Combatant Group (GICM) and to the Iraqi insurgency through Ansar al-Islam,"[85] as well as to Al Qaeda.[86] In another example, the Hofstad Group, one of whose members assassinated Dutch filmmaker Theo van Gogh in broad daylight, had some relationship with counterparts in Italy, Spain, and Belgium as well as contacts with extremists in Morocco, through a member who was affiliated with the GICM."[87]

The flexible nature of membership in these informal networks means that it can be difficult to distinguish members from nonmembers, and even if members are identified, it can be hard to differentiate between those who are engaged in violent activities and those who are not. Furthermore, network activities themselves as not always directly related to terrorism. This is particularly evident in the various Sharia4 networks described at length in chapter 9. While some of their members have become involved in acts of terrorism, most of the networks' activities are not illegal. As a result, governments face considerable difficulties in their efforts to identify the most dangerous elements within these networks, and the work of the prosecutors is also inhibited.[88]

Decentralization

Another common feature of these informal networks is their decentralized nature. Whereas formal terrorist organizations have clearly identifiable leaders who, by and large, exercise formal authority, many (although not all) informal networks are marked by decentralized authority.

Social network analysis conducted on Palestinian suicide networks, for example, has shown that networks can possess several highly connected nodes, or hubs, instead of a single leader. These hubs can help to diffuse power by creating local clusters of power, each of which can attract members to the network or carry out attacks on its own.[89] Informal jihadist networks in the Netherlands also illustrate this decentralized character well. According to Dutch intelligence, "The Hague, for example, has had a loose jihadist 'circle' for some years now. So too has Arnhem. . . . These and similar clusters elsewhere usually comprise [sic] groups of friends and acquaintances with a shared belief in the ideology of jihad. . . . Comparable clusters are also found online, in the form of Facebook communities."[90] Additionally, the overall network of jihadists in the Netherlands has "little hierarchy" and "few clear leaders." According to the report, "a few influential jihadists in the Netherlands possess the charisma, the knowledge and the relationships needed to play a role of some significance. Within a circle of friends, they are able to expound an appealing religious and ideological vision or to advise on its 'correct' interpretation. They can also lead media campaigns, logistical activities and fundraising efforts. . . . However, even they rarely exercise hierarchical leadership."[91]

TERRORIST ENTREPRENEURS

For better or worse, one of the most salient consequences of globalization has been the empowerment of individuals. The concept of the *terrorist entrepreneur* captures one aspect of this process and relates it to the newly expanded capabilities of some individuals to plan, execute, or support acts of terrorism. Like informal networks, terrorist entrepreneurs are not a new phenomenon. Historically, a number of terrorists have displayed an ability to plan and execute highly innovative attacks, build novel forms of organizations, and adopt new strategies designed to advance their political and ideological objectives. Some of these terrorist entrepreneurs were closely associated with formal terrorist groups. George Habash and Osama bin Laden, for example, founded and led the Popular Front for the Liberation of Palestine (PFLP) and Al Qaeda, respectively.[92] Abu Nidal formed the Fatah Revolutionary Council (also known as the Abu Nidal Organization [ANO]), while Wadie Haddad led the PFLP-External Operations group. Others had more loose organizational affiliations. While the infamous Carlos the Jackal joined the PFLP in 1970, he also functioned—as did Abu Nidal and George Habash—as a terrorist freelancer linked to a variety of groups and governments.[93]

Although these terrorist entrepreneurs, who are sometimes referred to as terrorist "masterminds" in the literature, have been an integral part of the complex web of international terrorism since the late 1960s, their ability to wreak havoc has grown exponentially since the 1990s due to the information revolution, the arrival of new technologies, the miniaturization of weapons, and similar developments. Along with their transformative power, the agency of these actors has multiplied in importance.

Nevertheless, there are surprisingly few theoretical reflections available on terrorist entrepreneurs in the existing terrorism studies literature.[94] An exception to this is Sherzod Abdukadirov, who describes entrepreneurs by contrasting them to what he calls ordinary "shopkeepers." The most important difference, he argues, is the very motivation to start an enterprise. Thus, ordinary "shopkeepers" frequently open up, or maintain, a business due to lack of other opportunities. If given a chance, they would possibly prefer an alternative employment. As a result, their businesses tend to remain relatively small. Entrepreneurs, on the other hand, are described as highly motivated individuals in constant search of opportunities. They seek to maximize profits and grow in size. Unlike "shopkeepers," entrepreneurs may have plenty of alternative opportunities for employment, but have made a deliberate choice to embark on a particular project.

Entrepreneurs are frequently described as innovators and inherent risk-seekers. Constantly on the lookout for new opportunities, they can help identify new products or raise the quality or efficiency of existing products. In business, the result of this greater efficiency tends to be economic growth.[95]

Using the above characterization as a starting point, I define terrorist entrepreneurs as independently minded, highly motivated, and resourceful individuals dedicated to exploiting existing opportunities and seeking novel ways to execute, plan, or support acts of terrorism. Accordingly, enterprising terrorists who are members of formal organizations and not independently minded are excluded. Describing terrorist entrepreneurs as "highly motivated" underscores their freedom of choice, while characterizing them as "dedicated" emphasizes the substantial amount of time and effort they generally devote to achieving their objectives, which they frequently pursue with great zeal. Entrepreneurs are activists in the sense that they care deeply about an issue, even to the point where they are willing to incur enormous cost to their lives.[96] They are also "resourceful," not so much in having financial means, but in terms of possessing less tangible, but no less important qualities such as advanced technological skills, the ability to think strategically and "out of the box," and other traits that abet terrorist innovation at the tactical, organizational, or strategic level.[97]

As stated above, many of history's most notorious terrorist entrepreneurs had organizational affiliations. For the present purposes, however, I focus on organizationally independent terrorist entrepreneurs because my goal is to examine cooperation between different types of agents. This requires drawing a distinction among agents at the individual, informal network, and organizational level. Once a terrorist entrepreneur joins an informal network or is a formal member of a terrorist or insurgent group, for present analytical purposes I consider his agency to be subsumed within that of informal networks or formal terrorist/insurgent organizations, respectively.

Given the potential of terrorist entrepreneurs to bring about transformative change, there is no doubt that terrorist entrepreneurs can be considered to possess agency. The 9/11 mastermind Khaled Sheikh Muhammad embodies the notion of terrorist entrepreneurship particularly well. As the *9/11 Commission Report* states, KSM was an ingenious, dedicated terrorist who placed a high premium on his independence—so much so that he initially refused to pledge allegiance to Osama bin Laden, although he subsequently joined the organization in late 1998 or 1999.[98]

Terrorist entrepreneurs can come in various forms. Some, including KSM, whom the *9/11 Commission Report* authors considered to "exemplif[y] the model of the terrorist entrepreneur" more than anyone else, or his nephew Ramzi Youssef, the mastermind of the first World Trade Center bombing in 1993, have been actively involved in the planning and execution of attacks.[99] Terrorist entrepreneurs, however, can support acts of terrorism without necessarily "getting their hands dirty." Here, as will be discussed below, the Internet has played an increasingly important role in recent years in empowering a growing number of individuals to serve as "force multipliers" who can significantly abet terrorism in various ways short of planning innovative attacks. Terrorist ideologues such as Omar Bakri Muhammad or Anwar al-Awlaki, for example, have radicalized thousands of youth, especially in Western countries, through in-person or online sermons.

The Internet, and especially social media platforms such as Facebook and Twitter, have provided a major boost to the ability of individual actors to abet terrorism and therefore to inflict great potential harm. It has served as a force multiplier not only to more recognized jihadi ideologues, but also to various self-starters, who can serve as critical links between various terrorist actors or help spread terrorist, especially jihadi propaganda and thereby contribute to the radicalization of countless youth.

TERRORIST AGENTS AND TERRORIST COOPERATION

The growing diversity of terrorist agents has very clear implications for terrorist cooperation. As the above discussion has indicated, many of the characteristics of terrorist entrepreneurs and informal networks enable them to establish ties to other terrorist actors—entrepreneurs, organizations, and other networks—more easily and efficiently, when compared with more formal organizations, and to do so in a conspiratorial and secretive fashion, under the radar of authorities. Furthermore, the structural flexibility and mobility of these informal actors, which enables easier physical diffusion of their participants, contributes to the establishment of transnational ties—a major catalyst for terrorist cooperation, even if the Internet and social media platforms are playing a growing role in this regard.[100] Since informal actors face fewer barriers for establishing an international presence, they are also better able to exploit opportunities afforded to them in other areas, such as the legal realm or, as we will see in the next chapter and case studies in chapter 9, in places where armed conflict prevails and territories are poorly governed.

The flexible structure of networks also affords them the benefit of establishing more variegated types of relationships with other actors, which may range from purely ideological support to more concrete, logistical, or operational forms of collaboration. Flexibility can also facilitate the creation of network ties to a variety of support structures that can promote terrorism. Phil Williams has noted the ability of criminal networks to draw, for instance, on "groups that provide false documentation, front companies, transportation, and a financial infrastructure that can be used to move the proceeds of crime."[101] Such support structures can be harnessed by and can benefit terrorist networks just as well.

The relative ease with which informal networks are able to share ideas and information both within and outside of the network helps advance ideological cooperation and the exertion of ideational influence over other actors and can also abet the diffusion of "hard" know-how, such as the use of certain tactical innovations as exemplified in the spread of suicide bombings.

The informal nature of the ties among network members enables easier contact with other actors. Of special importance here is Granovetter's prominent concept of "the strength of weak ties."[102] Informal networks, like all other networks, usually possess a core and a periphery. While the ties among participants are the strongest at the core, the periphery of networks is usually marked by more loose interactions, but these "weak" ties have a critical "strength": They enable the network to expand its reach. This has important implications for the ability of these groups to engage in a host of activities in promotion of their goals, including the sharing of ideas and cooperation with other actors. In fact, a network's weak ties are the predominant mechanism through which informal networks interact with their environment.[103]

Finally, network-based terrorist cooperation can have an impact on the nature and execution of terrorist activity. Not only are informal networks likely to become increasingly involved in conflict due to the ease with which they can turn into larger, multi-actor networks, but they can affect tactics and operations as well. Networked cooperation, for example, can support "swarming," which John Arquilla and David Ronfeldt define as "an emerging mode of conflict . . . in which the protagonists use network forms of organization and related doctrines, strategies and technologies attuned to the information age. These protagonists are likely to consist of dispersed organizations, small groups, and individuals who communicate, coordinate, and conduct their campaigns in an internetted manner, often without a precise central command."[104] Swarming entails the ability of multiple actors to converge on a target and strike from all directions and then to disperse rapidly while maintaining their readiness to re-converge for a new strike.[105]

In sum, the above discussion has shown that actors other than formal terrorist organizations are active today, and this has important implications for contemporary terrorist cooperation. Informal actors can establish a greater variety of cooperative ties with other actors more efficiently and can utilize these ties more effectively, thereby raising the overall threat posed by terrorist collaborations.

* * *

This chapter has argued that agency in terrorism has evolved significantly and that this evolution has implications for the way that new terrorist actors cooperate. And yet, these actors do not operate in a vacuum.

Rather, they are active in a broader environment that enables and constrains these actors' behavior and that, in turn, is affected by these actors. The next chapter sets out to describe in greater detail those structural and environmental factors that have a bearing on how contemporary actors cooperate.

3

SHIFTING ENVIRONMENT

Ideology, Social Media, and Armed Conflicts

T HE PREVIOUS CHAPTER highlighted the changing nature of agency in
terrorism, one of two key trends underlying the evolution of terrorist
cooperation in recent decades. Equally critical, however, is the second trend, which involves broader environmental developments that have
accompanied and interacted with this increasingly complex array of terrorist actors. Describing this enabling environment is a daunting task for
two reasons. First, there is a multitude of environmental, or structural,
factors at play—more than could possibly be addressed in this book. For
this reason, I will limit my description to a select number of environmental variables that I believe influence contemporary terrorist cooperation
the most. The second problem facing researchers in this regard is the dynamic nature of this environment. Even the best descriptions of what political scientists term "structure" are limited in their ability to fully grasp
an environmental context that is in constant flux. Therefore, my analysis
does not purport to be forward looking. It instead attempts to provide a
simplified and selective overview of structural factors that have affected
terrorist cooperation from the 1990s, and to the present.

Acknowledging the relevance of a broader structure that provides the
setting for contemporary terrorist cooperation is necessary because the

activities of terrorist actors—like those of all agents—do not occur in a vacuum; they cannot be divorced from their broader context.[1] The present discussion of environmental factors helps account for the growing diversity of actors described in the preceding chapter and promotes our understanding of why and how they cooperate. To those ends, I will highlight three key aspects of the context in which terrorist entrepreneurs, informal networks, and formal terrorist and insurgent organizations collaborate. The first is jihadi ideology, which, I argue, constitutes the main *cause*, or motivation, for contemporary jihadi cooperation. The second is the Internet and the new social media, which embody the main *medium* of terrorist collaboration. Third, I will briefly highlight the role that armed conflict plays in providing significant *opportunities* for terrorist cooperation.

STRUCTURE, TERRORISM, AND TERRORIST COOPERATION

Social scientists frequently refer to the term "structure" to describe the circumstances that shape the interests, choices, and actions of agents. Structure is broadly understood not only as enabling, but also as constraining these choices and actions.[2] In international relations, the most influential conceptualization sees "rules and resources" as the main elements of structure.[3]

David Dessler defines "rules" as the media through which agents communicate and coordinate their activities.[4] These rules, which generally derive from language, can be codified (or explicit), or unwritten (implicit). The latter are common in everyday social interactions.[5] As far as resources are concerned, realists and neorealists have viewed these attributes of structure largely in terms of the distribution of material capabilities.[6]

Structurationist and constructivist scholars, on the other hand, have argued that structure can be based on both material and nonmaterial capabilities. Anthony Giddens, for example, distinguishes between two types of resources: allocative resources, which are more tangible and include material objects such as territory, raw material, weapons, or technology; and authoritative resources, which are immaterial factors, such as positions of power in hierarchies that can enable human agents to exercise command over others.[7]

Colin Wight maintains that viewing structure merely as "rules and resources" ignores the motivations of agents. Motivations, according to Wight, are not limited to the level of agency. They have a structural dimension insofar as structural configurations can motivate agents to act in certain ways."[8] Alexander Wendt, in his later work, similarly argued that the ideational properties of structure help account for the motivations of actors.[9] In a 1995 article, he described social structures as "the shared ideas or common knowledge embodied in intersubjective phenomena like institutions and threat systems."[10] These social structures exist only in practice. Material resources, Wendt believes, continue to matter but are dependent on the structure of shared knowledge in which they are embedded in order to acquire meaning for human action. Most importantly for Wendt, social structures are defined, in part, by "shared understandings, expectations, or knowledge. These constitute the actors in a situation and the nature of their relationships, whether cooperative or conflictual."[11]

I distill several insights from this brief discussion on structure for the present analysis of terrorist cooperation. First, in line with the predominant view of structure as rules and resources, I will present those features of the contemporary environment that best describe a key *medium* in which contemporary terrorist action takes place and which presents prominent *opportunities* for contemporary cooperation to flourish. Second, in acknowledging the critique of the conventional description of structure as neglecting motivational and ideational aspects, I will describe what is in my mind the central structural *cause* affecting the motivations and behavior of contemporary jihadist terrorist actors to cooperate (see table 3.1). To be sure, these three environmental factors are mutually related and partially overlapping. Jihadi ideology (the cause), for example, is promoted through the medium of the Internet, while the Internet not only is a medium but also provides opportunities for action, and so forth.

TABLE 3.1 STRUCTURAL FACTORS FOR
CONTEMPORARY TERRORIST COOPERATION

STRUCTURAL FACTOR	SIGNIFICANCE FOR TERRORIST COOPERATION
Jihadi ideology	Cause
Internet and social media	Medium
Armed conflict	Opportunity

THE CAUSE: JIHADI IDEOLOGY

The global jihad can be understood as a broader social movement that brings together a large variety of individuals, cells, networks, and organizations, all of which are united in their belief that their actions are advancing the Islamic cause as they see it.[12] The common denominator connecting this broad array of jihadists is jihadi, or Salafi-Jihadi, ideology, which provides a common system of beliefs and values and suggests how to translate them into action.[13]

Jihadi ideology creates a fertile setting for terrorist cooperation. Two core functions of jihadism help foster this setting: The first is the attempt—successful by any objective measure—to create a community of believers who have similar norms, values, interests, and goals. The second is a programmatic function, and involves the calling upon this broad community of believers to join efforts—cooperate—in order to translate their ideological goals into practice.

True, jihadi groups are divided over a variety of issues ranging from tactics to strategy, and they have their share of personality problems and theological disagreements.[14] Jihadis of all stripes, however, are united by a common narrative that lies at the heart of global jihadi ideology.[15] The gist of that narrative is relatively straightforward: It is that Islam has been facing, and continues to face, a sustained military, political, cultural, and religious attack. Leading the charge on this anti-Islamic conspiracy is a three pronged enemy consisting of what jihadis call "Crusaders," meaning the Western, Christian nations led by the United States; "Zionists," meaning Israel and the Jews; and "Apostates," or nominal Muslims who have yet to accept the strict interpretation of Islam propagated by the jihadists. In order to defend the *umma*, or Islamic community of believers, from this attempted subjugation of Islam, it is incumbent upon every true Muslim to defend Islam through jihad. This individual duty (*fard ayn*) is foremost a militant effort. Even though the concept of *jihad* has broader meaning in Islam—it is usually defined as the exertion of an effort and can refer to militant and nonmilitant activity alike—jihadis employ the term almost exclusively in its militant sense.[16] The acceptance of this simple, yet powerful narrative is what unites jihadis in a self-described transnational community of Islamic believers, or *umma*.[17]

Several mechanisms have coincided in establishing jihadi ideology as a dominant force in recent decades. Not least of these is the jihadis' masterful employment of the Internet and the social media, which is discussed in the next section. Another is that jihadi ideology, like all ideologies, is a system of belief that can forge strong identities among its adherents, especially by raising the awareness of certain groups of people—typically during times of crisis—that a problem afflicting that group deserves the group's attention. Jihadi ideologues have long referred to a general crisis of Islam that affects both Muslims in the Islamic world and Muslim minorities in non-Muslim countries.[18] To these Muslims, and a growing number of converts, jihadi ideology is appealing in part because it offers simple answers to the existential questions that tend to plague men and women in their youth. Jihadi ideology, put differently, offers a solution to individuals in search of meaning and significance in their lives.[19]

The sense of crisis felt by those susceptible to jihadi ideology requires a common effort on the part of the self-described true adherents of Islam to rid the *umma* of the source of the crisis. This common endeavor helps strengthen the identity of the *umma*, a process further promoted by the tendency of all ideologies—jihadism included—to draw a sharp dividing line between in-groups and out-groups. For jihadis, the in-group consists of the true believers of Islam—that is, those who have adopted the jihadi

interpretation of Islam. The out-group consists of heretics and apostates—
or those who fail to accept the jihadi narrative. Jihadi ideology sharpens
these distinctions by ascribing superior characteristics to the in-group, and
juxtaposing these with the presumably inferior traits of the out-group.
Jihadi ideology utilizes the theological doctrine of *al-wala wa'l-bara* (loyalty and disavowal), among others, to highlight the distinctions between
Muslims and non-Muslims. According to this doctrine, "true" Muslims
are to be afforded loyalty and love, while infidels are to be renounced.[20]

Jihadi ideology serves as a glue that holds the jihadis' notion of the
umma together, and this community of believers is transnational in scope.
This is due in part to jihadis' adeptness in exploiting the tools of globalization, including modern technologies and in part to the way that jihadi
ideology actively seeks to portray local, seemingly isolated crises and their
corresponding grievances as part of a global problem—one that, consequently, requires global solutions. As Sidney Tarrow has shown, jihadis
are, by no means, alone in their ability to stoke transnational activism by
framing local issues in global terms,[21] but they nevertheless seem unusually good at it. One reason for this success lies in jihadism's status as a religious ideology, as opposed to a secular one. As such, jihadism describes its
adherents, its enemies, and its struggles in religious terms.[22] Even though
jihadis pick selectively from the Islamic tradition only those elements that
advance their narrow agenda, they nevertheless draw from the Quran,
hadith, and other religious sources that inform the lives and practices of all
Muslims. It is for this reason that non-jihadi Muslims—not to speak of
non-Muslims—find it particularly difficult to challenge jihadists without
being accused of speaking out against Islam as a whole.

Another mechanism that has enabled jihadi ideology to appeal to a
broad spectrum of people is that it defines the presumed enemies of jihad
broadly. As stated above, jihadis view their enemies in terms of a coalition
of Crusaders, Apostates, and Zionists, but individual jihadi writers will
draw the circle of enemies even wider to include international institutions,
multinational corporations, and other actors as part of the anti-Islamic
camp.[23] This broad conceptualization of enemies may seem incoherent to
outside observers, but jihadis try to portray this long list of enemies as part

of a cohesive conspiracy. More importantly, such a loose description of its enemies allows a wide range of individuals and groups with various grievances against particular aspects of that meta-enemy to latch on to the jihadi message.[24]

The fact that jihadi ideology is the common denominator for a transnational community has direct implications for terrorist cooperation. Ideologies do not merely function as systems that emphasize to a certain group of people that they suffer from a predicament, that they need to stick together, and that they are different from their enemies. Ideologies are also programmatic. They propose real world solutions to the problems supposedly afflicting their adherents. In the case of the jihadi community, that remedy is jihad, understood in its militant sense as the physical defense of Islam. Given that the perceived enemies of Islam are believed to have formed a powerful coalition, the defense against this coordinated anti-Islamic effort needs to be concerted as well. It needs to involve a broad variety of Islamic actors worldwide. Herein lies jihadi ideology's role in serving as the main cause of contemporary jihadist cooperation.

The imperative for Muslims to work together to repel a powerful, multidimensional enemy explains the frequent calls among jihadi leaders for unity among jihadists, even though in reality, such a unity remains elusive. Still, jihadi actors argue that the defense of Islam against its enemies requires cooperative efforts among all jihadi elements. In this effort to repel the presumed onslaught of the alleged anti-Islamic conspirators, the stakes are particularly high because jihad against the enemies of God is divinely ordained. This rationale creates a far greater sense of urgency for jihadists to join efforts in a common struggle against an enemy than secular political ideologies typically do. In the face of the perceived threat from the West, cooperation is a critical component in the struggle to safeguard Islam's future.

To most jihadis, participation in the struggle against the enemies of Islam outweighs in importance the more technical questions related to the struggle, such as which group a jihadi should join or in which theater a jihadi should fight. The members of the Hamburg cell that participated in the attacks of September 11, 2001, for example, were originally interested in joining the jihad in Chechnya, when a chance encounter on a German train led them to travel to Afghanistan instead.[25]

In another example, trial proceedings of a group of French jihadists who fought in Syria revealed that only days before they were set to depart for Syria, the men pondered whether to join the Mali, Libya, or Yemeni theaters of jihad instead.[26] Similarly, as Lorenzo Vidino has pointed out, it is of little concern to many European jihadists which jihadi group to join. Jihadis simply "want to fight jihad and care little about whether they do so with al Qaeda, the Islamic State, Al Shabaab, or any other group of the global jihadist community."[27]

THE MEDIUM: THE INTERNET

A second environmental factor of great importance for understanding contemporary terrorist cooperation—especially among jihadi actors—is the Internet. Since the Internet is the quintessential medium of globalization, I will briefly discuss the impact of globalization on terrorist cooperation, before focusing on the Internet.

Globalization, according to a prominent definition, entails the "widening, deepening and speeding up of worldwide interconnectedness in all aspects of contemporary social life, from the cultural to the criminal, the financial to the spiritual."[28] As this description suggests, while globalization harbors the potential for pro-social change, it has also produced unintended consequences that can be considered setbacks to human progress. This "dark side" of globalization, as it is sometimes referred to, includes the employment of elements of globalization—such as the Internet—in the service of terrorism.[29]

Globalization's supreme relevance to terrorism in general and terrorist cooperation specifically stems from its ability to affect power relations. As David Held, Anthony McGrew, David Goldblatt, and Jonathan Perraton observe, "In an increasingly interconnected global system, the exercise of power through the decisions, actions, or inactions, of agencies on one continent can have significant consequences for nations, communities, and households on other continents."[30] Globalization therefore "involves the structuring and restructuring of power relations at a distance."[31] This matters for terrorism because terrorism is "ineluctably about power," as Bruce Hoffman has put it—"the pursuit of power, the acquisition of power, and the use of power to achieve political change."[32] Globalization's impact on terrorism, therefore, derives from its potential to shift the power balance between terrorist actors and their enemies in the terrorists' favor.

Globalization has empowered terrorist actors in a variety of ways. It assists with the propagation of the terrorists' message, the mobilization of recruits, and planning of attacks, all of which boost the capacity of terrorist actors. Yet, perhaps nowhere is the impact of globalization on the capacity of terrorist actors greater than in their ability to cooperate. The reason is simple: The enhancement and strengthening of global interconnectedness is not merely a by-product of globalization, but arguably its essential feature.[33] Globalization, in other words, is so instrumental in advancing terrorist cooperation because interconnectivity is the central feature and purpose of globalization.

Moreover, economic conditions and technological developments associated with globalization have affected how terrorists cooperate in a number of ways. Cheaper air travel, for example, has enabled more individuals to travel and interact face to face. These interactions have helped build new networks and communities, which have in turn presented new opportunities for cooperation and transnational activism in general and for terrorists to establish regional or international links with their peers in particular.[34] Similarly, the miniaturization of technology, and especially the proliferation of portable communication devices such as Smartphones, allows individuals to be in constant touch with other individuals, networks, groups, and communities, from nearly any location worldwide.

If interconnectedness is the essential feature and specialty of globalization, then the Internet is the main medium for its development and growth. The Internet has also had an extraordinary impact on global terrorism, as scholars have recognized in recent years. Some have argued that the Internet has played an important role in supporting terrorist groups' efforts in gathering and disseminating information; indoctrinating their members and broader audiences; recruiting new members; fundraising; planning and executing terrorist attacks; providing online training; and, in the case of jihadists specifically, spreading jihadi ideology and forging a virtual community of jihadi believers.[35] While some scholars have questioned whether the overall impact of the Internet is an increase in terrorism,[36] most agree that the Internet is a force multiplier that offers a critical advantage to terrorists.

The following analysis focuses on the Internet's impact on cooperation among terrorist actors, not on terrorism writ large. I argue that the Internet has influenced terrorist cooperation in four main ways that, when taken together, have helped fundamentally transform the nature of terrorist cooperation. First, the Internet has influenced the emergence of new informal agents of terrorism and helped build the capacity of all terrorist agents to cooperate; second, the Internet has produced new online facilitators of and platforms for terrorist cooperation—from individual disseminators to jihadi forums, chat rooms, and social media platforms such as Facebook and Twitter; third, the Internet has helped forge a virtual identity among the broader jihadi community, which helps motivate cooperation; and fourth, the Internet serves as the main medium of communication for terrorist agents, platforms and facilitators, and the broader jihadi community (see figure 3.1).

BUILDING AGENT CAPACITY FOR TERRORIST COOPERATION

Social science scholars concerned with the relationship between social environments and the actors within them have long argued that structure and agents are mutually interdependent. For constructivist scholars, environments can affect the behavior of actors, their properties, and even their very existence.[37] As Peter Katzenstein puts it, contexts "help to constitute the very actors whose conduct they seek to regulate."[38]

Nowhere does this seem to be more applicable than in the case of the Internet, which offers capacities that, as George Michael writes, "allow for new, more flexible models of organization and mass collaboration."[39] Thus, the Internet has contributed significantly to the emergence of a new breed of terrorist entrepreneurs who are far more empowered than their counterparts in previous decades. It has also increased the overall number of

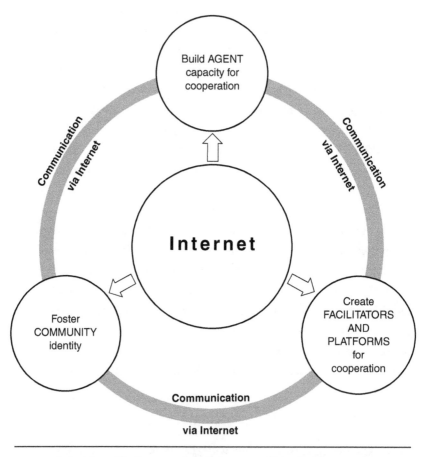

FIGURE 3.1 The Impact of the Internet on Terrorist Cooperation

individual actors who have the potential to rise to the level of terrorist entrepreneurs. In the first decades after the emergence of modern international terrorism in the late 1960s, terrorist entrepreneurs had to have high
motivation, a special skill set, and good connections to formal organizations or states in order to embark on successful careers. Nowadays, motivated individuals can, thanks to the Internet, inflict grave harm even in
the absence of special skills or links to established groups or states, for
example by helping to disseminate jihadist ideology via Facebook or
Twitter. Furthermore, the Internet enables these entrepreneurs to operate

in more consequential ways because it provides greater access to, and dissemination of, information, while offering these entrepreneurs a superior system of communication with other parties. In his interview with Khaled Sheikh Mohammed, for example, Al Jazeera investigative reporter Yousri Fouda noticed the large amount of laptops and cellular phones at the disposal of the 9/11 mastermind and his accomplice, Ramzi bin-al Shibh.[40]

While, the Internet has empowered individuals in unprecedented ways, it has also furthered the growing importance of informal networks. As Michele Zanini and Sean Edwards have pointed out, "new technologies have significantly reduced the cost of communication, allowing information-intensive organizational designs such as networks to become viable."[41]

By abetting the establishment of terrorist entrepreneurs and informal networks, the Internet has thus had a direct role in increasing the overall number of terrorist actors involved in cooperation. No less important, however, is that the Internet has helped boost the capacities of both emerging and existing agents of terrorism to cooperate with other actors and coordinate activities, thereby raising their overall ability to inflict harm on their enemies.

For one thing, the Internet enables terrorist actors to connect with more actors in more places more speedily and at a reduced cost. Employment of this medium helps different types of terrorist actors connect to each other across vast geographic distances using email, teleconferencing, chat rooms, interactive web sites, social media platforms, and the like, all of which can render irrelevant the need for any direct personal encounters when coordinating and planning attacks. These modes of communication can also affect the operational execution of terrorist attacks. Zanini and Edwards note, for example, that the Internet can affect speed of mobilization and can help groups adjust their tactics more frequently, thereby raising the overall flexibility of organizations.[42] Today's terrorists can communicate in real time, and they can do it at a fraction of the cost that traditional organizations incurred. As David Benson observes, "International communication was possible prior to the Internet, [but] it was either slow, expensive, or both, making the formation and maintenance of relationships difficult or impossible."[43]

A second way that the Internet helps facilitate terrorist cooperation is by offering vast improvements in the amount of information that groups can share. Providing greater bandwidth, the Internet allows terrorist actors to share greater quantities of more complex information with like-minded parties.

Furthermore, the Internet, and especially social media, helps terrorist organizations and networks expand their reach. Recruiters employ social media "to outsource recruitment to hubs of militants located outside the war zone," notes Jytte Klausen.[44] This helps organizations reach broader audiences through a cost-effective "echo chamber of lateral duplication across multiple platforms."[45] Recruiters can subsequently transfer these communications to private, encrypted contact points to heighten operational security.

Crucially, though, the Internet helps facilitate the internationalization of terrorist actors in the first place. The ease of communication streamlines the formation of geographically dispersed cells, which further provides distinct advantages. Cells can operate in areas that are poorly governed and establish links with local groups more easily. Transnational terrorist operations also complicate the mission of counterterrorism and law-enforcement operations because these operations cross jurisdictions.[46]

Finally, the Internet also offers these groups greater abilities to protect their communications using encryption programs and other technologies.[47] Terrorist groups are by nature conspiratorial and prefer anonymity, at least in the planning stage of their operations. The Internet, in the words of Bruce Hoffman, is therefore the ideal medium for terrorists—"anonymous but pervasive."[48] If anonymity cannot be attained, the Internet, at the very least, offers groups the ability to act pseudonymously.[49]

CREATING ONLINE FACILITATORS AND PLATFORMS OF COOPERATION

Another critical feature of the Internet is that it can be used as a tool to establish new platforms and facilitators for terrorist cooperation. Platforms for cooperation, of course, have existed and continue to exist in offline form. As noted in chapter 1, since the 1960s, terrorist training camps have served, inter alia, as a platform for terrorist cooperation. Front companies and charities have facilitated terrorist cooperation as well. As Matt Levitt explains, financial organizations such as Bank Al-Taqwa are "key nodes in [a] terrorist matrix" and "have become the preferred conduits used by terrorists from multiple terrorist groups to fund and facilitate attacks."[50]

Individual supporters and financiers of terrorism have played similar roles in connecting different terrorist groups to each other. While using the cover of a Hamas front organization named Al Aqsa International Foundation, for example, Mohammed Ali Hasan al-Moayad, the foundation's representative in Yemen, was arrested for funding Hamas while providing material and financial support to Al Qaeda recruits. Meanwhile, the foundation's Netherlands office reportedly raised funds for Hizballah.[51] Abdurahman Muahammad Alamoudi, the head of the American Muslim Foundation, played a similar role by providing financial support to both Hamas and Al Qaeda.[52]

As Levitt rightly emphasizes, facilitators of terrorism, be they institutions or individuals, play an underappreciated role in the terrorism nexus,[53] And this role has only increased with the advent of the Internet. Al Qaeda began harnessing modern information technology such as satellite telephones, e-mail, websites, and facsimiles around the time that its central faction, led by Osama bin Laden, returned from Sudan to Afghanistan in 1996.[54] By the time the war in Iraq began in 2003, jihadists were making use of the innovative capabilities of the Internet.[55] Thus, Marc Sageman describes how informal terrorist networks such as the Hofstad Group or the Madrid train bombers were inspired by and communicated through dedicated jihadi forums and chat rooms at that time.[56] Subsequently, the Internet has created a new breed of online facilitators, while also producing a broad new spectrum of platforms that further complicate the picture of how terrorists cooperate.

As far as online facilitators are concerned, since the time of the Iraq War in 2003 the Internet has vastly increased the power of individual actors to facilitate the violent activities of terrorist actors. These online facilitators include spiritual authorities who can provide inspiration and encouragement for would be jihadists to participate in jihadi activities, but oftentimes they are female supporters or wives of fighters.[57] By providing justification for and religious sanction to jihadis to participate in fighting, these facilitators play an essential role in radicalization and collaboration. A study by a team of researchers from the International Centre for the Study of Radicalisation (ICSR) at Kings College London highlighted the online influence of two such jihadi spiritual authorities on foreign fighters—Ahmad Musa Jibril, a U.S. based preacher, and Musa Cerantonio, an Australian convert to Islam.[58] According to the ICSR report, such "disseminators" have a number of advantages. They typically possess language skills that enable them to translate messages from official Arab accounts into English and other languages, thereby providing a "bridging function" between Arabs and non-Arabic speakers living in Western countries. Moreover, since they lack official ties to jihadi groups, they can receive information from numerous sources and thus serve as clearing-houses of sorts for credible information from jihadi theaters. In addition, they invest time and energy to communicate with their followers, which raises their status and profile in the jihadi online community.[59] As a result, these facilitators have amassed considerable influence not only among jihadists in the West, but also among foreign fighters, many of whom receive their information from these facilitators, rather than from official groups. "In this respect," the ICSR report concludes, "the ability of jihadist groups to control information has been significantly eroded while it is private individuals who now possess significant influence over how the conflict is perceived by those who are actively involved in it."[60]

Among the most important trends in the jihadi sphere is the emergence of a variety of communication platforms that help disseminate jihadi messages to broader audiences.[61] These platforms can be categorized as conventional Internet forums, which have been used widely for over a decade and consist of jihadi forums and jihadi chat rooms, and unconventional Internet forums, which consist of social media platforms, private websites and blogs, and gaming sites. While there has been a gradual shift from conventional to unconventional forums, conventional forums remain important.[62]

Conventional Forums

Conventional forums serve as platforms for official messages, sharing of news and operational information, and interactions among groups, in addition to other functions. Broadly speaking, terrorist actors use these forums in a top-down manner to publish propaganda, while broader communities of sympathizers and potential recruits tend to use them in a bottom-up or a lateral manner to post messages and respond to other posts.

According to Thomas Hegghammer, some five to fifteen jihadi forums are active at any one time, with most activities usually concentrated in one or two "market leaders."[63] Information posted by groups is frequently accompanied by a banner or logo and introduced through a series of promotional posts on the forum, creating hype and anticipation and drawing more attention to those messages the groups view as important. Upon sharing materials with members, the groups further disseminate these messages into other, less prominent, forums and popular social media platforms.

For example, the popular jihadi Ansar al-Mujahideen English Forum (AMEF) contain hidden sub-forums where discussions of software used by jihadists to hide their tracks and encrypt messages are pursued. Another hidden forum shares information that is gleaned from U.S. sources and may be of potential use to jihadis, such as U.S. efforts to counter jihadi activities, information on malware, firearms and explosives manuals, information about U.S. government actions against online jihadis, and so forth. Other posts discuss advanced weaponry around the world and teach online jihadists to avoid surveillance.

Another popular forum is the password-protected Al-Shumukh al-Islam, which is considered to be Al Qaeda's premier online forum.[64] Organized in sections such as news, messages, propaganda, and operations, the latter of which includes guidelines, manuals, and instructions, the forum also has a section of threads about different technologies, software manuals, and various tips for online safety. It was Al-Shumukh that first published Zawahiri's announcement that ISIS was no longer part of Al Qaeda. In the same statement, Zawahiri also "reaffirmed" that Jabhat al-Nusrah had sworn *bayah* to him and was hence directly subordinated to Al Qaeda's headquarters—and not a branch of what was then still Al Qaeda's Iraqi affiliate. The forum also released a joint statement by Al Qaeda in the Arabian Peninsula (AQAP) and Al Qaeda in the Islamic Maghreb (AQIM), in which all fighting groups in Syria were urged to put an end to internecine fighting and instead unite in their efforts against the main enemy, the United States and the West.[65]

Forums have also been used by jihadists to make calls to coordinate joint online activities. After drone strikes killed senior AQAP members Anwar al-Awlaki and Samir Khan, for example, a member of the Shumukh al-Islam forum issued a call to arms, especially to tech-savvy jihadists who could join forces to incapacitate social media platforms by flooding them with content about al-Awlaki and Khan. The announcement also asked jihadis to share their technological know-how with the rest of the forum members so that everyone could join the attack. Many members obliged.[66]

Another conventional online platform that can be used for cooperation among jihadis is the chat room, in which jihadis communicate on a personal, informal level and share ideas and content. Such chat rooms are frequently accessed by following specific forum instructions, which are typically provided to users after they have earned the trust of the forum administrators. Some chat rooms, however, use platforms that are unrelated to forums or jihadi websites in order to circumvent detection and infiltration. Since chat rooms are believed to be heavily infiltrated by security services, they are unlikely to feature operational cooperation by mid- or high-ranking members of terrorist groups, who often avoid using technology directly for fear of detection.[67]

Chat rooms were very common in the early 2000s, when they emerged as relatively open platforms for information-sharing in support of the cyber-jihadi struggle.[68] In recent years, chat room administrators have gradually restricted access to these platforms by imposing strict registration processes and other security barriers. As a result, the more extremist discourse has likely moved to the platforms that operate in the dark web and are difficult to access without prior knowledge of their precise web address.[69] As chat rooms have become more secure, the information exchanged in such virtual spheres has become more specific and now frequently include information on secure software and encryption tools, as well as actionable intelligence regarding the vulnerabilities of high-value enemy targets.

Chat rooms are widely employed for radicalization and for cooperation between terrorist actors. According to Finnish reports from 2013, for example, foreign fighters of Finnish origin have joined Al Qaeda affiliated organizations in Syria after conversing on chat rooms with operatives with alleged ties to both Al Qaeda and al-Shabaab.[70]

Unconventional Forums

In addition to conventional online spheres, recent years have witnessed a migration of terrorist communications from password-protected forums and secretive chat rooms to the unconventional open space of social media platforms, including social networking sites, webpages, blogs, and online gaming spheres. While forums and chat rooms remain important, the growing use of open social media platforms suggests that jihadists are interested in reaching broader audiences. Such platforms also act to strengthen terrorist actors' resilience against government efforts to shut down conventional jihadi platforms.[71]

Unconventional platforms are used mainly to spread propaganda, but military reports warn that they can also be used for real-time information sharing, facilitating attacks, providing GPS locations for operational purposes or as a deceptive technique, spreading malware, and infiltrating closed online communities by breaching private accounts and extracting valuable information from them.[72] The activity of the "Cyber Caliphate Army," an online entity that hacked news websites and private accounts on social networking sites to declare its allegiance to the Islamic State, provides one example of how unconventional platforms can be utilized by terrorist actors. Such hacks allow terrorist actors to threaten the virtual security of ordinary citizens by posting their private information stolen from compromised national databases and to glorify militant Islam.[73]

Using both top-down and bottom-up dissemination approaches, jihadis take advantage of social networking sites such as Facebook and Twitter. While online jihadis utilize accounts formally linked to terrorist entities, they also connect to private accounts of jihadi sympathizers, who act as force multipliers in the dissemination of jihadi materials. Social networking sites enable rapid and wide-scale distribution of information through such features as the "Like" or "Share" buttons. Furthermore, since social media sites such as Facebook and Twitter also allow personal messaging, they facilitate private communications within the same platform.

Cooperation between terrorist actors via social networking sites has an additional advantage. For, whereas communication on conventional online platforms was mostly secretive, communication on social media platforms is often public, and this means that the jihadi community can appear powerful and omnipresent and engender a shared online identity—an important tie that binds users to the goal of jihad.

Terrorist entities have employed social networking sites to claim support for groups, claim joint responsibility for attacks, praise certain activities, or express sympathies for the death of a martyr. Emerging groups often use such online platforms—at times several platforms at once—to declare their allegiance to other groups, who in turn can either accept these oaths or ignore them.[74]

One popular social networking site prominently used by jihadists is Facebook, which, according to a 2010 report, serves four main purposes: (1) sharing operational manuals and tactics such as homemade bomb recipes, firearms manuals, and other essential information; (2) providing links to online jihadi communities and attracting potential recruits into forums and chat rooms; (3) spreading propaganda to influence the broader jihadi community and intimidate its enemies; and (4) gathering intelligence on potential targets, attack schedules, and other operational material that can be used for terrorist activities.[75]

Since 2011, Facebook has also become a prominent sphere for foreign fighters. French foreign fighters in Syria and Iraq, for example, have communicated via Facebook, sharing details and information with fellow French fighters, while posting advice on how to get to Syria and Iraq, whom to contact, and how to join the fighting. Similarly, British foreign fighters have used Facebook for online questions and answers about their experience and to brag about their lives as foreign fighters, thereby creating an attractive image for potential recruits.[76]

In addition to Facebook, Twitter has become a favorite social networking site for jihadists to disseminate propaganda and communicate with like-minded individuals and groups. Twitter's popularity is due partly to its simple user interface and immediate public sharing function. The platform is used by a variety of jihadist groups, including Al Qaeda and all its affiliates, as well as associated groups such as the Taliban, and by rival jihadist groups such as the Islamic State and Boko Haram. Most of these groups use Twitter to share instant links to their official messages, which consist of further links and the banners of the group for purposes of authentication.[77]

Twitter is a particularly popular tool for distributing instant news about real time attacks, as seen for example in the case of Al Shabaab's attack on the Westgate Mall in Nairobi, Kenya, in September 2013. During the attack, members of the Somali group kept a running commentary on Al Shabaab's Twitter feed as the mass shooting attack unfolded.[78] Twitter was widely publicized by AQAP in its English-language online magazine *Inspire* in May 2013. Indeed, it became so popular that AQAP included a section called "AQTweets" in *Inspire*, which cited popular tweets from different actors in the jihadi sphere in order to highlight global support for jihadi activity.[79]

The January 10, 2012, announcement by the Muslim Youth Center of its support of Al-Shabaab via Twitter and a blog post is one instance of terrorist cooperation facilitated by Twitter. Another is Jabhat al-Nusra's declaration of allegiance to Al Qaeda Core in April 2013, published via its Twitter account.[80] Other emerging jihadi groups have used al-Nusra's Twitter account to show their support, upload pictures showing its flag alongside their own lesser-known flags, and to comment on its posts in order to gain recognition in the cyber sphere. Al-Nusra, in turn, has posted acknowledgements on Twitter of joint fighting alongside other rebel groups in its attacks against Assad's forces, as it did, for example, in a post about its strategic cooperation with the Islamic Front in the battle over the Qunaitra border passage in Syria in late August 2014, which included images of the groups celebrating their success.[81]

Apart from using social networking sites, jihadis are also known to have established private webpages and blogs, mainly to publish propaganda. Many groups today operate at least one personal webpage or blog, often by using open-source platforms such as WordPress, FileFlyer or other similar hosts for posting announcements, pictures, and videos. These platforms serve both as a security measure, in case certain forums and webpages are compromised or suspended, and as a backup for their own propaganda, to ensure that they can continue posting these materials through other media.

One of the most recent unconventional online social platforms with the potential to be used for cooperation is that of online gaming. While the existence of Jihadi-themed games available for download online is not new, the potential for cooperation using network-based games has created a novel threat. A confidential report leaked in 2013 has disclosed intelligence concerning potential terrorist use of networked virtual gaming spheres (Massively Multi-Player Online Role-Playing Game [MMORPG]) such as "Second Life" and "World of Warcraft" to recruit online gamers far from the eyes of data-monitoring intelligence agencies.[82] In the case of "Second Life," online gaming groups can use secretive measures to identify themselves as supporters of a certain group or ideology by designing special clothing pieces for their avatars or using key words and phrases to confidentially share information on the game's chatting system. This form of communication can be difficult to trace and requires the active participation of security agencies in the games. Another prominent threat posed by online games such as "Ultima Online" and "World of Warcraft," which trade in virtual currency on e-Bay, is that they can be used to raise funds in a nearly unsupervised manner.[83] This market, whose size in 2011 was estimated at up to $25 billion in the United States alone, should not be dismissed.[84] In this way, "armchair jihadis" can contribute to the jihadi efforts by playing games, which may also serve to entice them prior to their recruitment, as claimed by a father of two British foreign fighters.[85]

Furthermore, terrorist groups such as the Islamic State now use gaming slang to attract younger crowds and tempt them to fight in real life, uploading pictures of fighters with the title "this is our Call of Duty," for example, which is a clear reference to the popular fighting game series named "Call of Duty," in which players eliminate the "bad guys" to protect the good ones. This appeal to tech-savvy crowds is meant to convince them that contributing to IS's struggle in Iraq and Syria is a part of their duty and that just as in the game, they must fight to protect the "innocents."[86]

FOSTERING A VIRTUAL COMMUNITY OF BELIEVERS

The Internet's role in fostering a virtual community of individuals united by a common Jihadi identity also contributes to terrorist cooperation. It can be used both to target committed extremists and to proselytize aspiring jihadists.[87] This virtual communal bond can, in turn, intensify the motivations of a large, global group of like-minded individuals to seek cooperative interactions designed to achieve common objectives.

Jihadi entrepreneurs and facilitators utilize the Internet for the purpose of identity formation in three main ways: first, by highlighting collective grievances of the jihadi in-group; second, by drawing attention to the alleged evil doings of their enemies; and third, by contrasting the collective values and traits of the in-group with those of the out-group.

As a tool for highlighting the perceived grievances of Muslims—be they those living in Muslim majority countries or as minorities in the West and other regions—the Internet has proven to be of great value. It is cheap, widely available, and nearly egalitarian, allowing every member of the community to speak up, provided that they are connected. It can be used either discreetly or in a more public fashion, depending on the preferences of the user. It also allows jihadis to pick content selectively, ignoring alternative viewpoints and thereby reinforcing strongly held beliefs.[88] The Internet is, of course, also fast and can serve as a platform for the instantaneous transnational diffusion of grievances, with the result that local conflicts and tragedies can now be seen, watched, or heard by an unprecedented number of people in nearly all countries of the world. This has led some people who are far removed from the area of crisis or conflict to produce vicarious grievances—grievances that jihadis have not necessarily experienced personally, but ones with which they deeply identify and which can move them to action on behalf of the aggrieved.[89] One young man from Luton, England, who was interviewed shortly after the 2005 London bombings, put it as follows: "It's not just the BBC and ITV any more. We have al-Jazeera, we have the internet. If something happens to innocent people in Iraq, the Muslims of Luton will know about it and feel that grief."[90]

The Internet serves not only to highlight collective problems and grievances, but also to attribute blame on an out-group—the alleged enemies of Islam. As discussed earlier, the list of real or imagined enemies is long and ranges from "Crusaders" and "Zionists" to "apostates," "polytheists," and other infidels. Jihadi recruitment videos available on the Internet, in chat rooms and online forums, and through online magazines and other jihadi sources are replete with material drawing attention to perceived iniquities of the West.[91] A recent issue of the Islamic State's online English-language magazine *Dabiq* illustrates this point well. The foreword of the magazine's ninth issue, released in the second half of May 2015, concerned a shooting attack that took place in Garland, Texas, on May 3, 2015, when two jihadists opened fire outside an event titled "Muhammad Art Exhibit and Cartoon Contest," which was attended by several prominent critics of Islamism, including Dutch lawmaker Geert Wilders. The foreword begins as follows:

> As the crusaders continue to reveal their intense hatred and animosity towards Islam through their relentless bombing and drone campaigns on the Islamic State, a new breed of crusader continues shedding light on the extent of their hatred towards the religion of truth. This breed of crusader aims to do nothing more than to anger the Muslims by mocking and ridiculing the best of creation, the Prophet Muhammad Ibn 'Abdillāh (sallallāhu 'alayhi wa sallam), under the pretext of defending the idol of "freedom of speech."[92]

Finally, jihadists use the Internet to further consolidate their group identity by juxtaposing the presumably superior value system of the jihadis with the "corrupt" qualities of their enemies, especially the West. A subsequent passage of the same foreword exemplifies this contrast between the heroism of the jihadis and the godlessness of the West, while also showing how jihadis use this juxtaposition as an example that should serve to inspire other members of the jihadi community:

> The two lions of the Khilāfah arrived at the Curtis Culwell Center in Garland, Texas three weeks ago during a convention that featured a competition to draw the Prophet (sallallāhu 'alayhi wa sallam) in an attempt to mock and ridicule him. The two mujāhidīn came armed and ready to wage war, ignited a gun battle with the policemen guarding the center, and attained a noble shahādah in pursuit of vengeance for the honor of our beloved Prophet (sallallāhu 'alayhi wa sallam). Their determination to support the cause of Allah and punish those who insult the Prophet (sallallāhu 'alayhi wa sallam) should serve as inspiration to those residing in the lands of the crusaders who are still hesitant to perform their duty.

By using the Internet to highlight the alleged injustices inflicted upon Muslims, pointing at the perceived aggressions and depravity of the West, and contrasting the virtues of the jihadis with the vices of their enemies, jihadis bestow a sense of solidarity and identity, empowerment and pride, and a virtual utopia for the *umma*. The Internet serves as an ideal forum where jihadis and potential jihadis, many of whom feel humiliated, can regain a sense of solidarity and build a common identity. The new identity creates a feeling of empowerment and pride on this community, whose members can boast about apparent victory over their enemies. This serves the purpose of humiliating the enemy, while also reversing the jihadis' own humiliation. To jihadists and other Muslims striving to realize the global unity of Muslim believers in the form of an *umma*, the Internet presents itself as a virtual realization of such an imagined community. The virtual reality of the Internet helps present this imagined community as a just, egalitarian *umma*, "unified in an Islam purged of national peculiarities, and devoid of corruption, exploitation, and persecution. The appeal of this approximation of paradise," Marc Sageman further observes, "can become irresistible, especially to alienated young Muslims and potential converts suffering from isolation or from ordinary discrimination."[93] Practically speaking, these developments build communities united in their belief that the *umma*, indeed the jihadists' very identity, is under attack. This, in turn, requires a community wide response in defense of Islam. Because the stakes are so high and the problem affects them all, jihadists must work together—cooperate—to stem the anti-Islamic tide and safeguard the future of their religion and way of life.

ENABLING SYSTEM-WIDE COMMUNICATION

The discussion so far has clarified the revolutionary changes that the Internet has wrought for terrorist cooperation. The Internet serves as a force multiplier for terrorist agents and helps nurture a community of jihadists who view mutual cooperation as a sine qua non for warding off the concerted threat to their own existence. What renders the Internet even more powerful, however, is that it enables these jihadists and potential jihadists to correspond and collaborate. The Internet, in other words, is the medium of choice for communication among terrorist agents (organizations, informal networks, and entrepreneurs), jihadi facilitators and online platforms, and the broader jihadi community.

Examples abound. For instance, in 2013, some twenty leading figures of Al Qaeda, its affiliates, and associates—including Ayman al-Zawahiri and then-AQAP leader Wuhayshi—participated in a virtual "conference call" within a closed section of an Al Qaeda–linked forum. Among the subjects of discussion were pending terrorist plots, which led to the closing of twenty-two U.S. embassies across the globe.[94] To take another example, by 2014, Ask.fm, a social networking site in which users can pose anonymous questions to each other, had become a popular site in which jihadists radicalized and recruited other users. Foreign fighters in Syria also used Ask.fm to reach out to prospective foreign fighters in their home countries.[95]

Incorporating email, forums, chat rooms, social networking sites, voice-over protocol appliances such as Skype, and more, the Internet is a vast system of communication. It also differs from such media as letters and the telephone in that compared to its predecessors, the Internet is far more extensive, inclusive, interactive, efficient, and inexpensive—all of which have contributed to its ongoing capacity to revolutionize human relationships.[96]

THE OPPORTUNITY: THE PREVALENCE OF ARMED CONFLICT

So far, this chapter has described two structural factors that have affected the nature of contemporary terrorist cooperation. Jihadi ideology, I have argued, constitutes the main motivation for cooperation between today's terrorist actors, while the Internet is the central medium. In this section, I argue that besides having a unifying cause and an empowering medium, jihadi actors have also been able to exploit opportunities for cooperation. While the list of actual, as well as potential, opportunities is extensive,[97] I will briefly highlight those presented by armed conflict, especially civil wars and insurgencies.

Armed conflict matters for terrorism for an important reason: Terrorism rarely, if ever, occurs in isolation. Despite a tendency in the West to see terrorism as a self-standing phenomenon, acts of terrorism have historically been used as "part of a wider repertoire of struggle," as Paul Wilkinson points out.[98] Terrorism has been a common feature of both interstate and intrastate struggles.[99] But while terrorism has been used in all interstate wars of the modern era, including both World Wars,[100] over the course of the later twentieth and early twenty-first centuries, intrastate wars, including civil wars and insurgencies, have become more common, and they are the predominant form of conflict today.[101] Contemporary terrorism, therefore, is a tactic used most often in the context of civil wars and insurgencies.[102] According to recent data assembled and analyzed by Michael Findley and Joseph Young, most incidents of terrorism "take place in the geographic regions where civil war is occurring and during the ongoing war."[103] This trend is particularly apparent in the post-9/11 period, when civil wars and insurgencies have taken on an immense toll of destruction and human fatalities in places like Iraq, Afghanistan, Pakistan, Yemen, Somalia, Libya, and Syria. In all of these conflicts, terrorism has been rampant.[104]

Civil wars and insurgencies are not interchangeable concepts, but in practice they can overlap.[105] Scholars of civil wars commonly define them as armed conflicts between at least two warring parties, one of which is the incumbent state. Although civil wars frequently spill over to other countries, they are carried out mostly within the territory of a given state. The weaker party in a civil war must have strong local representation and be able to mount an effective resistance. To be considered a civil war, a conflict must attain a threshold of one thousand battle-related deaths per year, according to most scholars.[106]

An insurgency, on the other hand, can be defined as an "organized, protracted politico-military struggle designed to weaken the control and legitimacy of an established government, occupying power, or other political authority while increasing insurgent control."[107] Insurgencies can therefore occur either in the context of civil wars or in conflicts that do not amount to civil wars. Furthermore, some scholars distinguish classic insurgencies, which tended to be confined geographically to a single country, from neoclassical and global insurgencies, which have greater potential for spillovers to neighboring countries or have been designed as transnational insurgencies from the outset.[108]

Civil wars and insurgencies are also linked in terms of their causes. James Fearon and David Laitin were among the first to provide empirical support for the idea that civil wars tend to emerge in places where conditions exist that favor insurgencies. Such conditions include poverty, political instability, rough terrain, and large populations, all of which provide opportunities for rebels to mobilize and fight. Fearon and Laitin's argument has found much traction in subsequent years and has given rise to the common belief that fragile or failed states raise the likelihood for the onset of insurgencies and civil wars.[109]

Weak or failed states abet insurgency and civil war—and therefore also terrorism—because they are marked by ineffective governance—with "governance" meaning "the traditions and institutions by which authority in a country is exercised."[110] States plagued by ineffective governance raise the specter of insurgencies for three main reasons. First, their bureaucratic and political structures are defunct, and so the government cannot provide essential services to the population. The problems that are rampant under such circumstances, such as economic decline, corruption, and institutional malfunction, erode popular trust in the political system in general, and particularly in the government's ability to rule effectively. Second, the military and other security services of the government, suffering the effects of its eroding legitimacy, gradually lose their ability to establish effective control over the state's territory, or parts thereof. Third, as the government and its associated institutions weaken, nonstate actors such as insurgent organizations increasingly fill the vacuum that has been created. These actors oftentimes begin by increasing their control in peripheral areas neglected by the state, only to gradually expand the areas under their control.[111]

Scholars and analysts have used a variety of names for the armed nonstate actors that exploit these circumstances in order to challenge the state's monopoly on the use of force, including rebels, insurgents, militias, guerrillas, or terrorists. What all have in common is that they tend to employ terrorism—some more systematically, others less so—and do so frequently in conjunction with other tactics such as guerrilla or conventional warfare. Moreover, these nonstate actors typically rely on a broader strategy that combines both military and political means.[112]

Most important for our purposes is that civil wars and insurgencies provide opportunities for collaboration among nonstate actors. Shifting and oftentimes transitory alliances are commonplace. "Some of the most brutal and long-lasting civil wars of our times," writes Fotini Christia, "are associated with the rapid formation and disintegration of alliances among warring groups, as well as with fractionalization within them."[113] Consequently, a great deal of scholarly attention has been focused on alliance cohesion and disintegration in civil wars in recent years.[114]

The insurgencies and civil wars of the post-9/11 period exemplify the magnitude and complexity of the interlinking and varying forms of cooperation, especially between militant jihadi actors in the Middle East and North Africa. Data published by the Uppsala Conflict Data Program in June 2015, for example, showed that the years between 2009 and 2014 saw "a dramatic increase in organized violence, especially in the Middle East."[115] Meanwhile, civil wars and insurgencies in Afghanistan, India, Iraq, Libya, Pakistan, Somalia, Syria, and Yemen have given rise to a plethora of jihadist groups and an unfathomable number of alliances between them, many of them of a transactional or tactical nature.[116] A recent example from the Syrian civil war is Jaysh al-Fatah, a coalition of various Islamist groups, excluding the Islamic State, based in Idlib province. The group was formed in March 2015 and was said to consist of between 12,000 and 15,000 fighters. Member organizations included Al Qaeda's Syria affiliate Jabhat al-Nusra, Ahrar al-Sham, Jund al-Aqsa, Jaysh al-Sunna, and other groups.[117]

Conflict-ridden environments also become magnets for foreign fighters, who are able to travel to these places with few restrictions. Once there, arms are easy to obtain, again owing to the general weakness of governance. The result is the establishment of milieus that provide opportunities for a broad range of terrorist actors—individuals, informal networks, and formal organizations—to connect in different ways.[118] These connections, in turn, have defined much of the terrorist threat of the last two decades. As Petter Nesser has argued recently with regard to Europe, the history of jihadist terrorism there "is largely one of how interaction between local networks and militants in conflict zones produced attack cells."[119]

4

CONTEMPORARY TERRORIST COOPERATION

A Holistic Typology

I N THE PREVIOUS two chapters, I have relied on agency-structure theory to describe two fundamental developments that have been emerging since the 1990s and that, taken together, help illustrate how contemporary terrorist actors cooperate: the growing diversity of terrorist actors and the changing environment in which they cooperate. The present chapter will draw on the preceding theoretical discussion to formulate the main argument of the book—namely, that these changes have led to new and conceptually underexplored forms of terrorist collaboration, which I call *networked cooperation* and define as collaboration between at least two agents of terrorism in which one is an informal terrorist actor. Informal terrorist actors may be terrorist entrepreneurs or informal networks.

As the discussion in this chapter and the case studies of networked cooperation in chapter 9 will show, networked cooperation has increased in recent years, and this has important theoretical and policy implications that will be described in the conclusion of the book. Despite its growing importance, networked cooperation has not replaced or superseded traditional forms of cooperation between formal terrorist organizations. Instead, the analysis in this book demonstrates that these two forms of terrorist cooperation—networked and organizational—coexist, that this coexistence adds new layers of complexity to the threat of terrorism, and that new policy responses are necessary as a result.

To theorize and illustrate the advent of networked cooperation and its relationship to organizational cooperation, this chapter introduces a new holistic typology of terrorist cooperation.

TOWARD A NEW TYPOLOGY OF TERRORIST COOPERATION

As noted in chapter 1, several terrorism scholars have offered useful typologies of terrorist cooperation. Ely Karmon's identification, in his classic work *Coalitions Between Terrorist Organizations*, of three types of cooperation—ideological, logistical, and operational[1]—suggests a useful way to differentiate among types of activities that terrorist cooperation can encompass. However, he does not address the qualitative strength of the cooperative relationships, which is a critical consideration and one that Tricia Bacon has taken up, developing a typology that aims precisely at specifying the various kinds of relationships that can obtain in partnering groups. As discussed in chapter 1, Bacon's typology is built on several variables that help characterize cooperative relationships: how resources are treated; the time horizon for the relationship; the degree of independence/ autonomy of the partners; and the breadth and parameters of cooperation. Using these criteria, Bacon distinguishes among four types of alliance relationships: pooled, integrated, subordinate, and reciprocal.[2]

Building on these two important contributions, my typology accounts for different domains of terrorist cooperation and different types of relationships and, in addition, comprises a third dimension ignored in all previous typologies: the diversity of terrorist actors engaged in cooperative behavior.

This typology develops through two stages that, broadly speaking, correspond to two central facets of terrorist cooperation: the identity of the cooperating partners and the qualitative strength of the cooperation. In other words, the stages pertain to the questions of "who" cooperates, and "how."[3]

Stage 1 of the typology identifies the agents in the cooperating relationship. Whereas existing research has focused largely on cooperation between formal terrorist organizations, I argue that the changes described in the preceding two chapters—namely, the growing diversity of agents and the shifting nature of the environment—allow for a greater number of cooperative arrangements than those currently identified by scholars. These additional arrangements can develop between terrorist entrepreneurs and formal organizations, between informal networks and formal organizations, between terrorist entrepreneurs and informal networks, and so forth.

Stage 2 of the typology then addresses the qualitative strength of the cooperative relationship in each of these possible arrangements. Simply put, each of the arrangements identified in Stage 1 of the typology can result in different kinds of cooperative relations and activities. Stage 2 then introduces a distinction between "high-end" forms of cooperation, which include mergers and strategic alliances, and "low-end" forms of cooperation, which include tactical and transactional collaboration. In effect, this typology is based on the notion that to understand contemporary terrorist cooperation, two separate stages are required: The first involves identifying the agents that are cooperating (whether the parties are organizations, informal networks, or entrepreneurs); the second involves assessing the nature of their cooperative arrangements. After I discuss the two stages consecutively, I will then proceed to combine them in a single model. The process of developing this typology is summarized in table 4.1.

This typology offers three key benefits that existing typologies do not. First, it accounts for a diversity of terrorist actors beyond formal terrorist organizations. Second, it classifies cooperative arrangements in terms of their qualitative strength and places them on a spectrum that ranges from high-end to low-end cooperation. Third, the typology is dynamic in several respects. It allows for the fact that agents are not static and that their

TABLE 4.1 DEVELOPING A HOLISTIC TYPOLOGY OF
TERRORIST COOPERATION

	STAGE 1	STAGE 2	HOLISTIC TYPOLOGY
Key question addressed	Who cooperates?	How do these actors cooperate?	Who cooperates, and how?
Operationalization of key question	Distinguishing various cooperative arrangements based on identity of agents	Distinguishing different qualitative strengths of cooperation (high-end vs. low-end cooperation)	Combining Stages 1 and 2 into a model that accounts for agential identity and cooperative quality

cooperative relations do not necessarily remain the same. On the contrary, it recognizes not only that terrorist entrepreneurs can evolve into informal networks, and informal networks can develop into formal organizations, but also that cooperative relations can change according to the interests, preferences, and choices of the agents. Two groups may initiate a low-end form of cooperation, but may then decide to raise the level of cooperation and establish a strategic partnership or even a merger, both of which are high-end. The reverse is also possible, with two groups deciding on a strategic partnership or merger, only to scale back their level of cooperation to lower end forms if the previous, more intensive, relationship has proven difficult to maintain.

In sum, this typology makes two important contributions: First, it offers a novel theoretical approach to understanding terrorist cooperation—one that highlights the growing importance of networked cooperation alongside traditional interorganizational cooperation. Second, it can serve as a valuable tool for policymakers and counterterrorism analysts in their search for ways to make sense of an increasingly complex international terrorist nexus.

A HOLISTIC TYPOLOGY OF TERRORIST COOPERATION

As already noted, the typology I construct begins with two consecutive stages—Stage 1, which classifies terrorist cooperation according to the nature of terrorist actors, or agents, and Stage 2, which classifies terrorist cooperation according to the strength, or quality, of the cooperative relationships—and then goes on to combine them in one holistic typology. The discussion below is organized accordingly.

STAGE 1: IDENTITY OF AGENTS

The growing diversity of terrorist agents and the greater ability of these agents to cooperate thanks to a highly enabling environment present possibilities for new cooperative arrangements that are not limited to those undertaken by formal organizations. These arrangements, which I call "networked cooperation," can be broken down into five variants: cooperation between terrorist entrepreneurs (Variant 1); cooperation between a terrorist entrepreneur and a formal terrorist or insurgent organization (Variant 2); cooperation between a terrorist entrepreneur and an informal network (Variant 3); cooperation between a formal organization and an informal network (Variant 4); and cooperation between two informal networks (Variant 5). The full spectrum of these arrangements is illustrated in table 4.2.

Table 4.2 reflects the broad diversity of terrorist agents in both the horizontal and vertical columns. Each of the three types of terrorist agents identified in chapter 2—terrorist entrepreneurs, formal organizations, and informal networks—can cooperate with another terrorist agent, and this agent can also have any one of these three agential identities. Besides the five new variants of networked cooperation, the table also accounts for traditional cooperative arrangements between two formal organizations—the focus of the existing literature on terrorist cooperation. As table 4.2 illustrates, such organizational cooperation constitutes only one of six

TABLE 4.2 STAGE 1: COOPERATIVE ARRANGEMENTS BASED ON AGENT IDENTITY

	Terrorist Entrepreneurs	Terrorist/Insurgent Organizations	Informal Networks
Terrorist Entrepreneurs	Networked Cooperation (Variant 1)	Networked Cooperation (Variant 2)	Networked Cooperation (Variant 3)
Terrorist/Insurgent Organizations		Organizational Cooperation	Networked Cooperation (Variant 4)
Informal Networks			Networked Cooperation (Variant 5)

possible arrangements, once the diversity of terrorist agents is acknowledged. Moreover, in both theory and practice, additional arrangements are possible if other agents, such as states, are included in the analysis. While states are not identified in the above table, further consideration of how my typology extends to forms of state cooperation will be pursued in the conclusion to the book.

As the following discussion will show, the five variants of networked cooperation are not merely theoretical concepts; they have real-world counterparts. Take networked cooperation Variant 1, for instance, which involves cooperation between two terrorist entrepreneurs and results in the establishment of an informal network. It is exemplified by Ramzi Youssef and Khaled Sheikh Muhammad, two quintessential terrorist entrepreneurs, who cooperated for years on a plot to detonate nearly a dozen U.S. airliners, developing an informal network based mainly in the Philippines in the process. As is described in detail in chapter 9, the unsuccessful plan underscored the fascination of global jihadists with targeting the airline industry—a fascination shared by bin Laden.[4]

Networked cooperation Variant 2, in which a terrorist entrepreneur and a formal terrorist and/or insurgent organization cooperate, can be illustrated by the collaboration between the above-mentioned Khaled Sheikh Muhammad and Al Qaeda, which resulted in the attacks of September 11, 2001. Although the 9/11 attacks are not usually viewed as an example of terrorist cooperation, the concept of networked cooperation helps us reexamine them under a new light and see the success of the attacks as being conditional upon a successful collaboration between formal and informal terrorist actors.[5]

Networked cooperation Variant 3 involves cooperative activities between a terrorist entrepreneur and an informal network. It is exemplified in the role of the British jihadist entrepreneur Anjem Choudary in helping to establish a number of jihadist and Salafist network in Europe and other parts of the world, many including the "Sharia4" prefix in their names. Chapter 9 will examine in detail Choudary's cooperation with one of the most important "Sharia4" networks, Sharia4Belgium.

Networked cooperation Variant 4, in which an informal network cooperates with a formal terrorist organization, is exemplified by Sharia4-Belgium's cooperation with the Islamic State and Jabhat al-Nusra, two formal organizations. Sharia4Belgium is known to have helped these organizations by facilitating the movement of foreign fighters to Syria and Iraq starting in 2012, as is also detailed in chapter 9.

Finally, networked cooperation Variant 5 occurs among informal networks. It is exemplified by the Sharia4 movement, a constellation of various networks, many of which adopt the Sharia4 prefix, such as Sharia4Belgium.

In sum, Stage 1 of the typology suggests that the tendency in existing studies of terrorist cooperation to limit the analysis to formal terrorist organizations fails to capture the true extent of this phenomenon. Identifying the collaborating agents is a critical step that scholars and analysts should perform before examining the nature in which two or more terrorist actors cooperate. Agents, themselves, are subject to change, though, and so, too, are arrangements between them. Thus, informal networks can develop into formal organizations—as has indeed been the case for almost every formal terrorist and/or insurgent organization. Al Qaeda, prior to its founding meeting in August 1988, for example, was based on a network of jihadists surrounding Osama bin Laden and the training camp known as the Lion's Den (see chapter 5). Similarly, the Islamic State can be traced back to an informal network of jihadists around the person of Abu Musab al-Zarqawi—a network that predated even the first formal predecessor organization to the Islamic State, Jamaat al-Tawhid w'al Jihad.[6]

STAGE 2: QUALITATIVE STRENGTH OF COOPERATIVE ARRANGEMENTS

While Stage 1 of the typology classifies cooperative arrangements according to terrorist agents, Stage 2 addresses the characteristics of those arrangements. This has been the main, even exclusive, focus of existing typologies, from which the one presented here differs in several ways. First, characterizing different qualitative strengths is not the main focus; rather, it is one of two crucial building blocks for the typology. Second, my analysis differs from existing studies, including Bacon's, in that it examines cooperation more broadly, whereas most existing studies focus more narrowly on alliances or coalitions. Bacon defines alliances as "formal or informal relationships of security cooperation among two or more terrorist groups involving some degree of ongoing coordination or consultation in the future."[7] The typology offered here is based on a broader conception of terrorist cooperation. That is, besides extending to a variety of terrorist actors beyond formal organizations, my typology does not require that the cooperating partners will collaborate in the future (although they may well do so). Thus, the holistic typology also accounts for "transactional" forms of cooperation that may or may not recur.

Additionally, whereas Bacon omits ideological considerations from her typology, my model suggests that different types of terrorist cooperation can be distinguished in part based on the level of ideological affinity between groups. Ideology, I have argued, plays an important role as a shared cause for many contemporary terrorist actors. Moreover, not only do ideational factors influence the level of trust between partners, but the level of trust has a direct bearing on the quality of ties to which the cooperating parties aspire. Hence, the present typology also differs from Bacon's model in that it accounts for the level of trust inherent in each different type of terrorist cooperation.

The empirical and theoretical review of terrorist cooperation, which was presented in chapter 1, suggests that five main factors affect the quality of cooperative relationship between two terrorist entities. Given that the overwhelming empirical evidence in the literature on terrorist cooperation relates to formal terrorist organizations, I will illustrate the qualitative analysis of terrorist cooperation through examples of formal organizations. As will be argued later, however, and as several case studies of networked cooperation in chapter 9 will demonstrate, the factors analyzed also apply to networked cooperation.

The first of these is the expected duration of cooperation. Cooperative agreements between militant groups can differ substantially in terms of their expected time horizons. Cooperation can stretch over a considerable length of time, but is just as likely to occur over a short period.[8] On the lower end of the spectrum, groups may cooperate over a short time horizon—possibly even on a one-time basis—in order to complete a specific transaction. On the higher end of the spectrum, groups may envision collaboration enduring for a long time, and perhaps for an indefinite period if two groups merge into a single entity—the ultimate form of terrorist cooperation.

Cooperative relationships can also be distinguished in terms of the degree of interdependence between the collaborating entities. On the high end of the spectrum, groups that are merging pool their resources, unite their command and control apparatus, and eventually shed their autonomy. On the opposite end of the spectrum, groups that are engaged in specific transactions maintain their full independence. Between these two extremes are other kinds of relationships—strategic partnerships and tactical cooperation—in which the degree of interdependence varies.

A third factor to consider is the variety of cooperative activities in which groups can engage. Thus, two groups that have formed a strategic alliance can be expected to collaborate on a broader range of issues than groups whose relationship is limited to a single, or a few, transactions only. Higher-end collaborations such as mergers and strategic partnerships can thus be expected to encompass most or all of the domains of cooperation identified by Karmon—ideological, logistical, and operational. On the other hand, low-end cooperative relationships such as tactical or transactional ones can be expected to be limited to one or two domains only.

Ideological affinity is the fourth factor that affects the character of the collaborative relationships between groups. As chapter 1 has shown, the extent of ideational affinity can differ from one cooperative relationship to the other. Short-term relationships established for the purpose of specific transactions can obviate the need for an ideological common ground between the parties. Even tactical relationships between groups do not necessarily require that they share a worldview; having a common enemy can be enough. The same cannot be said for high-end relationships such as strategic partnerships and mergers, which are meant to be enduring and to encompass a wide variety of cooperative activities. Indeed, ideological ties can help overcome collective action problems that typically hinder stronger alliances from enduring.[9] No relationship can be expected to last unless the cooperating parties share a worldview, broadly defined. Clearly, the parties' ideological inclination does not have to be identical, but the stronger the alliance, the more ideological convergence we can expect.

Finally, cooperative relationships can also be distinguished in terms of the level of trust between the parties. Trust is related to ideational affinity because, all else being equal, groups that share a common ideological vision are more likely to trust each other than groups whose worldviews are incompatible. Trust, however, does not derive exclusively from ideological affinity. Other factors, such as the nature of the ties between individual members or common experiences predating the establishment of formal ties, can also affect the level of trust. So can rumors about the degree to which a group may be infiltrated by external agents, as was shown before. On the spectrum of terrorist cooperation, high-end forms are characterized

TABLE 4.3 HIGH-END AND LOW-END COOPERATION
AND THEIR SUBTYPES

QUALITY OF COOPERATION	SUBTYPE
High-end cooperation	Merger
	Strategic alliance
Low-end cooperation	Tactical cooperation
	Transactional collaboration

by greater levels of trust than low-end forms. It is hard to imagine two groups establishing a strategic alliance, much less contemplating a merger, unless they have developed a certain level of confidence about each other's reliability and good faith. Of course, such trust also helps strengthen transactional or tactical cooperation, but such low-end examples of cooperation have shorter expected time horizons to begin with, which makes full trust in the other party less critical.

Taking into account these five variables—expected duration; degree of interdependence; variety of cooperative activities; ideological affinity; and level of trust—we can distinguish two main qualitative types of terrorist cooperation (high-end and low-end) and subtypes of each (mergers and strategic alliances at the high end, tactical and transactional collaboration on the lower end) (table 4.3).

High-End Cooperation: Mergers and Strategic Alliances

High-end forms of cooperative relationships between militant groups include mergers and strategic alliances (or strategic partnerships). Mergers are the most complete type of cooperation because they entail the unification of the collaborating groups' command and control structure, the integration of their fighting forces, and the pooling of their resources (for a summary of the properties of mergers, see table 4.4).[10] The expected time horizon of groups that merge is indefinite, as the groups are essentially forming a single entity. As a result, the merging groups in essence shed their independence, while creating a new entity whose rules are binding to the resulting membership. Groups that merge cooperate ideologically, logistically, and operationally. Mergers are conditional upon the constituent groups sharing a common ideology. To the extent that ideological differences exist before the merger, the weaker group has to adopt the ideological guidelines of the senior partner. Failure to do so can jeopardize the success of the merger.

Mergers can be beneficial for militant groups plagued by financial woes, mobilization problems, or identity crises. When smaller organizations merge with larger groups, these organizations can adopt a highly desirable "brand" that can positively affect the group's efforts to recruit new personnel.[11] As Daniel Byman has noted, mergers and acquisitions—be they in the business world or the universe of militant organizations—can help promote organizational learning as they streamline the flow of ideas and solutions within the newly minted group. As more actors are able to exploit innovations at a lower cost and at greater speed, research and development will have greater dividends.[12]

Mergers, however, are not free of cost, the most obvious being the loss of autonomy, which applies especially to the weaker partner. Mergers also do not guarantee that members will establish and adopt a new identity or otherwise overcome divisions. Fractures over strategic, ideological, or tactical questions can remain and can result in a breakup of mergers. The two main Egyptian jihadist groups, Al-Jihad and Gamaa Islamiya, for example, briefly merged in 1980, only to split following the assassination of Anwar al-Sadat in October of the following year as a result of divisions over the leadership of the Blind Sheikh, Omar abd al-Rahman.[13]

The most successful mergers can result in the establishment of formidable terrorist and/or insurgent organizations. The Lebanese Hizballah, for one, was the result of a merger of members of different factions such as Amal, the Muslim Students Union, the Dawa party of Lebanon, and others. As Levitt explains, the group emerged as the "product of an Iranian effort to aggregate under one roof a variety of militant Shia groups in Lebanon as an umbrella movement."[14] The example of the merger between Ayman al-Zawahiri's Egyptian Islamic Jihad (EIJ) and Osama bin Laden's Al Qaeda to form a new group called Qaedat al-Jihad is another example.

A second type of high-end cooperation is the strategic alliance, a partially integrated relationship in which the collaborating groups share know-how and resources extensively. In contrast to mergers, strategic alliances do not mean that the two groups have united their command and control. Nevertheless, these groups find themselves in a moderately to highly interdependent relationship in which there is some degree of strategic coordination between them (for a summary, see table 4.4). Within this framework, strategic alliances can vary from moderately interdependent partnerships in which the groups retain most or all of their command and control powers to highly interdependent partnerships in which one or both parties may relinquish, or are expected to relinquish, some command and control. Strategic allies share similar or identical strategic objectives, and hence expect their partnership to last for an extended period of time. As in mergers, strategic allies expect to cooperate in multiple activities that usually span ideological and logistical domains and frequently the operational domain, too. The large variety of cooperative endeavors calls for frequent consultations between the leaderships, even though the security environment may not be conducive to frequent face-to-face encounters. As a result of the strong bonds between strategic partners, they may set up specialized infrastructures or point persons to manage their relations.[15] The relationship between Al Qaeda and most of its affiliates is a good example of strategic alliances.

Strategic alliances are dependent on a high degree of ideological affinity, although groups may differ over how ideological beliefs are to be applied in practice. Generally, however, strategic partnerships are marked by a high degree of ideological overlap and a general agreement on strategic issues (which may have prompted the alliance in the first place). As a result of this common vision, strategic partnerships are characterized by a relatively high degree of trust between the partners.

Strategic alliances between militant groups share similarities with strategic partnerships in the business world. Such partnerships between companies often consist of systematic forms of cooperation that benefit from a high degree of predictability and regularity and may take the form of joint ventures or licensing and franchise agreements. According to Phil Williams,

TABLE 4.4 STAGE 2: COOPERATIVE ARRANGEMENTS: SUBTYPES AND THEIR CHARACTERISTICS

TYPE OF COOPERATION	COOPERATION SUBTYPE	EXPECTED DURATION	EXPECTED DEGREE OF INTERDEPENDENCE	EXPECTED VARIETY OF COOPERATIVE ACTIVITIES	IDEOLOGICAL AFFINITY	LEVEL OF TRUST
High-end cooperation	Merger	Indefinite	Complete	Full	Congruent	Complete
	Strategic alliance	Long-term	Medium to high	Considerable	High	High
Low-end cooperation	Tactical cooperation	Variable	Low to medium	Small to medium	Variable	Variable
	Transactional collaboration	Variable	None	Small	Variable	Variable

such partnerships usually "involve fairly tight operating linkages, with the participants having a vested interest in each other's future, expectations that cooperation will continue over the long term, and significant competitive advantages for all parties."[16]

Examples of strategic partnerships include the alliance between the West German Rote Armee Fraktion (RAF) and the French group Action Directe (AD) during the 1980s.[17] More contemporary examples include those between Al Qaeda (Central) on the one hand and some of its affiliates on the other—Al Qaeda in the Arabian Peninsula (AQAP), Al Qaeda in the Islamic Maghreb (AQIM), al-Shabaab, and, at least until July 2016, Jabhat al-Nusra. These global jihadi partnerships and other forms of cooperation in the global jihad will be examined in greater detail in part 2 of the book.

Low-End Cooperation: Tactical and Transactional Collaborations

Low-end forms of cooperation, which range from tactical to transactional collaborations—differ from their high-end counterparts in terms of duration, interdependence, variety of activities, ideological affinity, and degree of trust. First, tactical or transactional collaborations typically have shorter time horizons than mergers or strategic alliances. Although some forms of tactical cooperation can endure or evolve into strategic partnerships, such relationships are usually subject to the vicissitudes of the actors' shifting interests. Second, partners in low-end forms of cooperation retain all or most of their independence. Third, they rarely encompass the full range of cooperative activities; more often, collaborations involve specific issues or domains. Fourth, in low-end types of cooperation, pragmatism prevails over ideological similarity. Transactional forms of cooperation can occur between ideologically incompatible groups, as can tactical cooperation, provided that other mundane interests are served. Fifth, tactical cooperation is rarely characterized by the same level of trust that accompanies high-end forms of cooperation such as strategic alliances and mergers.

Low-end forms of cooperation between militant actors can be either tactical or transactional, with the former denoting a more committed and encompassing form of relationship than the latter. Since the level of commitment falls short of that found in strategic alliances, tactical cooperation falls in between strategic alliances and transactional forms of cooperation.

Tactical cooperation differs from strategic cooperation in that strategic alliances are expected to last for a relatively long time, whereas no such expectation is inherent in a tactical cooperation (for a summary of the properties of tactical cooperation, see table 4.4). Tactical forms of cooperation are based on shared interests, but not necessarily on shared strategic objectives, which define strategic alliances. Since the interests of groups are far from static, a tactical cooperation can shift, and even end abruptly as the interests of the parties diverge. Tactical forms of cooperation may even be established with the express knowledge that such partnerships are not likely to endure, provided the parties identify areas of mutual gain in the short term.

Tactical forms of cooperation are particularly common between militant groups involved in civil wars and insurgencies, when transitory overlapping interests can result in a temporary "marriage of convenience" between groups that have divergent ideological orientations. The civil war in Syria, for example, has produced a myriad of such tactical partnerships, often at the prodding of foreign states.[18] These tactical partnerships can be composed of groups with varying backgrounds. Following the U.S. led invasion of Iraq starting in March 2003, for example, deposed Baathists and jihadists engaged in a tactical cooperation that had the immediate objective of ending the occupation. Furthermore, as Mohammed Hafez has pointed out, by 2006, hundreds of individual units of Iraqi (and some foreign) fighters had consolidated into a smaller number of eight umbrella groups, which took responsibility for the majority of violent attacks such as the Mujahideen Shura Council (MSC), the Islamic Army in Iraq (IAI), the Ansar al-Sunnah Group (ASG), and the Islamic Resistance Movement–1920 Revolution Brigades. Most of these groups consisted of a variety of "brigades" or "battalions," many of which operated in specific regions with limited coordination among themselves. Hafez provides a number of hypotheses as to why hundreds of so-called brigades seemed to coordinate their operations under a small number of umbrella movements, all of which point to the predominance of pragmatic interests. Thus, according to Hafez, one reason for the tactical partnerships was that the brigades simply joined the bandwagon led by broader movements that happened to enjoy an advantage on the battlefield. Another is that more powerful and well-funded groups enticed lesser "battalions" to join them by offering them continued financing. Third, some groups appeared to have joined larger umbrella movements in order to achieve better access to the shadow economies and criminal networks under the control of the umbrella groups. Finally, these groups may have cooperated tactically in a genuine belief that by joining forces they were better able to fight a superior enemy.[19]

As these examples indicate, a tactical cooperation is designed to meet particular needs and does not necessarily involve either extensive or systematic collaboration. It lacks the regularity of a strategic alliance, and as a result is less predictable. Collaborative tactical relationships can, however, develop into full blown strategic alliances if mutual interests are guaranteed and the parties have developed a necessary level of trust. Such a development is possible especially when the groups share similar world views.

The strength of the relationships in strategic and tactical forms of cooperation differs because strategic alliances depend on ideological affinity (such as adherence to Marxist or jihadi ideology), whereas tactical collaborations do not. An example that will be discussed at greater length in chapter 8 is the tactical cooperation between Al Qaeda, a Sunni group, and a Shiite constellation of actors that includes the Islamic Republic of Iran as well as its Hizballah proxy.

At the lowest end of cooperative relationships between militant groups are transactional relationships (table 4.4),[20] which can be material or ideological in nature. As far as material transactional relationships are concerned, their time horizon can vary from short, one-time exchanges to regular ones that are part of a contractual relationship. Generally speaking, transactional relationships do not involve expectations of longer-term mutual relationships, because their cooperative activities are limited to specific exchanges. In transactional relationships, the cooperating organizations maintain their full autonomy and usually cooperate in a single domain, which is often logistical, such as the transfer of weapons. Actors involved in transactional relationships therefore do not exchange memberships, do not need to share similar organizational goals, and do not necessarily share an ideological worldview.[21]

Exchanges in a transactional relationship occur on the basis of specific needs and may require very little interaction between the parties, but they can develop into more enduring forms of cooperation if the parties develop a solid basis of trust and overlapping interest. At the most fundamental level, transactional forms of cooperation can involve the demarcation of spheres of influence or territorial control. Such agreements are well known in the world of crime groups, and as Phil Williams's description of them suggests, they have parallels among terrorist groups.[22] Thus, agreements over spheres of influence "are about avoiding problems and conflicts, rather than generating mutual gains. . . . If successful, they can provide a basis for more active and ambitious forms of cooperation that seek not merely to avoid negative outcomes, but also to provide positive benefits for all concerned."[23] Agreements that include tacit or explicit arrangements not to target the other group fall into the same category. Rebel and insurgent groups that rely in part on terrorist tactics regularly engage in such low-end forms of cooperation, too.

Williams's distinction between transactional relationships that are more formal and involve contracts or service or supplier relationships, and those that are more informal and involve various forms of exchange or barter agreements in international criminal networks can also be applied to transactional arrangements between terrorist actors. Thus, insofar as contract relationships involve one group contracting for a specific service or good, and another group providing that service or good, sometimes on a regular basis, such relationships can develop between organized crime groups that depend on the supply of illicit goods and services and between militant groups that depend on a regular supply of goods such as ammunition or drugs. Contract relationships in the criminal world can also extend to services such as transportation, contract killing, or money laundering, all of which are relevant to terrorist and insurgent groups.[24]

Transactional relationships between terrorists tend, however, to involve more informal arrangements for the exchange of goods or services and thus tend to be more akin to barter.[25] Such was the case in the late 1970s, for example, when cooperative relations between the Red Brigades (RB) and the Palestine Liberation Organization (PLO) were at a peak and involved the transfer of four or five arms consignments from Fatah and the Popular Front for the Liberation of Palestine (PFLP) to the RB who, in return, agreed to store weapons in Italy for these Palestinian groups for possible future use.[26] Such barter relationships are also common in the global jihadist context. Al Qaeda, for example, frequently funded or trained local groups or cells. In return, the funded groups offered Al Qaeda safe houses, shelter, or sleeper cells. The relationship between Al Qaeda and the Indonesian Jemaah Islamiya (JI) is instructive. For JI, key benefits of its relationships with Al Qaeda were access to Al Qaeda training facilities, financial support, and ability to plan and carry out operations. Al Qaeda, on the other hand, benefited from JI's covert infrastructure to support terrorist attacks on targets in South East Asia. Al Qaeda's plans for undertaking bomb attacks on U.S. and Western interests in Singapore in late 2001, for example, depended on JI's clandestine infrastructure and local knowledge for surveillance of the targets and for building the truck bombs.

Transactional relationships, like other low-end cooperative relationships, are also characterized by a lack of ideological alignment, as the relationship between Hamas and the Islamic State's affiliate in Sinai, the so-called Sinai Province, known until November 2014 as Ansar Bayt al-Maqdis (ABM), illustrates.[27] According to Israeli and Egyptian sources, the Sinai Province group maintains a weapons cache on behalf of Hamas in the Sinai, where it is beyond Israel's reach, and helps Hamas smuggle these weapons, which originate in Iran and Libya, into the Gaza Strip. In return, it receives a certain percentage of these weapons, as well as financial compensation. Hamas also treats wounded members of the Sinai-based group in Gazan hospitals, and members of Hamas's Izzadin al-Qassem Brigades have reportedly provided training to their Egyptian colleagues.[28]

On the other hand, transactional relationships can also be limited to the ideological realm. Pledges of allegiance, for example, that do not (yet) involve further logistical or operational collaboration can be considered an ideological variant of transactional relationships. Unlike a material transactional relationship in which more tangible goods are exchanged, ideological cooperation revolves around the exchange of immaterial goods. A pledge of general support can be reciprocated, for example, by the pledging group's ability to adopt the brand of the senior partner. A further difference between material and ideological transactional cooperation is that ideological cooperation sends a stronger signal about the groups' intentions to engage in higher forms of cooperation in the future. The pledge of allegiance by Boko Haram to the Islamic State, which was formally accepted by the latter in March 2015, is an example of an ideological transactional relationship that may have subsequently developed into higher-end forms of cooperation.

A DYNAMIC TYPOLOGY

An important aspect of the typology is its dynamic nature. The model does not suggest that the boundaries between mergers, strategic alliances, tactical cooperation, and transactional cooperation are firm. On the contrary, the boundaries are soft, with areas of overlap between each qualitative type and its immediate neighbor, as figure 4.1 illustrates. Such an area of overlap between, say, a merger and a strategic alliance, can reflect a situation in which the partnership between the two actors is stronger than a typical strategic alliance, but has not yet amounted to a full merger. The strategic alliance between Al Qaeda and its Yemen-based affiliate, AQAP, serves as a good example. As will be discussed in detail in chapter 7, Al Qaeda Central's appointment of the former leader of AQAP, Wuhayshi, to serve as Al Qaeda Central's general manager—a position akin to the number two slot in the hierarchy of Al Qaeda Central—can be interpreted as an attempt to strengthen the strategic alliance even further, moving it in the direction of a merger. At the time of the appointment of Wuhayshi to serve as Al Qaeda Central's general manager, therefore, the relationship between the two groups can be considered to have been situated in the area of overlap between mergers and strategic alliances.

Similarly, the relationship between Al Qaeda Central and Al Qaeda in Iraq (AQI) arguably began as a strategic alliance when it was first formalized in 2004. Over time, however, as it became clear that AQI was not willing to submit itself to Al Qaeda's command and control, the relationship was probably situated in between a strategic alliance and a tactical cooperation—the central shaded area in figure 4.1.

The second way in which the typology I introduce is dynamic has already been suggested above, where I point to the fact that the characters of cooperative relationships can fluctuate over time. In figure 4.1, this process is graphically represented by the dashed arrow that spans the entire spectrum. Indeed, it is more likely for cooperative relationships to change over time than it is for them to remain static. The global jihad movement is loaded with examples of commitments and pledges of loyalties made and then broken.[29]

Regarding cooperative relationships that can strengthen over time—these include transactional relationships that develop into tactical ones; tactical ones that develop into strategic alliances; and strategic alliances that develop into full mergers. New affiliations forged between the Islamic State and lesser jihadi groups, for example, probably start as transactional collaborations, before they become tactical. Similarly, Al Qaeda entertained, over many years, tactical relationships with a multitude of groups, but it promoted only a handful to a formal affiliation, and thereby established the basis for the creation of a strategic alliance. Likewise, the relationship between Al Qaeda Central and the Egyptian Islamic Jihad, for example, did not begin as a merger, but gradually developed into one. Conversely, stronger cooperative relationships may turn into less intensive collaborations over time and can even lead to formal splits. The relationship between Al Qaeda and Al Qaeda in Iraq was at its peak when the latter became a formal affiliate (or strategic ally) in 2004. Gradually, however, AQI and its successor organizations—the Islamic State of Iraq (ISI), the Islamic State of Iraq and Greater Syria (ISIS), and the Islamic State (IS)—distanced themselves from their erstwhile ally, downgrading the relationship de facto to a tactical cooperation, before eventually splitting from Al Qaeda entirely.

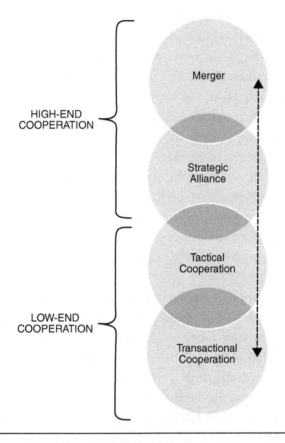

FIGURE 4.1 Stage 2: Qualitative Strength of Cooperation
in Dynamic Relation

COMBINING THE TWO STAGES INTO
A HOLISTIC TYPOLOGY

In Stage 2 of the typology, I distinguished four kinds of cooperation, divided into two broader qualitative groupings—high-end and low-end. While the above discussion relied on examples of interorganizational cooperation, the four categories and their subsets can be easily applied to other cooperative arrangements, such as networked cooperation, as the second case study in chapter 9 will illustrate. Examining the relationships between Khaled Sheikh Muhammad, a terrorist entrepreneur, and Al Qaeda Central, a formal organization, the case study will show how the relationship changed over time from a transactional collaboration all the way to a quasi-merger with KSM's eventual pledge of allegiance to Al Qaeda Central. In this case, and in other case studies that appear in the second half of the book, we can say with confidence that organizational or networked cooperation can adopt any of the forms of cooperation at the high-end (mergers, strategic alliances) and the low-end (tactical or transactional cooperation).

The two stages of the typology can now be merged in one holistic and dynamic typology, as is illustrated in table 4.5. In this table, each of the six cooperative arrangements identified in Stage 1—the five variants of networked cooperation and organizational cooperation—can vary in terms of their cooperative quality, ranging from mergers to transactional collaborations.

* * *

The introduction of the holistic typology of terrorist cooperation in this chapter concludes the discussion of part 1 of the book, which has offered a novel conceptualization of terrorist cooperation. The model I propose highlights the emergence of a new trend in terrorist cooperation—networked cooperation—which has been neglected in the scholarly literature to date. Networked cooperation matters because it is a growing feature of the contemporary terrorist threat. As such, it forms part of an increasingly complex picture in which formal organizations and informal actors interact, supported by new platforms and facilitators that serve as force multipliers to the cooperating agents.

Part 2 of the book (chapters 5–9) contains the empirical discussion that illustrates the concepts introduced in part 1. Before delving into the case studies, chapter 5 and 6 will provide a historical review of terrorist cooperation among the various elements of the global jihad movement—the preeminent terrorist threat today, and the empirical focus in this book. Then, while chapter 7 will consider a case study of high-end organizational cooperation—the cooperation between Al Qaeda and its Yemen-based affiliate, AQAP, chapter 8 will examine low-end cooperation, using the

TABLE 4.5 A HOLISTIC TYPOLOGY OF TERRORIST COOPERATION

	Terrorist Entrepreneurs		Terrorist/Insurgent Organizations		Informal Networks	
Terrorist Entre- preneurs	Networked Coop. (Variant 1)	Mergers*	Networked Coop. (Variant 2)	Mergers**	Networked Coop. (Variant 3)	Mergers
		Strat. Alliances		Strat. Alliances		Strat. Alliances
		Tactical Coop.		Tactical Coop.		Tactical Coop.
		Transact. Coop.		Transact. Coop.		Transact. Coop.
Terrorist/ Insurgent Organi- zations			Organizational Cooperation	Mergers	Networked Coop. (Variant 4)	Mergers
				Strat. Alliances		Strat. Alliances
				Tactical Coop.		Tactical Coop.
				Transact. Coop.		Transact. Coop.
Informal Networks					Networked Coop. (Variant 5)	Mergers
						Strat. Alliances
						Tactical Coop.
						Transact. Coop.

*A merger between two terrorist entrepreneurs amounts to the establishment of an informal network.

**A merger between a terrorist entrepreneur and a formal organization entails the incorporation of the entrepreneur into the organization.

example of Al Qaeda, Iran, and Hizballah. Finally, chapter 9 discusses networked cooperation as exemplified by five case studies, each of which illustrates one of the five variants of networked cooperation introduced in table 4.2.

PART TWO

TERRORIST COOPERATION
IN THE GLOBAL JIHAD

5

PRE-9/11 COOPERATION
IN THE GLOBAL JIHAD

PART 2 OF this book examines cooperative aspects of the global jihad movement. This chapter will introduce a broad overview from the founding period of Al Qaeda until the attacks of September 11, 2001. The next chapter will continue that historical review, covering the period from the 9/11 attacks until 2015.

The global jihad movement is the preeminent terrorist threat of modern times. It is a social movement in that is a "conscious, concerted and sustained" effort "by ordinary people to change some aspect of their society by using extra-institutional means."[1] It is also a transnational movement composed of individuals, cells, networks, and organizations tied by a common adherence to jihadist ideology, as described in chapter 3. Throughout most of the movement's existence, Al Qaeda has served as its nominal leader. By the end of 2014, the dramatic rise to power of the "Islamic State" challenged, and arguably eclipsed, Al Qaeda as the most influential and consequential entity within the movement.[2] Thus, after a quarter of a century in which the global jihad movement was best conceived as a nexus of jihadi actors with Al Qaeda at its helm, in 2015 and early 2016 global jihadism is better understood as a bifurcated movement. Its two main camps, centering on Al Qaeda and the Islamic State, respectively, are vying for power and influence. Nevertheless, cooperation remains a critical lens through which to examine the global jihad movement. For the competition for power and influence between these two camps is a function not only of their capacity to inflict violence on their enemies (as well as on each other), but perhaps even more importantly of their ability to establish cooperative partnerships through alliances, affiliations, and other forms of collaboration with like-minded militant groups.[3] In other words, even at a time when global jihad appears riven by conflict, the movement cannot be properly understood without examining the dynamic nature of global jihadi cooperation.

Notwithstanding the current competition, the origins of the global jihad movement as well as the rise of the so-called Islamic State (IS) are closely intertwined with the history of Al Qaeda. Formally established in late 1988, Al Qaeda embarked on a revolutionary strategic shift that marked the true beginning of global jihad during the mid-1990s. This shift involved a distancing of the jihadi movement from its traditional focus on the "near enemy,"—that is, local Arab regimes perceived by jihadis as un-Islamic. Henceforth, Al Qaeda's then-emir Osama bin Laden decided, the movement needed to refocus the jihadis' military and political efforts on the "far enemy"—the United States and its Western allies.[4]

For the next two decades, Al Qaeda served as the nominal vanguard of the global jihad movement and forged ties to a host of groups, commonly known as affiliates and associates.[5] The term *affiliate* in this book denotes a group that has formal ties to Al Qaeda or, for that matter, the Islamic State. Affiliates are formalized through the swearing of *bayah*—an oath of loyalty—to the leader of Al Qaeda or the Islamic State, who in turn must acknowledge and accept that oath in order for the affiliation to be officially established. Such oaths are not automatically accepted. For example, al-Shabaab swore allegiance to bin Laden, but did not receive a formal invitation from him to join the Al Qaeda movement. It was only under bin Laden's successor, Ayman al-Zawahiri, that al-Shabaab's pledge was formally accepted and the Somali associate became a formal Al Qaeda affiliate. In the case of the Islamic State, the process of formal affiliation appears streamlined. Groups swearing loyalty to IS are more likely to be accepted into its fold, and more quickly so, than groups pledging allegiance to Al

Qaeda, where the screening process is more stringent.[6] Affiliates can also differ according to how the senior partner seeks to employ them. Formal affiliates of the Islamic State establish so-called provinces, or *wilayat*, in an effort to help the Islamic State build out its caliphate as part of a strategy known as *baqiya wa tatamaddad*, or "remaining and expanding." Formal affiliates of Al Qaeda, on the other hand, have traditionally been expected to reinforce Al Qaeda's attempts to strike Western targets.[7]

Official affiliates of Al Qaeda sometimes adopt the Al Qaeda name, as in Al-Qaeda in the Arabian Peninsula (AQAP) and Al Qaeda in the Islamic Maghreb (AQIM), although not all formal affiliates do, as the examples of al-Shabaab and Al Qaeda's former Syrian-based affiliate, Jabhat al-Nusra, suggests.[8] Al Qaeda's affiliates in early 2016 included AQAP, AQIM, al-Shabaab, Jabhat al-Nusra, and Al Qaeda in the Indian Subcontinent (AQIS). As of July 2016, the Islamic State had formal affiliates in Afghanistan, Algeria, Chad, Egypt, Libya, Niger, Nigeria, Pakistan, Russia, Saudi Arabia, and Yemen, among other countries.[9]

Such affiliates are usually engaged in high-end forms of cooperation, especially strategic alliances with Al Qaeda or IS. One former affiliate, a faction of the Egyptian Islamic Jihad (EIJ), completed a merger with Al Qaeda prior to September 11, 2001. Even though formal affiliates are strategic partners by design, the quality of their relationship with their senior partner can vary, and may even fall short of a relationship that a senior partner has with an unofficial one. Before its formal break from Al Qaeda in February 2014, for example, Al Qaeda's affiliate in Iraq had a history of insubordination that proved extremely frustrating for Al Qaeda,[10] and the ties between the two were weaker than those Al Qaeda had with some of its unofficial partners, or "associates," such as the Haqqani Network.

The term *associate* in this book, refers to an entity that collaborates more or less regularly with Al Qaeda (or, more recently, with the Islamic State) without having become an official, formal affiliate. Associates may have sworn fealty to Al Qaeda, but as long as that *bayah* has not been formally acknowledged and accepted by Al Qaeda, the group remains an associate and does not cross the threshold into a formal affiliate. Association with Al Qaeda—as opposed to affiliation—can be short-term or long-term, and may involve groups that do not share Al Qaeda's Salafi-Jihadist worldview, such as the Afghan Taliban. Even groups that are ideologically opposed to Al Qaeda, such as the Shiite Hizballah, have had sporadic cooperative relationships with Al Qaeda, as will be shown in chapter 8. Associates can engage in low-end or high-end forms of cooperation with their senior partners. The Haqqani Network, for example, has not sworn *bayah* to Al Qaeda, but has nevertheless had a long-standing quasi–strategic alliance with Al Qaeda.[11]

Besides affiliates and associates, both camps—Al Qaeda and the Islamic State—include a variety of independent cells and networks, as well as individual supporters. Individual supporters include *adherents* who are inspired by the worldview propagated by Al-Qaeda or the Islamic State, or by their respective affiliates and associates, but who lack formal ties to any of these groups.[12]

Chapter 3 argued that cooperation within the jihadi movement is premised in part on a shared ideology. At the same time, adherence to the same beliefs does not preclude debates and disagreements over other issues, as is evident in the conflict between Al Qaeda and the Islamic State. Although all members of the global jihad movement share a core ideological narrative—most importantly the notion that Islam is under attack and hence in need of defense through militant jihad—movement participants differ regarding other important questions, such as what strategy and tactics to employ or which enemy to tackle first.[13] The global jihad is therefore a partially estranged brotherhood—an imperfect, fractured fraternity.

Internal strife within the global jihad movement is no less prevalent than global jihadi cooperation. Unlike cooperative aspects of the global jihad movement, however, the disagreements and fault lines that divide the movement have garnered more scholarly attention to date, including from this author.[14] Hence the focus on terrorist cooperation in this book, and the overview of cooperative aspects of the global jihad movement provided in this chapter and the next. While these two chapters do not aim to cover the history of the global jihad movement, its ideology, strategy, or structure, the discussion will naturally touch upon some of these issues.[15]

This chapter proceeds in chronological order, examining cooperative aspects in the global jihad movement in the pre-9/11 period. The next chapter will continue the discussion, covering the post-9/11 period until 2015. Before the rise of the Islamic State in 2014, this history centers in large part on Al Qaeda and its partners.

MAKTAB AL-KHIDAMAT, THE "LION'S DEN," AND THE FOUNDING PERIOD OF AL QAEDA, 1984–1992

Osama bin Laden's cooperative endeavors predate his formal founding of Al Qaeda on August 18, 1988. During the Soviet occupation of Afghanistan in the 1980s, bin Laden decided to contribute to the effort to rout the Soviet Army by collaborating with Abdulllah Azzam, a charismatic Islamic teacher and ideologue whom he had met at the university in Jedda in 1981 and who would become the "single most important individual behind the mobilization of Arab volunteers for Afghanistan."[16] Henceforth, the two decided, they would absorb foreign jihadists and place them in Afghanistan. To implement their plan, bin Laden and Azzam established the Maktab al-Khidamat (MAK), or Services Bureau, in 1984, an Islamic nongovernmental organization headquartered in Peshawar, Pakistan.[17] It received Arabs and helped recruit them for jihad on the battlefield, but it would also provide relief services such as food, healthcare, and education to Afghan refugees. Azzam served as the head of the organization, while bin Laden provided much of the funding. The MAK also served as the headquarters for Azzam's magazine, *Jihad*.

Bin Laden soon developed a desire to focus his efforts on the military aspects of the jihad in Afghanistan, and by the mid-1980s, he had begun entertaining the idea of establishing a separate Arab military force to help confront the Soviets. Azzam opposed the idea because he saw more value in the various Arab fighters being embedded throughout the various Afghan mujahideen factions, where they could spread the teachings of Islam to Afghans more effectively "and bring news of the Afghan jihad to wealthy donors in the Middle East."[18]

In October 1986, bin Laden began constructing a fortified training area near Jaji, in Eastern Afghanistan, known as the Lion's Den of Supporters (*ma'sadat al-ansar*). The Lion's Den would soon become known informally as *al-Qaeda al-askariyya*, the "military base," and it was from this name that the group that was formed less than two years later derived its name.[19] The training camp was set up with the help of two close associates, Ali Amin al-Rashidi (a.k.a. Abu Ubaidah al-Banjshiri) and Mohammed Atef (a.k.a. Abu Hafs al-Masri), and hosted several dozens of fighters.[20] In May 1987, bin Laden's fighters participated in the successful defense of the Lion's Den against two hundred Soviet special forces troops. The so-called Battle of Jaji became an important morale booster that helped drive up additional recruitment of Arab fighters to Afghanistan. The Battle of Jaji also reinforced bin Laden's belief in establishing an Arab fighting force, while foreshadowing a deepening rift with Azzam as well.[21] The rift was complete in the summer of 1988, when bin Laden secretly established a separate military organization for Arab jihadists under his leadership: Al Qaeda.

Bin Laden's split from Azzam had both strategic and ideological roots. Azzam believed that the jihad, which was now coming to an end in Afghanistan as the Soviets prepared for departure, should next be taken to Palestine in order to "liberate Jerusalem." Bin Laden's vision, in contrast, was to establish an international Islamic fighting unit that could be sent anywhere in the world where Muslims were in need. This strategic quarrel had ideological underpinnings. According to Vahid Brown, "For Bin Ladin and the growing number of Egyptian revolutionary jihadis that became his allies during this period, the legitimate zones of jihad were not limited to Muslim territories invaded by a non-Muslim aggressor—like Soviet-occupied Afghanistan or Israel-occupied Palestine—but included revolutionary struggles against apostate regimes within the Arab Muslim world."[22] Bin Laden's preference would eventually develop into a full-fledged global jihad model—the idea being to take the struggle directly to the "far enemy" and to employ more radical tactics, including terrorism. Compared to the mainstream, classical jihad model advocated by Azzam, which emphasized the defense of Muslim lands against non-Islamic aggressors, the global jihadi variant was an outlier,[23] which, according to Brown, never became mainstream jihad and therefore never managed to become a truly global phenomenon.[24]

Underlying Al Qaeda's conceptualization as a fighting force was the idea of a global community of Islamic believers. From its founding, Al Qaeda viewed itself as a being on the vanguard and inciting international waves of jihad. The hope was that this awakening would lead to a globally active jihadist movement that would help attain the utopian goal of reestablishing Islam's traditional form of government, the caliphate.[25] From its early days, Al Qaeda therefore regarded the establishment of links with other Islamist groups that adhered to a more or less similar worldview as an advantage. Cooperation, support, and coordination with other groups, Al Qaeda believed, would create a multiplier effect that would strengthen the Islamic community, or *umma*, against the infidels and apostates.

Al Qaeda's self-described goals were not only to protect the *umma*, but to actively foster this community of believers. Serving as a hub of cooperation and coordination between various like-minded individuals and groups was a critical part of this mission, as a number of Al Qaeda's internal documents, including its by-laws, indicate. In a section titled "Fundamentals," the group described its four general goals as follows:

1. To spread the feeling of Jihad throughout the Muslim nation.
2. Prepare and qualify the needed personnel for the Muslim world by training and practical fighting participation.
3. Support, aid and help the Jihad movements around the world as possible [*sic*].
4. Coordinate among the Jihad movements around the Islamic world in order to create a united global Jihad movement.[26]

The importance of jihadi cooperation and coordination was also clear in the original documents describing the functions of the various committees in charge of advancing Al Qaeda's agenda. Thus, the military committee's goals were listed as:

1. Preparation of young freedom fighting . . . men, their training, and organizing them for combat.
2. Organization and supervision for combat participation on the battlefield.
3. Preparation of programs and military procedures.
4. Offering what is needed of military mechanics for combat.[27]

In addition, one of three "special goals" to be pursued by the military committee was to "[make] Al Qaida an establishment for combat and training experts."[28]

Similarly, the political committee's mission included several clauses that clearly indicated the importance of inter-jihadi cooperation. One of the general goals of the political committee was the "interaction with Jihad movements in the world by communication with them and to spread their news," while another was "to spread political awareness" across the Islamic states.[29]

Among the official goals of Al Qaeda's information committee was "cooperation with the scientific, legal and Jihad groups," while a key mission of the administrative and financial committee was to provide logistical support, including support for the arrival of foreign trainees.[30]

As primary source documents thus show, the idea that Al Qaeda should cooperate with other jihadist actors was built into its organizational DNA from the very outset. To that end, Al Qaeda also tried to present itself as an Islamic movement that transcended some of the divides that have plagued the Islamic community for centuries. According to the biography of Fazul Muhammad Abdullah (aka Fadil Haroun), a high-level confidante of bin Laden, Al Qaeda's enterprise distinguished itself from that of other jihadi groups in that it was not emphasizing certain ideological, sectarian, or group affiliations. This applied, for example, to its guest houses, like Bayt al-Ansar, which hosted Muslims of various backgrounds. It also applied to Al Qaeda-run training camps, which, in contrast to those of other groups, was marked by a "cosmopolitan worldview" that sought to transcend divisions between jihadists and helped Al Qaeda adopt a "global identity" virtually from its inception.[31]

Despite its official proclamations, however, the early Al Qaeda was heavily influenced by Egyptian jihadists, especially Ayman al-Zawahiri—an important figure around bin Laden who had also received financial support from the Saudi millionaire at the time.[32]

From the group's inception, Al Qaeda's cooperative efforts were no selfless enterprise. While it provided support to jihadis, it eagerly sought cooperation with individuals and groups that could help fill Al Qaeda's gaps, especially in the military realm. Thus, many of the early trainers whom Al Qaeda hired had military experience, including the infamous Ali Muhammad (aka Haidara), who had also worked for the U.S. military. Subsequently, he professionalized Al Qaeda's military curriculum significantly.[33]

In order to "spread the feeling of Jihad throughout the Muslim nation," as was one of the group's main goals, Al Qaeda cast a wide net on possible recruits and was willing to provide military training for foreigners with few questions asked.[34] These were divided into different camps based in part on how much time they could spare to go to Afghanistan. Training courses in some camps lasted less than a week, while others lasted for months.[35] By receiving jihadis of various persuasions and with varying time commitments with open arms, Al Qaeda was aiming at building an international network of like-minded militants upon whom it could call in the future. It was also a plan that, as Nelly Lahoud said, "maximized the potential for global militancy."[36]

In the period between 1989 and 1991, bin Laden's efforts were still largely focused on Afghanistan, and he lacked a clear strategy concerning the future use of these trainees. He was also physically removed from the training camps in these years, spending his time in Saudi Arabia between November 1989 and early 1991, and then Pakistan between early 1991 and early 1992. In Saudi Arabia, bin Laden famously offered the Saudi royal family his jihadist fighters to help ward off a potential attack on the Kingdom by Saddam Hussein, whose Iraqi troops had invaded Kuwait in August 1990. The Saudis rejected bin Laden's offer and invited the United States to station its army on Saudi soil instead. Humiliated, the Al Qaeda leader vowed never to return to Saudi Arabia.[37]

Bin Laden brushed off early attempts by Zawahiri to take the jihad to Egypt. His main interest, in that period, was the collapse of the regime in Communist South Yemen, where he hoped to build a "massive Muslim presence . . . similar to the one in Afghanistan."[38] Bin Laden's attempt to establish a foothold failed because he was unable to shore up clerical support in Yemen, as local clerics questioned his religious credentials.[39]

In 1992, in light of increasing pressure Middle Eastern regimes placed on Pakistan to expel Arab militants, bin Laden and most other Al Qaeda members moved to the Sudan, although the group did retain some presence in both Pakistan and Afghanistan during the ensuing years. Among them was Abu al-Walid al-Masri, who remained behind to oversee the training of new arriving cadres, which included a disproportionately large number of jihadis from many of the newly independent Central Asian countries. Among these were members of the Islamic Movement of Uzbekistan (IMU) and the Tajik Nahda Party, who would later fight the Tajik government in the civil war of 1992–1997.[40] The training of the Central Asian jihadis—a project called "al-Furqan"—was itself based on terrorist cooperation. It was jointly administered by Al Qaeda and its long-time ally, the Haqqani Network, with Al Qaeda funding and arming the trainees and the Haqqanis taking charge of the ideological and religious indoctrination.[41]

THE SUDAN YEARS, 1992–1996

Prior to Al Qaeda's move to Sudan, the group's main cooperative efforts involved participating in the fighting in Afghanistan and training of the various Islamists who streamed into the country. In Sudan, where the group would remain for the next four years, the emphasis shifted. As far as cooperation with other militant substate actors was concerned, Al Qaeda's activities came to involve supporting military and, increasingly, terrorist operations; exerting influence; and providing financial, material, technical, and other assistance to like-minded actors. During that period, the group was able to expand its reach internationally by building relationships with many Islamist groups. These relationships were mostly of a transactional and tactical nature. With the exception of the Egyptian Islamic Jihad, Al Qaeda's attempts to forge strategic alliances of the kind that would materialize post-9/11 did not succeed.

From an operational point of view, Al Qaeda's years in the Sudan proved crucial for expanding the group's links with similar-minded partners. It increasingly shared its know-how, sometimes in innovative ways. For example, members of the groups began compiling the massive "Encyclopedia of the Afghan Jihad." Thousands of pages in length and spanning multiple volumes, the encyclopedia amassed the collective military and operational knowledge that the Afghan Arabs acquired during the fight against the Soviets. The manual was designed to be shared with other jihadis in Bosnia, Chechnya, and Kashmir. CD-ROMs of the encyclopedia were sold in Pakistani bazaars in the mid-1990s.[42] In subsequent years, copies of the original encyclopedia, as well as of other similar manuals, circulated among many other jihadis worldwide.[43]

While in Sudan, most of Al Qaeda's operational activities centered on establishing training camps for those bent on waging jihad against the "near enemy," especially against the Egyptian and Algerian regimes.[44] The scale of the camp system in Sudan, however, fell short of that in Afghanistan, probably due to the Sudanese government's opposition to Al Qaeda conducting training on its soil.[45] Some of the jihadists were members of local groups such as the Algerian Armed Islamic Group (GIA) or the Abu Sayyaf (ASG) in the Philippines, which had begun their jihad rather spontaneously, oftentimes under the influence of Afghan Arabs who had returned to these countries after the defeat of the Soviets.[46] Al Qaeda saw its role as coordinating these local movements by providing funds, training, and at times weapons.[47] Thus, for example, Al Qaeda transferred $100,000 to affiliates in Jordan and Eritrea and sent trainers to the Filipino Moro Islamic Liberation Front (MILF). It stepped up cooperation with the Armed Islamic Group (GIA), as well as with the Libyan Islamic Fighting Group (LIFG), some of whose fighters were in Sudan at the time. It maintained guest houses in Lebanon, and sent operatives to the Bekaa Valley to train with Hizballah on improvised explosive devices, intelligence, and security.[48]

Even if the magnitude of the training camp system in the Sudan fell short of that in Afghanistan, Al Qaeda was able to step up cooperation with other jihadists during that period. For the first time, it became involved in international terrorist and insurgent activities in various ways, including funding, operational support, guidance, and sometimes complete direction of attacks. These groups and individuals with various ties to Al Qaeda were present in such countries as Algeria, Bosnia, Eritrea, Ethiopia, Jordan, Philippines, Somalia, Uganda, and Yemen. Radical Islamists were also supported in Burma, Chechnya, Egypt, Lebanon, Libya, Kashmir, Pakistan, Saudi Arabia, and Tajikistan, among other places.[49] To manage these links, Al Qaeda formed the Islamic Army Shura, a coordinating body.[50]

One of Al Qaeda's main areas of interest during these years was Somalia. In late January 1993, Abu Hafs al-Masri sent scores of Al Qaeda's leading trainers—including Fadil Haroun—from the Sudan to Somalia to assess the possibility of using Somalia in place of Afghanistan as Al Qaeda's next safe haven for operations and training.[51] Cooperating with a local Islamist group, al-Ittihad al-Islami (AIAI), Al Qaeda was able to establish at least three training camps there, although it ultimately failed to create a safe haven in Somalia.[52] Another plan in Somalia was to sabotage the U.S.-led humanitarian intervention in the country, which had been announced in December 1992.[53] Al Qaeda training soon extended to teaching Somali clansmen how to shoot down helicopters using rocket-propelled grenades (RPGs); subsequently, they were able to shoot down two U.S. helicopters.[54] Keeping some of the trainers in Somalia even after the eventual withdrawal of U.S. forces in 1994, the Al Qaeda leadership charged them with establishing sleeper cells that would be activated against local, U.S., and Israeli targets.[55]

Many of the groups that received support from Al Qaeda during the Sudan years were focused on liberating lands that had once been under Muslim control, such as Kashmir and the Philippines. Others were fighting in places like Bosnia or Chechnya, where they believed Muslims to be under attack. Central Asia featured high on Al Qaeda's list of priorities. Leaders like Abu al-Walid sensed that enmity toward Russia in the aftermath of the collapse of the Soviet Union was a fertile ground for Al Qaeda to spread its influence, and to that end, it opened satellite offices in the region.[56]

Bosnia in particular offered an opportunity for the jihadists to make inroads into Europe proper. The country had declared its independence from Yugoslavia in 1992. When this move was followed by attacks from Serb militias, a few dozen Arab fighters traveled to Bosnia in 1992 to defend their Muslim brethren, who formed the largest minority in the multiethnic state.[57] By 1993, after Catholic Croats joined the battle, the number mushroomed to hundreds of Arab fighters, and the war in Bosnia became one the first major confrontations between Muslims and Christians of the post–Cold War period.

While Al Qaeda sent emissaries to Bosnia to investigate the conditions for a greater Al Qaeda involvement, it ended up playing only a marginal role in the Bosnian jihad. The Egyptian jihadist groups, notably the Egyptian Islamic Group (EIG) and Egyptian Islamic Jihad (EIJ), dominated the organization of foreign mujahideen in Bosnia. Bin Laden was not willing to meddle and decided to keep his focus on the Arabian Peninsula and the Horn of Africa for the time being.[58]

Besides sending emissaries, Al Qaeda had some financial influence on the war in Bosnia, funneling money through a number of charities. One was the Benevolence International Foundation (BIF), which had clear links to Al Qaeda through Enaam Arnaout, who had overseen logistics for Al Qaeda's early training camps, and Loay Bayazid, who was present during the founding meeting of Al Qaeda. BIF enabled jihadists to travel to conflict zones like Bosnia and later Chechnya, paid for uniforms and other equipment, and helped distribute propaganda material.[59]

In 1995, as the war in Bosnia was coming to an end, an Al Qaeda delegation headed by a member with the nom de guerre of Sayf al-Islam al-Misri was sent for training in Chechnya, which was in the midst of its first war with Russia. A couple of years earlier, bin Laden had hoped to gain the support of Ibn al-Khattab, a legendary Saudi fighter who had received military training in the Jawir Camp that was run by Al Qaeda in the late 1980s, before leaving after a quarrel with the camp leaders. Khattab was leading an international brigade in Chechnya in the late 1990s, but he was unwilling to join with bin Laden and fight under the Al Qaeda banner.[60]

In sum, Al Qaeda's failure to play a more central role in Bosnia and Chechnya was typical of its entire period in the Sudan. While it did manage to forge international links with a host of jihadi groups between 1992 and 1996, its aim to build a strong international jihadi alliance under its leadership ultimately failed. Its Somalian mission did not produce a new safe haven based on the Afghan model. Ties to several jihadi groups were severed. Its relationship with the GIA in Algeria was brought to an end when the latter descended into the massive killing of Muslims. Al-Qaeda's ties to the Libyan Islamic Fighting Group similarly ended disastrously when bin Laden acquiesced to the pressure of the Sudanese government to expel members of the group from Sudan, where LIFG members had relocated in the mid-1990s following Libyan government crackdowns. Other groups were ideologically incongruent with Al Qaeda. The Abu Sayyaf Group (ASG) in the Philippines, for example, shed its jihadi aspirations and turned toward criminal activities. The Moro Islamic Liberation Front (MILF), on the other hand, grew apart from Al Qaeda because its local focus was incompatible with Al Qaeda's global aspirations.

AL QAEDA'S GOLDEN ERA: AFGHANISTAN, 1996–2001

On August 23, 1996, three months after pressure from the Sudanese government forced bin Laden to leave Sudan and return to Afghanistan, the Al Qaeda leader declared war on the United States. Bin Laden laid out his case against the West in a lengthy statement.[61] On February 23, 1998, he followed up by proclaiming the establishment of a "World Islamic Front" dedicated to fighting the "Jews and the Crusaders."[62] These declarations against the "far enemy" signaled Al Qaeda's adoption of the global jihad as its main program of action. In the period from 1996 to 2001, Al Qaeda witnessed an unprecedented organizational growth that translated into a series of spectacular attacks against this "far enemy," including the bombings of U.S. embassies in Dar-es-Salaam and Nairobi in 1998, the attack on the USS *Cole* in 2000, and the attacks of September 11, 2001.

Much of the growth of Al Qaeda in the 1996–2001 period and the growing danger it posed to the West were due to its ability to forge cooperative ties with other entities, although these ties were almost exclusively tactical or transactional, and hence low-end in nature. According to Thomas Hegghammer, bin Laden had a "formidable ability to create alliances with other key players in the world of radical Islamism."[63] Hegghammer attributes this success to Al Qaeda's ability to offer highly valued commodities such as training, refuge, and money to interested parties, but clearly bin Laden also possessed personal traits that other jihadists valued, such as charisma, reputation, rhetorical skills, and a good sense of politics and windows of opportunity. This ability was "all the more remarkable given that the agenda he was pursuing—war against America—was actually shared by very few of his allies."[64]

In his efforts to build an international coalition of militant Islamists, bin Laden was increasingly willing to cooperate even with groups that did not necessarily share the Salafi-jihadist worldview. Bin Laden had assumed a rather pragmatic stance even during the Sudan years, as evidenced by his willingness to cooperate with ideologically opposed groups such as the Shiite Hizballah—an example of tactical cooperation discussed further in chapter 8. Now that Islamists had seemingly united for a common cause, namely, to fight the enemies of Islam, ideological purity was secondary to achieving the practical goals that Al Qaeda had set. Al Qaeda's ideological expectations of its partners would loosen even further in the post-9/11 period, when the U.S.-led campaign against bin Laden heightened Al Qaeda's urge to build alliances.[65]

Besides broadening the nexus of global jihad through intergroup cooperation, Al Qaeda also strove to become a source of inspiration for the global Islamic community. To that end, Al Qaeda intended to wake up Muslims from their "slumber" and instill the idea into the collective

Islamic psyche that Islam was under attack and that Muslims of all stripes had a duty to come to the defense of their religion.[66] First, however, bin Laden had to overcome the financial troubles that plagued the group upon its return to Afghanistan, which were caused by a combination of financial mismanagement and the expropriation of bin Laden's assets in the Sudan prior to his departure. These troubles were overcome fairly quickly, as a core group of financial supporters, known as the "Golden Chain," raised money for Al Qaeda from various donors and other fundraisers based mainly in Saudi Arabia and the Gulf States. Al Qaeda also managed to divert money from Islamic charities. In some cases, employees in these charities would siphon some money to Al Qaeda, while in other cases, Al Qaeda would control an entire charity.[67]

It was bin Laden's existing ties and his ability to establish new ties that helped him bridge the initial period of uncertainty. Upon his arrival in Afghanistan, he was hosted by Younis Khalis, a commander of a mujahideen faction that had fought the Soviets during their occupation. As the Taliban consolidated their power in Afghanistan in the course of 1996, bin Laden opted for a partnership with the group's leader, Mullah Omar. Over the next five years, Mullah Omar and the Taliban would provide Osama bin Laden a safe haven in Afghanistan. In return, bin Laden paid the Taliban an estimated $10–$20 million per year. Al Qaeda also supported various military operations of the Taliban and provided tactical training to the group in such areas as the use of suicide attacks.[68]

The relationship between the groups was troubled from the beginning, though. Some members of Al Qaeda looked at their Afghan hosts, who lacked Salafist credentials, with disdain.[69] Many in the Taliban, for their part, resented the foreign presence, and the Taliban leadership strongly preferred that bin Laden keep a low profile. Their appeals fell on deaf ears, however, as bin Laden was determined to use Afghanistan as a safe haven for terrorist attacks and as a platform to advertise his plans.

To offset the restrictions that the Taliban attempted to place on Al Qaeda, bin Laden maintained close ties to other groups such as the Haqqani Network (HQN). The Haqqanis, a Pakistan-based group operating on either side of the Pakistani-Afghan border, was aligned with the Taliban, but enjoyed some autonomy from it. HQN's relationship with Al Qaeda will be described in more detail in the next chapter.

All in all, Al Qaeda members enjoyed substantial freedom of movement over the next five years, running "something of a parallel state to that of the Taliban."[70] Using the state owned Ariana Airlines, for example, Al Qaeda managed to courier money into Afghanistan. According to the *9/11 Commission Report*, its members "could travel freely within the country, enter and exit it without visas or any immigration procedures, purchase and import vehicles and weapons, and enjoy the use of official Afghan Ministry of Defense license plates."[71]

Most importantly perhaps, the alliance with the Taliban enabled Al Qaeda to establish a sanctuary that the group used to train and indoctrinate an estimated 10,000–20,000 fighters over the next years; some were selected for advanced courses in terrorism. These fighters were not automatically members of Al Qaeda. Only several hundred of the best were formally invited to join the group.[72] Until 1999, Al Qaeda trained fighters in camps that were run by other jihadi outfits. Starting in 1999, the Taliban permitted Al Qaeda to set up its own camps. These included al-Faruq, which provided basic training to new recruits, and the so-called Airport Camp near Kandahar, which offered advanced courses.[73] Surpassing the camps of other groups in terms of size, quality of training, and skills of staff, Al Qaeda's camps were also unlike most other jihadi camps in that they were melting pots that brought together jihadists from many countries, established strong ties among the trainees, and built a strong sense of loyalty between them.

It is difficult, in fact, to overstate the centrality of the training camp system not only for the specific issue of cooperation within the global jihad movement, but for the self-understanding of Al Qaeda as a hub for the establishment of a global fraternity of Islamic activists that would internalize a militant understanding of jihad. As Hegghammer put it:

The camps "generated an ultra-masculine culture of violence which brutalized the volunteers and broke down their barriers to the use of violence. Recruits increased their paramilitary skills while the harsh camp life built strong personal relationships between them. Last but not least, they fell under the ideological influence of Usama bin Ladin and Ayman al-Zawahiri, who generated a feeling among the recruits of being part of a global vanguard of holy warriors, whose mission was to defend the Islamic world against attacks by the Jewish-Crusader alliance."[74]

In implementing his plans, bin Laden benefited from the existing infrastructure he had kept in place in Afghanistan since the pre-Sudan period. But the group now also benefited from the broader infrastructure established by a plethora of jihadist groups active in Afghanistan, with which Al Qaeda cooperated in varying degrees.[75] Using funds that flowed to Al Qaeda coffers, bin Laden sent trainers to many camps not formally run by Al Qaeda. Training in the camps differed, with some offering general guerrilla training, others offering training in mostly urban terrorism, and some even experimenting with nonconventional weapons.[76] Generally speaking, military training was the norm, and formal training in terrorism was the exception.[77]

The Afghan safe haven also gave Al Qaeda the ability to maintain ties to jihadi groups in Algeria, Egypt, Lebanon, Morocco, Somalia, Tunisia, and Yemen, with which it had linked up during the Sudan period.[78] It bolstered its presence in Central Asia and the Caucasus and reinforced its London office. It also established new ties with groups in South and Southeast Asia, including a variety of Pakistani groups that were involved in the struggle against India over Kashmir.[79]

The level of cooperation between Al Qaeda and other jihadi organizations varied from case to case, as well as over time. In some instances, Al Qaeda's links to other groups buttressed jihadist groups in places where a mujahideen presence had already been established. Al Qaeda's financial and material aid also supported the establishment of jihadi groups and movements in places where no such presence existed or where that presence was weak. Its most intimate cooperation was with the Egyptian Islamic Jihad, with which it formally merged in June 2001, subsequently renaming itself Qaedat al-Jihad (Base of Jihad).[80]

During the 1990s, in order to promote Al Qaeda's efforts to awaken Muslims from their "slumber" and enlist more of them in the struggle against the perceived enemies of Islam, Al Qaeda also established a security committee within its organizational structure, while subordinating a dawa apparatus to that new committee, which was in charge of recruitment and propaganda. The dawa apparatus consisted of a network of imams, many of whom had fought the Soviets in Afghanistan during the 1980s, who were placed in key cities around the world. Its mission was to find suitable candidates and facilitate their recruitment to training camps in Afghanistan. These clergymen became Al Qaeda's de facto "point-of-contact (POC) officers" around the world.[81]

Towards the end of the 1990s, bin Laden's organization in Afghanistan was able to benefit from the failure of jihadi enterprises in places such as Algeria, Egypt, or Libya, as well as the difficulty in accessing other theaters such as Chechnya.[82] This allowed Al Qaeda to "grow parasitically by absorbing jihadis from the margins of militant organizations in decline" and even to establish new training camps for them.[83]

In this time, Al Qaeda failed to unite all jihadists under its banner. Bin Laden's attempts to gain control over the Khalden camp, for example, which was run by Ibn al-Shaykh al-Libi and Abu Zubaydah, along with his efforts to gain the full allegiance of senior jihadi figures such as Abu Musab al-Suri and Abu Khabab al-Masri, who trained jihadists independently from Al Qaeda, did not succeed. Bin Laden also failed—although only for the time being—to bring Abu Musab al-Zarqawi and his group al-Tawhid w'al Jihad into his fold, despite the financial support that bin Laden provided to the group.[84]

Al Qaeda did manage, however, to step up its terrorist activities. It had already declared war on the United States in a 1996 fatwa, and it had supported operations against the United States in Somalia in 1993. In Afghanistan, Al Qaeda now had an opportunity to acquire weapons, funding, and the necessary know-how to embark on a broader strategy of terrorism focused especially on the far enemy.

In its drive to support terrorist operations, Al Qaeda was unusual in its openness toward various ideas for terrorist attacks from a variety of jihadi entrepreneurs and groups.[85] In the process, Al Qaeda internalized modern forms of business management such as a flat organizational structure and flexible strategy. As Bruce Hoffman observes, bin Laden's leadership style was similar to that of a president or CEO of a large multinational corporation. He issued strategic guidance by defining specific goals and overseeing their implementation. At the same time, however, bin Laden also "operated as a venture capitalist: soliciting ideas from below, encouraging creative approaches and 'out of the box' thinking, and providing funding to those proposals he th[ought] promising."[86] Proposals by local terrorist seeking funding for operations were vetted by Al Qaeda's military committee, which also provided some operational support. Al Qaeda preferred to provide seed money for terrorist operations, but in rare cases it did fund attacks in their entirety, eventually appropriating them as their own.[87] One proposal brought to bin Laden in mid-1996 was known as the "planes operation" and was concocted by Khaled Sheikh Muhammed. The ensuing cooperation that eventually led to the 9/11 attacks is discussed in detail in chapter 9.

During this period, besides conducting its own operations, Al Qaeda supported numerous efforts by associated terrorist cells and networks, which were seeking to carry out terrorist activities worldwide. Examples include the so-called Millennium Plot by Ahmed Ressam, who planned to blow up Los Angeles International Airport using RDX before being arrested and a Jordanian network of "Afghan alumni," which planned attacks against U.S. and Israeli tourists visiting Christian holy sites in Jordan and the Jordanian-Israeli border crossing.[88]

Despite the impressive comeback of Al Qaeda in this period, its ultimate goal of establishing itself as the vanguard of global Islamist resistance ultimately came to naught, as exemplified by the resounding failure of its 1998 declaration of the "World Islamic Front." With only a fraction of the groups operating in Afghanistan at the time signing on to the declaration—and with two of these signatories, the Egyptian Islamic Group and the Egyptian Islamic Jihad, retracting their agreement shortly thereafter—it became clear that bin Laden was unable to lead a global movement. Lacking a coherent ideology and strategy to unite the movement, he similarly failed to lobby other groups, including the Libyan Islamic Fighting Group (LIFG).[89]

From the standpoint of alliances, Al Qaeda's high-end merger with the Egyptian Islamic Jihad was its main success in this period. Although the merger followed a longer period of cooperation with EIJ, it was formalized only a few months prior to the attacks of September 11, 2001. Zawahiri was promoted to Al Qaeda's deputy emir, but ultimately the Al Qaeda–EIJ merger added only five people to the core membership of Al Qaeda— hardly a resounding success.[90]

6

POST-9/11 COOPERATION
IN THE GLOBAL JIHAD

O N SEPTEMBER 11, 2001, Al Qaeda was able to deliver a painful blow to the United States, but the aftermath of the attacks, which provoked a U.S. led invasion of Afghanistan, placed major challenges before the group. In the wake of the strikes of 9/11, Al Qaeda lost its safe haven in Afghanistan and along with it the ability to maintain the training camps that had been one of the cornerstones of its organization. Key leaders of Al Qaeda were now forced into hiding in the region along the Pakistan-Afghanistan border, while another group of senior leaders were granted access to Iran (see chapter 8). Mid-level and lower-level operatives were forced to disperse to various countries around the world. As the United States and other countries stepped up their counterterrorism campaigns over the following years, killing or capturing mid- and senior-level Al Qaeda operatives, while restricting the jihadists' ability to move and communicate, the impact on the organizational unity and ideological cohesion of Al Qaeda was detrimental.

To contend with these post-9/11 pressures, but also partly by design, Al Qaeda embarked on several evolutionary changes in strategy, ideology, and structure.[1] In the realm of strategy, Al Qaeda tried to compensate for the loss of the Afghan safe haven by stepping up its involvement in worldwide terrorist attacks. Throughout the post-9/11 period, the group continued to centrally plan and direct several attacks and plots, such as the London bombings of July 7, 2005, as well as the failed attempt to replicate the London bombings in the New York City subway in 2009.[2] More than carrying out attacks on its own, however, Al Qaeda after 9/11 tended to support terrorist activities by groups and networks with which it had varying degrees of ties, such as the Moroccan Islamist Combatant Group (GICM), which was involved in the Madrid train attacks of March 11, 2004. The Madrid attacks also showcase another trend of the 9/11 period, namely, the involvement of homegrown terrorists. As Bruce Hoffman and Fernando Reinares concluded from their review of key jihadist plots of the post-9/11 period, the "fusion of local, homegrown radicals with the directing hand of an al-Qaeda affiliate connecting to the core in Pakistan would become an enduring feature of post–September 11 international terrorism."[3]

In these plots, Al Qaeda was at times only the source of inspiration, as was the case in the 2006 plan to strike a variety of targets in Toronto.[4] In other cases, such as a plot disrupted in August 2006 to detonate at least seven airliners departing from Heathrow airport using liquid explosives, Al Qaeda played a more hands-on role.[5] In many cases, Al Qaeda operatives would redirect individuals who sought training in Pakistan and other jihadist hot spots to carry out terrorist strikes in the West.[6]

Another key strategic adaptation of the post-9/11 period was the increase in terrorism carried out by independent jihadi cells or individuals. This trend did not emerge by accident, but was part of a doctrine of *individual jihad* developed by Abu Musab al-Suri, one of the leading jihadi strategists of modern times. Suri introduced the concept in his 1,600-page *Global Islamic Resistance Call*, which has been referred to as "the most significant written source in the strategic studies literature on al-Qaida."[7] In advocating the use of individual jihad in various spontaneous operations spread over the globe, Suri was favoring a growing reliance on decentralized operations that would receive little, if any, direction and would therefore sow confusion in the enemy's ranks. Even if the enemy could apprehend some operatives, its doing so would "not influence the operational activities of others who are not connected to them."[8] Individual jihad, according to

Suri, has the added benefit of "awakening the spirit of jihad and resistance within the Islamic Nation,"[9] while the goal of the operations is to "inflict as many human and material losses as possible upon the interests of America and her allies, and to make them feel that the Resistance has transformed into a phenomenon of popular uprising against them. . . . The arena of the Islamic countries is the basic arena for the Resistance."[10]

Another strategic adaptation of the post-9/11 period was what Al Qaeda called *economic jihad*. In October 2004, bin Laden declared a "bleed-America-to-bankruptcy" plan, which involved such broad tactics as luring the United States to engage in expensive combat operations in the Middle East and targeting the Middle Eastern and Gulf state oil facilities that were considered the lifeblood of the U.S. economy.[11] This emphasis on economic targets was part of Al Qaeda's growing effort to take advantage of perceived weaknesses of the West. Thus, global jihadi strategists, such as al-Suri, studied Western strategic literature and familiarized themselves with Western policy debates, which they skillfully exploited to achieve strategic and ideological objectives.[12]

A growing reliance on the media for a variety of activities associated with terrorism, including recruitment, indoctrination, and propaganda, is an additional development of the post-9/11 period.[13] This strategy, like that of individual jihad, arose in part from Al Qaeda's changing fortunes on the battlefield, and was a way to compensate for the loss of its training camp infrastructure and its corresponding centrality among jihadist groups.[14] After 2003, Al Qaeda proved particularly skillful at exploiting widespread negative sentiment about the American invasion and occupation of Iraq. Subsequently, it seized on the Ethiopian occupation of Mogadishu in a similar way, urging the erstwhile Islamist militia turned jihadist group al-Shabaab to "fight on" as "champions of Somalia."[15] Meanwhile, in the ideological realm, Al Qaeda endeavored to widen the target audience of its recruitment and propaganda campaign. Whereas before 9/11, its appeals were directed exclusively to Muslims, after 9/11, Al Qaeda adopted a more populist rhetoric that included non-Muslims.[16] In an essay published in February 2005, for example, Zawahiri attempted to engage anti-globalization and environmental activists in the cause.[17] During this time, Al Qaeda also increased its ideological efforts to frame local grievances in accordance with its global narrative, and while this was not a new feature of its propaganda, more extensive and intensive media production has characterized Al Qaeda's growing attempts to aggregate disparate Islamist conflicts after 2001. Accordingly, Al Qaeda has sought to harmonize its propaganda with the grievance narratives associated with local and regional jihadist movements in Yemen, Somalia, the Caucasus, Pakistan, Afghanistan, Iraq, India, Central Asia, and Southeast Asia. While its ability to globalize these disparate conflicts has remained limited, isolated successes across a spectrum of theaters have increased the number of ideological pathways to participation in the global jihad, as, for example, in the case of the Tehrik-e Taliban Pakistan (TTP), which adopted attacks against Western targets after it became associated with Al Qaeda.[18]

In all, though, the most crucial developments facilitating the evolution from Al Qaeda to the global jihad movement in the post-9/11 period have involved several structural adaptations. As an organization, Al Qaeda changed in at least three significant ways during these years.

First, it became formally affiliated with geographically dispersed groups, which, in turn, fundamentally altered Al Qaeda. Rather than a single organization with cells spread in scores of countries, Al Qaeda became a multi-polar organization with a central hub in the Pakistani tribal areas and a small number of autonomous regional nodes. By aligning themselves with Al Qaeda, the organizations in these nodes extended Al Qaeda's ideological and operational influence in their respective regions, while also allowing Al Qaeda to engage in networking, propagandizing, and resource mobilization in active conflict zones. Thus, these nodes created resilience and dynamism in the movement and amplified the world's perception of Al Qaeda, while also being designed to provide a degree of redundancy should Al Qaeda continue to suffer devastating losses in Pakistan.

The most consequential results of this structural transformation were changes in the locations, targets, and tactics of terrorist violence. Thus, areas in proximity to the main territorial hubs of Al Qaeda Core and its affiliates, such as Afghanistan, Algeria, Iraq, Pakistan, Somalia, Yemen, and their neighbors, became the most likely targets of terrorist and guerrilla attacks.[19] Moreover, Al Qaeda tactics such as suicide bombings were introduced precisely in those regions where jihadist cells, including Al Qaeda affiliates, sprang up, such as Algeria, Somalia, and Yemen.[20] Besides the adoption of suicide attacks, the use of vehicle-borne improvised explosive devices (VBIEDs) offered additional evidence of knowledge transfer to these regional nodes.

Second, Al Qaeda stepped up the intensity of its informal partnerships with geographically co-located groups. While Al Qaeda had always valued associations short of formal affiliation with militant organizations, it began utilizing these associations more aggressively in the post-9/11 period in order to facilitate jihadist violence against Western interests.

Third, in addition to operational convergence, regional affiliates and associates began embracing the same types of information operations for which Al Qaeda had become famous. As a result, media organizations that produced the type of propaganda originally employed by Al Qaeda's official As-Sahab media organization multiplied. The proliferation of content on dynamic jihadist websites, the empowering nature of user-generated content, and the growing links between jihadist activity online and jihadist activity in the real world created another crucial structural shift in the global jihad, which has been addressed in chapter 3.

THE AFFILIATES SYSTEM:
AL QAEDA'S FRANCHISING MODEL

The relationships that Al Qaeda had built over the years proved useful as members of the group fled Afghanistan in the wake of the U.S. response to the 9/11 strikes. According to Michael Scheuer, the former head of the CIA's bin Laden unit, Al Qaeda used its ties to Pashtun tribes and to Afghan heroin smuggling networks for its dispersal. It was also assisted by members of Pakistan's bureaucracy and Islamists in Pakistan's army and security services, Islamic NGOs, and insurgent and terrorist groups in Kashmir, such as Jaish-e Muhammad (JEM), Lashkar-e Taiba (LET), and Hizb-ul Mujahideen (HM).[21] Some Al Qaeda leaders fled to Iran, aided likely by the Iranian Revolutionary Guard Corps.[22]

By late 2002, the global jihad movement, which had lost much of its orientation after losing its Afghan safe haven, found a new focus in Iraq. Al Qaeda had some ties to jihadist groups in Iraq dating to the pre-9/11 period, notably Ansar al-Islam, a Kurdish jihadist group located in northern Iraq.[23] Subsequently, however, the war in Iraq that began in March of 2003 created far greater opportunities for the global jihad movement to establish a foothold in the heart of the Middle East. During the ensuing years, Iraq became the most important theater in the battle against the perceived enemies of Islam, providing a new strategic and emotional focus for the movement.[24]

The Iraq War also improved Al Qaeda's conditions for establishing formal partnerships with groups, when compared to the pre-9/11 period, by solving an ideological problem: namely, Al Qaeda's inability thus far to convince jihadi movements, which were preoccupied with classical models of jihad, of the merits of global jihad. In Iraq, classical and global models of jihad would, within a short time, merge to create a hybrid version of jihad that allowed a variety of jihad movements to identify with a struggle that pitted jihadists simultaneously against the near and far enemy.[25] Because the Iraq War could be portrayed as a jihad against foreign intruders, a broader array of Islamist ideologies declared this jihad to be legitimate. In light of the hybridized nature of the jihad in Iraq, it is perhaps no coincidence that Al Qaeda's new franchise model—its decision to step up efforts to identify suitable affiliates and rely on them as a force multiplier to achieve the group's objectives—was first implemented in that country. No other adaptation would be more important in guiding Al Qaeda's strategy of cooperation in the post-9/11 period.

Al Qaeda's affiliate system emerged in 2004, when the group formally affiliated with Abu Musab al-Zarqawi's al-Tawhid w'al Jihad. Its new franchising model had not emerged in a vacuum, but was a continuation of Al Qaeda's previous efforts to seek partnerships with like-minded organizations. Whereas such attempts generally failed before 9/11, with the notable exception of its merger with a faction of the Egyptian Islamic Jihad (EIJ), after 9/11, they were more successful, at least on the surface. Within a decade, Al Qaeda managed to establish formal strategic alliances with several organizations, although fractures with these partners were common from the start.

Al Qaeda's ability to establish more formal affiliations in the post-9/11 period was also due to Al Qaeda's growing ideological flexibility. Previously, Al Qaeda had requested that organizations seeking formal affiliation fully adopt its global jihadist agenda—a problematic request, given the predominance of local concerns among jihadi groups. After 9/11, facing the pressures of Western counterterrorism campaigns against the group, bin Laden decided to loosen the ideological requirements for affiliates. Potential partners were no longer expected to abandon their local focus, but would only have to broaden their agenda. Affiliates were now able to continue to fight the local enemy, as long as they would also conduct occasional attacks against the far enemy. Leaders of the new affiliates also had to present "a united front, stay on message, and be seen to fall under al Qaeda's authority—all crucial for demonstrating the organization's power and attracting others to its cause."[26]

According to Australian terrorism researcher Leah Farrall, Al Qaeda gave up on attempts to micromanage the affiliates, and instead tried to manage relations broadly, especially with regard to external operations.[27] Subsidiaries were "to seek approval before conducting attacks outside their assigned regions and . . . before assisting other militant groups with external operations."[28] Suicide missions, Farrall adds, became a preferred tactic, as did "strikes on preapproved classes of targets, such as public transportation, government buildings, and vital infrastructure. Once a location ha[d] been authorized, the branch and the franchises [we]re free to pursue plots against it. But al Qaeda still emphasize[d] the need to consult the central leadership before undertaking large-scale plots, plots directed against a new location or a new class of targets, and plots utilizing a tactic that ha[d] not been previously sanctioned, such as the use of chemical, biological, or radiological devices."[29]

From the start, it became clear that the franchising model afforded Al Qaeda a number of distinct advantages, such as helping it implement its growing support of terrorist strikes in the post-9/11 period. Affiliates and associates could serve as force multipliers that extended Al Qaeda's ability to strike, or seek credit for strikes, in multiple locations. Affiliates would also benefit Al Qaeda by helping to propagate its global jihadist vision. Moreover, given their local roots, they could both serve as sanctuaries and reach more potential recruits. In sum, the arrangement not only maintained, but also enhanced Al Qaeda visibility and apparent power, afforded greater legitimacy to the movement, and therefore expanded its brand. Given the weakened state of the group's core group, these were significant benefits.[30] At the same time, affiliation with what Western analysts increasingly referred to as Al Qaeda Central (AQC) afforded junior partners with benefits as well. These included access to funds; technical know-how related to the use of weapons or advanced media operations; and access to international logistics network. In addition to these operational and logistical advantages, benefits to junior partners extended to the ideational realm and included the ability to spread propaganda through affiliation with a well-known brand and to employ the senior group's media infrastructure.[31]

Branching out, however, turned out to be a costly strategy. The empowerment of affiliated organizations increased the chances that these groups would develop interests and strategies not entirely aligned with AQC, which led to principal-agent problems.[32] Slow and irregular communication between AQC and its affiliates added to these challenges. As a result, headquarters were poorly informed about the activities of the affiliates and could not issue directives efficiently; this, in turn, led affiliates to second guess AQC's ability to lead an increasingly amorphous global jihadi movement.

The affiliates also ran risks by formally affiliating themselves with AQC. These included the obvious risk of attracting the attention of the United States and other countries bent on fighting global jihadi groups. Affiliates also risked alienating some of their local constituents, many of whom were more concerned with local problems and not with AQC's global agenda.

Aware of these and other disadvantages of its franchising model, AQC has therefore carefully selected the groups with which it has been willing to establish formal strategic partnerships. Where it found the risks of formal affiliation to be excessive, it declined offers of formal affiliation, or held out on acknowledging the pledge of loyalty. AQC preferred to strike formal alliances with groups that were the lead organizations in a given theater, while shunning affiliations with groups whose viability it deemed uncertain.[33] Several of the most prominent alliances are discussed below; that of Al Qaeda with Al Qaeda in the Arabian Peninsula (AQAP) is examined in detail in the next chapter.

AFFILIATION WITH JAMAAT AL-TAWHID W'AL JIHAD, 2004

One of the groups whose long-term ability to survive Al Qaeda did not question was Jamaat al-Tawhid w'al Jihad, a network based around Jordanian jihadist Abu Musab al-Zarqawi. In 2004, after pledging *bayah* to bin Laden, the group became Al Qaeda's first formal affiliate under that franchise model. Subsequently, however, some of the tensions inherent in the model began to surface. While renaming itself Al Qaeda in the Land of the Two Rivers (commonly referred to as Al Qaeda in Iraq, or AQI), the group then set itself apart from AQC by its more extremist interpretation of Islam and geographic focus on the Levant.

Bin Laden had made overtures to Zarqawi already prior to 9/11. Since 1999, Zarqawi had been running training camps in Western Afghanistan, which had attracted many jihadists from Europe, Lebanon, and Syria, due in part to the group's regional focus, which appealed to the more regionally-minded Levantene jihadis. In the course of 2001, when Al Qaeda was providing financial support for Zarqawi's training camps in Herat, bin Laden tried to establish a formal alliance with Zarqawi, in part to boost his credentials as a serious potential challenger to Israel. Sayf al-Adel was tasked with approaching Zarqawi to seek "coordination and cooperation to achieve our joint objectives," but Zarqawi was not yet willing to forgo his group's independence.[34] Then, in 2003 or 2004, it was Zarqawi who proposed to bin Laden the idea of a formal affiliation.[35]

After some ten months of deliberations, bin Laden agreed, and Zarqawi's outfit, by then based in Iraq, became a formal affiliate in October 2004. AQI's involvement in the Iraqi insurgency made it a highly visible jihadist actor, capable of attracting much donor money. By affiliating with the Iraqi group, AQC could claim active involvement in the jihad against the American enemy in what was now the main theater of jihad. According to Daniel Byman, affiliation with AQI offered AQC "enhanced specialization via access within the Iraqi market, branding outside it, learning, and legitimization—all the expected rewards of a relationship."[36] Thus, AQI not only gained greater legitimacy and respectability by affiliating with the leading brand in the fight against the infidels and apostates, but also tied into a broader logistical and propaganda infrastructure. Furthermore, affiliation with AQC bolstered AQI financially, as well as enabling it to draw greater numbers of foreign fighters, many of whom would be used for the group's suicide operations.[37]

From the very beginning, though, the relationship between the groups was a rocky one. AQI did not live up to Al Qaeda's expectations that new affiliates should devote their efforts to attacking the United States and other Western targets, Rather than global jihad, AQI's primary concern was the local struggle in Iraq, where the bulk of its operations took place. Moreover, Zarqawi embarked on a campaign to target the Shiite population of Iraq in an effort to stir sectarian tensions, increasingly employed a series of gruesome tactics, such as beheadings, and did not stop short even of killing many Sunni Iraqis.[38] The AQC leadership and influential jihadi ideologues soon came to view AQI's actions as excessively violent and counterproductive to the jihadist cause.

Al Qaeda's relationship with AQI remained problematic after Zarqawi's death in June 2006, when AQI and its successor organization, the Islamic State of Iraq (ISI), failed to consult with Al Qaeda on various activities. Bin Laden, for that matter, viewed Zarqawi's successors to be even more dangerous and objectionable.[39]

AFFILIATION WITH THE SALAFIST GROUP FOR PREACHING AND COMBAT (GSPC), 2007

Algerian Islamists have played an integral role in the global jihad movement dating back to the anti-Soviet jihad in Afghanistan. Between 1,200 and 2,000 sought to participate in the fighting against the Soviets, while thousands have reportedly received instruction in Afghan and Pakistani training camps since the 1980s. Subsequently, Algerians were prominent in every major jihadi theater, particularly in Bosnia, Iraq, and Syria.[40]

The Algerian Salafist Group for Preaching and Combat (GSPC) emerged in 1998 as a supposedly more moderate splinter group of the Armed Islamic Group (GIA), possibly at the goading of Osama bin Laden.[41] Whereas its predecessor organization had made a dubious name for itself by declaring virtually all Algerians who did not adopt the GIA's ideology to be infidels, the new splinter organization declared that in its goal of overthrowing the Algerian government—which it shared with the GIA—it would predominantly target military and political institutions, as opposed to civilians. In less than a decade the GSPC broke its promise. In 2007, the group formally joined Al Qaeda and renamed itself Al Qaeda in the Islamic Maghreb (AQIM).[42]

The GSPC's adoption of a global jihadist agenda evolved gradually, starting shortly after the turn of the millennium.[43] At the time when Al Qaeda struck the United States on 9/11, the GSPC, whose traditional focus had been on Algeria and France, had already established a number of cells in several European countries. On the second anniversary of 9/11, the group, now under a new leadership, announced that it included the United States among its enemies, stating that "We strongly and fully support Osama bin Laden's jihad against the heretic America."[44] The GSPC also began vocally supporting various global jihadi groups, notably Chechen jihadists fighting Russia, as well as AQI after October 2004. The latter cooperation proved particularly fruitful. The GSPC was able to draw more recruits to Algerian training camps, while sending some for training to Iraq. It also copied AQI's tactics, even establishing a suicide brigade based on AQI's model. All in all, the GSPC's cooperation with AQI further paved the way toward the Algerian group's formal association with Al Qaeda.[45]

In May 2006, the GSPC threatened to attack U.S. military bases in Mali and Nigeria, warning that planning for these operations was already under way.[46] On September 11, 2006, the fifth anniversary of the 9/11 attacks, Zawahiri announced the formal integration of the GSPC into the Al Qaeda network. In late January 2007, the group renamed itself Al Qaeda in the Islamic Maghreb (AQIM), thereby formalizing its transition to a global jihadist organization.

The newly established Al Qaeda affiliate was quick to fully adopt the global jihadi agenda in both word and deed. In a communiqué released by the group in 2007, its emir, Abdelmalik Droudkel (a.k.a. Abu Musab Abdul Wadud) labeled France a participant in the "Christian crusade" to dominate the Muslim world and deprive Muslims of their religious values.[47] In May 2007, he followed up with a statement calling upon Muslims to make a commitment to martyr themselves in the cause of Islam.[48] The adoption of the global jihadist agenda was also visible in AQIM's evolving target selection. While the group had previously focused its activities on the Algerian army and the government, after the announcement of the self-described "merger" with AQC, the group began targeting United Nations installations.[49] It had also trained operatives who attacked the Israeli embassy in Nouakchott, Mauritania.

Al Qaeda's affiliation with the GSPC serves as an example of what Al Qaeda stood to gain, in theory, from such strategic alliances.[50] Al Qaeda hoped to exploit the GSPC/AQIM's existing reach into Europe, where the group enjoyed well-established connections, as well as into the Sahel, where vast ungoverned spaces provided opportunities for fundraising and training.[51] It also hoped to use the Algerian group as a force multiplier for its operations. This was evident, for example, from an intercepted message in which Ayman al-Zawahiri asked AQIM leader Droukdel to help exact revenge against Denmark after a Danish newspaper, *Jyllands-Posten*, published twelve editorial cartoons that depicted the Prophet Muhammad.[52]

On another occasion, in the wake of the civil strife in Libya following the collapse of the Qaddhafi regime, Zawahiri encouraged the AQIM leadership to keep resources flowing into Libya in order to spread violence across North Africa.[53] Droukdel, meanwhile, hoped that affiliation with Al Qaeda would confer "swagger and ferocity" to the GSPC and strengthen his own position within the fractured organization.[54]

Yet, the affiliation with the GSPC has failed to meet Al Qaeda's expectations. As Yoram Schweitzer and Aviv Oreg have argued, as of 2014, "AQIM has desisted from exploiting the entire arsenal at its disposal, especially the extensive infrastructure the organization enjoys in Europe and North America (Canada), and has limited its operations to sporadic attacks on Western targets in the margins of its sphere of activity in the Sahel region."[55] AQIM has also increasingly turned to kidnapping and other forms of crime, especially as funding from AQC began to decrease.[56]

AFFILIATION WITH AL-SHABAAB, 2012

In 2012, following years of courting Al Qaeda, the Somali group al-Shabaab became the fourth organization to become a formal affiliate of the group (after Al Qaeda in the Arabian Peninsula, as discussed in detail in the next chapter). Previously, bin Laden had refused to bring the Somali group into Al Qaeda's fold, feeling at odds with the group's style of governance, which included harsh applications of Sharia law.[57] Bin Laden's successor, Ayman al-Zawahiri—less stringent and cautious than his predecessor as far as formal affiliations were concerned—acknowledged al-Shabaab's pledge of *bayah* and turned al-Shabaab into Al Qaeda's official partner in the Horn of Africa.

As noted in the previous chapter, Somalia had been of great interest to Al Qaeda early on in the group's history.[58] In the early 1990s, Abu Ubayda al-Banshiri, bin Laden's first deputy leader, envisioned turning Somalia into the "new Afghanistan."[59] Al Qaeda's attempts to establish a foothold in Somalia date back at least to 1992, when a mysterious Al Qaeda figure known as the "Chinese brother" first traveled to the region to explore the feasibility of establishing training camps there. The previously mentioned Fadil Haroun, who would later be promoted to the position of Al Qaeda's confidential secretary, became Al Qaeda's point man in the region.

Al-Shabaab's historical origins are disputed, but it is established that some of its leaders were members of the first generation of foreign fighters who had spent time in Afghanistan during the Soviet occupation. Upon their return to Somalia, they brought along ideas of pan-Islamism that had not been prevalent at the time.[60] Al-Shabaab was also historically connected to Al-Ittihad al-Islami (AIAI), a militant Islamist group with ties to Al Qaeda. Aden Hashi Ayro, Mukhtar Robow, and key al-Shabaab figures had fought for AIAI in the early 1990s. According to Stig Hansen, al-Shabaab in fact emerged out of a small subgroup of AIAI, which had been dominated by the Somali "Afghan Arab" contingent.[61]

In the late 1990s, Ethiopa invaded Somalia, defeating the AIAI. To establish some order in the chaos that reigned in the capital of Mogadishu, several local, clan-based Islamic courts arose, which also contained the Somali Afghanistan veterans. In 2000, the courts, which are also known as the Sharia courts, united to form the Islamic Courts Union (ICU). The ICU instituted a system based on the strict application of sharia law. When, in 2003, a more pragmatic faction of the ICU attempted to become a political party, the militant wing of the group, known as the al-Shabaab, rose in rejection. In 2006, in the wake of another Ethiopian invasion of Somalia, the ICU collapsed, paving the way for al-Shabaab's separation from the ICU and its formal establishment as an independent organization.[62]

Al-Shabaab suffered from a number of divisions from the outset, including conflict between a faction guided by mostly local concerns and a wing that adhered to global jihadi interpretations, led by Mukhtar Ali Zubayr, also known as Ahmed Abdi Godane.[63]

According to Haroun, Al Qaeda took no part in the formation of the group and had no ties to it until 2009.[64] Later, several senior Al Qaeda operatives, including Haroun and Sallah Ali Nabahan, provided technical assistance to al-Shabaab.[65] Both Haroun and Nabahan boasted operational experience, having earlier participated in several high-profile attacks by Al Qaeda Central. Whereas Haroun had masterminded Al Qaeda's attacks on the U.S. embassies in Kenya and Tanzania, Nabahan took part in Al Qaeda's attack in Mombasa in 2002, which targeted an Israeli-owned hotel and an Israeli Arkia airliner, which was brought down when Nabahan fired one of the shoulder-to-air missiles aimed at it.[66] Additionally, Haroun provided operational training to new recruits that arrived from Europe, North America, and Australia. While some of these recruits joined the local insurgency against the Ethiopians, most were trained in terrorist tactics. According to Schweitzer and Oreg, Haroun thus had a visible impact on al-Shabaab's ability to become an international terrorist organization.[67]

By 2008, Al-Shabaab was able to control most of southern Somalia, and two years later it had extended its control to the capital of Mogadishu. In September 2009, al-Shabaab released a video addressing bin Laden as the sheikh and emir of the group and stating, "We await your guidance during this advanced stage of jihad."[68]

Between 2009 and 2012, Al Qaeda had an ambivalent relationship with Al-Shabaab. While it was clearly impressed with the group's geographic expansion, bin Laden harbored doubts about the group's long-term prospects for success. The resulting policy toward Al-Shabaab was what Barak Mendelsohn described as a "balancing act," where Al Qaeda maintained strong links with Al-Shabaab while refraining from offering the Somali group a formal affiliation with Al Qaeda.[69] It was only after the death of bin Laden in early 2011 that Al Qaeda, now under the leadership of Zawahiri, invited Al-Shabaab to formally join Al Qaeda. Unlike his predecessor, Zawahiri set a lower threshold for accepting new groups to the Al Qaeda fold.

According to Mendelsohn, the merger between AQC and al-Shabbab addressed the weakness that beset the two organizations. It provided al-Shabbab with potential access to resources and compensation for declining local support while providing AQC with access to al-Shabbab's Western foreign fighters and the media exposure it lost.[70]

INFORMAL PARTNERSHIPS

Besides formally affiliating with jihadi organizations, Al Qaeda pursued an additional strategy of inter-group cooperation: striking informal partnerships with mostly co-located groups such as the Taliban, the Haqqani Network (HQN), the Tehrik-e Taliban Pakistan (TTP), the Islamic Jihad Union (IJU), Lashkar-e Jhangvi (LeJ), Harkat-ul-Jihad al-Islami (HUJI), Hizb-I Islami Gulbuddin, and other groups.[71] Such associations were no novelty in Al Qaeda's strategic toolkit. What was new was the intensity with which Al Qaeda pursued these partnerships and exploited them to advance its goals.

Of all its informal partnerships, AQC's closest association has been that with the Haqqani Network, a jihadist group present in Pakistan's Waziristan region as well as the Afghan provinces of Paktia, Paktika, and Khowst. A major player in the region since the 1980s, HQN maintains an abundance of cooperative relationships with a host of militant Islamist groups, including the Taliban, the TTP, and the IJU. Its relationship with Al Qaeda is historical and dates back to the Soviet occupation of Afghanistan.[72]

HQN has established itself as a regional platform for jihadi groups by providing ideological and operational training, as well as greater ease of access to various locations. For example, HQN helps the TTP project power logistically and militarily to Afghanistan, while helping the Quetta Shura Taliban spread their influence and power to the southeastern region of Afghanistan. In return, it obtains various benefits from these groups, such as access to infrastructure, manpower, and expertise.[73]

The Haqqani Network has played a key role in helping AQC survive the post-9/11 period by providing the group with access to a safe haven, as well as training foreign fighters and local jihadis alike. It has also offered AQC opportunities to expand its brand through filmed battlefield footage. AQC, meanwhile, has assisted HQN with technical expertise and training, suicide bombers, and a more extensive network of potential donors.[74]

Another AQC associate in Pakistan is the above mentioned TTP, an umbrella group of various Pashtun-based jihadist organizations formed in December 2007. Compared with AQC's relationship with the Haqqanis, the one with the TTP has been less cordial. Letters seized from bin Laden's compound in Abbottabad, for example, revealed bin Laden's reservations regarding the TTP's indiscriminate targeting of civilians, as well as complaining about other "errors" and "lapses" in "ideology, methods, and behavior."[75] Still, AQC has entertained operational ties and has carried out joint attacks with the group. Following TTP operative Faizal Shahzad's attempt to set off a car bomb in New York's Times Square in May 2010, for example, then-senior White House counterterrorism adviser John Brennan told Fox News that AQC and the TTP "train together, plan together, plot together. They are almost indistinguishable."[76]

Al Qaeda's ties with the Taliban serves as a good example of how Al Qaeda associations with co-located groups have intensified in the post-9/11 period, resulting in a growing political, ideological, and tactical convergence. In return for safe haven, AQC helps the Taliban build its capacity as an insurgent force, while the Taliban has adopted signature Al Qaeda tactics such as suicide bombings and improvised explosive devices (IEDs). In addition, it has become more media-savvy and enhanced its online presence, as well as benefiting from AQC's ability to increase funding due to its extensive ties to wealthy donors from the Gulf and other regions. While the Afghan groups have expressed support for AQC's global jihadi aspirations, senior AQC members, including bin Laden, swore allegiance to Mullah Omar, the head of the Afghan Taliban.[77]

In sum, AQC's informal associations with groups, especially in the Afghan and Pakistani region, represent an alternative strategy to formal affiliation. It enables the group to exert influence and create military coalitions,[78] while providing AQC with redundancy through safe havens.

THE GLOBAL JIHAD MOVEMENT AFTER THE "ARAB SPRING": JABHAT AL-NUSRA AND THE RISE OF THE "ISLAMIC STATE"

By the spring of 2011, Al Qaeda Central was able to boast a growing number of formal and informal partnerships with jihadi groups both near and far. Its true state of affairs, however, was far from rosy and was about to change dramatically when, on May 11, a U.S. special operations team killed Osama bin Laden in his safe house in Abbottabad, Pakistan.

The elimination of the charismatic leader coincided with dramatic upheavals in the Middle East whose net impact on Al Qaeda, at least in the short term, appeared to be negative. Thus, not only was the turmoil predominantly nonviolent in its early phase; it also generated hopes that revolutionary change in the Middle East could come about via peaceful means, which was a repudiation of AQC's emphasis on using violence to achieve political change. But AQC's problems only began here. Besides bin Laden, the group lost a series of other senior operatives to the U.S. counterterrorism campaign, which heavily relied on drone strikes to kill top terrorist operatives. Moreover, his successor, Ayman al-Zawahiri, lacked the charisma and leadership qualities of bin Laden. As documents captured from bin Laden's safe house in Abbottabad disclosed, Al Qaeda also suffered from ongoing branding problems caused by the large percentage of Muslims killed in attacks by groups operating under the Al Qaeda name, as well as by AQC's failure to repeat a spectacular 9/11-style attack against the West.[79] The Abbottabad documents further revealed that bin Laden had even toyed with the idea of changing Al Qaeda's name.[80] The proliferation of various Salafi-Jihadist and Al Qaeda proxy groups that deliberately avoided using the Al Qaeda moniker and instead adopted the name Ansar al-Sharia (Supporters of Sharia Law) further underscored Al Qaeda's reputation problems.[81]

Regardless, the Abbottabad documents painted a portrait of bin Laden as the unchallenged leader of AQC up until his death. Bin Laden dispatched instructions via highly trusted couriers, closely supervised AQC's broader strategy, and even issued guidance on proper behavior to the leaders of AQC's affiliates. However, the Abbottabad documents also suggest that already under bin Laden, the group's ability to control the affiliates had begun to slip. Bin Laden lamented the tendency of the affiliates to act in ways that were not in accordance with AQC's strategic guidance, such as continuing to direct violence at Muslims. He also believed that some of the affiliates were incompetent, and this resulted in internal divisions between bin Laden and other senior AQC leaders over how the group should respond.[82]

Under bin Laden's successor, Ayman al-Zawahiri, the center of gravity of the global jihad movement shifted even farther away from AQC to its partners, who increasingly pursued local agendas rather than the global jihad that had been AQC's trademark.[83] These affiliates and associates waged mostly local insurgencies as opposed to campaigns of terrorism. Thus, the struggle of various jihadi groups against local regimes in places like Mali, Nigeria, Somalia, Yemen, and Syria amounted to insurgent campaigns that relied on a mix of guerrilla and terrorist tactics.[84] Meanwhile, acts of terrorism taking place in the West became increasingly rare, with the exception of the group's Yemen-based affiliate, AQAP, which appeared bent on striking the West on its home turf. Most attacks against Western targets now occurred locally. Examples include the attacks on the U.S. Embassy in Benghazi, Libya, in September 2012; the attacks on a gas facility near In Amenas, Algeria, in January 2013; and al-Shabaab's attack on the Westgate mall in Kenya in September 2013.

In the post–Arab Spring period, Al Qaeda's affiliates and associates have evolved into new hubs of jihadi activity themselves, as has become manifest in Somalia, Iraq, Yemen, Mali, and Syria, among other places. Some, such as AQAP, appeared poised to eclipse AQC in terms of its capacity and success in challenging local regimes.[85] Apart from cooperating among themselves, these local jihadi groups have formed their own local alliances with smaller jihadi organizations, thereby turning into what Tricia Bacon has labeled "alliance hubs."[86] Aware of the somewhat tarnished image of Al Qaeda among moderate Muslims, these affiliates have been working through local, organic proxy forces far more capable of mobilizing local populations. Unlike the Al Qaeda organization at the time of the 9/11 attacks, most of these groups realize that continued mobilization of the local population requires a modicum of governance and the provision of social services.

In their alliances with local and far-flung groups, Al Qaeda's affiliates and associates, as well as other jihadi groups unaffiliated with Al Qaeda, have provided resources, logistics, and advice to their junior partners or established splinter groups of their own. Examples include the Islamic State of Iraq's essential role in founding Jabhat al-Nusra in Syria (although failing at its later attempt to subsume it); AQIM's relationship with local groups such as the Movement for Oneness and Jihad in Africa (MUJAO) and its erstwhile alliance with Ansar Addine, which it used to expand into Southern Mali;[87] and AQIM's attempt to influence or establish even more distant militant Islamist groups such as Ansar al-Sharia in Tunisia or the Uqba ibn Nafi Brigade.[88] Boko Haram, an associate of Al Qaeda before it became an affiliate of the Islamic State in early 2015, similarly spawned smaller movements such as Jamaat Ansar al-Muslimin fi Bilad al-Sudan and maintained a wealth of cooperative relations in northern Mali, the Sahel, Somalia, and other Muslim countries.[89]

This new reality has further complicated attempts to understand the more recent nexus of jihadi cooperation. Thus, affiliates and associates are not only cooperating with their senior partners—that is, Al Qaeda or the Islamic State—but have established alliances of their own. AQAP, for example, has served a communication and coordination function between Zawahiri and al-Shabaab, according to revelations by Omar Hammami, a senior American member of al-Shabaab who was killed in September 2013. Likewise the most capable jihadi groups in Africa cooperate with each other. According to the former commander of USAFRICOM, General Carter Ham, Boko Haram in Nigeria, AQIM, and al-Shabaab have all shared trainers and copied each other's tactics.[90] Furthermore, a blurring of organizational boundaries has accompanied this trend. Thus, while the weakening of Al Qaeda's traditional stronghold in Pakistan has led to an atomization of the jihadi threat, this development has in turn abetted cross-fertilization among the affiliates and their progeny. The memberships of the newer groups are more numerous, more dispersed geographically, and more willing to cooperate with each other; they also have access to more weapons. Thus, in a guidance letter written by AQIM leader Abdelmalik Droukdel and intercepted in 2016, Droukdel urged his followers to integrate with local movements and to "extend bridges" with Arabs, Tuareg, and Zingiya.[91]

While the global jihad movement went through a number of dramatic changes throughout most of its existence, Al Qaeda still managed to remain at the helm. But when the turmoil of the so-called Arab Spring reached the Levant and found its new focus in Syria, the structure of the global jihad movement shifted in fundamental ways.

It was in Syria in April 2013 that AQC was able to forge its next formal affiliation with the group named Jabhat al-Nusra, which was formed earlier, in August 2011, as a secretive faction of AQC's Iraq affiliate, the Islamic State in Iraq (ISI).[92] Jabhat al-Nusra's origins date back to a decision by Abu Bakr al-Baghdadi, the ISI's emir, to secretly dispatch Abu Muhammad al-Joulani, a young ISI officer who had risen through the group's ranks to become "governor" of Ninewa province, to Syria to exploit the chaotic situation in the neighboring country to ISI's advantage and form a secret faction of the ISI in Syria.[93] Baghdadi provided Joulani with money, weapons, and some elite soldiers, and subsequently the group was founded in a series of meetings in Homs and Damascus in October 2011, although its existence was not made public until January 2012.[94] By the second half of 2012, Jabhat al-Nusra (JN), as the offshoot was called, became the most formidable fighting force in Syria. By the spring of 2013, with JN continuing to score successes on the battlefield, Abu Bakr al-Baghdadi apparently decided that the time had come to check JN's power, while preempting Ayman al-Zawahiri from claiming ownership of JN for Al Qaeda Central.[95] On April 8, 2013, he declared, with immediate effect, the unification of JN and the ISI into a single organization, to be renamed the Islamic State of Iraq and Greater Syria (ISIS).

Two days after Baghdadi's pronouncement, JN leader Joulani released an audio message in response. Rather than accepting al-Baghdadi's declaration, Joulani pledged *bayah* to Zawahiri. According to Charles Lister,

JN's main decision-making body, the Shura Council, had decided against the formal association with what was now called ISIS "for fear of losing the support they had worked so hard to gain across parts of opposition-controlled Syria."[96] On May 23, 2013, Zawahiri declared that the formation of ISIS as a merger between the ISI and Jabhat al-Nusra was made without prior approval and was hence null and void. Zawahiri instructed Baghdadi to limit his group's operations to Iraq, while all Syria-related activities were to be coordinated and led by JN, which had now become Al Qaeda's formal affiliate in Syria.

Baghdadi now began to prepare ISIS for the inevitable break from JN and Al Qaeda. The writing had been on the wall for years, with the erstwhile allies having increasingly turned into competitors over time. AQC's Iraq affiliate had always been the most insubordinate of all of Al Qaeda's formal partners, and it had grown even more distant and unruly after the death of Osama bin Laden.[97] In February 2014, Zawahiri announced the formal split between the two groups when he declared that ISIS was no longer part of Al Qaeda.

COMPETITION AND COOPERATION: TOWARD A POLARIZED JIHAD MOVEMENT

In the dramatic rise to power that was to follow the official break from Al Qaeda, ISIS relied on the support of former elements of Iraq's Baath party. A critical role was played by a former member of Saddam Hussein's aerial intelligence services, Samir al-Khlifawi, better known as Haji Bakr, who reportedly devised the strategy for the Islamic State's takeover of Syria and for the setup of the group's bureaucratic infrastructure.[98]

The rise of the Islamic State has dramatically altered the balance of power within the global jihad movement. For the first time, there are two formidable camps in the global jihad movement, each vying for power and influence, and their respective alliances and collaborations play an important role in the race for dominance in the global jihad. For the time being,

Al Qaeda has been able to maintain its affiliations with AQAP, AQIM, al-Shabaab, and JN, and in September 2014, AQC announced another affiliate, Al Qaeda in the Indian Subcontinent (AQIS). In the first year since that affiliation, however, AQIS's activities were limited to a number of assassinations, mostly against liberal bloggers. AQIS also suffered a setback when its deputy leader was killed in an airstrike in January 2015.[99] The Islamic State, for its part, has attracted the allegiance of dozens of jihadi organizations and established footholds in Afghanistan, Algeria, Egypt, Libya, Nigeria, Saudi Arabia, and Yemen. While most of these "provinces" do not appear to have dramatically boosted the Islamic State's capacity, ISIS has managed to establish a relatively strong presence in the Sinai and Libya, although its survival in either one is not guaranteed. Toward the end of 2015 in Libya, for example, "local conditions [made] the expansion of doubtful endurance," according to one noted analyst.[100]

In 2015, as the Islamic State faced growing pressures on the battlefield in Iraq and Syria, the group's leadership increased calls for terrorist attacks against the West.[101] These calls led to a growing number of plots that included both centrally directed attacks and others that were inspired by the group.[102] Among the most notable was an elaborate terrorist strike that hit Paris on November 13, 2015, targeting a soccer match, a pop-music concert, and several cafes. Not only were these attacks the deadliest to have occurred on European soil since the Madrid attacks of 2004, but they also exhibited ominous signs of central Islamic State direction and control.[103] In the meantime, the rift between Al Qaeda and the Islamic State has deepened. In the northwestern Syrian province of Idlib, Jaysh al-Fatah, an Islamist alliance that includes local elements of Jabhat al-Nusra, targets Syrian Army positions but is also involved in clashes with the Islamic State,[104] which has itself made few attempts to hide its contempt for Al Qaeda, even to the point of killing an official Al Qaeda emissary who was ordered by Zawahiri to mediate between Al Qaeda and ISIS.[105]

Their mutual enmity notwithstanding, there have been instances of low-level cooperation between Jabhat al-Nusra/Al Qaeda and the Islamic State. In the spring of 2015, for example, JN fighters assisted ISIS in the Battle of Yarmouk.[106] Several months before, Amedi Coulibaly, who killed four people in the kosher Hypercacher supermarket in a Parisian suburb, had coordinated his attacks to follow shortly after those on the headquarters of *Charlie Hebdo*, a satirical magazine that had regularly poked fun at religious figures, including the Prophet Muhammad. The perpetrators of the *Charlie Hebdo* murders, brothers Saïd and Chérif Kouachi, had ties to AQAP, while Coulibaly had pledged allegiance to the Islamic State.[107] Furthermore, Coulibaly and Chérif Kouachi had befriended each other in prison and also shared a common mentor in Djamel Beghal, who at some point had been known as Al Qaeda's chief recruiter in Europe.[108] While it is doubtful that the coordination of these attacks was part of an organizational strategy, what these attacks do show is that for many ordinary jihadists, cooperation that can lead to action in pursuit of the jihadist cause trumps strict organizational affiliations.[109]

The rivalry between the Islamic State and Al Qaeda is unlikely to disappear anytime soon. In their competition for dominance in the global jihad movement, both Al Qaeda and the Islamic State have comparative strengths and weaknesses, and here, the kinds of cooperative arrangements each of them pursues may well influence which of these two organizations will prevail in the longer term. In this respect, the two groups have radically different policies for building alliances. Whereas the Islamic State tends toward intimidation of other rebel group as part of its attempt to expand its hold on territory, JN—which renamed itself Jabhat Fath al-Sham (JFS), or Front for the Liberation of the Levant, on July 28, 2016— has adopted a more sophisticated approach by trying to embed itself more deeply within the Syrian insurgency. As JN/JFS expert Jennifer Cafarella has argued, the attempt to establish a network of rebel relationships—in other words, to establish powerful relationships of cooperation with other militant groups—is the "central component" of the group's strategy in Syria.[110] For JN/JFS, cooperation is a means to an end. Using these alliances, the group seeks to "embed itself into the fabric of the Syrian opposition and use its influence to direct the evolution of rebel forces and governance activities."[111]

JN/JFS, according to analysts, has been quite successful in this endeavor, for two main reasons. First, its fighters boast a high level of skill, including a "special forces" capacity that helps both generate trust in JN/JFS and increase other rebel groups' dependence on the Al Qaeda affiliate, thereby further deepening their mutual relationships. JN/JFS, in other words, has earned its respect with other groups—an approach that contrasts starkly with the Islamic State's proclivity for dominating its allies.[112] Second, JN/JFS seems to have adopted a tailored approach that adjusts the level of cooperation depending on the size and ideological orientation of the partner, thus playing a more direct, command-centric role with smaller groups that are more ideologically aligned and a less direct role as facilitator of operations with larger and more powerful groups.[113]

The Islamic State has also been able to forge alliances, but unlike allies of JN/JFS, those affiliated with the Islamic state appear to be driven to join by intimidation or for opportunistic reasons. Tribes in both Syria and Iraq, for example, have been coopted with money, but the Islamic State's momentum on the battlefield has also been a factor, at least in 2014. According to Lina Khatib, what has helped the Islamic State build local alliances is that "tribes and clans often ally themselves with the strongest actor in the pursuit of self-protection. In Syria, as the militant group gained prominence, many tribes saw it as stronger than the Syrian regime and shifted their allegiances accordingly."[114]

The Islamic State has also been far more outspoken than JN/JFS. Highly effective in its employment of communications, especially social media platforms, to achieve its objectives, the Islamic State has been able to gain an extraordinary amount of attention, creating a media buzz that perpetuates the notion that the Islamic State is unstoppable. Moreover, the Islamic State often seems to exaggerate even minor battlefield successes, while rarely admitting its own weaknesses. As Bridget Moreng and Daveed Gartenstein-Ross have argued, "The Islamic State's louder strategy has allowed it to snatch up a couple of important Al Qaeda affiliates, Boko Haram and Egypt's Ansar Bayt al-Maqdis," but some of these successes rest on a deliberate misrepresentation of the group's real capabilities and successes.[115]

Other things remaining equal, it seems reasonable to believe that JN/JFS's more subdued approach to alliance building and cooperation will pay dividends in the long-term. This assessment can also be extended to Al Qaeda more broadly, whose long-game strategy appears more sustainable in the long term than the Islamic State's approach of shock and awe. Given that the Islamic State's relationships are based on intimidation, opportunism, and the ability of the group to make a lot of noise, it stands to reason to believe that such alliances are naturally more brittle, and will not survive if put to serious tests, such as a continuing decline of the Islamic State's fortunes.

7

HIGH-END COOPERATION

Al Qaeda and Al Qaeda in the
Arabian Peninsula (AQAP)

THIS CHAPTER EXAMINES a case of high-end cooperation between Al Qaeda Central (AQC) and Al Qaeda in the Arabian Peninsula (AQAP). While there have been two different groups known as Al Qaeda in the Arabian Peninsula, the chapter focuses on AQC's relationship with the second generation of AQAP, a group based in Yemen. The original Al Qaeda in the Arabian Peninsula, which was based in Saudi Arabia, will be referred to here under the acronym QAP to avoid confusion. AQAP's formal existence was announced in early 2009 as a result of a merger between a Yemen-based group tied to Al Qaeda and the Saudi-based QAP. QAP had made jihadi history in November 2003 when it became the first militant jihadist outfit to operate while adopting Al Qaeda as part of its official name. More so than AQAP, QAP had been formed as an official branch of AQC, and the two entities are often considered as part of the same organization. Hence the chapter's focus on the more independent AQAP.[1]

I argue that the relationship described in this chapter best fits the description of a strategic cooperation, or strategic alliance, as introduced in chapter 4. Strategic alliances are high-end forms of cooperation in which the command and control functions of the cooperating terrorist actors tend to be partially integrated. Cooperative activities in a strategic alliance typically extend into a variety of areas, oftentimes spanning the ideological, logistic, and operational domains. Strategic alliances are built on a high degree of ideological affinity, although groups may harbor differences as to how ideological beliefs should be translated into practice. The ideational affinity between the groups—an affinity that does not necessarily apply to low-end forms of terrorist cooperation—results in a common strategic vision and a relatively high degree of trust between the cooperating parties, especially when compared to more unpredictable, low-end forms of terrorist cooperation.

The chapter assesses the nature of the cooperative ties between AQC and AQAP by relying on primary and secondary sources, including recently declassified correspondence between and within the respective leaderships of these two groups. It is important to keep in mind that only a selection of AQC's internal correspondence has been published to date. Assessments of the nature of the relationship between groups relying primarily on internal documents must therefore be made with caution, and are tentative pending the release of other documents detailing the nature of AQC's ties with its affiliates and associates.

The chapter begins with a brief background discussion about AQAP and the various networks and organizations from which it surfaced in 2009. The chapter will then delve into a more detailed and substantive examination of the AQC-AQAP relationship, in terms of the main characteristics of strategic cooperative ties introduced in chapter 4—namely, the expected duration of the cooperative relationship; the degree of interdependence between the groups; the variety of cooperative activities undertaken by the parties; the groups' ideological affinity; and the level of trust apparent from the mutual relations between the parties.

BACKGROUND

The Arabian Peninsula had always been close to the heart of Osama bin Laden, who was born in Saudi Arabia to a family with Yemeni origins. As mentioned in chapter 5, one of bin Laden's first ventures as Al Qaeda leader was his attempt to establish a Sunni Islamic foothold in Yemen in the early 1990s.[2] While bin Laden failed in his initial effort, he succeeded in establishing some presence on the Arabian peninsula later in that decade. In 1997, the Al Qaeda leader was able to set up an Al Qaeda network in the Hejaz region of Saudi Arabia, shortly after issuing a statement decrying the "Zionist-Crusader" occupation of the kingdom.[3]

The Saudi network included Abd al-Rahim al-Nashiri (a.k.a. Abu Bilal), a Saudi veteran of the Afghanistan war who would rise to direct Al Qaeda operations on the peninsula over the next five years. Al-Nashiri later coordinated the 2000 bombing of the American destroyer USS *Cole* in the Yemeni port of Aden, among other attacks. Saudi authorities arrested al-Nashiri in November 2002, at a time when hundreds of Saudi veterans had just returned to the kingdom, heeding a call by bin Laden to step up attacks in Saudi Arabia. Al-Nashiri's capture was of minor consequence for jihadi activism on the peninsula because bin Laden had drawn up contingency plans to render the network more resilient. By 2002, the Al Qaeda leader had already established a second, parallel network in Saudi Arabia that operated under the radar of the Saudi security services, thereby evading the authorities' dragnet. Led by the charismatic and capable Yusuf al-Ayeri, a former Al Qaeda training camp instructor and bin Laden's personal secretary, the second network conducted its first attack on May 12, 2003. Operating under the name Mujahidun on the Arabian Peninsula (MAP), it carried out a coordinated bombing of a residential compound in Riyadh populated by Westerners. The attacks killed thirty-five people and injured hundreds more.[4] According to Thomas Hegghammer, the attacks were externally directed by the core Al Qaeda leadership. The "top-down" nature of the plot was evident in part from the fact that most of the plotters, and the core cohort of the network, had spent time in Afghanistan before 2002. More important, several of the core conspirators of the Riyadh attacks, including Khalid al-Juhani, Muhammad al-Shihri, and al-Ayeri, had long-standing, close ties with AQC in Afghanistan.[5]

It was from the MAP that the Saudi-based Al Qaeda in the Arabian Peninsula (QAP) would formally announce its existence in November

2003, becoming the first group to insert the Al Qaeda label into its name.[6] The group was an "in-house creation, based on al-Qaeda's own forces and led by al-Qaeda operatives"[7] and is therefore better viewed as a branch, rather than as an affiliate, and hence as an integral part of Al Qaeda, rather than as a separate outfit.[8] Its existence was short-lived, in part because the Riyadh bombings provoked a heavy-handed security crackdown. Al-Ayeri, who had pleaded with bin Laden to hold off on the attacks because his network lacked robustness, was killed along with many of his cohort, while others were detained.[9] Subsequent attacks by the group proved equally self-destructive. Striking mostly Saudi rather than Western targets, QAP lost public support as the number of Muslim victims rose. By mid-2005, only a year and a half after its formal announcement, QAP lay in tatters. Those members of QAP who had not been killed or detained moved to neighboring Yemen.

Between 2006 and 2009, as it became clear that Al Qaeda's jihad in Saudi Arabia had failed, the center of gravity of jihad in the Arabian Peninsula shifted to Yemen. First-generation Al Qaeda operatives, drawn mostly from jihadists who had been recruited in the late 1990s for training in Afghanistan, had already been present in Yemen at the time. Bin Laden had also increased Al Qaeda activities in Yemen around 1999, after temporarily suspending operations in Saudi Arabia. By late 2003, U.S. and Yemeni counterterrorism efforts had succeeded in crushing the first generation of Al Qaeda in Yemen.[10]

It was a prison break in the Yemeni capital of Sanaa in early 2006 that presented Al Qaeda's Yemen contingent with a chance for a comeback. On February 3, twenty-three jihadi activists, including several commanders of Al Qaeda, escaped from a high-security prison in Sanaa. The escapists included Nasir al-Wuhayshi, a.k.a. Abu Basir, a former bin Laden body guard who would rise to become the formal leader of the group in early 2007,[11] as well as Qasim al-Raymi, a Yemeni who had trained in Al Qaeda training camps during the 1990s and who succeeded Wuhayshi as AQAP's emir upon the latter's death in June 2015.

Within two years of the prison break, Wuhayshi had rebuilt the Al Qaeda network in Yemen by relying on members from various backgrounds.

Some, including Wuhayshi and al-Raymi, who had been high-level operatives with ties to Al Qaeda's leadership, took command of the network's
political and military arms. Others were Yemeni jihadists who had returned from the war in Iraq. The group also attracted young Saudi militants who had managed to evade the authorities and sought refuge in Yemen. Finally, it recruited individuals locally.[12]

During the 2007–2008 period, the reinvigorated Al Qaeda network in
Yemen appeared to operate under two different names: Al Qaeda on the
Arabian Peninsula–Soldier's Brigade of Yemen (AQAP-SBY), and Al Qaeda
in the Southern Arabian Peninsula (AQSAP). According to Yemen specialist Gregory Johnsen, the two groups were not separate entities but
"more like loose cells of the same organization."[13] The network specialized
in attacking such targets as foreign embassies and tourist groups in Yemen,
as well as Western oil installations. Among its major operations was an attack carried out under the name AQSAP against the U.S. Embassy in Sanaa on September 17, 2008, in which six civilians and six policemen died, in
addition to six attackers.[14] By 2008, it relied increasingly on guerrilla operations against Yemeni police and military targets. Among its most commonly used tactics were armed attacks, attacks using improvised explosive
devices (IEDs), and suicide bombings.[15]

In November 2008, Al Qaeda's then–deputy leader Ayman al-Zawahiri
blessed the newly regrouped Yemen-based Al Qaeda and called Wuhayshi
the "Amir of the Mujahideen."[16] Zawahiri's blessing was followed by an
announcement of an official merger between the leftover Saudi-based
QAP and the Yemen-based Al Qaeda network led by Wuhayshi. The new
entity was named Al Qaeda in the Arabian Peninsula (AQAP). Unlike its
Saudi predecessor organization, QAP, the newly formed AQAP made its
headquarters in Yemen.

The merger was announced in a nineteen-minute video released on January 23, 2009. The video featured two Yemenis, Wuhayshi and Raymi, as
well as two Saudis, Said Ali al-Shiri and Mohammed al-Awfi, both of
whom were former inmates at Guantanamo Bay.[17] To Al Qaeda's deputy
leader, the merger symbolized "a revival of Jihad in the Arabian Penin-

sula."[18] Indeed, by August 2009, the newly minted AQAP demonstrated its ability to attack high-profile targets in Saudi Arabia when a Saudi member of AQAP, Abdullah al-Asiri, detonated a concealed explosive device while meeting the Saudi Deputy Minister of the Interior, Prince Muhammad bin Nayef.[19] During the ensuing years, AQAP not only revived jihad in Arabia, but also rose to become Al Qaeda's most trusted and important affiliate. As far as attacks on Western targets were concerned, AQAP eclipsed even Al Qaeda Central.

For example, on Christmas Day 2009, the group dispatched a Nigerian man, Omar Farouk Abdulmutallab—later dubbed the "Underwear Bomber"—to detonate an explosive device hidden in his underwear during Northwest Airlines Flight 253 from Amsterdam to Detroit. In October 2010, after receiving intelligence from Saudi officials, two plastic explosive devices hidden inside printer cartridges were discovered aboard two separate cargo planes that were headed from Yemen to the United States. AQAP took responsibility for the plots. Later that month, AQAP was also believed to be behind the attempt to send explosives-filled packages to several synagogues in Chicago.[20] In January 2015, the group claimed credit for the attack by two gunmen, Cherif and Said Kouachi, on the headquarters of the French satirical magazine *Charlie Hebdo*. The attack killed eleven people, injured eleven more, and apparently provoked an additional series of attack (claimed by the Islamic State) that same week, including one on a kosher supermarket in the Port de Vincennes suburb of Paris.

AQAP did not limit its activities to terrorist attacks, however. In addition, the group began waging an insurgency against the Yemeni government, which relied heavily on guerrilla operations. In the process, AQAP managed to expand its hold over areas in the south of the country, and it established a proxy by the name of Ansar al-Sharia, to create a semblance of governance in the places it controlled.[21] In May and June 2012, a government counteroffensive temporarily repelled AQAP from certain areas in south Yemen, but in 2015—in the wake of a Saudi invasion of Yemen—Al Qaeda was able to regain control over parts of Hadramaut and other southern provinces in Yemen.[22]

AQAP also became known for its skillful employment of media in the pursuit of its objectives. Over the course of its existence, AQAP developed high-profile mechanisms to propagate its messages, recruit more jihadists to its fold, and seek to incite like-minded individuals to conduct attacks against Al Qaeda's declared enemies—oftentimes providing bomb-making instructions and how-to manuals in its magazines, as well as contact information for jihadists wishing to connect to the group. To that end, the group released an English language magazine, *Inspire*, and an Arabic equivalent, *Salah al-Malahim*. The magazines justified campaigns of violence against the West and encouraged solo attacks by providing how-to manuals, bomb-making instructions, and contact information to enable recruits to connect to the Al Qaeda network.

COOPERATION BETWEEN AQ AND AQAP

Like its predecessor organizations, AQAP had close ties to Al Qaeda Central from the very outset. As will be seen, these ties were built into its organizational DNA because of longstanding and deep personal connections between AQAP's and AQC's leaders. In 2013, Zawahiri, who had assumed the leadership of Al Qaeda following the killing of Osama bin Laden in 2011 by U.S. Special Forces, further consolidated these ties when he declared that henceforth, AQAP emir Wuhayshi would concurrently serve as Al Qaeda's general manager—the second highest position in AQC. As such, Wuhayshi managed AQC's overall infrastructure and its relationships with its affiliates.

As the following analysis shows, the cooperative relationship between AQC and AQAP most closely resembles that of a strategic alliance for the following reasons: The cooperative partners expressed an expectation for a long-standing relationship; they share some degree of interdependence in their command and control; they cooperate along ideological, logistical, and operational domains; they share a high degree of ideological affinity; and their relationship exhibits signs of a relatively high degree of mutual trust.

EXPECTED DURATION

Strategic partnerships are alliances between groups that have a vested interest in the longevity of their cooperative relations and in the mutual survival of the groups. Statements attributed to both AQAP and AQC offer clear indications that the groups expect to cooperate over the long term and are committed to their strategic alliance. Thus, in a message released by Al Qaeda Central on February 22, 2009, on the occasion of the formal merger that brought forth AQAP, AQC's then–deputy leader Zawahiri accepted the merger and called upon God to protect the new entity and turn it into a "thorn in the throats of the Crusaders and their agents."[23] Meanwhile, indications of AQAP's commitment to a long-term strategic partnership with its parent organization can be found in the group's *Inspire* e-magazine, where AQAP leaders articulate their admiration of, and absolute obedience to, Osama bin Laden and his successor.[24] Articles by prominent AQC figures, such as bin Laden and Zawahiri, often appear before those of AQAP's leaders. In addition, writings reiterating a deep commitment to AQC, such as Anwar al-Awlaki's 2010 "Why Did I Choose Al-Qaeda?" have been serialized.[25] After the death of bin Laden, the eleventh issue of *Inspire* celebrated his martyrdom and welcomed Zawahiri as his rightful successor, thereby reaffirming AQAP's commitment to AQC.

In addition, the high expectations for the long duration of AQAP-AQC cooperation is further supported by the close personal links between AQAP and AQC leaders, which will be discussed in greater detail below.

DEGREE OF INTERDEPENDENCE

One of the key characteristics of strategic alliances is that one or both of the cooperating parties typically relinquish some degree of their independence. Strategic alliances can vary from moderately interdependent partnerships, in which the weaker group concedes a relatively small portion of its command and control powers, to highly interdependent partnerships, in which the weaker party relinquishes, or is expected to relinquish, a relatively high portion of its command and control. The interdependent nature of the relationship distinguishes such strategic partnerships from a tactical cooperation, in which the two cooperating entities usually retain their full independence.

Correspondence between the leaders of AQC and AQAP indicates at least a moderate degree of interdependence between the groups. For one thing, bin Laden, and later Zawahiri, provided guidance and instructions on a range of strategic and tactical matters and clearly expected the AQAP leadership to abide by these guidelines. The AQAP leadership, in turn, fell in line on some issues, accepting bin Laden's and, later, Zawahiri's guidance, while on others they balked or ignored the instructions altogether, suggesting that the group maintained a degree of its command and control powers.

Letters seized by U.S. Special Forces during the May 2011 raid on Osama bin Laden's safe house in Abbottabad, Pakistan, disclose that in the years after 2010, the strategic guidance bin Laden gave AQAP was often at odds with its leadership's preferences. One of the differences of opinion concerned the question of replacing the central government in Yemen with an Islamic state. "If you want Sana'a," AQAP emir Wuhayshi urged bin Laden sometime around 2010, "today is the day."[26] In a reply to Wuhayshi, bin Laden discouraged AQAP from overthrowing the government in Yemen and establishing a state of their own. "We do not see escalation as necessary at this point because we are in the preparation stage," he wrote. Therefore, "It is not in our interest to rush in bringing down the regime."[27] Bin Laden instead urged Wuhayshi to focus on the far enemy, the United States. "I need to remind you," he wrote, taking a somewhat condescending attitude, "about the general politics of al-Qa'ida concerning the military sector and media. Al-Qaida concentrates on its external . . . enemy before its internal enemy."[28] This required a concentration of jihadist forces in places other than Yemen. According to bin Laden, America's "strength to destroy an Islamic State in the region remains high during this time. . . . Therefore, we need to be proactive and face all of their plans and continue to deplete and exhaust it throughout the open battlefield in Afghanistan and Iraq to . . . stop it from destroying the country that we want to establish."[29] In another letter bin Laden sent to his general manager at the time, Attiyah Abd-al Rahman, the Al Qaeda leader explained his rationale in greater detail. Bin Laden's main argument against an overthrow of the regime of Yemeni President Saleh was that such an effort would be doomed to fail for several reasons. For one, the United States would prevent a jihadi uprising in Yemen at all costs, given the country's proximity to "other oil nations. . . . At the same time, the capabilities of our brothers there are not yet such that they can enter this sort of struggle [against the United States], neither in terms of their administration or their financial resources."[30]

Bin Laden believed that a successful attempt to establish a state in Yemen or even to hold territory required an ability to maintain control. This was a function not only of military capacity, but also of the ability to provide basic services to the population. This was absolutely necessary to keep the Yemeni population from turning against AQAP—an eventuality bin Laden deemed especially likely to happen because Saudi Arabia would invest considerable resources into crippling AQAP's state-building efforts. From letters penned by the Al Qaeda leader, it is clear that bin Laden was haunted by the long history of jihadi failures in Afghanistan, Algeria, Egypt, Saudi Arabia, and other places and was determined to avoid having to add another failed jihadist project to the list.[31] At the same time, focusing on Yemen, rather than on the "far enemies," would diminish Yemen's ability to serve as a supply line to other jihadi theaters and hence detract from its role as the "center of gravity in supporting [other jihadi] fronts with men."[32]

Bin Laden shared with the AQAP leader his alternative plan for Yemen. Until such time as "the enemy becomes weak,"[33] bin Laden preferred Yemen to remain a safe haven that would harbor jihadists for the eventual battle. Yemen had already shown itself useful in this respect: Jihadists were able to "target America from Yemen," and the country provided an opportunity for Al Qaeda "to assign our brothers to conduct international operations."[34] Rather than focus on a military campaign, bin Laden believed that AQAP should emphasize other efforts, notably in the realm of media, general preparations (*idad*) for the eventual battle, and outreach to the population (*dawa*).[35]

Bin Laden offered additional directives to the AQAP leader that leave little doubt that he expected AQAP to follow them. "Avoid killing anyone from the tribes. . . . Do not target military and police officers in their centers unless you receive an order from us."[36] To ensure compliance with his various directives, most importantly the need to focus jihadist energies on "external work" (that is, terrorist attacks) in Western countries, bin Laden planned to dispatch the head of Al Qaeda's external operations at the time, Shaykh Yunis al-Mauritani, to Yemen and Algeria. He also instructed his general manager, Attiyah to make it clear to the respective leaders of AQAP and AQIM that they should "put forward their best in cooperating with Shaykh Yunis in whatever he asks of them."[37] Attiyah was also tasked with delivering the message to all affiliates that operations outside of their respective regions must be coordinated with the Al Qaeda senior leadership, through Attiyah. Bin Laden added that such coordination was necessary "so there will [be] no conflicts between operations or failures where the brothers could be exposed or captured."[38] In the case of Yemen, bin Laden emphasized, the need for prior coordination extended to sea-based operations in the territorial waters surrounding the peninsula, which were "to be considered external work" for these purposes.[39]

Bin Laden also meddled in AQAP's personnel decisions. When Wuhayshi suggested that the Yemeni-American jihadi preacher, Anwar al-Awlaqi, was worthy to succeed Wuhayshi as AQAP leader, bin Laden politely told Wuhayshi to hold his horses. While complimenting Wuhayshi on his competence, he nevertheless asked the AQAP leaders for "further assurances" regarding al-Awlaqi's qualifications, raising in particular Awlaqi's lack of experience fighting on the ground. Al Qaeda headquarters, he wrote in a message to Wuhayshi, is "generally assured after people go to the battlefield and are tested there."[40]

To what extent has the AQAP leadership heeded bin Laden's and, later, Zawahiri's directives? Initially, AQAP appears to have taken a middle ground, accepting some of bin Laden's guidance, while ignoring other directives. In early 2011, protests sparked by the uprisings in other Arab countries and related to the Arab Spring began to appear in Sanaa. With the central government and military appearing to collapse, AQAP was quick to exploit the ensuing turbulence and occupied parts of southern Yemen. In line with bin Laden's recommendations, the group did not declare a state, but it did establish several Islamic substate provinces, so-called emirates, in the regions they now controlled. As Will McCants observed, by doing so, AQAP was "breaking with the spirit of the advice in the letters from Bin Laden and al-Qaeda's senior leaders."[41]

It would be premature, however, to conclude that AQAP has tended to act out of sync with AQC's guidelines for several reasons. First, AQAP leaders have stated explicitly and repeatedly that they are bound by the guidelines provided by the Al Qaeda leadership, and also appear to have acted accordingly.[42] For instance, one of AQAP's most senior officials, Nasser bin Ali al-Ansi, has consistently confirmed that AQAP stands by the directives of Ayman al-Zawahiri. When AQAP assumed responsibility for the attacks against the *Charlie Hebdo* headquarters in Paris in early 2015, al-Ansi stated that these were in compliance with the command of God, as well as with the "order of our general emir" Zawahiri and the "will" of bin Laden.[43] When asked whether Zawahiri lost control over Al Qaeda's affiliates, al-Ansi denied that this was the case and assured the interviewer that Zawahiri was still issuing guidance to AQAP.[44]

In response to a different question as to why AQAP conducted an attack in Sanaa targeting Shiites, when such a modus operandi did not seem to be in line with Zawahiri's guidelines, al-Ansi said that Wuhayshi "gave clear instructions to the operating cells to avoid attacking mixed gatherings and to focus on armed Houthis."[45] The group's fighters, he added, were "abiding by this rule as far as we know" and focusing on places "where their military armed forces exist" and on "their headquarters, and their other posts." They were told to avoid targeting mosques and other "areas where common Muslims are found."[46] Then, on March 20, 2015, when the Islamic State conducted a dual suicide bombing attack against two Houthi mosques in Sanaa, the AQAP leadership issued a statement in an attempt to distance itself from the Islamic State and reaffirm its allegiance to AQC, which said that the group remained "committed to the guidelines" issued by Zawahiri to avoid "targeting mosques, markets, and public places out of concern for the lives of innocent Muslims, and to prioritize the paramount interests," namely the fight against the infidels.[47]

There are also strong indications that AQAP has not only adopted the rhetoric of the guidelines, but also internalized those directives. One of the indications is that AQAP has passed these guidelines on to other jihadist groups. In 2012, for instance, Wuhayshi suggested to his counterpart Abdel-Malik Droukdel, leader of Al Qaeda in the Islamic Maghreb (AQIM), to adopt a "hearts and minds" campaign while establishing sharia law gradually. "Try to avoid enforcing Islamic punishments as much as possible, unless you are forced to do so," he advised his colleague.[48] In addition, more than any other Al Qaeda affiliate, AQAP has attempted to strike Western targets, as noted earlier. Internal Al Qaeda documents leave no doubt that AQC placed utmost importance on its affiliates carrying out strikes against the "far enemy," and in this regard, AQAP stands out as the only affiliate that has consistently done so, even out-performing AQC. The AQAP leadership has even issued formal apologies when AQAP fighters appear to have ignored AQC's rules. In early 2013, for example, fighters associated with AQAP stormed a military hospital located on the Defense Ministry compound in Sanaa. In the course of the attack, the group killed several medical personnel and patients. The attacks, which were caught on camera, caused an uproar among many Yemenis. Later in December, AQAP's military chief, Qassem al-Raymi, issued an apology for the attack on the medics and patients, saying that the group "do[es] not fight this way, and this [is] not what we call on people to do, and this is not our approach. . . . The attack was on the ministry of defense, it was not on the hospital."[49] Al-Raymi blamed a renegade AQAP fighter for the mistake, offered the group's "apologies and condolences," and gave assurances that AQAP would take "full responsibility" for the attack, including through the payment of blood money to compensate the victims' families.[50]

A further indication of the degree of interdependence of Al Qaeda and AQAP is the integration of personnel at the senior level of the groups. Under Zawahiri's leadership, AQC has promoted several leaders of AQAP to senior command positions in AQC, thereby partially integrating the groups' command and control functions and consolidating cooperation between the two groups by. The most dramatic step in this direction occurred in 2013, when Zawahiri promoted the AQAP leader, Wuhayshi, to serve as general manager of Al Qaeda, the second highest position in AQC.[51] Wuhayshi, who had served as one of bin Laden's secretaries in the past and who had always had close ties to the central leadership of Al Qaeda, is not the only senior AQAP official to have been formally integrated into Al Qaeda Central. The above mentioned Nasser al-Ansi, a senior official and spokesperson of AQAP who was killed in a drone strike in May 2015, had served as a deputy general manager within AQC since 2010. According to Thomas Joscelyn, Wuhayshi's and al-Ansi's twin roles in both movements turned the two de facto into "core" Al Qaeda leaders.[52] Wuhayshi's successor, al-Raymi, swore *bayah* to Ayman al-Zawahiri on July 9, 2015.

VARIETY OF COOPERATIVE ACTIVITIES

Strategic alliances are high-end cooperative relationships, and as such the cooperating groups collaborate on a host of activities that usually span ideological, logistical, and operational domains and call for frequent consultations between the leaderships, security restrictions permitting. As the following discussion demonstrates, evidence strongly indicates that AQC and AQAP have cooperated across all three domains.

Ideological Cooperation

In the ideological domain, AQAP's English-language newsletter, *Inspire*, showcases several concrete examples of cooperation between the two groups. The journal's introductory issue, for example, includes messages from the two most prominent and important members of AQC, Osama bin Laden and Ayman al-Zawahiri.[53] AQAP's media arms hence serve as a platform to propagate not only its own messages, but also those of Al Qaeda Central.

Furthermore, the groups regularly express support of one another, as well as heaping praise on each other. Following the Islamic State's dramatic announcement of the establishment of a new caliphate under the leadership of Abu Bakr al-Baghdadi in 2014, for instance, AQAP released a tribute to Zawahiri in the form of a poem posted on an online twitter feed (@bashaer_Audio) that frequently released AQAP messages. In the tribute, which was accompanied by a *nasheed*, or anthem, AQAP leader Wuhayshi referred to Zawahiri as he who "continues to hold fast" to the "flag [of jihad]," a "skillful teacher, seasoned veteran, and expert commander." He further extolled Zawahiri as a leader who is "nursed by wisdom and reveled in it"; the "apple of the eyes of mujahideen of this time"; "the theorist of the jihadist movement, its orator"; and "Sheikh father."[54]

AQAP and AQC also provide mutual ideological justification and support for their activities. Following AQAP's attempt to detonate IEDs hidden in printer cartridges aboard Western commercial aircraft, for example, the group devoted the third issue of *Inspire* entirely to the celebration of the plot, which it termed "Operation Hemorrhage." The operation, AQAP stated, was part of a new strategy of inflicting a "death by a thousand cuts" to America, which entails more frequent strikes that are individually cheaper and faster to produce. While each of these is less destructive than attacks such as those of September 11, 2001, together, they are designed to "bleed the enemy to death."[55] In the same issue, AQAP praised the 9/11 attacks as the "blessed operation of Washington and New York" and "the greatest special operations in the history of man."[56] Furthermore, in its official statement of responsibility for Operation Hemorrhage, the group quoted statements by Osama bin Laden, thereby clearly suggesting that the plot was inspired by bin Laden's doctrine.

Following the death of Wuhayshi in a drone strike on June 12, 2015, his successor, Qassem al-Raymi, reaffirmed his allegiance to AQC leader Zawahiri on July 9. Raymi called Zawahiri "the eminent sheikh" and "the beloved father" and reiterated that the fight against the United States was his and AQAP's highest priority. Addressing his supporters, he said: "All of you must direct and gather your arrows and swords against [America]."[57] Zawahiri responded in an audio message released on a jihadist forum on September 9, 2015, thanking the leaders of AQAP and AQIM for a joint letter urging jihadists to stop fighting each other in Iraq and Syria.[58] In another audio message published in early December of the same year, Zawahiri praised the *Charlie Hebdo* attacks and asked Allah to reward AQAP for supporting "this blessed work" and to support AQAP against their various enemies such as "the crusaders" and the Houthis.[59]

Logistical Cooperation

Apart from ideological cooperation, AQ and AQAP cooperate extensively in the logistical domain. Perhaps the most striking example of this is Zawahiri's abovementioned promotion of AQAP emir Wuhayshi to the position of general manager of Al Qaeda Central, effectively turning him into its deputy leader.

Logistical cooperation between the two groups has also taken the form of financial collaboration. AQAP, for example, reportedly provided financial support on behalf of Al Qaeda Central to a group known as the Nasr City Cell, which plotted a number of attacks in Egypt and was also involved in the attacks on the U.S. Embassy in Benghazi, Libya, on September 11, 2012. In October 2012, a raid on an apartment in Nasr City, a neighborhood in Cairo, uncovered several pieces of correspondence between one of the cell members, Muhammad Jamal al-Kashef, and Al Qaeda emir Zawahiri. In one letter, which was first published in Cairo's *Al Yawm al-Sabi*, Jamal acknowledged to Zawahiri that he received a certain amount of money from AQAP, but complained that it was "much less than what is required" to fund attacks in the Sinai Peninsula if the families of the jihadists are to be adequately compensated.[60] As Clint Watts observes, AQAP's proximity to Gulf donors and its relative safe haven in Yemen makes it perfectly suited to transfer funds on behalf of AQC.[61]

AQAP has also served as an intermediary for communication between AQC and third parties. For example, as noted earlier, Wuhayshi provided guidance to AQIM leader Abdulmalik Droukdel about the need to provide basic services to the local population, the virtues of a gradual application of sharia law, and the wisdom of refraining from declaring a state in Mali—all directives that were in line with Zawahiri's strategic guidance and likely provided to Droukdel by Wuhayshi at Zawahiri's request.[62]

Another letter indicating AQAP's role as an intermediary for communication was one from the above-mentioned Nasr City Cell leader, dated August 18, 2012, which suggests that he contacted three high-ranking AQAP members, asking them for their help in getting him in touch with Zawahiri.[63]

Operational Cooperation

Finally, the strategic cooperation between Al Qaeda and AQAP also extends to the operational domain. According to the statements of AQAP leaders themselves, several of its most high-profile terrorist attacks have been conducted with some level of cooperation with Al Qaeda. Top-ranking AQAP leader Said al-Shihri, for example, stated in an audiotape released by the group's media institute Al-Malahem on February 8, 2010, that the so-called Christmas Day plot of December 25, 2009, in which an AQAP member attempted to detonate explosive devices hidden in his underwear while aboard a plane to Detroit, was coordinated with Osama bin Laden.[64]

Another operation in which there may have been some degree of operational cooperation involving members of AQAP as well as individuals affiliated with the AQC-linked Nasr City Cell were the attacks on the U.S. diplomatic compound in Benghazi, Libya, on September 11, 2012. The attacks killed U.S. ambassador Christopher Stevens as well as a U.S. Foreign Service information management officer. According to an interim report published by the U.S. Senate Select Committee on Intelligence in early 2014, members of several groups participated in the attacks on the compound, including AQAP, the Mohammad Jamal (or Nasr City Cell) Network, AQIM, and Ansar al-Sharia. The report also stated that the attack was made in an opportunistic manner and that it was still "unclear if any group or person exercised overall command and control of the attacks or whether extremist group leaders directed their members to participate."[65]

A further indication of operational cooperation between Al Qaeda headquarters and AQAP came in August 2013, when U.S. intelligence services picked up electronic communications between Zawahiri and Wuhayshi, in which the Al Qaeda emir and the AQAP leader discussed plans for an imminent attack. The communications, in addition to other streams of intelligence, prompted a security alert that led to an unprecedented temporary closure of nearly two dozen embassies in the Middle East and Africa. According to U.S. officials quoted in the *New York Times*, the intercepted conversations revealed "one of the most serious plots against American and Western interests since the attacks on Sept. 11, 2001."[66]

If AQAP leaders are to be believed, the attacks on the headquarters of the *Charlie Hebdo* satirical magazine in Paris on January 7, 2015, were also the product of operational cooperation between AQAP and Al Qaeda Central. An article providing an operational analysis of the *Charlie Hebdo* attacks and presumably penned by AQAP chief bomb-maker, Ibrahim al-Asiri, claims that in the first stage of the operation, "The central leadership began by selecting a particular target—in this case, caricature artists defaming the religion and Prophet Muhammed—they made consultations and resolved in selecting two methods in achieving this goal i.e. Assassinating the targets."[67] The division of labor between the two groups is described in more detail later in the article: "Selection of the target was from the central leadership (AQ). The planning and initiation of the operation was in the Arabian Peninsula."[68]

IDEOLOGICAL AFFINITY

Strategic alliances, like mergers, presume a high degree of ideological affinity, and the relationship between Al Qaeda and Al Qaeda in the Arabian Peninsula indeed exhibits a common ideological worldview. For example, in the first edition of its English-language magazine, AQAP describes *Inspire* as the mouthpiece of a Salafi-jihadist organization that has a global outlook and seeks to revive Islam and reestablish the caliphate:

> This Islāmic Magazine is geared towards making the Muslim a mujāhid in Allāh's path. Our intent is to give the most accurate presentation of Islām as followed by the Ṣalaf as-Ṣālih. Our concern for the ummah is worldwide and thus we try to touch upon all major issues while giving attention to the events unfolding in the Arabian Peninsula as we witness

it on the ground. Jihād has been deconstructed in our age and thus its revival in comprehension and endeavor is of utmost importance for the Caliphate's manifestation.[69]

AQAP also presented its ideological outlook in a nineteen-minute video released by the group on January 24, 2009, shortly after the merger that established the Yemen-based organization. Titled "From Here We Begin . . . And at al-Aqsa We Meet," the video presents AQAP's ideology and goals, which fall squarely in line with those of Al Qaeda, as described in chapter 3.[70] In the message, the narrator states that the mujahideen united to form a jihadi group "in defense of the Muslim world, and to liberate the Noble Aqsa Mosque."[71] Subsequently, deputy commander of AQAP, Said al-Shihri, appears, commemorating deceased jihadists and promising that AQAP will "tread their path until we establish the Islamic State, the Prophetic Caliphate, until we establish the laws of Allah, or until our blood mixes with theirs."[72] Next, al-Shihri lists the various enemies of the *umma*, which overlap entirely with Al Qaeda's declared enemies: "the spiteful Zionist Jews," their "Crusader" allies, and the "traitorous rulers of the region" who provide protection to the Zionists and the Crusaders. Al-Shihri also warns the *umma* to beware of the "numerous deviant scholars who misguide others, who have sold us to the Jews, Christians, and the Magian Rejectionists [Shiites] for a measly price."[73] He calls upon the *umma* to set out on *jihad fi sabil Allah*, jihad for the sake of God, and to that end travel to Yemen and all other Muslim lands.

AQAP's first message also features the group's first emir, Wuhayshi, who describes the AQAP as the avengers of God. Consequently, jihad must be fought using violent means: "There is no meaning to life while you see the Jews commit all sorts of atrocities against your brothers, children and women, and then in reaction only fast for day or two or scream our lungs out in protest, only to return to our homes as if we have defended our children, lifted the siege of Gaza and prevented the massacre of its people. Rather, these protests must turn into explosions, and civil disorder must turn into military rage."[74]

Despite broad ideological agreement, AQC and AQAP have not been entirely immune to differences in opinion. A close examination of their differences shows that the disagreements between these organizations are over strategy and tactics, however, rather than over doctrinal ideological matters.

Bin Laden's objection to the establishment of an Islamic state in Yemen, and his preference for using Yemen as a base of operations, for example, was rooted in pragmatic considerations. "It is well known that one of the requirements for plunging into wars is to have a reserve army and to continue exhausting the enemy in the open fronts until the enemy becomes weak, which would enable us to establish the state of Islam," he argued.[75] "Therefore, the more we can escalate operations against America, the closer we get to uniting our efforts to establish the state of Islam, God willing."[76] Once America was defeated, Al Qaeda's "next step would be targeting the region's leaders who had been the pillar of support for that American hegemony."[77] Meanwhile, bin Laden also argued that AQAP dis not have the necessary resources to establish a state and that without these resources it will not be able to win over the population. "A revolutionary movement today needs more than just military might to topple a government or control a country," he wrote.[78] "While putting aside the external enemy, a movement needs to have the resources in place to meet the needs and demands of the society, as it makes its way to controlling a city or a country."[79] Thus, it is clear that bin Laden's objections to erecting a state in Yemen were not ideological, but strategic and that his differences with AQAP had to do with the imperative to avoid yet another failure of the jihad movement because, as he said, "The public does not like losers."[80]

Similarly, Al Qaeda leaders have not taken issue with AQAP's description of the ruling powers in Sanaa as heretics. In February 2010, for example, Abu Yahya al-Libi, then considered to be third highest ranking Al Qaeda member, condemned the "heretical" Yemeni government, which he accused of collusion with Washington.[81] For his part, bin Laden acknowledged that Yemen's president was an "apostate," but an "ineffectual one." This weakness, he said, "gives jihadists room to maneuver. It is not in our interest to rush in bringing down the regime. In spite of this regime's mis-management, it is less dangerous to us than the one America wants to exchange it with."[82] Noting that "if the Yemeni government attacks the jihadists, then they should defend themselves," bin Laden went on to say that "they should not go on the offensive against the government, which would only turn the population against their enterprise."[83] As far as the assessment of the Yemeni President is concerned, Bin Laden therefore sees eye to eye with the AQAP leadership. Saleh is an apostate; indeed, their shared ideological interpretation cannot but portray him as such. The differences between bin Laden and the AQAP leadership are not about Saleh being an apostate, but over the best way to deal with this particular apostate leader at the present time.

LEVEL OF TRUST

Strategic partnerships are high-end forms of cooperation that are marked by interdependence between the parties and an expectation that the partnership will be long-term. Trust, which entails a subjective belief in mutual reliability, affects both of these factors. Trust is a key ingredient in a host of alliances, and especially in terrorist alliances, where it helps mitigate the uncertainties and risks that are inherent in relationships between militant, conspiratorial actors.[84] At the same time, strategic alliances are also based on ideological affinity, which in turn reinforces trust between the parties. "Identity affinity signals trustworthiness," as Tricia Bacon observes.[85] It "may act as an early indicator to both groups that it is safe to try to build trust, especially when personal ties have not yet formed or reputations are not well established. Affinity cannot substitute for trust, yet without it, opportunities to build trust and personal relationships are less likely to be capitalized upon by prospective allies."[86]

Citing studies from both political and business alliances, Bacon argues that trust can be reinforced by three main factors: interaction between the parties, personal relationships, and reputation.[87] The strategic alliance between Al Qaeda Central and AQAP is striking in these regards in that it showcases a number of examples of personal relationships, which include long-lasting, face-to-face interactions at the highest levels of the organizations. For instance, it has already been noted that Saudi-based QAP, which later merged with its Yemeni counterpart to form Yemen-based AQAP, was established as a branch of Al Qaeda. Yusuf al-Ayeri, who was responsible for recruitment in the network, was an "old friend" of bin Laden who later served as one of his bodyguards and traveled with him to Sudan in the mid-1990s. In the second half of 2000, he began working with Al Qaeda even more closely.[88]

Likewise, close personal relations continued between the senior leadership of AQC and the second generation of AQAP formed officially in 2009. For as long as he was alive, Wuhayshi had particularly close personal ties to Osama bin Laden. Their connection began in 1998, when Wuhayshi traveled to Afghanistan from his native Yemen to join a jihadi training camp near Khost. There, an Al Qaeda scout noticed him and arranged a meeting with bin Laden. Wuhayshi "found himself falling under bin Laden's spell" and soon pledged allegiance to the Al Qaeda leader.[89] He was appointed to serve as bin Laden's personal secretary, and his responsibilities included handling bin Laden's correspondence and diary. Bin Laden, recognizing the potential of the young Yemeni, groomed him for a future leadership position.[90] For the next four years Wuhayshi was "bin Laden's shadow," as Yemen expert Gregory Johnsen has noted.[91] Soon, other Yemenis joined him in Al Qaeda training camps in Afghanistan—the same jihadists who, together with Wuhayshi, were responsible for establishing AQAP a decade later.[92]

Wuhayshi's successor as emir of AQAP, Qasim bin Mahdi al-Raymi, is a more obscure character, even though he is a long-time participant in global jihadi activity. Al-Raymi served as the military chief of Al Qaeda in the Arabian Peninsula after the 2009 merger that formed AQAP, and he succeeded Wuhayshi as emir of the group in June 2015. Al-Raymi had trained in the al-Farouk training camp near Kandahar, where he also claims to have met bin Laden, and is cited as one of the hardliners in AQAP.[93]

Another top-ranking member of AQAP with personal ties to the Al Qaeda leadership was Said al-Shihri. Before he was killed by a drone strike in July 2013, he served as Wuhayshi's deputy and appeared in many of the group's videos, including its first official one, released in January 2009, in which he was featured alongside Wuhayshi and al-Raymi. Al-Shihri had been a detainee at Guantanamo Bay. He was also a veteran of Afghanistan, where he helped facilitate the arrival of jihadists after 2000, and he later also helped coordinate Al Qaeda activities in Iran.[94]

Another senior AQAP leader mentioned earlier, Nasser al-Ansi, also had close ties to bin Laden. According to Abd al-Razzaq al-Jamal, a journalist for *al-Wasat* with well known connections to jihadists, al-Ansi had been in Afghanistan during the 1990s, where he also worked for bin Laden. In 1998, bin Laden tasked him with overseeing an Al Qaeda guest house in Kabul and later assigned al-Ansi to a "secretive mission" in the Philippines.[95]

AQAP's religious leader, or *mufti*, Ibrahim al-Rubaysh, also had close relationships with Al Qaeda. A Saudi by origin, al-Rubaysh left for Afghanistan in the fall of 2001 and trained at the al-Farouk camp near Kandahar. He subsequently fought at Tora Bora, but was eventually captured by Pakistani forces and ended up a prisoner in Guantanamo Bay before being transferred to Saudi Arabia in December 2006.[96]

There can be little doubt that these kinds of personal relationships make Al Qaeda's ties with AQAP as strong as any between Al Qaeda and its other affiliates. They have generated a level of trust between senior leaders and reinforced both groups' expectations that theirs is an ironclad cooperative relationship. The personal ties between the leaderships also probably account for AQAP's apparent internalization of Al Qaeda's ideological and strategic preference to strike Western targets.

* * *

While the ties described above are an important reason why the strategic alliance between AQC and AQAP is so strong, another important factor is that AQAP has acted in ways that are "closer to the al-Qaeda ideal" than has any other affiliate, as McCants observes.[97] Unlike some other affiliates that have rather bluntly disregarded Al Qaeda's general instructions and helped erode Al Qaeda's brand name, AQAP has stuck relatively close to the Al Qaeda script. It has largely avoided targeting Muslim civilians, including tribesmen, sought cooperation with other jihadist groups, and refrained from advertising executions of prisoners. It has also attempted to service the local population, and in comparison to most other affiliates, it has relied less on harsh punishments in the areas under its control. Providing ideological backing to Al Qaeda on numerous occasions and performing important communication functions as an intermediary between AQC and other affiliates, AQAP is also the only affiliate that has consistently attempted, and sometimes succeeded, in supporting Al Qaeda's key objective of targeting the far enemy, both as an end in itself and as a means for pressuring Western states to cease supporting local "apostate" regimes.[98]

Given these special ties, Zawahiri's promotion of AQAP emir Wuhayshi to Al Qaeda's general manager—a move that represented an attempt to upgrade the relationship closer to a merger—comes as little surprise. At the same time, however, the relationship between AQC and AQAP also demonstrates that divisions remain even among terrorist actors that have unusually close ties. In the case of AQC and AQAP, we have seen that these differences revolve mainly around strategic and tactical issues, rather than doctrinal ones. Upon closer inspection, it is clear that AQAP has at times sought to maintain a degree of independence and at other times has had difficulty ensuring that all of its lower-ranking members abide by AQC's strategic directives. AQAP's adherence to AQC's guidelines has also been uneven in that on the one hand, it has "collaborated with local rebel groups and sought the support of the tribes" in accordance with AQC guidelines, while on the other, "it also killed tribesmen who worked with its enemies. It beheaded opponents and spies but usually didn't broadcast the acts. It bombed two Shii religious processions, but such attacks were rare."[99]

As far as governance of areas under its control is concerned, here too AQAP appears to have tried to stick to Zawahiri's regulations, although it also seems to have had difficulty reining in some of its rank and file members. In line with AQC's directives, AQAP has "tried to provide public services and to manage the . . . local economies" of their territories, but in contrast to the headquarters' guidelines, AQAP "was not lenient when applying the *hudud* punishments," although its leaders "later came to regret" that failure.[100]

In sum, the above discussion describes an usually close partnership between two like-minded organizations. As this case study also shows, however, even the most cordial of terrorist alliances are not immune to disagreements.

8

LOW-END COOPERATION

Al Qaeda, Iran, and Hizballah

T HIS CHAPTER EXAMINES a case of low-end cooperation involving Al
Qaeda, Iran, and Hizballah. In 2012, a report published by the
Combating Terrorism Center at West Point, a research institution
devoted to the analysis of the evolving global jihad movement, described
the relationship between Al Qaeda and Iran as "one of the least understood aspects about al-Qaʾida's history."[1] Following the attacks of September 11, 2001, analysts, insiders, and pundits have indeed entertained a broad
range of views about the existence and quality of ties between two camps
that, at first glance, appear deeply divided along sectarian lines: a militant
Sunni camp comprising Al Qaeda and its associated entities on the one
hand; and a militant Shiite camp consisting of elements within Iran as
well as Hizballah on the other. Assessments and opinions regarding the
existence and quality of cooperation between these two camps have spanned
a broad spectrum. On one end, some have raised serious doubts about the
possibility of these ideologically opposed camps cooperating in any meaningful way. On the other, some have described the relationship between
these entities as a full-fledged alliance.[2]

The existence of some kind of ties between these two camps has been
firmly established at least since the release of the *9/11 Commission Report* in
July 2004, which was unequivocal in this regard. At the same time, the

authors of the report insinuated that the precise nature and extent of the cooperation between these parties remained shrouded in mystery. The authors therefore suggested that the U.S. government further investigate the matter.[3]

This chapter argues that the cooperation between Al Qaeda and Iran/Hizballah is best understood as tactical. As described in chapter 4, a tactical cooperation is a low-end form in which the partners pursue a number of common interests, while maintaining their autonomy. In contrast to high-end forms of cooperation such as mergers or strategic alliances, tactical collaborations are not dependent on a shared ideology or worldview and hence do not necessarily involve the pursuit of common strategic goals. In examining and evaluating the cooperative ties between these two camps, this chapter draws on an abundance of primary and secondary sources, including declassified documents seized during the raid on Osama bin Laden's safe house in Abbottabad, Pakistan. The puzzle of the relationship between the global jihad movement and Iran/Hizballah continues to miss many important pieces. Nevertheless, the available information on cooperation between the Al Qaeda camp and the Iran-Hizballah camp strongly supports the conclusion that they have entertained a relationship that extends beyond isolated transactions, but at the same time falls short of a real strategic alliance. It also confirms the assessment that these camps have engaged in tactical cooperation based largely on perceptions of common interests and common enemies—perceptions that are in constant flux and have therefore rendered the relationship highly uneven and unpredictable.

PRE-9/11 COOPERATION

The existence of ties between Al Qaeda-associated individuals and elements within Iran—notably the Iranian Revolutionary Guards Corps (IRGC) and Ministry of Intelligence and Security (MOIS)—as well as between Al Qaeda and Hizballah has predated the 9/11 attacks by roughly a decade. Several accounts date initial relevant contacts to April 1991, when Egyptian Islamic Jihad (EIJ) leader (and future Al Qaeda emir) Ayman al-Zawahiri is believed to have secretly visited Iran and indicate that the establishment of ties between them appear to have been based on mutual respect, even admiration. Zawahiri had been a supporter of the 1979 Islamic Revolution in Iran and had hoped that Egyptians would follow the Iranian example and set up a theocratic regime of their own.[4] The Iranians, for their part, had celebrated the 1981 assassination of Egyptian President Anwar Sadat by an EIJ operative, Khalid Islambouli, and even named a street in Tehran in the assassin's honor.[5]

On his secret trip to Iran, Zawahiri asked his Iranian interlocutors to support his group's attempted overthrow of the Egyptian regime of President Hosni Mubarak, a coup the EIJ had been planning since 1990. In return, Zawahiri offered information to the Iranians about a plan by the Egyptian government to storm several Gulf islands whose status was disputed between Iran and the United Arab Emirates (UAE). As former Al Qaeda trainer Ali Muhammad told a U.S. court, the Iranians granted Zawahiri's request and began training EIJ members in both Iran and the Sudan, while also providing $2 million in financial support.[6] According to Ronen Bergman, an Israeli journalist with close ties to the Israeli intelligence services, Zawahiri also met Hizballah's notorious military commander, Imad Mughniyeh on his April 1991 visit. Mughniyeh impressed Zawahiri with Hizballah's technical expertise in conducting suicide operations. Following these meetings, Zawahiri also sent several EIJ members, including Muhammad, to train with Hizballah in Lebanon, under Mughniyeh.[7]

In late 1991 or 1992, the discussions between the EIJ and Iran began to include Al Qaeda. The discussions were the fruits of a growing friendship between Zawahiri and Al Qaeda leader Osama bin Laden and were held in the Sudan, where the EIJ, Al Qaeda, hundreds of IRGC members, and members of Hizballah and dozens of other militant and terrorist entities were in residence—a situation that greatly facilitated cooperation between these various groups. As the 9/11 Commission has reported, the meeting between Al Qaeda and the Iranian operatives "led to an informal agreement to cooperate in providing support—even if only training—for actions carried out primarily against Israel and the United States. Not long afterward, senior al Qaeda operatives and trainers traveled to Iran to receive training in explosives."[8]

In 1993, Hizballah operative Mughniyeh visited Sudan and met bin Laden. In the fall of that year, another Al Qaeda delegation left for the Bekaa valley in Lebanon "for further training in explosives as well as in intelligence and security."[9] According to the *9/11 Commission Report*, "Bin Ladin reportedly showed particular interest in learning how to use truck bombs such as the one that had killed 241 U.S. Marines in Lebanon in 1983."[10] The Al Qaeda delegation that left for Lebanon in the fall of 1993 included top members affiliated with the group's military committee, as well as other members who would help execute the suicide bombing on the U.S. Embassy in Nairobi, Kenya, on 7 August 1998.[11] As the *9/11 Commission Report* later noted, the training Al Qaeda received in Lebanon gave it the "tactical expertise" needed to carry out the dual embassy bombings of 1988 in Kenya and Tanzania. In fact, thirteen years after the bombings, the U.S. District Court for the District of Columbia found the government of Iran liable for (although not necessarily directly linked to) the 1998 bombings. Judge John D. Bates wrote in his decision:

> The government of Iran aided, abetted and conspired with Hezbollah, Osama bin Laden, and al Qaeda to launch large-scale bombing attacks against the United States by utilizing the sophisticated delivery mechanism of powerful suicide truck bombs. . . . Al Qaeda desired to replicate Hezbollah's 1983 Beirut Marine barracks suicide bombing, and bin Laden sought Iranian expertise to teach al Qaeda operatives about how to blow up buildings. . . . Prior to their meetings with Iranian officials and agents Bin Laden and al Qaeda did not possess the technical expertise required to carry out the embassy bombings in Nairobi and Dar es Salaam. The Iranian defendants, through Hezbollah, provided explosives training to Bin Laden and al Qaeda and rendered direct assistance to al Qaeda operatives. . . . In a short time, al Qaeda acquired the capabilities to carry out the 1998 Embassy bombings, which killed

hundreds and injured thousands by detonation of very large and sophisticated bombs.[12]

In his testimony, former Al Qaeda trainer Ali Mohammed suggested that the "deal" between the parties had several elements. On the Sunni militant side, it involved both the EIJ and Al Qaeda—two friendly, but separate organizations. On the other end, it involved two Shiite entities, namely Hizballah and its Iranian sponsor. "Hezbollah provided explosives training for al Qaeda. Iran supplied Egyptian Jihad with weapons. Iran also used Hezbollah to supply explosives that were disguised to look like rocks."[13] The EIJ also received training in Lebanon, including training in conducting suicide operations. It is highly likely that that training led to one of the first suicide attacks by a Sunni jihadist group in August 1993, when the EIJ attempted to kill the Egyptian minister of the interior, Hasan al-Alfi, in a suicide mission. The EIJ had an axe to grind with Al-Alfi, who had been a key organizer of the crackdown against Egyptian jihadi groups in Egypt.[14]

Zawahiri was not only responsible for the initiation of the Al Qaeda-Iran link, but also remained an important middleman in that relationship over the next decades.[15] In addition to Zawahiri's help, bin Laden's decision to collude with Iran and Hizballah was enabled by the efforts of Hassan al-Turabi, a Sudanese Islamist ideologue affiliated with the Muslim Brotherhood. As head of the Sudanese National Islamic Front, al-Turabi was chiefly responsible for Sudan's shift towards militant Islamism in the 1990s, during which time the country turned into a safe haven and meeting ground for myriad terrorist groups. Despite his personal dislike of al-Turabi, bin Laden bought into the Sudanese Islamist's idea that the fight against the West required Sunnis and Shiites to put aside their differences and join a common cause. Accordingly, the Al Qaeda leader instructed Abu Hajer al-Iraqi, his close friend and religious adviser, to convey this message to members of Al Qaeda.[16]

Several other individuals kept the communication lines between the Iranians and Al Qaeda open. By 1995, Mustafa Hamid (Abu al-Walid al-Masri), an Al Qaeda member with EIJ origins, became another important intermediary between Al Qaeda and Iranian officials. Al-Masri had remained in Afghanistan during the 1992–1996 period, when most of his fellow Al Qaeda members were in Sudan, in order to oversee Al Qaeda's various operations there (see chapter 5). Al-Masri reportedly visited Iran in 1995, and he spent almost a decade in the country after 9/11 under some form of house arrest.[17]

Bin Laden was interested in maintaining the relationship with his Shiite partners even after he returned to Afghanistan in 1996, and the *9/11 Commission Report* confirms the persistence of these contacts after that year.[18] In July 1996, for example, after bin Laden's departure from Sudan and his return to Afghanistan, he tried to contact Iranian intelligence officers in Afghanistan in order to seek their cooperation in attacks against U.S. targets. To that end, he dispatched his close ally Abdullah Nuri, leader of the Islamic Renaissance Party of Tajikistan, to liaise with the Iranians. The Iranians were willing to meet with bin Laden in the Afghan city of Taliqan, close to the Tajik border. Bin Laden declined, citing concerns for his safety.[19]

Iran's relationship with Al Qaeda grew more problematic after Al Qaeda partnered with the Taliban, whom the Iranians despised. Iran-Taliban relations reached their low point in 1998, when Iran mobilized 200,000 troops along its border with Afghanistan after the Taliban killed nine Iranian diplomats who worked with the Taliban's main challengers, the Northern Alliance. Still, Iranian officials were often willing to grant transit through Iran to Al Qaeda members seeking to travel into or out of Afghanistan. Iranian border inspectors were instructed not to stamp the passports of the jihadists in transit.[20]

Iran has also been accused of playing a role in setting up Al Qaeda's network in Yemen, and thereby facilitating the bombing of the USS *Cole* in October 2000—a suicide boat attack that killed seventeen U.S. servicemen. In April 2015, U.S. District Judge Rudolph Contreras, ruling in Washington, found Iran responsible for the bombing of the American vessel. Contreras wrote in a fifty page opinion that "in the years leading up to the Cole bombing, Iran was directly involved in establishing Al-Qaeda's Yemen network and supported training and logistics for Al-Qaeda in the Gulf region."[21] After the bombing, Iran made what the *9/11 Commission*

Report's authors have called a "concerted effort to strengthen relations with al Qaeda."[22]

These efforts were mutual. For Al Qaeda, improving cooperation with the Iranians became more important when, in early 2000, the group helped Abu Musab al-Zarqawi set up a jihadist training camp outside the western Afghan city of Herat, near the border with Iran. Although Zarqawi was no formal affiliate of Al Qaeda at this point, bin Laden had already identified his potential value and hoped that the charismatic Jordanian jihadist would pledge allegiance to him. The location of the training camps was chosen in part for its convenience for current and future jihadists traveling through Iran. To that end, senior Al Qaeda member Sayf al-Adl, who would rise to become the group's operational commander after 2002, and Zarqawi discussed establishing two guesthouses in Tehran and Mashhad, which were eventually set up to facilitate the transfer of jihadists to Herat. The route was "safe to travel," as al-Adl wrote in his biography.[23] Said al-Shihri, who would later become deputy leader of AQAP, helped facilitate the travel of jihadists at the Mashhad guesthouse.[24]

The presence of the Zarqawi-run, Al Qaeda–funded camp near the Iranian border stoked Al Qaeda's interest in "building good relations with some virtuous people in Iran to coordinate regarding issues of mutual interest," according to al-Adel.[25] He acknowledged that "coordination with the Iranians was later achieved with sincere individuals who were hostile to the Americans and the Israelis."[26]

IRAN, HIZBALLAH, AND THE 9/11 ATTACKS

The 9/11 Commission found "no evidence that Iran or Hezbollah was aware of the planning for what later became the 9/11 attacks," but the persistence of contacts between Iranian security officials and senior Al Qaeda figures in the decade from 1991 to 2001 raised important questions that the commission believed warranted further investigation by the U.S. government.[27] Unsubstantiated rumors about possible Iranian foreknowledge of the 9/11 attacks continued to appear in subsequent years, fueling further speculation about the responsibility for the 9/11 attacks.[28]

The 9/11 Commission did have evidence, though, that among the jihadists who passed through Iran between October 2000 and February 2001 were eight to ten of the fourteen Saudi muscle hijackers. In October 2000, one muscle hijacker, Ahmed al-Ghamdi, flew to Beirut on the same flight as a senior Hizballah operative, although the *9/11 Commission Report* acknowledges that this may have been a coincidence. One month later, three future muscle hijackers traveled together from Saudi Arabia to Beirut and then to Iran. On the second leg of the trip, an "associate of a senior Hezbollah operative" was also on the flight. "Hezbollah officials in Beirut and Iran," the report goes on, "were expecting the arrival of a group during the same time period. The travel of this group was important enough to merit the attention of senior figures in Hezbollah."[29] The 9/11 mastermind Khaled Sheikh Muhammad (KSM) and Ramzi bin-al-Shibh, a member of the Hamburg cell who traveled to Tehran less than a week before the attack, later admitted that several of the 9/11 operatives passed through Iran. They denied any relationship between the hijackers and Hizballah and said that the only reason the hijackers passed through Iran was that Iranian border officials were known to refrain from stamping Saudi passports.[30]

POST-9/11 COOPERATION

Following the attacks of September 11, 2001, members of Al Qaeda fled Afghanistan. While most of the senior leadership moved to Pakistan, Iran provided "safe passage" to many jihadists, as al-Adel acknowledged.[31] These jihadists were part of a first wave of "Afghan Arab" fighters who, along with their families, entered Iran shortly after the attacks of September 11, 2001. They included hundreds of people, both formal Al Qaeda members and other jihadists not formally associated with the group, such as Abu Musab al-Suri and Abu Musab al-Zarqawi.[32]

According to both Western and jihadist sources, the Iranians were not passive recipients of the jihadist "refugees." Instead, they had "dispatched a delegation to Afghanistan to guarantee the safe travel of operatives and their families to Iran."[33] Organizing these transports was the Quds Force—an IRGC unit in charge of external operations such as direct action, subversion, training, and advising.[34] Iranian officials then appeared to select a core group that would remain in Iran, while deporting the other jihadists. This was also expressed in a meeting with Al Qaeda in December 2001, during which Iranian officials indicated their willingness to provide "shelter" to some two dozen Al Qaeda members, while allowing the other jihadists to transit through the country to other locations.[35] Of those who were allowed to stay in Iran, up to a dozen individuals, including bin Laden's son Saad, reportedly found refuge in the northern Iranian resort town of Chalus, on the Caspian Sea.[36] Al-Adel said that he was in charge of securing passage to Iran for Al Qaeda members, who were mainly jihadists from Saudi Arabia, Kuwait, and the UAE. Gulbuddin Hekmatyar, a prominent veteran of the anti-Soviet jihad in Afghanistan who had been living in exile in Iran since 1996, was also involved in making travel and housing arrangements.[37]

One month after his State of the Union Address of January 2002, when President George W. Bush referred to Iran as part of an "axis of evil,"[38] Iran provided access to another group of Al Qaeda–linked jihadists and their families who had arrived from Pakistan, where they faced growing pressures. The movement of this second wave of jihadists to Iran was reported by several jihadist sources, including a letter by Anas al-Subayie—known by the *kunya* (alias) Abu abd al-Rahman—an Al Qaeda operative who had been detained in Iran and released in May 2010.[39] Al-Subayie's letter, which was declassified and released by the U.S. Office of the Director of National Intelligence in 2015, was addressed in all likelihood to bin Laden and written in response to his request that al-Subayie provide a detailed report about his experiences in Iran, and those of other Al Qaeda members. Accordingly, Al-Subayie reported that upon arriving in Iran, the second group of "brothers" and their families spread out across several cities, including Zahedan, Shiraz, Mashhad, Tehran, and Karaj.[40] His account suggests that the Iranians at first allowed the members of the second group to roam relatively freely, but then began to step up their efforts of "locating" the jihadists in Iran in late 2002.[41]

During 2002, when members of Al Qaeda enjoyed relative freedom in Iran, several core Al Qaeda operatives in Iran established a "management council" charged with providing strategic support to the main leadership in Pakistan. This council was one of two that reported directly to bin Laden, the other being the consultative (*shura*) council.[42] Management council members included Sayf al-Adel, Sulayman abu Ghayth, Abu al-Khayr al-Masri, Abu Muhammad al-Masri, and Abu Hafs al-Mauritani.[43] Other Al Qaeda members in Iran included Ali Salah Hussain, whom the U.S. Treasury Department accused of smuggling Al Qaeda associates through networks in Zahedan, Iran,[44] and Muhammad Raba al Sayid al Bahtiyti, a longtime member of EIJ and Al Qaeda who was reportedly involved in Al Qaeda's 1995 bombing of the Egyptian embassy in Islamabad, Pakistan.[45] Abu al-Walid al-Masri, the longtime middleman between Al Qaeda and Iran, was also part of the management council and would continue to play a major role as an interlocutor between the Iranians and Al Qaeda. In January 2009, the U.S. Treasury Department designated him under Executive Order 13224, which targets terrorists and those providing support to terrorists or acts of terrorism, stating that he was harbored by the IRGC and played a key role in negotiating a secret agreement between bin Laden and Iran that would ensure safe transit for Al Qaeda members through Iran.

During the run-up to the U.S. invasion of Iraq in March 2003—perhaps out of concern that the United States could seek regime change in Iran next—these jihadists were reportedly allowed to prepare the resistance against the coalition forces while in Iran.[46] The relative freedom enjoyed by those Al Qaeda members who were allowed to remain in Iran, which included the ability to communicate with each other, lasted until the spring of 2003. Thus, Sayf al-Adel and Saad bin Laden, among others, communicated with the cell that planned and executed the attacks of May 2003 on a Western housing complex in Riyadh, Saudi Arabia, using three truck bombs.[47] Shortly after the attacks, the United States reportedly delivered a message to Tehran via Switzerland, demanding that Iran transfer the Al Qaeda leaders to the Saudis or alternatively to third states that would then hand them over to the United States. Tehran replied with a proposal of its own, proposing to deliver the Al Qaeda members to the United States in return for the United States extraditing members of Mujahedeen al-Khalq, an Iranian opposition group that attempted to overthrow the government of the Islamic Republic, to Iran. Washington declined the offer.[48]

Just a few days after the Riyadh attacks, on May 16, 2003, fourteen suicide bombers struck several targets in Casablanca, killing forty-five people in what was the most deadly terrorist attack on Moroccan soil. Saad bin Laden is believed to have been implicated in these attacks as well.[49]

It was after the attacks in Riyadh and Casablanca that the lax treatment of the Al Qaeda contingent in Iran began to change. Iranian authorities apprehended the remaining Al Qaeda members relatively quickly after the bombings—a fact that suggested, as Kenneth Pollack has pointed out, that Iran's decision to let the Al Qaeda members roam in Iran relatively freely until then had been a conscious one.[50] Thereafter, when all members of Al Qaeda's management council and their families were apprehended, the conditions under which they were detained varied significantly, with some being quite harsh, according to Al-Sibayie.[51] In his letter to bin Laden, he described the "tightly secured and fortified detention centers" near Tehran, which were run by the IRGC and the MOIS, in addition to the prison authorities, where jihadists were detained with their families. According to Sibayie, resources were scarce, and children were not able to receive education.[52] Four years later, the group was moved to another compound that was part of an "airport training facility" in Karaj, in the Kihan Mahr area, where twelve housing units were fortified with six- or seven-meter high inner fences, finished off with barbed wires, cameras, and large metal gates, and two outer fences. All in all, Al-Sibayie reported, living standards there were better than in the initial detention facility.[53]

According to Seth Jones, others were placed under a loose form of house arrest, which enabled them to continue to communicate, travel, and even raise funds.[54] Al-Subayie's report to bin Laden confirms that some members of Al Qaeda were moved to "fortified houses" in Tehran "where the treatment was better."[55]

In addition, Iran continued to let Al Qaeda operatives pass through the country in subsequent years. By June 2008, for example, Adel Muhammad Mahmoud Abdulkhaleq, an Al Qaeda operative and member of LIFG, had traveled to Iran five times since 2004, according to the U.S. Department of Treasury. Similar activities were uncovered by the Bahraini government, which said that several members of an Al Qaeda–linked cell traveled from Bahrain to Afghanistan via Iran and met with Al Qaeda operatives at Tehran airport.[56] Additionally, in 2010 a trial in Germany of Ahmad Wali Siddiqui, an Al Qaeda operative who had extensive ties to the 9/11 Hamburg cell, revealed that two of his co-conspirators in a planned mass shooting attack in Europe, Rami Makanesi and Maamen Meziche, were regularly traversing Iran on their way to Pakistan in order to evade apprehension.[57]

Indeed, throughout the period following the detention of Al Qaeda members in Iran, Al Qaeda apparently was able to use Iran as a "facilitation hub," according to General David Petraeus, then commander of US-CENTCOM. Testifying before the Senate Foreign Relations Committee on March 16, 2010, Petraeus stated that Al Qaeda "continues to use Iran as a key facilitation hub, where facilitators connect al-Qaida's senior leadership to regional affiliates. . . . And although Iranian authorities do periodically disrupt this network by detaining select al-Qaida facilitators and operational planners, Tehran's policy in this regard is often unpredictable."[58]

Another aspect of Iran's unpredictable policy with regard to the Al Qaeda contingent on its soil was the sporadic release of some Al Qaeda members. According to the German newspaper Die Welt, Saad bin Laden was released on July 28, 2006, in the wake of the Israel-Lebanon war, and sent to the Syria-Lebanon border, perhaps with the purpose of recruiting Lebanese refugees in the fight against Israel.[59] Another newspaper, Al-Elaph (UAE), reported that Iran dispatched Saad bin Laden to build cells for Hizballah from the refugees in regional camps.[60] He apparently returned to Iran, but left again in 2008, when Iran seemed to loosen its grip on more Al Qaeda members.[61] While the members of the management council remained in Iran under a limited form of house arrest and received instructions to maintain a low profile and abstain from attacking Iran, they were also allowed "some freedom to fundraise, communicate with al Qaeda central in Pakistan and other affiliates, and funnel foreign fighters through Iran."[62]

Correspondence between bin Laden and his most trusted emissary, Atiyyah abd al-Rahman, who also served as bin Laden's liaison with the Al Qaeda members in Iran, revealed that Iran continued to release groups of jihadists associated with Al Qaeda in batches in mid-2009.[63] At the same time, Iran's refusal to release all Al Qaeda members and its treatment of some of them caused major consternation among senior Al Qaeda leaders, including Osama bin Laden, who complained in a letter that the Iranians had not released his daughter Fatima.[64] In another letter written by bin Laden's son Khalid to Iranian Supreme Leader Ayatollah Khamenei, Khalid called for the release of the remaining members of his family and plainly expressed his frustration that numerous earlier requests had been ignored by the Iranian government.[65]

In the spring of 2010, *Der Spiegel* reported Iran's release of top Al Qaeda officials,[66] including Sayf al-Adel; Abu Muhammad al-Masri, who had played a key role in the 1998 embassy bombings; Sulaiman Abu Ghaith, a prominent Al Qaeda fundraiser and spokesman, as well as Osama bin Laden's son-in-law; and Abu Hafs al-Mauritani, a leading Al Qaeda member who had served on the group's shura council before the 9/11 attacks.[67] The release was presumably part of a prisoner exchange agreement between Iran and Al Qaeda's Pakistani leadership. In November 2008, Al Qaeda had kidnapped the commercial counselor in the Iranian consulate in Peshawar, Pakistan, Heshmatollah Attarzadeh-Nyaki, and then later demanded that Iran release Al Qaeda figures from detention, most importantly members of bin Laden's family.[68] Bin Laden's confidant, Atiyah, believed that the sporadic Iranian release of some "mid-level" Al Qaeda members and their families starting in 2009, were proof that Al Qaeda's pressure tactics against the Iranians worked.[69] Atiyah may have had a point. Subsequently, when Iran released five additional senior Al Qaeda members in 2015, including Sayf al-Adl, the release was reportedly part of a prisoner swap with AQAP. In return, Al Qaeda's Yemeni affiliate released Nour Ahmad Nikbakht, an Iranian diplomat whom the group had kidnapped in Sana in July 2013.[70]

A report issued by the Combating Terrorism Center at West Point suggested that the pressure tactics and Iran's unwillingness to release all Al Qaeda members from custody suggested that the relationship between Al Qaeda and Iran was antagonistic, at least in 2009–2010.[71] In fact, however, Iran's relationship with Al Qaeda remained deliberately ambivalent. Despite the antagonism, the Iranians provided at least some Al Qaeda members in Iran an opportunity to use Iran as a base, as long as the Sunni militants were pursuing goals that aligned with Iran's own interests. This became evident in late July 2011, when the U.S. Treasury Department provided additional details on Iran's role as a facilitation hub. According to its report, the Iranian government had entered into an agreement with Al Qaeda operatives to use Iran as a transit point for funneling money and people from the Gulf to Pakistan and Afghanistan. Outlining extensive fundraising operations involving Iran-based operatives who drew from donors in oil-rich Gulf countries such as Kuwait and Qatar, the Treasury report named several Al Qaeda operatives in this context. These included Ezedin Abdel Aziz Khalil, a.k.a. Yasin al-Suri, who collected money from Gulf donors and transferred it to Al Qaeda in Iraq and Afghanistan. The Treasury report also named five other operatives who contributed to Al Qaeda's activity in Iran, including the prominent bin Laden emissary Atiyah Abd al-Rahman, whom bin Laden appointed as Al Qaeda's envoy in Iran before tasking him with commanding Al Qaeda in Pakistan's tribal areas.[72]

Within a few months after the Treasury's revelations, Yasin al-Suri was reportedly placed in protective custody by Iranian officials. In late 2011, he was replaced by a new Al Qaeda leader in Iran, Muhsin al-Fadhli. According to Treasury, Fadhli "began working with al Qaeda's Iran-based facilitation network in 2009 and was later arrested by the Iranians," who subsequently released him in 2011.[73] A close confidant of bin Laden's of Kuwaiti background, al-Fadhli later became part of the Khorasan Group nested within Al Qaeda's Syrian affiliate Jabhat al-Nusra. He was killed in a U.S. airstrike in Syria in July 2015.[74] While in Iran, his deputy, according to Treasury, was Adel Radi Saqr al-Wahabi al-Harbi. Treasury further revealed that Fadhli and other Al Qaeda operatives in Iran were "working to move fighters and money through Turkey to support al-Qa'ida-affiliated elements in Syria."[75] It also offered additional details about the agreement between Iran and Al Qaeda during the time of Yasin al-Suri's involvement:

> Under the terms of the agreement between al-Qa'ida and Iran, al-Qa'ida must refrain from conducting any operations within Iranian territory and recruiting operatives inside Iran while keeping Iranian authorities informed of their activities. In return, the Government of Iran gave the Iran-based al-Qa'ida network freedom of operation and uninhibited ability to travel for extremists and their families. Al-Qa'ida members who violate these terms run the risk of being detained by Iranian authorities. Yasin al-Suri agreed to the terms of this agreement with Iran with the knowledge of now-deceased al-Qa'ida leader 'Atiyah 'Abd al Rahman.[76]

News reports at the time of the leadership transition within Al Qaeda in Iran also claimed that Iran was supplying Al Qaeda with training in the use of advanced explosives as part of the above-named deal, which was first struck in 2009 and had reached "operational capacity" by 2012. Citing a "secret intelligence memorandum," *Sky News* stated that "Iran has significantly stepped up its investment, maintenance and improvement of operational and intelligence ties with the al Qaeda leadership in Pakistan in recent months."[77]

The benefits of the Iran–Al Qaeda deal were not lost on the Al Qaeda leadership. In a letter to an unknown jihadist called "Karim," dated October 18, 2007, and declassified by the U.S. Director of National Intelligence in March 2016, Osama bin Laden, the presumed author, described Iran as "our main artery for funds, personnel, and communication, as well as the matter of hostages."[78] According to other declassified correspondence, Al Qaeda continued to suggest Iran as a safe haven for several of its operatives as late as 2011. In a letter from Atiyah dated April 5, 2011, bin Laden's trusted emissary suggested Iran as a place where "Sheikh Yunis," referring most likely to top Al Qaeda terrorist planner Younis al-Muritani, could "easily hide."[79] He also mentioned other jihadis who traveled to Iran recently, such as "brother [Abdallah Rajab] al-Libi" as well as "Brother [Abu al-Samah] al-Masri" who recently left for Iran from where he "resumed media activities and communications under the title 'Jama'at alJihad.'"[80]

Furthermore, Al Qaeda members had multiple occasions for using Iran as a staging ground for attacks against the West. One such plan was the so-called "Europlot," which was overseen by Osama bin Laden and envisioned commando-style attacks in Germany, France, and the United Kingdom, before being foiled in 2010 by U.S. and European authorities.[81] The Europlot conspirators included German and British jihadists who traveled to the Waziristan region of Pakistan to receive training. The plotters traveled through Iran, and relied on Yasin al-Suri and his network for transit support. After the foiled attacks, some of the network's members found refuge in Iran for a limited time.[82] In another case related to Al Qaeda's Iran-based group, Canadian authorities disrupted a plot in April 2013 to derail a passenger train heading from New York to Toronto. According to the assistant commissioner of the Canadian Royal Mounted Police, the two suspects had received "direction and guidance" from "Al Qaeda elements living in Iran," although there was no evidence that Iran had sponsored the plot.[83]

In February 2012, The U.S. Treasury Department designated the MOIS for human rights abuses and support for terrorism. Treasury stated that the MOIS "has facilitated the movement of al Qa'ida operatives in Iran and provided them with documents, identification cards, and passports. MOIS also provided money and weapons to al Qa'ida in Iraq (AQI), a terrorist group designated under E.O. 13224, and negotiated prisoner releases of AQI operatives."[84] Two years later, in February 2014, Treasury designated yet another member of Al Qaeda active in Iran, while adding that the Al Qaeda network "also uses Iran as a transit point for moving funding and foreign fighters through Turkey to support al Qaeda-affiliated elements in Syria, including the al-Nusrah Front."[85]

ANALYSIS

The preceding discussion has outlined the relationship between two camps whose mutual antagonism, one would think, would preclude any meaningful mutual cooperation. Nevertheless, an abundance of evidence establishes beyond any reasonable doubt that some degree of cooperation between Al Qaeda and related jihadi groups on the one hand, and Iran and Hizballah on the other hand, has existed since at least 1991, and perhaps before.[86] This evidence is drawn from declassified internal jihadi communications; court proceedings; U.S. government–sponsored inquiry commissions; U.S. Department of Treasury designations; and scholarly and journalistic accounts. As Iran specialist Patrick Clawson has pointed out, the evidence presented in the *9/11 Commission Report* and in U.S. Treasury designations about these links "have not been contradicted by any significant figures in the U.S. government. There simply is no ambiguity or unclarity in U.S. government statements about this matter."[87]

Statements on the part of Al Qaeda members and Iranian officials themselves have further corroborated reports of a collaboration between these two camps or, at the very least, indicated that these parties harbor open-minded views about mutual cooperation. In 2008, for example, Zawahiri admitted that Iran and Al Qaeda had collaborated "on confronting the American-led Zionist-Crusader alliance."[88] Four years later, Iranian Supreme Leader Ayatollah Khamenei said that Iran "will continue to support any nation or group that fights or confronts the Zionist regime, and we are not afraid of saying this."[89] Longstanding Iranian support for Sunni anti-Israel groups such as Hamas has given further credence to Khamenei's statement.[90]

If the existence of ties between these two camps is well established, the more pertinent question now concerns the nature of these ties. I argue that they are best understood as a low-end tactical cooperation. As I discussed in chapter 4, in low-end cooperative arrangements, the partners pursue a limited number of common interests. Tactical partnerships may develop into strategic alliances if the cooperating partners develop mutual trust and identify common strategic objectives. This clearly has not occurred between Al Qaeda and its associates and the Iran-Hizballah camp, whose ideologies and strategic objectives are so incompatible. Given their being so at odds, the real puzzle is why they cooperated in the first place.

Before addressing this question, I will first assess the extent to which the findings of this case study correspond to the characteristics of tactical cooperation that I introduced in chapter 4. These characteristics pertain to the duration of the cooperation; the degree of interdependence between the cooperating parties; the variety of their cooperative activities; their ideological positions; and their level of trust.

EXPECTED DURATION

In chapter 4, I argued that since the common interests identified by the partners in a tactical cooperation are subject to shifts, the cooperating parties do not necessarily expect the tactical cooperation to endure over a prolonged period of time. Moreover, tactical cooperation is based on the identification of common tactical and operational goals, not on common strategic objectives. Thus a tactical cooperative arrangement allows the partners greater flexibility in choosing when and how to cooperate, when compared to strategic alliances or mergers. Because common tactical or operational interests emerge or disappear at short notice, the characteristics of the relationship between parties can vary considerably. While it can be enduring in some cases, in others it may be sporadic, as parties recalibrate their short-term interests according to the ebbs and flows of changing geopolitical events. Periods of more intensive collaboration are likely to be interrupted by periods of few interactions. If two parties are ideologically incompatible in the first place, the periods in between more intensive cooperation can even be marked by outright enmity. Nevertheless, it is also possible for the parties to entertain a cooperative and conflictual relationship at one and the same time. No wonder, then, that to outside observers, such relationships can seem puzzling.

The collaborative relationship between Al Qaeda and associated groups on the one hand, and Iran and Hizballah on the other, fits the template of a tactical cooperation between two ideologically opposed camps. It has also been highly uneven. An early peak of cooperation occurred in the earlier 1990s, when both parties engaged in joint training in Iran and Lebanon. Then, upon Al Qaeda's return to Afghanistan in 1996, the relationship appeared to ebb, probably as a result of Al Qaeda's alliance with the Taliban, a movement loathed by the Iranians, and then it seems to have picked up again toward the end of the 1990s, possibly as a result of Al Qaeda's ability to humiliate the United States repeatedly with attacks against its embassies in several African countries, Yemen, and elsewhere, which Iran likely viewed as a favorable development.

We can discern similar patterns after 9/11. While Iran appeared to detain jihadists at times when placating the United States seemed to be in its best interests, it released jihadists from custody to lash out against the United States in revenge or when blackmailed by Al Qaeda to do so. At the same time, however, its actions appeared to be contradictory in that while it held most Al Qaeda members and their families in detention, it allowed others to meet, facilitate travel, and communicate, and possibly to plan and execute attacks. Iran's policy appeared so erratic that even Al Qaeda members failed to understand its rationale. Iran's detention of Al Qaeda members, Sayf al-Adel once admitted, "confused us and foiled 75 percent of our plan."[91]

DEGREE OF INTERDEPENDENCE

One of the key characteristics of a tactical cooperation is the ability of the parties to maintain their full independence. Unlike mergers, where at least one of the parties loses its status as an independent actor, and unlike strategic alliances, where one party usually loses some aspect of its independence, in a tactical cooperation both parties remain fully autonomous. In one sense, of course, Al Qaeda members in Iran were clearly not independent— they were held in detention, unable to leave the country as they pleased. As far as their cooperation is concerned, however, there is no evidence to suggest that either party transferred resources to the other or shared command and control functions. On the contrary, their mutual distrust, as further discussed below, strengthened the parties' determination to maintain their full independence.

VARIETY OF COOPERATIVE ACTIVITIES

As I argued in chapter 4, we can further distinguish high-end forms of cooperation from a low-end form of cooperation in terms of the variety of cooperative activities in which the parties engage. Parties in a strategic alliance, and certainly groups that have conducted a formal merger, co-operate in all the main domains: ideological, logistical, and operational. In contrast, the relationship between entities engaged in tactical or transactional collaboration rarely extends over this full spectrum.

The relations examined in this chapter confirm this proposition. Cooperative activities of the Al Qaeda camp and Iran/Hizballah have been limited to the logistical, and possibly the operational domain, but no more. Western officials have concluded much the same. In June 2002, for example, intelligence officials quoted in the *Washington Post* said that Hizballah and Al Qaeda teamed up for logistics and training in a relationship that was "ad hoc and tactical," involving "mid- and low-level operatives" and including "coordination on explosives and tactics training, money laundering, weapons smuggling and acquiring forged documents."[92]

Thus, based on the known and openly available evidence, cooperation between Iran and Al Qaeda has been mainly logistical. It included Iran's provision of material and financial support to Al Qaeda and associated groups such as the EIJ in the pre- and post-9/11 period, as well as provision of a safe haven, travel assistance, and training after 9/11. Insofar as some of these activities may have directly supported acts of terrorism carried out by Al Qaeda, the cooperation may have extended to the operational domain, but there is no evidence to suggest systematic cooperation of this kind.[93]

On the other hand, ideological cooperation between the parties has been out of the question because of their incompatible worldviews. Furthermore, any cooperation at the ideological level runs the risk of alienating the parties' respective constituencies. Thus, for example, after Ayman al-Zawahiri, then deputy leader of Al Qaeda, invited journalists and jihadists to pose questions to him via main jihadi web forums in December of 2007, many jihadists asked Zawahiri to explain why Al Qaeda had so far failed to attack Iran.[94]

Not only is ideological cooperation between the two camps off the table, but both sides have tried to "downplay the depth and nature of the relationship," as Daniel Byman has noted, "because antagonism on both sides is considerable."[95] Besides losing the confidence of its supporters, Al Qaeda would also run the risk of alienating potential donors if the relationship with Iran was to be revealed. Iran, too, has had an interest in keeping its relationship with Al Qaeda quiet. Many Shiites would loathe the idea of a powerful Shiite-majority country collaborating with militant organization of Sunni persuasion.

IDEOLOGICAL AFFINITY

While it is likely that two given entities involved in terrorism and cooperating with each other share a common worldview, tactical cooperative engagements distinguish themselves from high-end forms of cooperation in that there is no requirement for the groups to see eye to eye in ideological terms. The relationship between Iran and Al Qaeda, and their respective proxies and affiliates, is perhaps the paradigmatic example of the fact that tactical cooperation allows the partners ideological flexibility.

Jihadis have an endemic religious quarrel with the Shia, with direct strategic consequences for relations between these sects. In recent years, Sunni rebel groups, including several jihadist groups among them, found themselves fighting a Shiite coalition in Syria, where the Alawite regime of Bashar al-Assad is propped by Iran and Hizballah.[96]

Nowhere have the Sunni-Shiite tensions found a more striking expression than in post-2003 Iraq, where the insurgency waged against the U.S. occupation forces and the Shiite government established after the collapse of the Baath party produced some of the most bloody sectarian violence in modern memory.[97] In mid-January 2004 American officials obtained a detailed proposal directed at senior leaders of Al Qaeda and believed to hail from then-AQI leader Abu Musab al-Zarqawi. In the seventeen-page letter, found on a CD seized in a Baghdad safe house, Zarqawi asked the Al Qaeda leadership for help in waging a "sectarian war" in Iraq. Zarqawi said the extremists failed to mobilize sufficient support inside Iraq and failed to rout the U.S. forces. The document suggested that a counterattack be waged against the Shia community in Iraq, a step that would rally Sunni Arabs to the religious extremists. "The solution, and only God knows, is that we need to bring the Shia into the battle," the letter read. "It is the only way to prolong the duration of the fight between the infidels and us. If we succeed in dragging them into a sectarian war, this will awaken the sleepy Sunnis who are fearful of destruction and death" at the hands of the Shia.[98] Zarqawi promised the Al Qaeda leaders that "if you agree . . . and are convinced of the idea of killing the perverse sects, we stand ready as an army for you to work under your guidance and yield to your command."[99] In future letters, Zarqawi confirmed his repugnance for the Shia. In one dated June 15, 2004, to bin Laden, for instance, Zarqawi referred to the Shia as "the lurking serpent, the cunning and vicious scorpion, the waylaying enemy, and the deadly poison."[100]

The Islamic State has carried on Zarqawi's legacy of Shia hatred, and in the summer of 2015 targeted Shia mosques in Kuwait in Saudi Arabia to "to rid the Arab peninsula of all the 'polytheists' and 'rejectionists.'"[101] In an audio message released in November 2014, its self-styled caliph, Abu Bakr al-Baghdadi, called upon the newly formed Islamic State to "deal with the *rafidah* [a derogatory term for Shia] first, wherever you find them. . . . Dismember their limbs. Snatch them as groups and individuals. Embitter their lives."[102] According to Toby Matthiesen, the Islamic State targets Shiites in order to fuel sectarian strife, trying to push them toward Iran in order to gain the support of more Sunnis in return.[103] Meanwhile, the civil war in Yemen has led to repeated clashes between Iranian-backed Houthi rebels on the one hand and AQAP on the other, and the Yemen's Islamic State branch has targeted Houthi mosques such as the al Balili mosque in Sanaa on September 24, 2015.[104]

Despite this troubled history, the Al Qaeda-Iran connection demonstrates, as the 9/11 Commission put it, that "Sunni-Shia divisions did not necessarily pose an insurmountable barrier to cooperation in terrorist operations."[105] There are several reasons for this. First, despite their enmity, the parties share some common interests. Al Qaeda and Hizballah, for example, are united by a common hatred of the United States, which they accuse of being responsible for the humiliation of Islam, as well as by a common opposition to Israel's existence. As Bernard Haykel has pointed out, both Hizballah and Al Qaeda have come to the realization that "wide appeal cannot be generated from ideological sectarianism. It can only be generated by spectacular and effective attacks against Western and/or Israeli targets."[106]

Second, even within the global jihad movement, the degree of hatred of the Shiites varies, and there is an ongoing debate over the extent to which Shiites should be legitimate targets. As Haykel explains, Al Qaeda is the product of two ideological and religious streams that are often in tension with each other, especially over the treatment of the Shiites. The first is the Muslim Brotherhood; the second is the more puritan Salafi stream. It is only the Salafis, however, who believe that hatred of Shiism is a condition for being a good Muslim. The Muslim Brotherhood, in contrast, has "continuously stressed Muslim unity and opposed delving into intra-Muslim differences for fear of weakening the effort to establish a state in which the sharia is implemented."[107] This trend of peaceful relations with the Shia dates back to Hassan al-Banna, the founder of the Muslim Brotherhood, and it "persisted with Sayyid Qutb, the godfather of all of [the Muslim Brotherhood's] radical and militant offshoots."[108] The Shiites, Haykel notes, simply do not appear on Qutb's list of the "enemies of Islam that must be fought."[109]

Third, Al Qaeda and its affiliates and Iran/Hizballah are able to cooperate because their mutual ideological antagonism is trumped by pragmatism. By granting Al Qaeda access to Iran, for example, Iranian elements may have identified a potential source of income or an opportunity to recruit some jihadists as agents who could be used in various operations. Byman reasons that cooperation affords Iran "options for possible or even unforeseen contingencies."[110] Iran may thus have calculated that a presence of Al Qaeda members on its territory would allow it to "hedge its bets" against the United States, as Kenneth Pollack has argued. After the U.S.-led invasion of Iraq, fearing that it might be the next target, Iran could employ Al Qaeda members on its territory to lash out against the United States as punishment for its actions. Iran may have also utilized Al Qaeda to stir up trouble in advance of a possible attack on Iran, in order to signal the high costs that such an attack would incur.[111]

It is also likely that members of the IRGC, the MOIS, and other Iranian agencies in charge of relations with Al Qaeda calculated that holding Al Qaeda members would provide Iran leverage against Al Qaeda's striking Iran. As letters found in bin Laden's safe house show, these calculations were accurate.[112] By holding senior members of Al Qaeda in captivity, Iran did in fact protect itself from Al Qaeda attacks, even in the face of open calls by Al Qaeda members asking the group to strike the despised Shiite-majority state. Thus, a letter sent by Zawahiri to Zarqawi chastised the former head of AQI for targeting Shiites, while confirming Al Qaeda's inhibitions to strike at the country that holds many of its members captive:

> And why kill ordinary Shia considering that they are forgiven because of their ignorance? And what loss will befall us if we did not attack the Shia? And do the brothers forget that we have more than one hundred prisoners—many of whom are from the leadership who are wanted in their countries—in the custody of the Iranians? And even if we attack the Shia out of necessity, then why do you announce this matter and make it public, which compels the Iranians to take counter measures? And do the brothers forget that both we and the Iranians need to refrain from harming each other at this time in which the Americans are targeting us?[113]

Al Qaeda's calculations in cooperating with Iran and Hizballah were similarly pragmatic. Iran was a convenient safe haven when it opened its doors to jihadists in the aftermath of the 9/11 attacks, and it also served as a shield against aggressive U.S. counterterrorism efforts.[114] As a declared enemy of the United States, Iran was unlikely to meet any U.S. requests to arrest or extradite suspected Al Qaeda members. Al Qaeda members would also enjoy protection from drone strikes, as the United States would clearly refrain from acts of targeted killings on the soil of a country that would view these strikes as an act of war. In addition, Iran's geographic location, between Iraq and Afghanistan, and next to the Gulf, Pakistan, Turkey, and other countries with an important jihadist presence or other strategic opportunities, offers Al Qaeda additional strategic advantages.

Communication between leaders of Jaysh al-Islam, a Gaza-based jihadi group, and bin Laden's trusted emissary Attiyah offers a more recent example of Al Qaeda's pragmatism. In a letter written in the fall of 2006, the representative of Jaysh al-Islam asked Attiyah whether it was permissible for the group to receive funds from Iran, "in exchange for which we are to work with them and participate jointly in qualitative operations."[115] In his response, Attiyah wrote that the Prophet Muhammad himself and his companions "ate of the food and gifts of Jews and other infidels, and they did not ask them [about the nature by which they were obtained]."[116] He further states that Iran is "to us an infidel state, and accepting monies from infidel states and kings is permitted, in and of itself, unless another prohibiting factor arises."[117]

LEVEL OF TRUST

Since tactical cooperative relationships involve actors who have only logistical or operational interests in common, while possibly also having opposing long-term goals steeped in different worldviews, such relationships can be marked by open distrust between the parties. Recently declassified letters seized from bin Laden's hideout in Abbottabad provide a window into the deep mistrust that Al Qaeda leaders harbor vis-à-vis the Iranians. In a letter from bin Laden to his confidante Attiyah dated late May 2010, for example, bin Laden referred to some jihadists who had been recently released from custody in Iran and said that these former detainees "should be warned on the importance of getting rid of everything they received from Iran, like baggage or anything, even as small as a needle, as there are eavesdropping chips that are developed to be so small that they can even be put inside a medical syringe; and since the Iranians are not to be trusted then it is possible to plant chips in some of the coming people's belongings."[118] In another letter presumably written by Attiyah to Osama bin Laden and dated November 24, 2010, Attiyah confirmed that when bin Laden's wife, referred to as "Um Hamzah," was informed by the authorities that she could leave Iran, she was briefed about not taking any belongings with her, for fear that the Iranians may have installed listening devices in them. Attiyah even informed bin Laden that Um Hamzah's teeth were filled under the "supervision of a doctor who is associated" with the captors of bin Laden's wife. Although Attiyah doubted that "there would be anything [in the fillings]," he said that he wanted to report the situation to bin Laden "in order for you to be aware and we can consult when need be."[119] Clearly concerned, bin Laden wrote to his wife, telling her to report to him "about anything that bothers you about any hospital in Iran or any suspicions . . . about chips planted in any way. . . . One of the ways, the syringe can be of the same size, but its head is slightly bigger than normal, that way, as I previously mentioned to you, they can insert a small chip in it to implant under the skin."[120] Adding that "the size of the chip is about the length of a grain of wheat and the width of a fine piece of vermicelli," bin Laden said that he needed "to know the date you had the filling, also about any surgery you had, even if it was only a quick pinch."[121]

Any possibility for trust to develop between the parties appears to have been further undermined by the off-and-on nature of their communication. In a letter to bin Laden dated June 11, 2009, Attiyah complained about the Iranians, saying that "the criminals," as he referred to them, "did not send any messages to us, and they did not talk to any of the brothers about [the release of Al Qaeda members from Iran]. . . . Of course, this is nothing strange coming from them; in fact, this is their mentality and method. They don't want to show that they are negotiating with us or reacting to our pressure."[122]

The tension between the parties has also come to the fore in instances in which they apparently tried to outdo each other in terms of their anti-Americanism. In September 2011, when then-President Mahmoud Ahmadinejad gave a speech at the United Nations in which he said that the U.S. government, not Al Qaeda, was responsible for the 9/11 attacks, Al

Qaeda's partner in Yemen responded angrily. In the English-language magazine *Inspire*, published by AQAP, one Abu Suhail labeled the Iranian charge "ridiculous. . . . If Iran was genuine in its animosity towards the United States," he added, "it would be pleased to see another entity striking a blow at the Great Satan but that's not the case. For Iran, anti-Americanism is merely a game of politics. . . . Iran and the Shi'a in general do not want to give Al Qaeda credit for the greatest and biggest operation ever committed against America because this would expose their lip-service against [*sic*] the Great Satan."[123]

* * *

The above discussion has shown that the cooperative relationship between Al Qaeda and Iran fits the pattern of a tactical cooperation as described in chapter 4. Alternating between periods of more or less intensive cooperation interrupted by periods of tension, the relationship, as Director of National Intelligence James Clapper has memorably described it, is like a "longstanding . . . shotgun marriage."[124] Despite their divergent ideological and strategic objectives, both Al Qaeda and Iran identified, at various moments in their shared history, tactical or operational interests that could be advanced by mutual cooperation and were important enough to override any doctrinal reservations that could hinder cooperation. Indeed, despite deep ideological antagonisms that preclude a strategic alliance from forming, both sides have been keen on advancing their interests even if these fly in the face of core ideological or doctrinal beliefs.

9
NETWORKED COOPERATION

From Bojinka to the Sharia4 Movement

T HE FINAL CHAPTER of this book is devoted to illustrating the concept of networked cooperation, an underexplored yet increasingly important type of cooperation involving at least one informal actor. In chapter 4, I introduced five different variants of networked cooperation, each featuring a different constellation of cooperating agents. Accordingly, the present chapter is divided into five sections reflecting these variants.

The first case study illustrates cooperation between two terrorist entrepreneurs by focusing on the so-called Bojinka plot—a plan to detonate over ten U.S. airliners over the Pacific Ocean in the mid-1990s. The plot was hatched in tandem by two of the most notorious terrorist entrepreneurs of modern history, namely Khaled Sheikh Muhammad (KSM) and his nephew Ramzi Youssef. The pair is best known for masterminding the 9/11 attacks and the 1993 World Trade Center bombings, respectively.

The second case study, which illustrates cooperation between a terrorist entrepreneur and a formal terrorist organization, demonstrates how the 9/11 attacks exemplify this variant through the respective roles played by KSM and Al Qaeda.

The remaining three case studies of this chapter involve informal networks and center on the figure of Anjem Choudary and the broader Sharia4 movement he helped spawn. The discussion reveals the elusive nature of cooperation between an increasingly complex array of actors that at times produces terrorism, but more often does not cross the threshold to terrorist violence. The discussion also sheds light on how structural factors described in chapter 3—ideology, the Internet, and contemporary conflict environments—afford new opportunities to these diverse actors to cooperate more often, more easily, with more actors, and arguably to greater effect. The implications of these findings will be discussed in greater detail in the book's concluding chapter.

NETWORKED COOPERATION VARIANT 1: THE BOJINKA PLOT

Networked cooperation Variant 1 describes terrorist collaboration centering on two terrorist entrepreneurs—that is, two independently minded, highly motivated, and resourceful individuals dedicated to exploiting existing opportunities and seeking novel ways to plan, execute, or support acts of terrorism. In the context of the global jihad movement, it is difficult to find two individuals to whom the moniker "terrorist entrepreneur" can be more appropriately applied than Khalid Sheikh Mohammed (KSM) and Ramzi Youssef. In 1994 and 1995, KSM and Youssef were at the center of a conspiracy known as the Bojinka plot (also known as Oplan Bojinka or the Manila Air Plot), which is examined here.

Khalid Sheikh Mohammed, the mastermind of the 9/11 attacks, fits the description of a terrorist entrepreneur so well that the authors of the *9/11 Commission Report* described him as a terrorist entrepreneur par excellence.[1] Evidence of his independent mindedness can be gleaned from the fact that for most of the 1990s he resisted formally joining Al Qaeda.[2] The *9/11 Commission Report* further describes KSM as a capable terrorist mastermind, steeped in technical and managerial skills and with an ability to generate ideas. KSM was experienced, highly motivated, and did not shy away from getting his own hands dirty. He had honed his terrorist skills years before 9/11 in a number of attacks, such as car and aircraft bombings, assassinations, hijackings, and poisonings.[3] He also carried out attacks himself, including the 2002 beheading of *Wall Street Journal* reporter Daniel Pearl.[4]

The career of Abdul Basit Mahmoud Abdul Karim, better known as Ramzi Youssef, closely paralleled that of KSM. Youssef was a Kuwaiti-born son of a Pakistani father of Balochi extraction who was married to KSM's sister. Youssef had done well in school, particularly in mathematics, physics, and chemistry. As a teenager, he became fascinated with chemicals and later studied electrical engineering in Wales.[5] He later turned his passion to sinister ends, undergoing training as a bomb maker at bin Laden–funded camps,[6] and then ended up pursuing a career as a master terrorist with a "dark and grandiose imagination."[7] In 1993, he master-minded the first World Trade Center bombing, which killed six people and injured more than a thousand others. Afterward, FBI investigators concluded that the van that Youssef detonated underneath the North Tower contained the "largest improvised explosive device the bureau had ever encountered."[8] Youssef's plan had been to make the North Tower collapse onto the South Tower; to that end, he had parked the rented Ford van in the southeast corner of the garage. He hoped that the collapsing Twin Towers would bury 250,000 people—a number he believed would reflect that of Palestinians suffering from America's support for Israel.[9]

True to form for a terrorist entrepreneur, Youssef worked on improving his skills after the 1993 World Trade Center bombing and prior to the Bojinka plot. Immersing himself in texts on chemistry and explosives, he became particularly interested in producing bombs out of objects that seemed innocuous and could easily pass airport security—objects such as wrist watches that could be used as timers and contact lens solution bottles holding liquid components for nitroglycerine.

The Bojinka plot originated as a result of cooperation between Youssef and his uncle KSM. Most of the planning for the plot occurred in 1994, after Youssef had gained notoriety for the bombing in New York. Inspired by the sudden fame of his nephew, KSM decided that he, too, would de-vote his efforts to strike at the United States—a country that he, like his nephew, despised because of its pro-Israel stance. This was the first time that KSM took an active part in plotting an act of terrorism, although it was not the first time he had cooperated with Youssef. In late November 1992, he had wired $660 to an accomplice of his nephew to help fund the 1993 World Trade Center bombing.[10]

The Bojinka plot consisted of three phases of attacks, all to be carried out within a short time period. The first was the assassination of Pope John Paul II, which was scheduled for January 15, 1995, when the pope was visiting the Philippines as part of the 1995 World Youth Day celebrations. According to the plan, a suicide bomber was to dress up as a priest and detonate himself as the pope's motorcade proceeded to San Carlos Seminary in Makati City.

The second, and more ambitious, phase of the Bojinka plot involved what prosecutors later called wreaking "48 hours of terror in the sky."[11] KSM's and Youssef's scheme was to detonate eleven improvised explosive devices hidden in as many U.S. commercial airliners in midflight. To that end, a cell of five members—consisting of KSM, Youssef, and three co-conspirators, would board U.S. flag aircraft operating on routes in Southeast Asia and heading for the United States, with a stopover en route. Each attacker was to board a separate airliner and assemble an explosive device in midair during the first leg of his respective flight. He would then set the timer for the detonator so that the device would explode during the second leg of each flight. Then attackers would board additional flights to other destinations and follow the same steps again. In preparation of the bombing of the commercial airlines, Youssef and KSM acquired detailed flight data on the relevant flights, including departing times, flight durations, and aircraft type, and cased target flights to Hong Kong and Seoul that had continuing legs to cities in the United States. They also rented several apartments in Manila, where Youssef and other cell members prepared the explosive devices,[12] which were then tested on the ground and in the air.

On December 1, 1994, an Afghan co-conspirator of the Bojinka plot acting on behalf of Youssef, Wali Khan Amin Shah, placed a bomb under a seat of the Greenbelt Theater in Manila, to be detonated by Youssef's newly invented digital watch timer. Several patrons were injured in the bombing.[13] Following up by testing the assembly of an explosive device in mid-air, Youssef boarded Philippine Airlines Flight 434 from Manila to Tokyo, with a stopover in Cebu, on December 11, 1994. During the first leg of the flight, Youssef built a bomb in the lavatory, using liquid explosives concealed in a contact lens solution bottle with a cotton ball stabilizing agent and a timer in the form of a wristwatch, and left the bomb inside the life jacket under his seat before disembarking at Cebu. Youssef's bomb detonated as planned, four hours after he left the airplane. The blast occurred over Okinawa, killing a Japanese businessman who was in the seat that Yousef had previously occupied, and injuring five additional passengers. The blast damaged the aircraft's hydraulic system, but the pilot was able to perform an emergency landing in Okinawa that saved the remaining 272 passengers. In an attempt to minimize the amount of attention the bombing would spark—his goal had been merely to test the functionality of his new device—Youssef had decided to use a small charge that would not destroy the entire aircraft. Even though the aircraft did not crash, Youssef was nevertheless surprised by the severity of the damage.[14] Following the blast, Youssef telephoned the Associated Press in Manila, claiming that the attack had been carried out by Abu Sayyaf. As a long-time friend and co-conspirator of Youssef later told the police, it was Youssef who had made the call "as part of a long-term cooperation arrangement" between him and the Philippine jihadist group.[15]

In building the devices, Youssef had synthesized triacetonetriperoxide (TATP) and nitroglycerin—both highly sensitive explosives that terrorists had not dared carry onto an airplane before.[16] According to Daniel Benjamin and Steven Simon, "The overall assembly was an unrivaled piece of terrorist tradecraft: with only negligible amounts of metal and no high-density materials, it would be all but impossible to detect using any existing security system."[17] Luckily, however, this phase of the Bojinka Plot never came to pass, nor did the assassination of Pope John Paul II.

On January 6, 1995, about two weeks before the attacks were to take place, a fire broke out in the apartment on Quirino Avenue where Youssef and Abdul Hakim Murad—an old school friend who had earlier assisted with the 1993 plot to blow up the World Trade Center—had mixed chemicals for the preparation of the bombs. Thanks to a suspicious policewoman, officers arrived soon after the fire was extinguished to investigate the scene. They found bomb instruction manuals, a foot-long pipe bomb with a Casio wristwatch timer, and a "cornucopia of explosive ingredients" among other incriminating information.[18] In the bedroom, the police found Bibles, crucifixes, and pictures of Pope John Paul II, as well as additional Casio timers.[19] It was not difficult to conclude that the apartment had been a bomb factory and that its inhabitants had conspired to target the pontiff, who was scheduled to pass on his motorcade just hundreds of yards away from the apartment within a few weeks.

The police also seized a laptop computer and several diskettes belonging to Ramzi Youssef, and it was the analysis of that electronic information that revealed to the investigators the full scale of the cell's mission and future plans. Of particular interest to the investigators were the contents in a file on Youssef's computer labeled "Bojinka." The document detailed the plans to detonate up to a dozen airliners over the Pacific Ocean, which, U.S. investigators later assessed, could have cost the lives of 4,000 people.[20] The document used code names for the five cell members who were to place the bombs on the planes. It also discussed additional long-term goals, including plans to "hit all U.S. nuclear targets."[21]

That same night, Murad, a Pakistani by origin who was supposed to take part in the second phase of the Bojinka plot, was arrested and then held in custody for the next six weeks.[22] Undergoing interrogation, Murad was pressed to explain why he had attended flight school and had a pilot's license. Murad admitted that it was for the third phase of the Bojinka plot, in which he was to conduct a suicide attack on CIA headquarters by crash-landing a small, explosives-laden airplane on the agency's premises in Langley, Virginia. Murad further confessed that the cell had planned to strike additional targets, including the Pentagon, Congress, and the White House, but had not trained enough pilots yet.[23] This suicide mission targeting CIA headquarters—the third phase of the Bojinka plot—foreshadowed the 9/11 attacks. During the ensuing years, KSM would continue to refine the design of this plan and develop it into a full-scale proposal that he would present to bin Laden as the "planes operation."[24]

While two highly determined, ingenious terrorist entrepreneurs were at the center of the Bojinka plot, it was in fact a complex undertaking that defied simplistic explanations. Thus, Philippine investigators believed that the Abu Sayyaf organization provided some logistical support to Youssef and may have offered to provide operatives for the plan.[25] According to Zachary Abuza, a leading authority on jihadist groups in Southeast Asia, more than fifteen individuals had some knowledge of the Bojinka Plot. Besides Youssef and KSM, the main members of the cell included Wali Khan Amin Shah, an associate of Osama bin Laden whose main role was to manage the cell's finances and provide logistical support; Murad, the Pakistani, Kuwait-born childhood friend and apprentice of Youssef's who helped assemble the devices in the latter's apartment; and Adel Annon, suspected to be a brother of Youssef's. In addition, several individuals served roles as financial conduits for the cell, including Munir Ibrahim, a wealthy Saudi Arabian from Jeddah, and Amein Mohammed, a Pakistani who helped Wali Khan establish a firm in Malaysia called Konsojaya, which was used to funnel money to the cell. One of the individuals who served on the board of Konsojaya was Riduan bin Isumuddin, better known as Hambali, who was the military leader of Indonesian jihadist group Jemaah Islamiya. Besides Konsojaya, Yousef and Wali Khan created a second shell company known as the Bermuda Trading Company, which served as a cover to purchase chemicals.[26] Five days after the fire in Youssef's apartment, the police arrested Shah, who disclosed under interrogation that he had links with the Abu Sayyaf group as well as Mohammed Jamal Khalifa, a Saudi Arabian businessman and brother-in-law of Osama bin Laden, who was also tied to Murad.

Philippine investigators eventually came to believe that the Bojinka plot was funded by Osama bin Laden.[27] One of the clues was found through Wali Khan Amin Shah, who lived in an apartment linked to cell phone numbers found on the hard drive of Ramzi Youssef's computer. Wali Khan, the financial officer of the cell, regularly laundered incoming funds using bank accounts belonging to his girlfriend and other local women. Wali Khan admitted under interrogation that he funneled the money to Youssef via Omar abu Omar, a Syrian employee at the International Islamic Relief

Organization (IIRO). The IIRO, a charity widely believed to have served as a front for the financing of terrorism, was run by Muhammad Jamal Khalifa, a Saudi businessman and a brother-in-law of Osama bin Laden who at one point was bin Laden's closest friend.[28] Khalifa's business card was found in the apartment on Quirino Street, and it was Khalifa who had paid for the rent of that apartment.[29] Khalifa was tied to several jihadist organizations in the Philippines, including Abu Sayyaf and the Moro Islamic Liberation Front (MILF), as well as to Jemaah Islamiya (JI) in Indonesia and jihadist organizations in Malaysia.

NETWORKED COOPERATION VARIANT 2: THE PLANNING OF THE 9/11 ATTACKS

This variant, which involves cooperation between a terrorist entrepreneur and a formal terrorist or insurgent organization, is exemplified by he 9/11 attacks, which were an outcome of cooperation between terrorist entrepreneur KSM and the Al Qaeda organization.[30] Although much has been written about the planning of the 9/11 attacks, the brief reexamination of this case is valuable for two reasons. First, while existing studies tend to depict these strikes as an Al Qaeda Central plot, the present case study highlights the critical role of terrorist cooperation, which was a necessary condition for the success of the 9/11 attacks. Second, this case is important because it demonstrates particularly well that the quality of a cooperative relationship does not necessarily remain static, but can evolve over time—a key insight of the holistic typology introduced in chapter 4. In the case of KSM and Al Qaeda, their relations changed over time from a low-end to a high-end form of cooperation.

KSM's 1996 proposal to bin Laden regarding the "planes operation" was no less spectacular than his plans for the Bojinka plot. He envisioned hijacking ten aircraft and then crashing them into targets on both U.S. coasts. KSM's initial targets included the World Trade Center, the Pentagon, Congress, the CIA's and the FBI's headquarters, nuclear power plants, and the tallest buildings in California and the state of Washington. KSM himself intended to land the tenth plane on a U.S. airport, kill all adult male passengers on board, and hold a press conference before the assembled media in which he would denounce U.S. support for Israel, Arab governments, and the Philippines.[31]

When KSM made his initial proposal to bin Laden in mid-1996, he believed that the Al Qaeda leader would be receptive to it because he was "in the process of consolidating his new position in Afghanistan while hearing out others' ideas, and had not yet settled on an agenda for future anti-U.S. operations."[32] In hindsight, it is also clear that what enabled KSM to approach bin Laden in the first place were the innovative organizational attributes of Al Qaeda.[33] Chief among these were bin Laden's very openness to accepting proposals for terrorist attacks from a variety of jihadi entrepreneurs. This openness is not a matter of course for terrorist groups; for reasons that include operational security, they usually prefer to keep operational planning in house. Al Qaeda, however, has never been an ordinary terrorist organization. More so than other groups, it had internalized modern forms of business management such as a flat organizational structure and flexible strategy, and as Bruce Hoffman observes, bin Laden's leadership style was similar to that of a president or CEO of a large multinational corporation, with responsibilities including strategic guidance, as well as defining specific goals and overseeing their implementation. At the same time, however, bin Laden also "operated as a venture capitalist: soliciting ideas from below, encouraging creative approaches and 'out of the box' thinking, and providing funding to those proposals he [thought] promising."[34]

Bin Laden eventually agreed to KSM's proposal, but only after limiting the plan to striking targets on the East Coast, as well as shedding KSM's grandiose vision of steering the last plane himself and giving an interview to the world media in which he would explain the motives of the attacks.[35] Bin Laden agreed to provide funding, and he would select the hijackers. He also invited KSM to pledge *bayah*, which would turn him into a formal Al Qaeda member. For the time being, however, KSM was keen on retaining his independence. He told U.S. interrogators years later that he wished to reserve for himself the option to work with other jihadist groups—a fact that underscores the need to view KSM as a terrorist agent separate from Al Qaeda, and the 9/11 attacks as the result of cooperation between two distinct terrorist agents.

The success of the 9/11 attacks was due in part to the highly complementary skill set that KSM and bin Laden brought to the table. KSM possessed significant technical and managerial skills, and he was an avid idea generator. Yosri Fouda, an investigative reporter for Al Jazeera who interviewed KSM in 2002, later said that KSM "likes being on top of a certain operation, directing people here and there, thinking of targets and stuff. . . . It doesn't surprise me [that KSM organized 9/11]. It's not exactly bin Laden's territory. He's not very fond of details."[36] That is not to say, however, that bin Laden's role was marginal. On the contrary, bin Laden's input was no less critical, given that he selected the operatives for the attack and funded the operation. Moreover, it was thanks to bin Laden's unique leadership skills that the plans to conduct the 9/11 attacks were implemented. Bin Laden had to contend with significant objections to the 9/11 attack plans from the Taliban and his own ranks. Critically, however, he insisted that the operation go forward despite the dissent.[37]

Bin Laden's ability to make difficult decisions was also critical to the success of the 9/11 plots. KSM told interrogators that bin Ladin "could assess new trainees very quickly, in about ten minutes, and that many of the 9/11 hijackers were selected in this manner."[38] Thus, it was with a "remarkable" speed that bin Laden selected the German cell members Marwan al-Shehhi, Ziad Jarrah, and Ramzi Binalshibh, as well as Muhammad Atta, who was designated the operational leader of the team. "They had not yet met with KSM when all this occurred," the *9/11 Commission Report*'s authors marveled.[39] The report further states that the Al Qaeda leader, with the help of Muhammad Atef, Al Qaeda's operations chief, personally selected all the future muscle hijackers, asking each one to swear *bayah* to him.[40] In addition to his decisiveness, bin Laden was also pragmatic, as is apparent from his reducing KSM's original megalomaniacal plan to hijack ten planes to the more realistic plot eventually executed on 9/11.[41] According to reports from KSM's interrogation, bin Laden had not only been worried about the initial plan's scale and complexity, but also had to weigh these plans against other proposals for terrorist and insurgent strikes that Al Qaeda kept receiving.[42] Furthermore, bin Laden was also shrewd enough to outsource most of the operational planning of the 9/11 attacks to KSM. This long-standing, innovative practice of the Al Qaeda leader is known as "centralization of decision and decentralization of execution."[43] According to this principle, which has an equivalent known as "mission command" in military organizations, bin Laden "decided on the targets, selected the leaders, and provided at least some of the funding. After that, the planning of the operation and the method of attack were left to the men who would have the responsibility of carrying it out."[44]

Ultimately, what this management style meant for the planning and execution of terrorist attacks was that Al Qaeda's "worldwide terrorist operations relied heavily on the ideas and work of enterprising and strong-willed field commanders who enjoyed considerable autonomy,"[45] as the *9/11 Commission Report* put it. Both KSM, the mastermind of the 9/11 attacks, and Muhammad Atta, the field commander and lead hijacker, enjoyed such autonomy in carrying out the mission.

As the originator of the plot, KSM naturally played an important role in overseeing the execution of the "planes operation." Atta was chosen by bin Laden directly to become the tactical commander of the group, and bin Laden met with him on several occasions to provide him with instructions, including an initial list of targets.[46] According to KSM, Atta was "the only 9/11 hijacker who knew the entire scope of the operation from the outset"—which means that information about the 9/11 plan was strictly compartmentalized.[47] His role was to finalize the operational decisions of the attack. He reported to KSM and bin Laden through an intermediary, Ramzi Binalshibh.[48] Meanwhile, KSM also helped train some of the future hijackers. Following initial training at the Mes Aynak camp in Afghanistan, several of the initially selected team members traveled to Karachi, Pakistan, where KSM took over, teaching the future hijackers basic English words and phrases, as well as how to read phone books, interpret airline timetables, use the Internet, use code words in communications, make travel reservations, and rent an apartment. One of the recruits later reported that they also used flight simulator computer games in order to familiarize themselves with aircraft models and functions and identify security holes. They also viewed videos that featured hijacking scenes. Another topic of discussion was surveillance, with KSM recommending that the team "watch the cabin doors at takeoff and landing, to observe whether the captain went to the lavatory during the flight, and to note whether the flight attendants brought food into the cockpit."[49] An additional important skill they were taught was to avoid drawing attention to themselves.[50]

In hindsight, the cooperation between KSM and the Al Qaeda organization, led by Osama bin Laden, appears to have been crucial for the successful implementation of the attacks of September 11, 2001. The above case study sheds important light on the ability of terrorist entrepreneurs and formal organizations to boost their mutual capacity through cooperation, with devastating consequences. As mentioned above, however, the analysis of the cooperative relationship between KSM and Al Qaeda is also illuminating for another reason, namely the dynamic nature of terrorist cooperation.

As information gleaned from the *9/11 Commission Report* suggests, the quality of the relationship between KSM and the Al Qaeda organization was far from static, and instead spanned across the entire spectrum of collaboration, gradually evolving from low-end to high-end forms of cooperation. Thus, the *9/11 Commission Report* states that when KSM visited Sudan in mid-1995, at a time when bin Laden was present in the country, KSM's attempts to meet bin Laden did not bear fruit. However, he did manage to meet with Mohammed Atef (a.k.a. Abu Hafs al-Masri), Al Qaeda's then-military chief, who "gave [KSM] a contact in Brazil."[51] Although few additional details are disclosed in the report, there is no evidence to suggest that at this point the relationship between Al Qaeda and KSM was anything more than transactional. Additionally, bin Laden, as has been suggested earlier, may have been involved in funding the Bojinka plot through his associate and brother-in-law, Muhammad Jamal Khalifa, but there is no conclusive evidence to support this.

Roughly a year later, in mid-1996, KSM first approached bin Laden with the plan that would eventually become the 9/11 attacks. At that time, the *9/11 Commission Report* states that KSM and bin Laden "did not yet enjoy an especially close working relationship," although bin Laden was clearly intrigued by KSM and asked him to formally join Al Qaeda, which KSM declined.[52] At this point, the relationship involved greater interaction between KSM and the Al Qaeda organization, as well as the prospect for more intensive cooperation in the long run. For example, KSM "ma[de] himself useful, collecting news articles and helping other al Qaeda members with their outdated computer equipment."[53] In effect, the relationship was evolving from a transactional to a tactical form of cooperation.

Around mid-1998, it evolved even further. Following Al Qaeda's double suicide bombings targeted at the U.S. embassies in Nairobi and Dar-es-Salaam, KSM became convinced of bin Laden's true commitment to jihad. Bin Laden, for his part, informed KSM after the bombings that he formally accepted KSM's idea to conduct a "planes operation" targeting the United States. Subsequently, their relationship moved toward a high-end form of cooperation. As the *9/11 Commission Report* relates, "KSM then accepted Bin Ladin's standing invitation to move to Kandahar and work directly with al Qaeda. In addition to supervising the planning and preparations for the 9/11 operation, KSM worked with and eventually led al Qaeda's media committee. But KSM states he refused to swear a formal oath of allegiance to Bin Ladin, thereby retaining a last vestige of his cherished autonomy."[54] Thus, the two were now engaged in a full-fledged strategic partnership—one that is marked by some overlap in terms of command and control, given KSM's role in managing a department within the Al Qaeda organization. Then, when KSM did finally pledge allegiance to bin Laden at some point in late 1998 or 1999,[55] their relationship became a de-facto merger that subsumed KSM within the Al Qaeda organization.

NETWORKED COOPERATION VARIANT 3: ANJEM CHOUDARY AND SHARIA4BELGIUM

Networked cooperation Variant 3 reflects a growing trend of collaboration between terrorist entrepreneurs and informal networks, which is exemplified by the relationship between Anjem Choudary and Sharia4Belgium, an informal network of Salafists and jihadists based in Belgium.

Anjem Choudary is a London-born militant Salafist preacher of Pakistani origin who was sentenced on September 6, 2016, at the Old Bailey Central Criminal Court to five years and six months in prison. Choudary was found in violation of Section 12 of the United Kingdom's Terrorism Act 2000 by inviting support for a proscribed organization, the so-called Islamic State.

Choudary had a long history as a rabble-rouser with Salafist and jihadist leanings. After the London bombings of July 7, 2005, Choudary gradually became the most well known, and one of the most controversial, activists associated with the British, as well as the broader European Salafist and Jihadist scene.

As the last three case studies will show, Choudary has also been a driving force behind the creation of a variety of informal Salafist networks, both in the United Kingdom and outside of it. Furthermore, mutual cooperation between these various informal networks has become one of their defining features, and has contributed to an international "network of networks" known as the Sharia4 movement. While the repertoires of action of the Sharia4 movement are usually limited to nonviolent tactics such as sit-ins and protests, scores of movement members have made the transition to political violence. They include dozens of members who have participated in acts of terrorism in Europe and abroad, as well as foreign fighters who have traveled to regions of conflict such as Syria and Iraq to participate in a self-described militant jihad. Given Choudary's role as a key sponsor of this jihadist nexus, a report published in 2014 by the nonprofit organization HOPE Not Hate described him as the "single biggest gateway to terrorism in recent British history."[56]

The present case study—networked cooperation Variant 3, which involves collaboration between an entrepreneur and an informal network— examines the cooperative relations between Anjem Choudary and Sharia4Belgium, a Belgium-based informal jihadist network that is part of the Sharia4 movement and was charged with being a terrorist entity in 2015. The case study begins by tracing the militant Islamist trajectory of Choudary's career, starting when he was a leading member of the U.K. branch of Al-Muhajiroun (the Emigrants, AM), a Salafist and jihadist organization currently headquartered in Lebanon. Although its U.K. branch was formally banned in 2005, the group has continued to make reappearances in the United Kingdom under various guises. The case study then moves on to describe Sharia4Belgium, and examine in depth the collaborative relationship between this network and Anjem Choudary.

The rise of Anjem Choudary to jihadist stardom, especially in Britain and other parts of Europe, cannot be divorced from Al-Muhajiroun, a group founded in 1986 by Omar Bakri Mohammed, a Syrian-born Salafist preacher and activist. AM was established as a spin-off organization of Hizb ut-Tahrir (Liberation Party, HT), a secretive, cult-like Sunni pan-Islamic movement founded in 1953 in Jerusalem, which Bakri had joined in 1977. Between 1979 and 1986, Bakri lived in Saudi Arabia, where he attempted to mobilize Muslims for HT's cause of establishing a caliphate, the traditional form of Islamic governance. After ignoring HT's tradition of quiet activism and falling out with the global HT leadership, Bakri was suspended from HT in the early 1980s, but he continued to be active under the newly founded group, Al-Muhajiroun-Wilayat al-Jazira al-Arabiyya (the Emigrants, Arab Peninsula Province). In 1986, after six years in Saudi Arabia, Bakri was deported for anti-Saudi activities and then settled in London,[57] where he began organizing a local HT branch. Within four years, he succeeded in increasing the group's membership to around four hundred.[58] Bakri drew much publicity by organizing highly visible and provocative events, such as one held in Trafalgar Square in August 1995, in which he called for Queen Elizabeth to convert to Islam and promised the audience that the "black flag of Islam" would one day fly over Downing

Street.[59] Similar publicity stunts designed to draw the attention of the media would become a staple of the soon-to-be relaunched Al-Muhajiroun.

The second iteration of Al-Mujahiroun was formed in January 1996, within a few days after Bakri's resignation from HT over differences about his overt and controversial tactics. The new U.K.-based AM initially consisted of only three members, but it soon grew to become the most prominent Islamist movement in the United Kingdom, in part by attracting many disillusioned members from HT. While its formal membership consisted of less than 160 members, roughly 700 followers took weekly religious lessons with AM leaders, and the group's broader rolodex of contacts reached into the thousands. These included followers and sympathizers not only in about thirty cities and towns across the United Kingdom, but also in other countries, including Lebanon, Ireland, Pakistan, and the United States.[60] Choudary, a lawyer by training, played a key role in AM's U.K. branch by serving as Bakri's assistant.

The group set itself apart from its predecessor organization by arguing that efforts to establish the caliphate should be conducted in all countries, not only in those where success was most likely, and by favoring a more overt approach over HT's traditionally secretive form of activism. Unlike HT, AM also pronounced its active support for jihad by "hand, tongue, or heart."[61] Besides the global ambitions to establish the Islamic caliphate, Choudary also stated that AM's goals include the overthrow of the British government, using nonviolent means, and its replacement with an Islamic state ruled according to Sharia law.[62] In subsequent years, not only would AM rise up to become the most outspoken jihadist group in the United Kingdom, but its members would be linked to numerous acts of violence, including several high-profile terrorist plots in the United Kingdom and abroad. According to a report published by the Henry Jackson Society, 18 percent of all Islamic-related offences in the United Kingdom between 1998 and 2010 were linked to AM.[63] According to Joe Mulhall, a senior researcher at *HOPE Not Hate*, more than seventy people in AM's orbit have "either been convicted of planning terrorist attacks or have actually been successful,"[64] making Choudary's network a "gateway to terrorism as well as a conveyor belt for British jihad fighters abroad."[65]

Terrorists with ties to AM include Bilal Ahmed, the first British suicide bomber, who detonated himself in Kashmir in December 2000; the London bombers of July 7, 2005, Muhammad Siddique Khan and Shehzad Tanweer; Mohammed Chowdhury and other members of a cell of nine individuals connected to the so-called Christmas Bomb Plot, which envisioned a series of bombings at popular sites such as Big Ben, the London Stock Exchange, Westminster Abbey, and the London Eye; Omar Khyam, the ringleader of the so-called Fertilizer Bomb Plot, which involved plans to attack the Bluewater shopping center in Essex, the Ministry of Sound nightclub in London, and the domestic gas network; "shoe bomber" Richard Reid, who attempted to detonate a plastic explosive device hidden in his shoes aboard a flight from Paris to Miami in December 2001; and two Britons who traveled to Israel in April 2003 with plans to detonate themselves at the Mike's Place bar on the Tel Aviv beach front (one of whom succeeded).[66]

More recently, the May 2013 murder in broad daylight of a British off-duty soldier, Lee Rigby, in the streets of Woolwich, London, was carried out by two perpetrators with links to AM and Bakri. The brutality of the attack, in which two British Muslims of Nigerian descent first ran over Rigby with a car, then stabbed and hacked him to death using knives and cleavers, and then attempted to behead him, sent shockwaves throughout the United Kingdom. Choudary later admitted that one of the attackers, Michael Adebolajo, attended meetings of AM from 2005 to 2011 and "was on our ideological wave-length."[67] The other attacker, Michael Adebowale, was caught on video attending an AM-linked demonstration on Christmas Eve 2012.[68]

Shortly after the 7/7 bombings in London, AM was banned in Britain, and Bakri fled to Lebanon. Despite the official ban, however, AM continued to evolve through a steadily growing number of front groups that operated under various names, but were largely run by the same small circle of leaders who had been involved in the founding of AM. Although the front groups had, on paper, a separate leadership, the groups were now under the de facto control of Anjem Choudary. The names of the groups usually co-existed as online domains.[69]

Choudary made no secret of this cat-and-mouse game. He admitted to a British interviewer that the group uses "different platforms, as . . . the important thing is not the name, the important thing is that you plant the seeds in the heart of the people."[70] He also acknowledged that the names of various front groups, such as the Society of Muslim Lawyers, Shariah Court U.K., and Al Ghurabaa, are "all us. . . . We use different platforms depending on what we are dealing with."[71] Indeed, in a study published in 2006, Islamism scholar Quintan Wiktorowicz found at least fifty platforms connected in some form to AM and used to continue public outreach efforts.[72] These tend to adopt innocent-sounding names such as Society of Muslim Parents, Global Truth, and Peaceful Society and are "intended to facilitate movement access to public spaces," which has become more difficult since 9/11.[73] Wiktorowicz further found that these platforms were not administratively tied to AM "in the sense of shared bylaws and bureaucratic structure," but that "they are connected at the level of individual activists. The founders and leaders of the platforms are what Omar [Bakri Muhammad] terms the 'A-team' of Al-Muhajiroun—the top elite of the movement."[74]

Once Bakri left for Lebanon, Choudary took the lead of this A-team. In his upper thirties around the time of the 7/7 bombings, Choudary had served as the U.K. national leader of AM and as assistant to Bakri, who was then emir (religious leader) in the United Kingdom.[75] After Bakri's departure, Choudary assumed that role, too. Bakri, meanwhile, continued to top the hierarchy of the organization as worldwide emir of AM, based out of Lebanon.[76]

Following the ban of AM, the group initially reconstituted itself under the names Al-Ghurabaa (the Strangers) and al-Firqat un-Naajiyah (the Savior Sect, or Saved Sect). After these two groups were banned in July 2006, a new group emerged almost immediately called Ahlus Sunnah wal Jamaah (Adherents to the Sunnah and the Community). In 2009, the group, which was otherwise active mainly on the Internet, gained notoriety by staging a protest against returning British soldiers in Luton—a protest that provoked the formation of the far-right English Defence League.[77] Thereafter, Choudary attained growing prominence as a virulent Salafist rabble-rouser with a deliberately confrontational and provocative style. He has regularly condemned Western countries and the values they represent, arguing that their political and value systems, are incompatible with true Islam and will eventually be replaced by Islamic governance in accordance with Sharia law. In 2009, for instance, he said that Buckingham Palace should be turned into the seat of the new caliph. He was also behind the release of mock-up photos indicating a jihadist takeover of the "White Masjid," a thinly veiled reference to the White House. Other photos depicted the Statue of Liberty in New York harbor draped in a burqa and Choudary in front of the White House, waving a black flag of Islam.[78]

Subsequently, his name became linked to additional organizations that sprang up and focused their efforts on "street dawa," an attempt to spread Choudary's uncompromising interpretation of Islam on the streets of European cities and villages using leaflets, demonstrations, and the like. One of these newly minted entities was called Islam4UK. In early January 2010, the group announced its plans to organize a protest in Royal Wootton Bassett, a town were public mourning is held for corteges of U.K. armed forces personnel killed in active duty. Islam4UK planned to have five hundred group members carry black coffins to represent the thousands of Muslims killed "in the name of democracy and freedom."[79] The outcry among the broader population was enormous, and Choudary later admitted that the plans were a publicity stunt.[80]

Islam4UK was proscribed in due course, but a new group under Choudary's leadership surfaced soon thereafter called Muslims Against Crusades (MAC). Combining militant Islamist ideologies with a tendency to provoke, MAC announced its plans to establish independent Islamic emirates in various cities in the United Kingdom, where Sharia law would be imposed. By November 2011, MAC was also banned by British authorities, and then it, too, was replaced by other groups such as the Sharia Project, Need4Khilafah, and the Islamic Dawah Association. On June 26, 2014, the U.K. Home Office banned these entities, specifying them as "aliases of the proscribed organization known as Al Ghurabaa, The Saved Sect, Al Muhajirouin and Islam4UK." The order further stated that

AM and related groups were proscribed "for glorifying terrorism and we are clear it should not be able to continue these activities by simply operating under alternative names."[81] Other groups included the London School of Sharia, Muslim Prisoners, and the Islamic Emergency Defence, a self-styled defense organization.

Until around 2010, Choudary's network was based mainly in the United Kingdom, even though smaller groupings associated with AM had existed in mainland Europe and the United States since the late 1990s. It was not until 2010, however, that Choudary began exporting a new brand outside of the United Kingdom: it became known as the Sharia4 movement.[82] Its Belgian franchise, Sharia4Belgium, developed as one of the first networks associated with it. This informal network is separate from Choudary's U.K. movement, although it is closely connected to and inspired by it. As Belgian jihadism expert Pieter van Ostaeyen notes, "Sharia4Belgium copied a lot of the rhetoric of Anjem Choudary and other inspiring leaders of Islam4UK."[83] As will be seen, however, Choudary's influence upon Sharia4Belgium went beyond inspiration and included more concrete cooperative activities, including strategic and operational guidance, financial support, and ideological training. Of key importance in this regard were the personal relations between Choudary and the Belgian movement's leader, Fouad Belkacem, a.k.a. Abu Imran.

It is not coincidental that the internationalization of Choudary's network began in earnest in Belgium—a country that had long been known as a hotbed of European jihadism. Belgium had multiple encounters with jihadism dating back at least to 2001. Two days before the attacks of September 11, 2001, two suicide bombers posing as cameramen killed the Afghan commander of the Northern Alliance rebel movement, Ahmed Shah Massoud. One of the attackers was the first husband of Malika El Aroud, a Belgian woman of Moroccan origin who rose to become one of the most celebrated and influential female jihadists to date.[84] Two and a half years later, Belgian jihadists from Maaseik were part of the Moroccan Islamist Combatant Group (GICM) cell connected to the Madrid train bombings. In November 2005 in Iraq, meanwhile, it was a Belgian convert to Islam, Muriel Degauque, who became the first female Western suicide bomber in

Iraq. In May 2014, twenty-nine-year-old French national Mehdi Nemmouche opened fire on the Jewish Museum in Brussels, killing four. Following terrorist attacks in Paris in January against the *Charlie Hebdo* headquarters and the Hypercacher supermarket, and again in November at multiple targets including the Bataclan Theater and the Stade de France, Belgian authorities conducted high-profile raids against jihadist networks in places like Verviers and Molenbeek. When Belgian authorities suspected that Belgian-born Moroccan-Frenchman Saleh Abdeslam, the driver of the cell that conducted the November 2015 attacks in Paris, was hiding in Brussels, they imposed a security lockdown that lasted several days. Abdeslam was eventually caught in Molenbeek after hiding in the Brussels municipality for more than four months. Within less than a week of his arrest, on the morning of March 22, 2016, Belgium suffered its worst terrorist attack in history, when three coordinated bombings rocked Brussels. Two bombs detonated at the terminal area of the Brussels Airport in Zaventem, while a third device exploded inside a carriage at the Maalbeek metro station, in close proximity to the headquarters of the European Commission. The coordinated attacks killed 31 people and wounded 340 more.

Most Belgium jihadists are descendants of migration guest workers who came mainly from Morocco and Turkey in the 1960s to work in the steel and coal industry. When the industry declined, most of these workers stayed. In the 1980s and 1990s, many of their offspring were socially marginalized and disproportionately likely to engage in crime, theft, and drug dealings.[85]

Belgium has also turned into a jihadist hub for geographic reasons. Its central location in Europe makes it ideal for logistical purposes, while the highly diverse Muslim population in the country allows potential terrorists opportunities to hide and recruit in Belgium.[86]

As if these structural problems were not enough, many Muslims in Belgium have also been under the impression that the state is curtailing their right to practice their religion, citing bans on wearing headscarves in public schools and public service, as well as plans to ban private halal slaughter, among other issues.

It is within this context that a small network of activists mostly from Antwerp established Sharia4Belgium in early 2010. The group formed around a young Belgian-born jihadist of Moroccan extraction, Fouad Belkacem, who recruited mainly young Muslims and converts through street preaching. He was known to Belgian authorities due to a rap sheet that included theft and assault, as well as time spent in prison.[87]

In establishing Sharia4Belgium, Belkacem availed himself of assistance from an ideological fellow traveler, Anjem Choudary, who was more than happy to offer his support, helping facilitate the establishment of Sharia-4Belgium and its ongoing operations. As Choudary told journalist Ben Taub, Belkacem came to London in March 2010 to ask him for advice on how "to start something in Belgium." Choudary then enlightened Belkacem about the history of AM. Shortly after the meeting, Belkacem returned to Belgium and organized an informal network, Sharia4Belgium.[88] According to the *Daily Mail*, Choudary continued to provide guidance to Belkacem "on the phone," presumably after Belkacem's return to Belgium, about how to cultivate followers.[89]

The British jihadist entrepreneur's input did not stop there. Police reports later identified Choudary as a financial supporter of Sharia4Belgium. Moreover, Choudary offered support to Belkacem by helping the Sharia-4Belgium leader conduct ideological training as part of an "intensive twenty-four-week program" in which new network members had to participate. As part of this ideological indoctrination, Choudary lectured regularly to members of Sharia4Belgium using Paltalk, a video chat website, as did Omar Bakri Mohammed from Lebanon.[90]

Choudary's endorsement of Sharia4Belgium was open and official. In March 2010, he stated: "We support our brothers in Belgium under the banner of Sharia4Belgium and we are ready, whatever they need to send more people to support them in their activities, in their duty, and fulfilling their responsibility."[91] Subsequently, the ideological cooperation between the British jihadist entrepreneur and the Belgian informal network continued unabatedly into 2013, until the formal dissolution of Sharia4Belgium. When Belkacem was arrested in April 2013, Choudary released a video on YouTube in which he warned Belgian authorities that "if Muslims will be persecuted, there will be a revolution, and only Allah knows what the consequences will be for Belgium. . . . Whomever [sic] will force Muslims to keep quiet will face problems. An entire new generation will arise and will do far more than merely talk, because its voice has not been heard. Do not provoke Muslims!"[92]

Choudary also initiated an exchange program between members of his U.K.-based network and Sharia4Belgium. The arrangement was that the members of Belkacem's network would travel to England to study with Choudary, while Choudary's followers in the United Kingdom would visit the headquarters of the Belgian group on 117 Dambruggestraat in Antwerp.[93]

The group's main goal was the imposition of Islamic sharia law throughout Belgium. As a militant Salafist and jihadist network, Sharia4Belgium was fundamentally opposed to the Belgian state and the Western, democratic values it stood for, and it decried the perceived curtailing of rights of Muslims, such as the right for female Muslims to wear the burqa. In their opposition to Western governance and values, members did not shun verbal or physical violence. Frequently referring to non-Muslims as monkeys and pigs, the group indicated a readiness to meet "anti-Islamic" policies such as the burqa ban with "physical confrontation."[94] In a video release, the group even threatened to kill Dutch politician Geert Wilders. The Jewish community was also a frequently threatened target.[95]

The tactics employed by this informal network were eerily similar to those of Choudary's old AM network in the United Kingdom. Network members held a political vision of Islam, according to which Muslims must "display their religion in the public space."[96] Confrontational and provocative by design, the group was hungry for media attention. Its activities, like Choudary's, revolved around "street dawah," in which public demonstrations and rallies at times turned violent. The network also regularly disrupted events and lectures by allegedly "anti-Muslim" speakers such as the Dutch writer Benno Barnard, Dutch Green Party MP Tofik Dib, and the feminist advocate Irshad Manji.[97] Moreover, many of its events were designed as publicity stunts. In September 2011, the network said that it established an Islamic sharia law court in Antwerp with the aim of creating a parallel legal system.[98] Group leaders also issued statements meant to shock the general population, such as warning that the Atomium in Brussels would be destroyed because it represented a form of idolatry (*taghut*). In the video released in late December 2011, in which Belkacem made this threat, he also stated that the black flag of Islamic jihad would "soon be flying on top of all the palaces in Europe."[99]

In June 2012, Belgian authorities arrested Belkacem, later sentencing him for incitement of hatred and violence against non-Muslims. Then, on October 7, 2012, Sharia4Belgium announced its disbandment on its website, although a Belgian court would later establish that Sharia4Belgium continued to function as a recruitment network as late as 2013.[100]

Not too long after the announcement of Sharia4Belgium's dissolution, authorities realized that many of its members had already moved to Syria to fight on behalf of insurgent and terrorist organizations like the Islamic State and Jabhat al-Nusra. Belgian prosecutors then began the largest terrorism trial in the country's history in September 2014, charging forty-six adherents of Sharia4Belgium with membership in a terrorist organization. Only eight of the accused were present in court, with the majority believed to be in Syria. In February 2015, the court ruled that Sharia4Belgium was a "terrorist organization" and found forty-five members of the network guilty of terror charges. Belkacem, who was ruled to be the "undisputed" leader of the network, was sentenced to twelve years in prison.

The Belgian journalist Guy Van Vlierden later charged the Belgian government of having neglected the Sharia4Belgium threat when it first appeared. When they finally acted towards the end of 2012, it was too late, with too many young jihadists having been radicalized already. Just when the network's leaders were imprisoned and the group could no longer engage in overt activity, "the Syrian war presented itself as an alternative outlet for radicals; young people who had absorbed the group's message that Belgian society did not want them and that it offered no space for Islam, saw the Syrian jihad as a worthy way out."[101]

NETWORKED COOPERATION VARIANT 4:
SHARIA4BELGIUM, THE ISLAMIC STATE,
AND JABHAT AL-NUSRA

In recent years, there have been growing indications that Sharia4Belgium and several other European informal jihadist and Salafist networks have encouraged their members to travel—and facilitated that travel—to conflict regions such as Syria, Iraq, Mali, and Yemen to join insurgent and terrorist organizations active there. In February 2015, for example, when a correctional tribunal in Antwerp found forty-five members of Sharia4Belgium guilty of terrorism charges, the judge noted that "Sharia4Belgium recruited young men for armed combat and organized their departure for Syria."[102] Europol's annual terrorism report for 2015 similarly noted that members of Sharia4Belgium, among those of other European networks, "are suspected of facilitation and recruitment activities."[103] It cited, for example, Sharia4Spain's active involvement in the "recruitment of fighters for jihadist groups in Mali."[104] Independent scholars have confirmed these trends. Raffaello Pantucci, an expert on European jihadism, stated in the summer of 2015 that the European networks connected to the so-called Sharia4 movement are "increasingly proving to be at the heart of Europe's radical Islamist community connected with Islamic State and the conflict in Syria and Iraq."[105] Likewise, Lorenzo Vidino, who directs the Program on Extremism at George Washington University, has observed "a new turn, particularly in continental Europe, since the beginning of the civil war in Syria," whereby the Sharia4 networks "transformed from simply jihadist-leaning to fully involved in mobilizing for combat."[106]

The present case study examines these trends in greater detail and shows how they illustrate networked cooperation Variant 4, that is, cooperation between informal networks and formal terrorist and/or insurgent organizations. The focus here is the informal network Sharia4Belgium and its role as a facilitator of Western foreign fighters to Syria and Iraq, where its members have joined the Islamic State, Jabhat al-Nusra, and other formal terrorist and insurgent organizations.

The ongoing conflicts in Syria and Iraq have had tragic consequences first and foremost for the Syrian and Iraqi civilian population. But they have also presented new concerns to the West. In addition to the influx of refugees from these countries, thousands of Westerners, mostly youth, have traveled to Syria, Iraq, and elsewhere to fight alongside rebel groups and terrorist organizations. According to several sources, between 20,000 and 30,000 foreign fighters traveled to fight in Syria and Iraq between 2011 and 2015.[107] Of these, the majority are citizens of countries in the Middle East and North Africa,[108] but between 3,400 and 4,500 are from Western countries. In Syria and Iraq, most of them have joined the Islamic State or the Al Qaeda–affiliated Jabhat al-Nusra. According to Peter Neumann, the director of the International Centre for the Study of Radicalisation (ICSR) at Kings College London, 10 to 15 percent of the Western foreign fighters have died in these conflicts, while others have vowed never to return to their countries of origin. Extrapolating from figures of German foreign fighters, Neumann estimates that between a quarter and up to 40 percent of foreign fighters are returning to their countries of origin, although these numbers have to be approached with caution.[109] Analyses by different Western scholars have shown that historically speaking, only a minority of the returnees, between 11 percent and 26 percent have engaged in terrorist activities back in their countries of origin.[110]

While several European countries are plagued by high numbers of foreign fighters in absolute terms, smaller countries like Belgium, Sweden, Norway, Denmark, and Austria face the greatest problems given their high per capita ratio of jihadist foreign fighters. Among Western European countries, Belgium has topped this negative list with the highest ratio of jihadists fighting abroad—about forty jihadists per million inhabitants.[111] Many of these Belgian foreign fighters, including some who have participated in the most gruesome violence, such as beheadings, have been associated with Sharia4Belgium. Some have gained worldwide notoriety, including Abdelhamid Abaaoud, a Belgian jihadist of Moroccan background who traveled to Syria as a foreign fighter in 2013 and again in January 2014, and who joined the Islamic State in the process. Abaaoud's terrorist career includes actual or suspected involvement in several plots.[112] In January

2014, for example, he communicated with Mehdi Nemmouche three months before the latter entered the Jewish Museum in Brussels, where he shot to death two museum employees and two visiting Israeli tourists. He was also suspected of having organized and financed a terrorist cell affiliated with the Islamic State in the Belgian town of Verviers. The cell was raided by Belgian authorities in January 2015 before it could realize its plans to kill Belgian police officers. Finally, Abaaoud gained worldwide notoriety in November 2015, when French authorities identified him as the presumed mastermind of the November 13 attacks in Paris that killed 129 individuals and injured more than three hundred.[113] Abaaoud was killed five days after the Paris attacks in a firefight in the Parisian suburb of Saint Denis.

Experts on Belgian jihadism argue that it is precisely because of Sharia-4Belgium's role as an incubator of jihadism that Belgium has produced jihadists such as Abbaoud.[114] According to data collected by Pieter van Ostaeyen and Guy Van Vlierden, 553 Belgians, aged 14 to 69, with an average age of 25.9, have been active in Syria or Iraq between 2011 and December 2015. Six percent of them are converts to Islam. At least 78 of the total number have been killed in that period, while 120 are believed to have returned.[115] Seventy-nine out of the 553 Belgians (14.2 percent) in this period have previously been associated with Sharia4Belgium, the most important (though not the only) Belgian network recruiting foreign fighters for jihad abroad. These recruits include 52 women (11 percent), 14 of whom (27 percent) have a "proven affiliation with Sharia4Belgium."[116] Moreover, out of the 79 Belgian foreign fighters associated with Sharia-4Belgium, 35 have a "proven affiliation with the Islamic State."[117] Several members of Sharia4Belgium paid the ultimate price for their activities. In May 2014, for example, Van Ostaeyen noted that a third of the 27 Belgians known to have been killed fighting were members of Sharia-4Belgium. Of the 20 returnees at that point in time, half were affiliated with Sharia4Belgium.[118]

According to Van Vlierden, these figures probably underestimate the actual influence of Sharia4Belgium. He believes that about two out of every three Belgian jihadists who traveled to these conflict zones "have at least been influenced by Shariah4Belgium, even if they have not been directly recruited by the organization."[119]

While three quarters of all the Belgians who have gone to Syria and Iraq are believed to have joined the Islamic State, their affiliations have not always been fixed over time. Until the summer of 2013, for example, many of the foreign fighters joined what was then an independent jihadist militia known as the Majlis Shura al-Mujahideen in Aleppo Province.[120] When this organization formally joined the Islamic State, many of the Belgians decided to switch their allegiance to Jabhat al-Nusra, though some of these later joined the Islamic State.[121]

Sharia4Belgium's involvement in the conflict in Syria began in 2011, when Fouad Belkacem, the group's leader, and Nabil Kasmi, another member of the network, traveled to London to meet with Anjem Choudary. According to an Antwerp police official, Choudary helped Belkacem and Kasmi contact AM's global emir, Omar Bakri Mohammed.[122] In November 2011, Kasmi traveled to the Lebanese coastal city of Tripolis to meet Bakri, who was under house arrest there. Antwerp police officials say that Bakri put Kasmi in touch with militant groups fighting in Syria.[123] After a few months in Lebanon, Kasmi returned to Belgium, but then revisited Lebanon in March 2012.[124] Just when Kasmi returned to Lebanon, two suspected Sharia4Belgium members traveled to Yemen. Local authorities believed that they had ties to al-Shabaab and were about to join AQAP, and detained and subsequently deported them.[125]

Kasmi entered Syria in May 2012 and reported back to the Sharia-4Belgium headquarters that he was now "in Syria to fight."[126] According to a report in the *New Yorker* magazine, a Lebanese military court later declared that Bakri and Kasmi facilitated the movement of a few European jihadists from Lebanon to Syria, where they established themselves among Al Qaeda–linked groups. A Belgian security official cited by the *New Yorker* said that "once they were ready to go to Syria, . . . they had a whole operational network" thanks to Sharia4Belgium's cooperative relationship with Bakri and Choudary.[127]

Choudary and the AM network had prior experience facilitating the movement of jihadists to conflict regions. During the 1990s, the destination was Chechnya. Choudary boasted about "recruiting people standing in Trafalgar Square to send them abroad."[128] Vidino notes that there is plenty of evidence to support Choudary's claims. AM members are known to have established training camps in Pakistan and otherwise recruited jihadists for various terrorist activities. Bakri and Choudary, however, have always managed to evade the authorities by remaining "one step removed from these activities," Vidino states, adding however that "the role of the individuals who were immediately close to them is well documented."[129]

Following his first stint in Syria, Kasmi briefly returned to Belgium, but left again for Syria on August 20, 2012. The next day, five members of Sharia4Belgium followed him to Syria. After Sharia4Belgium formally dissolved in October, dozens of additional Sharia4Belgium members made the trip to Syria.[130] These self-styled jihadists established a Belgian faction within a group known as Majlis Shura al-Mujahideen (MSM), but Sharia4Belgium members also joined Jabhat al-Nusra (JN).[131] Those who joined MSM were settled near Aleppo in a walled villa that had earlier belonged to a senior official of the Assad regime. In addition to the Belgians, the villa also housed Dutch and French jihadists.

The European contingent within MSM, including the Sharia4Belgium members, participated in beheadings and established training camps where they trained for jihad. Apart from fighting on the battlefield, the foreign fighters also set up roadblocks and stole money and belongings from non-Sunnis. They frequently held non-Sunni Syrian civilians for ransom, demanding large sums for their release. Those whose families would not or could not pay were killed. The European jihadists filmed many of these murders, which often involved gruesome beheadings.[132]

MSM was led by a Syrian extremist, Amr al-Absi (a.k.a. Abu Asir), who was considered a high-ranking member of ISIS. The Belgian faction was led by a young Belgian jihadist from Vilvoorde, Houssien Elouassaki (a.k.a. Abu Fallujah), who also participated in the beheadings.[133] Following Elouassaki's death in August 2013, the Belgian foreign fighters left their base in the Aleppo countryside and began dispersing across various groupings, including the Islamic State and Jabhat al-Nusra.[134]

It was also in 2013 that Belgian police first realized that dozens of Sharia4Belgium members had left for Syria.[135] Concerned about the consequences, Belgian authorities began arresting jihadists who had been monitored, in addition to detaining those fighters who were beginning to return to Belgium.[136] Despite these efforts, many Belgian foreign fighters continued to flock to Syria and Iraq in 2013 and 2014. They included many sympathizers and "second-tier" Sharia4Belgium members, as well as acquaintances and friends of those already fighting in Syria.[137] Oftentimes leaving in batches, these people received instructions via text messages from compatriots already in Syria, who picked them up from a meeting point set in advance.[138]

Unlike the first wave of Sharia4Belgium members who ended up in Syria, but who had been interested in fighting alongside groups in Somalia, Yemen, or Chechnya, subsequent waves of foreign fighters expressed a clear desire in joining the Islamic State (IS), particularly after the group's dramatic territorial expansion in the summer of 2014.[139] These jihadists included a growing number of women. Some of the male jihadists, including Kasmi, achieved high positions in the Islamic State's organization.[140]

Sharia4Belgium's networked cooperation with formal jihadist groups in Syria and Iraq took a number of forms. One, as described above, involved Sharia4Belgium's mobilizing its own members to join these groups and establishing facilitation networks through its contacts. Another was the key role played by returning foreign fighters in leveraging their existing and newly acquired contacts for further foreign fighter movement. In addition, these returnees also supported fundraising efforts to provide financial support to those wishing to travel to Syria and Iraq to join local fighting organizations.[141]

Sharia4Belgium also facilitated the movement of other jihadists not affiliated with the Belgian network to Syria and Iraq. As a report by the Dutch Intelligence service AIVD suggests, Sharia4Belgium's involvement especially in Syria served as a blueprint of sorts for members of Dutch informal networks Behind Bars and Street Dawah. Those two networks formally ceased their operations in the Netherlands in late 2012—just when the first wave of Dutch jihadists departed for Syria. According to the AIVD report, this successful departure "was probably attributable to the close contacts between Behind Bars/Street Dawah and Sharia4Belgium. Individuals associated with the two movements were at the heart of that sudden exodus."[142] Along with adherents of Sharia4Holland, these Dutch networks continued throughout 2013 to facilitate the travel of young men and women to Syria, where they joined Jabhat al-Nusra, ISIS, and other groups.[143]

Finally, Sharia4Belgium and other informal networks associated or influenced by Anjem Choudary and AM are involved in online cooperation with IS, JN, and other groups. As research by Brandeis University professor Jytte Klausen and her team revealed, Twitter feeder accounts associated with IS, JN, and various Sharia4 movement networks have played a "controlling role" among foreign fighters based in Western Syria. A database established by Klausen's research team consisting of 29,000 Twitter accounts connected with jihadist foreign fighters in the first three months of 2014 revealed that authority in the broader network of Western foreign fighters derived "primarily from organizations in the Al-Muhajiroun network and from media accounts belonging primarily to ISIL and secondarily to Jabhat al-Nusra."[144] These findings, in other words, indicated a very high level of online cooperation between the networks associated with the Sharia4 movement on the one hand and formal jihadist organizations on the other.

NETWORKED COOPERATION VARIANT 5: THE GLOBAL SHARIA4 MOVEMENT

In early 2010, when Fouad Belkacem sought advice from Anjem Choudary on how to establish a Belgian-based network similar to Sharia4UK and its various AM-linked predecessors, Choudary already harbored visions of facilitating the formation of networks similar to Islam4UK throughout Europe and beyond. Within a few years, that vision turned into reality when a host of networks that emerged in Europe and other parts of the world appeared to copy the militant Salafist and jihadist ideologies propagated by Anjem Choudary's U.K.-based network and Sharia4Belgium. The totality of these various informal networks is known as the Sharia4 movement—a movement that has gained much prominence in recent years for preaching a militant form of Salafism and for its ties to terrorism and insurgency in Europe, the Middle East, and elsewhere. This final case study focuses on the lifeblood of this movement, namely the cooperative activities among its various constitutive informal networks. In other words, this last case study considers the Sharia4 Movement as an example of networked cooperation Variant 5, which involves cooperation among informal networks.

In early January 2010, around the time when Anjem Choudary provided his counsel to Sharia4Belgium founder Fouad Belkacem, the U.K.-based preacher tied to the global AM network hinted at his visions to spread his interpretation of Islam beyond Belgium in an interview with a Western researcher: "The whole of Europe is virgin territory for people like us who want to call for the Sharia," he said. "If they are worried about the minarets in Switzerland . . . then I think we can bring their fears to fruition."[145] Choudary hinted at the impending internationalization of the AM-inspired network—one that would adopt the notion of sharia and turn it into a brand.

Choudary started making good on his promise in 2010, just at a time when Omar Bakri Mohammed, the global emir of AM, was becoming more isolated in Lebanon.[146] The internationalization of the movement proceeded through the export of a new brand, "Sharia4." Groups adopting the ideology, strategy, and brand of Islam4UK and Sharia4Belgium appeared on the scene, calling themselves Sharia4Holland or Shariah4Andalus (a.k.a. Sharia4Spain). The movement soon spread to outside of Europe, encompassing groups such as Sharia4USA, Sharia4Australia, Shariah4Southafrica, and Sharia4Pakistan. At times, these networks adopted names that did not contain the Sharia4 prefix, such as Jama'at al Tawhid (Organization of Monotheism) in France, Straatdawah (Street Dawah) in the Netherlands, Kaldet til Islam (Call to Islam) in Denmark, and Profetens

Ummah (Prophets of the Ummah) in Norway.[147] The movement also included networks that functioned mostly online, such as Sharia4Bangladesh, a YouTube channel, and websites such as International Sharia Movement or Salafimedia.com.[148]

The various nodes that constitute the Sharia4 movement are informal networks and at times virtual networks present merely on the Internet. Vidino described these various entities as "spontaneous and fluid formations of like-minded individuals without a clear leadership and structure."[149] Furthermore, these networks disproportionately attract individuals from lower socioeconomic strata, including youth with backgrounds in criminal behavior and gang activity. Many of their participants are second- or third-generation Muslims, as well as converts to Islam.[150]

If Choudary is to be believed, these networks evolved organically. In an interview with Joe Mulhall, Choudary stated that after Belkacem approached him in early 2010 about how to set up Sharia4Belgium, he then

> initiated Sharia4Holland and then people in France wanted to be part of it and people in other countries and basically it spread like that without us. Many people started to attribute themselves to us, they started wanting to know more about us. I started to be invited to different places. I went to Indonesia, I went to Belgium. It was a natural thing. The globalization of the Sharia4 brand was not something we initiated it was something that was initiated because of the public profile. I mean there are people in countries we have never been to that we never had any contact with that said we have a Sharia4Algeria or Shari4 this or that and that's fantastic.[151]

Whether the movement emerged organically or was centrally steered, its ideological affinity to Choudary and AM is beyond doubt. A research team led by Jytte Klausen found that over a period of three months in early 2011, forty-one YouTube channels examined "posted jihadist content and carried brand names with a family resemblance to incarnations of the British-based banned organization, al-Muhajiroun. Twenty-one used some version of the Shariah4 label, playing on the name of Islam4UK, a banned organization in the al-Muhajiroun clan."[152]

Research by Klausen and her team strongly suggests that even if some of the Sharia4 informal networks emerged independently, they are becoming gradually absorbed into a centrally steered movement associated with Choudary. As far as the ideological content on these YouTube channels is concerned, there is "a single production entity behind most of the propaganda."[153] Many of the websites associated with these networks, including the channels for Muslim Against Crusades, Jamaat al-Tawheed, and AnjemChoudary.com, were all hosted by the U.S.-based Dynadot web hosting company, through which these sites enjoy the rights guaranteed under the First Amendment.[154] Thus, Klausen and her collaborators conclude that one of the main purposes of the Sharia4 movement is the creation of redundancy. "While the various groups are portrayed, truthfully or not, as independent start-ups, they are soon officially brought into the network"[155] in order "to make removals by the *YouTube* administrators or government officials ineffective."[156]

The Sharia4 groups tend to express their views and identity in a provocative manner, while attempting to obscure their links with terrorism by preventing their members from openly inciting individuals from committing acts of terrorism. Nevertheless, a 2013 Europol report determined that the Sharia4 groups "praise terrorist groups and present perpetrators of terrorist attacks as heroes. Through such activities, the Sharia4 groups contribute to spreading a highly intolerant interpretation of Islam, including the support of violent acts in the name of religion, in the public sphere, thereby exposing vulnerable individuals to radical ideas."[157] The report further warned that the ideology spread by Sharia4Belgium and like-minded groups "has contributed to the radicalisation and engagement of EU citizens in the Syrian conflict."[158] The Europol assessment is supported by abundant examples. To cite just a few, videos posted by Sharia4Australia feature the Al Qaeda flag, which also appears on the backdrop of Sharia4Belgium videos. The Belgian group's leader, Belkacem, held a memorial prayer service for bin Laden, in which he lauded the Al Qaeda leader, while Shariah4USA regularly posted content supportive of Al

Qaeda on its Facebook page and YouTube channel.[159] Dutch Sharia4 networks also often express sympathy for jihadists who have committed acts of terrorism in Europe, such as Mohammed Merah, a twenty-three-year-old French national of Algerian origin who killed three French soldiers before attacking a Jewish school in Toulouse in March 2012 and killing an additional four people, including three children.[160]

Their informal network characteristics, coupled with their ability to walk a tightrope between the permissible and the illegal, add to the complexity of these groups and "epitomiz[e] the heterogeneity of Islamism in the West," as Vidino observes.[161] Their repertoires of actions are controversial, radical, intimidating, and provocative, but save for occasional skirmishes with other groups or the police, the groups by and large assume a nonviolent stance. That being said, there are growing indications that individuals associated with these networks have subsequently resorted to acts of terrorism. Moreover, Vidino states that in some instances leaders of these networks "have transformed from headline-grabbing agitators (dismissed by most as buffoons) into full-fledged jihadists actively involved in combat in Syria and Iraq."[162]

It appears that following the establishment of Sharia4Belgium, the movement expanded next to the Netherlands by inspiring local jihadists from places like The Hague, Delft, and Amsterdam to establish several informal networks known for their provocative propaganda.[163] The most well-known of these was Sharia4Holland, followed by networks called Straatdawah (Street Dawah) and Behind Bars. The last of these was founded by Muslims who regularly prayed at the As Soennah mosque in The Hague—a hub of Dutch Salafists that, according to local authorities, had previously linked with terrorism.[164]

In Denmark and Norway, meanwhile, groups known as Kaldet til Islam (Call to Islam) and Profetens Ummah (Prophets of the Ummah) appeared in 2010, closely resembling their U.K., Belgian, and Dutch counterparts in terms of ideology and style.[165] Kaldet til Islam, for one, boasted about regularly communicating with Bakri. In addition, their use of slogans such as "Democracy Is Hypocrisy," and its plans to create "Sharia-Zones" in Denmark, parroted the language and activity of Sharia4 partners abroad.[166]

Kaldet, however, also called upon its sympathizers to wage jihad abroad, especially in Syria, where the group called for the overthrow of Bashar Assad and his regime's replacement with a caliphate.[167]

The informal networks that compose the Sharia4 Movement usually adopt Choudary's sermons and propaganda, which appear on the websites and Facebook pages of the various networks and on associated YouTube channels.[168] The various informal networks constituting the Global Sharia4 movement differ, however, in terms of their level of activity and the nature of their connection with Choudary. In terms of their activity level, some constituent networks take the form of blogs, websites, Facebook pages, or YouTube channels, while others function as quasi-organizations.[169] In terms of their connection with Choudary, the networks can be placed along a spectrum. On one end are those that seem to be directly controlled by him, including Sharia4Hind, Sharia4Pakistan, and Sharia4Finland. On the other end are those that are fully independent, but nevertheless have links with Choudary and are certainly inspired by the ideology and strategy of the various incarnations of Al-Muhajiroun that have influenced and socialized Choudary. These include networks such as Profetens Ummah in Norway; Forsane Alizza (Knights of Pride), a small French Salafist network established in Nantes in early 2010; and Millatu Ibrahim (Abraham's Path), a German-based network that eventually became a "breeding ground for foreign fighters in Syria."[170] In terms of these groups' connections with Choudary, Profetens Ummah has few administrative ties, but by his own admission Choudary provided guidance and mentorship to the group.[171] Similarly, Sharia4Italy, a small and short-lived informal network, was set up by a young Moroccan-born Italian amateur rapper named Anas el-Abboubi, who became intrigued with the style of Salafism preached by Choudary and began an online communication with him. El-Abboubi also contacted members of Millatu Ibrahim in Germany and Sharia4Belgium via Facebook and Twitter and made plans to visit Sharia4Belgium members in Brussels.[172]

In between these ends of the spectrum are affiliated networks that, according to Mulhall, have been established independently, but have "adopted the branding and operate within the Al-Muhajidoun framework."[173] This category includes Sharia4Belgium, Sharia4Holland, Sharia4Italy,[174] Sharia-4Indonesia, Sharia4Australia, and Jamaat al-Tawhid (formerly Sharia-4France). Research by Ineke Roex, for example, describes Sharia4Holland as a network that was set up not by Anjem Choudary, but by Dutch Is-lamists who were inspired by Sharia4Belgium. "Compelled by [Sharia-4Belgium's] message, several young Dutch Muslims started following them online and visited them in Antwerp. Soon, the idea to found a Dutch group was born. . . . Their ideology and style of activism were based on Al-Muhajiroun and Islam4UK."[175]

The more autonomously functioning networks oftentimes pursue more local agendas in addition to their common cause with the other networks. Sharia4Belgium, for example, which is composed of many Moroccan immigrants, has protested Moroccan government policies. The French network Jamaat al-Tawhid, on the other hand, has frequently decried the French law banning the burqa.

The various Sharia4 and related informal networks that are part of the Sharia4 movement collaborate in various domains. Particularly striking is the heavy reliance—even dependency—on the Internet and social media platforms in order to effect these forms of cooperation. In fact, the Sharia4 networks' heavy utilization of the Internet for the purpose of mutual cooperation renders the Sharia4 movement the quintessential example of the complex ways in which contemporary jihadists actors cooperate today.

In terms of the ideological domain of cooperation, these groups share an affinity for a highly political and activist form of Salafism that aims to establish an Islamic caliphate as the remedy to the perceived predicaments facing the global Islamic community of believers. In the process, Western states and their perceived corrupt and un-Islamic values, which stand in the way of achieving that goal, must be shunned. More concretely, ideological cooperation among these informal Salafist networks is apparent in their common branding, and especially the frequent adoption of the "Sharia4" prefix. In addition, many of the groups use similar logos, usually showing the map of a country on which the black Islamist flag is superimposed to signal the impending reign of Islam over that particular territory.[176]

The ideological cooperation between these networks further expresses itself in the sharing and cross-posting of ideological content, especially on the various Internet platforms associated with these networks. The French group Forsane Alizza, for example, which sometimes used the name Shariah4France, "openly advertised its ideological proximity to the British-based *Islam4UK* organization," and its website regularly posts statements of Sharia4Belgium.[177] Research by Klausen and her team shows that Forsane Alizza is representative of the entire Sharia4 movement, whose networks have associated YouTube channels that all feature "strikingly similar" content. "Over images of Muslims suffering at the hands of western military forces, the sound track broadcasts *anasheed* [chants] . . . and texts from the Koran, or a voice-over explaining the righteous path."[178] Their research also points to the central ideological and logistical role played by Anjem Choudary and Omar Bakri Muhammad, as well as Abu Hamza al-Mari, an Egyptian Salafist cleric who had close ties with Al-Muhajiroun, functioned as the imam of the Finsbury Park mosque in London, and was sentenced to life in prison in May 2014 after being found guilty of eleven charges of terrorism. The trio, according to Klausen and her team, were "the most frequently used speakers" in the videos and clips.[179] Moreover, they also found that the various YouTube channels in the Sharia4 network cross-posted many of the same videos. The most active of these included Sharia4Belgium (and its successor channels), Sharia4Holland, Shariah4Australia (and its successor channel), Sharia4Poland, Shariah4Pakistan, and Shariah4AlAndalus.[180] Many more such channels with similar content appeared shortly after the uprisings in parts of the Arab world that were initially labeled the "Arab Spring." These included Shariah4Tunisia, Sharia4Egypt, and Sharia4Yemen.[181]

The informal networks of the Sharia4 movement also cooperate in the logistical domain, adopting joint strategies and tactics. Here, too, examples abound. Thus, even the smaller networks have a strong Internet presence on all social networks and professional websites and post videos of major events.[182] Their websites, social media pages, and YouTube channels feature similar images of prominent icons from various Western countries—such as the White House in Washington, DC, or Big Ben in

London—with a black flag flying above them. The websites are also replete with videos in which representatives of one group address their counterparts in another and offer guidance and support.

Choudary and Omar Bakri Muhammad serve as logistical hubs of the movement. This is evident from the contact pages of these websites. That of the Shariah4USA website, for example, features contact information for Choudary and Bakri, as well as for the head of Sharia4Australia, Ibrahim Siddiq Conlon.[183]

Finally, the various informal networks cooperate in the "operational" domain—not in the sense of overt terrorist activity, but in terms of predominantly nonviolent (albeit extremist) collective action. Until his arrest, Choudary, for example, abetted operational cooperation among constituent networks within the Sharia4 movement through his frequent travels. In one instance, Choudary and some of his British supporters traveled to the Netherlands, where Choudary lectured to members of both Sharia4-Holland and Sharia4Belgium about the "methodology to overthrow the [un-Islamic] regimes."[184] Choudary did not mince words before the assembled Belgian television crew, stating: "I come from England in order to radicalize the youth in this country." One of the Sharia4Belgium members was overheard telling a British colleague during the visit that "sometimes you need laptop, sometimes you need Kalashnikov."[185]

Operational cooperation frequently involves joint protests, demonstrations, and other publicity stunts. Social networking platforms are the main means for organizing these events. In April 2011, for example, Jamaat al-Tawheed invited Choudary and two of his colleagues to participate in a Paris march to protest the French ban on the public wearing of the *niqab*. The French group also invited other prominent members of the Sharia4 movement to the demonstration, including Sharia4Belgium's Belkacem, who attended the event and was arrested by French authorities.[186] Another demonstration in The Hague half a year later organized by Behind Bars featured protesters affiliated with Sharia4Belgium and Sharia4Holland.[187]

CONCLUSION

ONTEMPORARY TERRORIST ACTORS cooperate in myriad ways that defy simplistic characterizations and explanations. This applies particularly to global jihadist actors, the empirical focus of this study. Contemporary terrorism is marked on the one hand by a growing diversity of actors and on the other by an enabling environment in flux.

As far as actors are concerned, formal terrorist organizations—nearly the exclusive focus in existing studies on terrorist cooperation—no longer have a monopoly on the planning and execution of terrorism. A growing variety of other actors capable of effecting transformative change by supporting, planning, or executing acts of terrorism have entered the picture. These include both informal actors such as terrorist entrepreneurs and informal networks, as well as other, more traditional actors such as states. As the empirical cases in this book have shown, these diverse actors cooperate with one another and thereby create a highly intricate web of terrorist relationships. Studies focusing exclusively on cooperation between formal terrorist organizations capture only a slice of that complex nexus of terrorist connections.

Contemporary terrorism is also evolving due to developments at the environmental, or structural, level, which also affect cooperation between today's terrorist actors. I have argued that today's environment is highly conducive to terrorist cooperation for three reasons. First, it features a formidable and persistent ideology—jihadism—that serves as a key *motivator* for cooperation. Second, the Internet, and especially new social media platforms, provide a cheap and effective *medium* for cooperation. Third, new and enduring armed conflicts, typically in areas of limited statehood, offer ample *opportunities* for militant actors to collaborate in various ways on the ground.

These broader transformations provided the setting for the book's main argument: While contemporary terrorist actors continue to cooperate in established forms of interorganizational cooperation, they also engage in novel forms of *networked cooperation*, a form of collaboration between militant and terrorist actors that involves at least one informal actor—that is, a terrorist entrepreneur or an informal network. As illustrated both theoretically and empirically, networked cooperation can come in at least five variants: cooperation between two terrorist entrepreneurs; cooperation between a terrorist entrepreneur and a formal organization; cooperation between a terrorist entrepreneur and an informal network; cooperation between an informal network and a formal organization; and cooperation between two (or more) informal networks. As I will argue shortly, the model can be extended to incorporate additional agents.

I further proposed that contemporary forms of terrorist cooperation should be distinguished not only in terms of the varying types of actors that collaborate, but also in terms of the qualitative strengths of their respective relationships. After all, any pair of terrorist actors can cooperate in a variety of ways depending on the nature of their relationship. Thus, in addition to distinguishing between organizational and networked cooperation, I have added the categories of high-end cooperation and low-end cooperation, each of which has two additional subcategories. Thus, high-end cooperation can take the form of mergers and strategic alliances, while low-end cooperation includes tactical and transactional collaborations.

A comprehensive typology of contemporary cooperation, I argued, must simultaneously account both for differences in the types of actors that collaborate and for varying qualitative strengths of cooperation. The holistic typology presented in chapter 4 merges these two dimensions. It also shows that organizational cooperation and the five variants of networked cooperation contain four additional subcategories (mergers, strategic alliances, tactical cooperation, and transactional cooperation). Thus, altogether, we can theoretically distinguish twenty-four subtypes of cooperation (see table 4.5).

The case studies in this book illustrate the two differences between high-end and low-end cooperation (chapters 7 and 8) and between organizational and networked cooperation (chapters 7 and 9).

It is time now to consider the implications of this project both for the study of terrorism and for policy.

IMPLICATIONS FOR THE STUDY OF TERRORISM

My study of terrorist cooperation furthers our understanding of the broader phenomenon of terrorism in four main ways. First, it offers a new theoretical model for the analysis of terrorism; second, the conceptual model is able to capture a highly dynamic and constantly evolving threat; third, by broadening the scope of terrorism, my study offers a more nuanced understanding of terrorism in its broader context; and finally, it strengthens calls for interdisciplinary approaches to studying the phenomenon of terrorism.

OFFERING A NEW THEORETICAL MODEL FOR THE ANALYSIS OF TERRORISM

Theoretically, this book has contributed to the study of terrorism by applying the important but underutilized agency-structure model to terrorist cooperation in several innovative ways. First, structure-agency theorists have pointed out that despite the prominence of the agency-structure debate, the concept is rarely applied to illuminate contemporary problems of international relations because scholars have had difficulties operational-izing the concept in practical terms. Second, the relatively few attempts made to date to do so have applied the concept of agency mostly to state actors, rather than to nonstate actors. Third, even among those studies that have applied the agential element of the agency-structure debate to nonstate actors, none that I am aware of has explicitly and systematically applied the concept to examine terrorism.

Adopting the agency-structure debate as a framework of analysis for terrorist cooperation offers several analytical benefits for our understand-ing of terrorist cooperation and terrorism more broadly. First, it offers new conceptual avenues through which to identify emerging types of terrorist actors and analyze their broader significance. Second, it serves as a con-ceptual tool with which to describe larger environmental forces that wield varying levels of influence on terrorist cooperation and on terrorism more broadly. Finally, it also illuminates the mutual relationship between environment and actors. Consequently, it has certain advantages over other, similar frameworks of analysis such as the "levels of analysis" approach, which has been applied to the study of terrorism in a number of studies, in-cluding by this author. The levels of analysis approach is valuable for its ability to break up highly complex phenomena into analytical categories that can be more easily examined. However, it is limited in that it does not address the relationships between the various levels. Agency-structure frameworks, in contrast, address this mutual relationship conceptually by assuming that structure and agents are inherently co-constituted.

CAPTURING A DYNAMIC THREAT

Because the typology I construct in this book is dynamic by design, it is well suited to grasping intellectually the constantly evolving threat of terrorism.

Thus, the typology explicitly acknowledges that the nature of coopera-tive relationships can change over time. As illustrated in figure 4.1, a tacti-cal relationship between two terrorist actors, for example, can gradually evolve into a strategic relationship; conversely, high-end forms of cooperation such as mergers or strategic alliances can weaken over time, regressing into tactical or transactional forms of cooperation and even leading to splits and competitions between erstwhile partners. This first dynamic aspect of the typology can help scholars and policymakers better understand how the intensity of groups' collaborations strengthen or weaken their mutual ties and shed light on the ways in which relationships between groups shift from cooperation to competition, and vice versa.

This typology is also explicit in stating that there are no hard separations between types of cooperation. Instead, they should be seen as occupying a spectrum ranging from mergers, at the highest end, to transactional cooperation, at the lowest end. Along this spectrum, each category overlaps with (rather than borders) its neighboring categories (see figure 4.1). Using this model allows both scholars and policy analysts to identify certain cooperative relationships that do not necessarily fall directly within one of the four ideal types. Cooperative relationships between, say, Al Qaeda and Al Qaeda in the Islamic Maghreb, can thus be situated in between strategic and tactical partnerships, which means that in this case, as in others, the typology allows for a considerable nuance for understanding the precise quality of a given collaboration between two actors.

In addition, the typology can be used to conceptualize dynamic changes in the agency of terrorist actors. Terrorist entrepreneurs, for example, are described as individual actors in the present study. It is not inconceivable, however, that such individual agents draw others to themselves and that their agency thereby evolves into an informal network. Similarly, some formal organizations, including Al Qaeda in Iraq (AQI)—the predecessor organization to the Islamic State—evolved out of informal networks. The typology introduced in chapter 4 can therefore help us trace not only changes in the types and degrees of cooperation, but also shifts in constellations of actors. For example, cooperation between an informal network and an organization (networked cooperation Variant 4) can be conceptualized as making a shift toward organizational cooperation once the informal network evolves into a formal organization. This can help portray the events of 2004, when Abu Musab al-Zarqawi's network Al-Tawhid w'al Jihad formally pledged allegiance to Al Qaeda, and subsequently formalized its existence as an organization formally affiliated with Al Qaeda.

A final benefit of the typology that I present crystallizes from the case studies on networked cooperation in chapter 9. The discussion of the nexus of jihadist militancy associated with Anjem Choudary in particular highlights the fact that the various types of cooperation identified in this book are not mutually exclusive, but coexist. In the last three case studies in chapter 9, I have first traced the links between terrorist entrepreneur Anjem Choudary and the informal network known as Sharia4Belgium. I have then examined the ties between Sharia4Belgium and two formal terrorist organizations, the Islamic State and Jabhat al-Nusra, before discussing how a multitude of informal actors cooperate under the Sharia4 umbrella. Although separating these three variants of networked cooperation was analytically helpful, a key finding of the consecutive examination of these cases is that these different variants converge. In other words, the highly intricate ties that bind the broader nexus of global jihad together integrate multiple forms of cooperation between a variety of actors. The model I offer is dynamic enough to allow us not only to disaggregate various types of cooperation—organizational cooperation as well as different variants of networked cooperation—but to reassemble them to better understand the complex picture of global jihadist ties. This is an important contribution because existing studies of terrorist cooperation have mostly limited their focus to bilateral cooperative ties. The framework I offer allows examination of ties that extend beyond dyads. Given that the contemporary jihadist threat picture involves multilateral cooperation, rather than mere dyadic cooperation, this contribution has clear implications for understanding, and addressing, today's most pressing terrorist challenges.

In sum, given its dynamic nature, the holistic typology serves as a valuable intellectual tool that can help situate, describe, and trace processes that are central to the identity of terrorist actors involved in cooperation; to the nature of their relationship; and to changes in the nature of their cooperation over time.

BROADENING THE SCOPE OF TERRORIST COOPERATION

Insofar as this book analyzes terrorist cooperation in a way that far exceeds the conceptual boundaries of existing studies on this topic, its broad scope allows for the inclusion of actors and structural factors that receive only scant attention, if any, in existing studies of terrorist cooperation. Informal actors such as terrorist entrepreneurs and informal networks are a good case in point. Even though the concept of terrorist entrepreneurs has been introduced elsewhere, existing studies have not discussed terrorist entrepreneurs in the context of terrorist cooperation. Similarly, much has been written in the post-9/11 period about terrorist networks, but network analysis is strangely absent from the literature on terrorist cooperation, despite its obvious relevance. This has prevented much of the existing research on terrorist cooperation from recognizing the central role that these informal actors play in this regard.

The limitations of an exclusive focus on formal organizations in studies on terrorist cooperation—and the advantages of this book's more inclusive approach—are particularly apparent in the case studies of networked cooperation presented in chapter 9, which show it operating in various ways among foreign fighters, Salafist networks, and online jihadist entrepreneurs, as much as, if not more than among formal terrorist organizations. While studies of foreign fighters or militant Salafist networks do, of course exist, their broader relevance to terrorist cooperation is usually ignored. Instead, studies of foreign fighters typically consider the issue of terrorist recruitment, the rising threat of homegrown terrorism, or the future threat posed by returning fighters, while studies of Salafist or militant jihadist networks often focus on questions of radicalization; tactics and strategies; or Western dilemmas in addressing these problems.

Apart from broadening the scope of terrorist cooperation at the level of actors, the study also broadens the scope of terrorist cooperation at the structural, or environmental, level. It illuminates and theorizes about the role of social media in establishing new platforms for cooperation and empowering new online facilitators of cooperation. While a large and growing body of studies on how terrorists use the Internet to achieve their objectives is available, few have assessed the implications of these new platforms and facilitators for how terrorists cooperate.

PROVIDING AN INTERDISCIPLINARY PERSPECTIVE

Finally, the insights gleaned from the more inclusive approach to the analysis of terrorist cooperation adopted here suggest that the problem of terrorist cooperation, and terrorism in general, is best examined from an interdisciplinary perspective. Thus, this book has drawn from a number of areas of study, ranging from terrorism and jihadism studies to the literature on insurgencies and civil wars, in addition to network and globalization theory, to name but a few. The present study adds additional evidence to claims that disciplinary boundaries are becoming increasingly porous, and that approaches that limit themselves to single areas of studies are analytically restrictive. Luckily, there is a growing trend among younger scholars to transcend disciplinary boundaries, as is evidenced in the burgeoning, cross-disciplinary fields of conflict studies and peace studies. Addressing an inherently multifaceted problem such as terrorism from various disciplinary angles allows analysts to pool the insights and best practices from academic fields that have too often remained divided.

IMPLICATIONS FOR POLICY

The theoretical and empirical discussions in this book imply that the overall threat posed by terrorist cooperation is on the rise. Insofar as the book shows that contemporary terrorist cooperation involves diverse types of terrorist agents, such as entrepreneurs, informal networks, and formal organizations, as well as states, and that each of these various agents can cooperate with one or more of the others, it points to an opening of an unprecedented number of new channels of terrorist cooperation. To illustrate, whereas traditional channels of terrorist cooperation linked two formal organizations, the advent of networked cooperation implies new possibilities of cooperation between organizations and networks; organizations and entrepreneurs; networks and networks; entrepreneurs and networks; and two sets of entrepreneurs. Moreover, these channels, as we have seen, are not mutually exclusive, but can and do coincide to create a highly complex web of multichannel cooperation, as exemplified by the militant jihadist nexus surrounding the figure of Anjem Choudary. Along these multiple channels of cooperation, these actors can engage in a plethora of cooperative activities related to terrorism. Coupled with highly enabling environmental factors such as jihadist ideology, the rise of social media, and the prevalence of armed conflict, the overall threat posed by cooperation between contemporary terrorist actors in terms of quantity, diversity, and efficiency rises significantly.

Here, I will highlight a number of ways that the analysis of terrorist cooperation can help policymakers address this growing threat.

LOOKING BEYOND THE TERRORIST ORGANIZATION

This book suggests that counterterrorism policy must heavily rely on an accurate analysis of the cooperating actors. Hence, the units of analysis must be properly identified. In this regard. it is apparent that gathering and analyzing data using "terrorist organizations" as the single, or main, unit of analysis is no longer adequate. Counterterrorism analysts should adopt a more comprehensive approach that conceives of the threat of terrorism as emanating from a variety of actors. Failure to do so could, in extreme cases, blur analysts' ability to identify other types of actors that can abet terrorism, including informal networks or terrorist entrepreneurs that are active relatively independently of existing groups, which could lead to consequences that might include missing the next terrorist attack.

To illustrate this point, consider the cooperation between Al Qaeda and Khaled Sheikh Muhammad that led to the attacks of September 11, 2001. Had Western analysts kept close tabs not only on Al Qaeda in the pre-9/11 period, but also on Khaled Sheikh Muhammad, chances of preventing the attacks of 9/11 would have increased. But KSM's lack of formal association with Al Qaeda, or any other terrorist group for that matter, may have rendered him a low-priority target of observation. What makes tracking the movements of these unconventional and loosely affiliated terrorist agents even more pressing is that future terrorists are more, not less, likely, to have fluid organizational attachments and act with relative autonomy.

The findings in this book further suggest that good counterterrorism policy is dependent not only on broadening the scope of data-gathering, but also on obtaining more granular data. Due to inherent limitations of manpower, counterterrorism practitioners could benefit from outsourcing at least part of their data-gathering efforts to reliable commercial partners, including those specializing in the gathering, processing, and analysis of "big data"—even though such a step would raise other problems related to privacy.

Counterterrorism policy also faces new challenges because of the international character of many contemporary terrorist actors. While this is not an entirely new problem, it has become more common in the wake of globalization. The ease with which terrorist entrepreneurs can travel, for example, presents law enforcement agencies with challenges in prosecuting terrorists due to jurisdictional ambiguities. Similarly, as was described in chapter 2, many of the informal networks have participants in different countries—a fact that greatly impedes governmental efforts to monitor terrorism suspects. For all these reasons, countering contemporary terrorist cooperation requires international cooperation, especially among counterterrorism and intelligence services of the various states affected by this problem. The bombings at Brussels airport and the Maalbeek metro station in Brussels in March 2016, which were carried out by an international jihadist cell that traversed several European countries, were only the latest reminder of the need to foster international security cooperation. Only cooperation that is strong and confident enough to share information on terrorism freely will be able to face a global jihadist movement that seeks to exploit Western liberalism and openness for its own sinister ends.

Security services, however, have their work cut out for them in another respect. Counterterrorism practitioners should not only broaden their focus beyond the terrorist organization to new, unconventional terrorist actors, but also recognize that terrorist actors increasingly interact with radical elements that may not rely on violence or have not yet crossed the threshold to violence. The various Sharia4 entities discussed in chapter 9 illustrate this problem well. Even if most of these Salafist networks have not crossed the threshold to terrorism, they are playing an important role as real or potential interlocutors between their participating members and actual terrorist actors. Furthermore, even if most of these Salafist and jihadist networks remain largely within the boundaries of legality, they clearly attract individuals who are predisposed to adopting radical ideologies that may streamline a later transition toward illegal activity, including terrorism. Therefore, governments that face stronger Salafist activity ignore these movements at great risk, as the discussion of Sharia4 Belgium in chapter 9 has shown. Here too, governments should rely on surveillance, where justified. In addition, governments especially in the West should establish relationships of trust with local Muslim communities—relationships based on a common understanding that jihadism threatens non-Muslims as well as the vast majority of Muslims alike, for only a small fringe of the Muslim population identifies with the Salafist and jihadist stream of Islam.

CONSTRAINING THE ENABLING ENVIRONMENT

In addition to adjusting existing approaches related to the actors involved in terrorist cooperation, Western governments would also be well advised to seek ways to constrain the environmental factors that enable today's increasingly diverse terrorist actors to collaborate with one another. Chapter 3 suggested that among the main challenges related to terrorist cooperation today are the persistent appeal of jihadist ideology, the ability of actors to communicate using the social media, and ongoing armed conflict. Unfortunately, there are no quick fixes to any of these structural challenges.

As far as ideology is concerned, jihadism has proven powerful and stubborn. But rather than despairing over jihadism's staying power as an idea, policymakers should seek ways to counter the ideological appeal without offending the broader Muslim population in the process. Here, it is worth recalling that Western governments have scored some successes in the decade after 9/11, when they faced a global jihad movement that was spearheaded by Al Qaeda. Although they have not been able to eradicate jihadist ideology—a goal that, if at all possible, is best pursued by Muslims themselves—they have been able in some ways to contain jihadism's appeal. Western scholars and governments, along with many brave Muslims, have highlighted the high costs of jihadism first and foremost to Muslims themselves by pointing, for example, to the large numbers of Muslims killed as a result of jihadist violence. Arguably, however, the value of such an approach is questionable in the case of the Islamic State, which uses brutality as a strategy not only to intimidate its enemies, but also to mobilize potential supporters. For a group that glorifies violence and prides itself for its systematic campaigns of rape and beheadings, a strategy of highlighting behavioral misconduct is pointless.

What is more likely to succeed in stemming the ideological appeal of the Islamic State is forcefully preventing the group from fulfilling its ideological promises to its hoped for constituency. The revival of the Islamic caliphate has motivated many would-be jihadists to join the Islamic State, even if the caliphate's legitimacy is recognized by only a minority of Muslims. At the same time, the Islamic State's keystone project is also its Achilles' heel, given that one of the greatest ideological setbacks for the movement would result from the very failure of the caliphate to survive. Hence, ensuring that it does fail should be the top priority for governments threatened by the Islamic State.

If, on the other hand, ensuring the survival of the caliphate is critical for the Islamic State's ongoing ability to mobilize recruits, as of the fall of 2016, its survival is hardly a foregone conclusion.[1] Hence, for a global jihadist movement that is arguably dominated by the Islamic State, the destruction of the Islamic State organization—and along with it the end of its declared caliphate—will help deal at least a temporary blow to the overall appeal of jihadist ideology, and therefore to one of the key motivators for contemporary terrorist cooperation.

It is less clear what Western governments can do to stem the ability of jihadists to exploit the Internet and social media platforms for their own ends. Any measures taken in this regard raise civil liberties concerns and other legal and ethical issues. Furthermore, while shutting down Twitter or Facebook accounts of militant organizations may be a nuisance for them, doing so can also harm government analysts who use the same accounts to gather open-source intelligence. Counterterrorism professionals must walk a fine line between seeking to shut down accounts that are highly valuable for jihadist groups in terms of recruitment, propaganda, and operations and not shooting themselves in the foot by destroying some of the most useful means of gathering intelligence about jihadist networks.[2]

As far as the prevalence of armed conflict is concerned, the post–Arab Spring period in particular has made it painfully evident that ignoring civil wars and insurgencies can incur significant humanitarian, political, financial, and other security costs. Massive waves of refugees not only present daunting humanitarian and economic challenges to the affected countries, but can also tear at the social and political fabric of the countries concerned, for example, by provoking a dangerous ascendance of right-wing extremism in the West.[3]

The discussion in this book has highlighted the risks inherent in these civil wars and insurgencies to produce areas of limited statehood and poor governance—a welcome situation for militant actors who are adept at exploiting such opportunities for their own ends. That the resulting chaos creates formidable alliances is nowhere clearer than ever in Syria, where, it is worth recalling, the most significant challenges to the Assad regime were posed by alliances of militant groups, such as Jaysh al-Islam or Jaysh al-Fatah, as opposed to by groups acting largely on their own.

DISRUPTING TERRORIST COOPERATION: A TAILORED APPROACH

Unless there are political or countervailing security concerns that speak against seeking ways to break up terrorist alliances and other forms of cooperation among militant actors, counterterrorism practitioners will likely conclude that it is generally a good idea to do so. To that end, the distinction of terrorist cooperation made in this book into four basic qualitative types—mergers, strategic alliances, tactical cooperation, and transactional cooperation—can provide a useful tool for counterterrorism practitioners to develop an approach that is tailored to exploit the specific weakness of each of these types of cooperation.

Mergers, for example, are predicated on a relatively high degree of ideological affinity and agreement over strategy. In such a situation, divisions along ideological and strategic lines will be hard to identify. Mergers might instead be most vulnerable to personality rifts, especially between the leaderships of the two merging groups.

Strategic alliances usually involve a shared world view but, as the example of strategic alliances between Al Qaeda and its affiliates suggest, such alliances may feature ongoing divisions over strategic and tactical choices, in addition to possible personality rifts or agency problems. Strategic alliances might therefore be broken up most effectively by deepening strategic and tactical rifts between the partners.

In a tactical cooperation, on the other hand, the survivability of the relationship is conditional upon the partners' ongoing perception that tactical collaboration continues to serve their respective parochial interests—interests that can fluctuate due to shifting circumstances. This suggests that states trying to break up tactical alliances may succeed by trying to influence the cost-benefit calculation of these groups to remain in such alliances. States may consider both positive incentives and negative sanctions in trying to influence these groups' ongoing rationale for maintaining tactical relationships.

Transactional cooperative relationships come in different forms, but are generally the least intensive form of cooperation. Some material transactional forms of cooperation may be of minor importance, and best left unaddressed. Ideological affiliations, such as Boko Haram's pledge of *bayah* to the Islamic State, may pose a greater potential threat, and may therefore best be addressed by attempts to highlight ideological differences between the groups, or otherwise reduce trust between the parties. The goal for policy makers should be to prevent a low-end cooperation from turning into a high-end cooperation.

EXTENSIONS: INCORPORATING STATE ACTORS

The typology I introduced in this book has focused on three different types of terrorist agents, but it can easily be adjusted to fit differing perspectives of terrorist actors or specific needs of counterterrorism practitioners. To demonstrate this point, this final section of the book will extend the typology introduced in chapter 4 to incorporate state actors as agents of terrorist cooperation. Doing so has obvious benefits for counterterrorism practitioners and academics. No less important, policy analysts and scholars can, with relatively little effort, extend the model further to include still other types of actors and/or agents.

Table C.1 expands upon table 4.2 (chapter 4) by including state agents and showing that they can cooperate with any of the other types of terrorist agents, as well as with other states supporting terrorism. By taking account of state actors, table C.1 suggests the extent to which the international nexus of terrorist cooperation is even more complex than has been described so far.

As table C.1 shows, states can cooperate with at least four additional types of agents. They can cooperate with terrorist entrepreneurs in what can be termed state sponsorship Variant 1; with formal terrorist/insurgent organizations (state sponsorship Variant 2); with informal networks (state sponsorship Variant 3); and with other states (state cooperation). Identifying these possibilities is not just a theoretical exercise. In the early 1990s, for example, Sudan provided a safe haven to Carlos the Jackal, a notorious terrorist entrepreneur, and entertained a relationship that fits the description of state sponsorship Variant 1.[4] Cooperation between a state and a formal organization (Variant 2), which can be considered the classic form of state sponsorship, is exemplified by Al Qaeda's relationship with Iran, as discussed in chapter 8; Pakistan's support for a variety of jihadist groups, such as Lashkar-e Taibeh, is another example, among many others.[5] Iranian support of Abu Musab al-Zarqawi and his informal network of jihadists after September 11, 2001, first reported by the German magazine *Cicero* using leaked German intelligence documents, exemplifies state sponsorship

TABLE C.1 TYPOLOGY EXTENSIONS:
INCORPORATING THE ROLE OF STATES

	Terrorist Entrepreneurs	Terrorist/ Insurgent Organizations	Informal Networks	States
Terrorist Entrepreneurs	Networked Cooperation (Variant 1)	Networked Cooperation (Variant 2)	Networked Cooperation (Variant 3)	State Sponsorship (Variant 1)
Terrorist/ Insurgent Organizations		Organizational Cooperation	Networked Cooperation (Variant 4)	State Sponsorship (Variant 2)
Informal Networks			Networked Cooperation (Variant 5)	State Sponsorship (Variant 3)
States				State Cooperation

Variant 3.[6] Finally, Iranian-Syrian coordination on Hizballah represents an example of state cooperation per se.

* * *

Fifteen years after the attacks of September 11, 2001, struck the United States and President George W. Bush declared a war on terrorism, it is painfully obvious that terrorism shows no signs of subsiding. On the contrary, in the aftermath of the dramatic rise of the so-called Islamic State in the summer of 2014, it seems as if terrorism has become a tragic constant of modern life.

To pursue their goals, terrorist actors and their broader support networks seek ever more innovative ways to collaborate with each other. The attacks in late March 2016 at the Zaventem airport and Maalbeek metro station in Brussels, which killed at least thirty-five people and wounded some three hundred others, took place as I was writing the final sentences of this book. The Brussels attacks and the November 2015 attacks in Paris were carried out by one and the same network—one whose modus operandi is symptomatic of the innovative and inter-connected character of modern terrorism.[7]

This book has attempted to shed some light on the multifarious ways in which these terrorists cooperate by examining terrorist cooperation in its broader context. Only by grasping the fundamental transformations that terrorist actors have undergone in a constantly shifting environment can we trace the evolution of terrorist cooperation over time and understand its contemporary forms.

Terrorist actors continue to evolve, as does the broader environment in which they operate. At a minimum, this requires that analysts keep tracking these developments closely. More than ever before, however, the fast-paced social transformations we are witnessing require analysts to also keep questioning their basic assumptions. Defining *terrorism*, *terrorist organizations*, or *terrorist cooperation* is useful as long as analysts recognize that these phenomena are themselves undergoing change and that our attempts to understand them must evolve along with them.

This book has been, in part, an attempt to frame the discussion of terrorist cooperation in new ways—away from static models that focus on bilateral relationships between formal terrorist actors. It is to be hoped that the preceding discussion has succeeded in providing a more comprehensive, nuanced analysis of how contemporary militant actors cooperate. At the same time, it is important to recognize that despite its broader scope, this book has limitations.

Cooperation between actors engaged in terrorism occurs within far more complex webs of relationships than any single book is able to describe. These complex webs link terrorist actors to other actors that may support terrorism financially or ideologically, but may not carry out terrorist activities themselves. As discussed in chapter 9, radical jihadist ideologues like Anjem Choudary have skillfully managed to avoid and/or hide direct involvement in acts of terrorism, but nevertheless play a critically important

role as international hubs of jihadist militancy.[8] A multitude of less prominent jihadist sympathizers are active in cyberspace, sharing the ideological
content of terrorist organizations such as the Islamic State to thousands of
followers. Still other activists, from individual financiers to banks and front
companies, are cooperating with terrorist actors by providing financial support to these groups, or serving as financial interlocutors that channel funds
to militant jihadist groups.[9] More research is needed to understand terrorist
cooperation in all of these facets. Specifically, future studies of terrorist
cooperation should examine ties between an even broader array of terrorist
actors—those actors defined as agents in this book—and other important
actors, such as online facilitators, jihadist ideologues, and independent
financiers.

Finally, an additional fruitful avenue for research is a broader examination of the relationship between terrorist actors not only in terms of their
cooperation and competition, but also in terms of the interplay between
these two.[10] More research on the conditions that shift a given relationship
from one of cooperation to one of competition, and vice versa, will help us
inch closer toward an understanding of the dynamics of terrorism.

NOTES

INTRODUCTION

1. National Commission on Terrorist Attacks Upon the United States, *The 9/11 Commission Report*, 1st ed. (New York: Norton, 2004), 154 (hereafter cited as *9/11 Commission Report*).
2. *9/11 Commission Report*, 150, 154.
3. KSM did eventually pledge allegiance to bin Laden and formally joined Al Qaeda, but only after bin Laden's formal acceptance of his proposal. *9/11 Commission Report*, 150, 154.
4. Barak Mendelsohn, *The al-Qaeda Franchise: The Expansion of al-Qaeda and Its Consequences* (Oxford: Oxford University Press, 2015), 9.
5. In July 2016, Jabhat al-Nusra renamed itself Jabhat Fath al-Sham. As this book covers the period until 2015, however, I will refer to the group as Jabhat al-Nusra.
6. Daniel Byman, "ISIS Goes Global," *Foreign Affairs*, March/April 2016.
7. Eric Schmitt and Mark Mazzetti, "Qaeda Leader's Edict to Yemen Affiliate Is Said to Prompt Alert," *New York Times*, August 5, 2013.
8. *Ad-Diyar*, October 4, 2015, cited in Meir Amit Intelligence and Terrorism Information Center, "Spotlight on Global Jihad, September 22–October 8, 2015," 10.
9. Colin Elman, "Explanatory Typologies in Qualitative Studies of International Politics," *International Organization* 59, no. 2 (April 2005): 294.
10. Research teams that I directed have systematically reviewed all main terrorism journals for data on terrorist cooperation up until and including the year 2015. These journals include *Studies in Conflict & Terrorism, Terrorism and Political Violence, Perspectives on Terrorism*, and the *CTC Sentinel*. In addition, research teams have mined the vast collection of books on terrorism in the Marc Rich Library at the Interdisciplinary Center Herzliya for information on terrorist cooperation.

11. Documents released up to March 1, 2016, including the 113 documents found in Osama bin Laden's safe house in Abbottabad, Pakistan, are covered in this book. These and previously released documents are available on the website of the DNI at http://www .dni.gov/index.php/resources/bin-laden-bookshelf?start=1. Other documents are available at the CTC's website, at https://www.ctc.usma.edu/programs-resources/harmony -program.

12. Alexander Wendt, "The Agent-Structure Problem in International Relations Theory," *International Organization* 41, no. 3 (Summer 1987); David Dessler, "What's at Stake in the Agent-Structure Debate?" *International Organization* 43, no. 3 (Summer 1989); Colin Wight, *Agents, Structures and International Relations: Politics as Ontology* (Cambridge: Cambridge University Press, 2006).

13. Kate O'Neill, Jörg Balsiger, and Stacy D. VanDeveer, "Actors, Norms, and Impact: Recent International Cooperation Theory and the Influence of the Agent-Structure Debate," *Annual Review of Political Science* 7 (2004): 168.

14. O'Neill, Balsiger, and VanDeveer, "Actors, Norms, and Impact."

15. Compare Tricia L. Bacon, "Strange Bedfellows or Brothers-In-Arms: Why Terrorist Groups Ally," (PhD dissertation, Georgetown University, November 2013), 13.

16. Compare Kanisha D. Bond, "Power, Identity, Credibility and Cooperation: Examining the Development of Cooperative Arrangements Among Violent Non-State Actors" (PhD dissertation, Pennsylvania State University, August 2010), 4.

17. Bacon, "Strange Bedfellows," 13.

18. Assaf Moghadam, *The Globalization of Martyrdom: Al Qaeda, Salafi Jihad, and the Diffusion of Suicide Attacks* (Baltimore, MD: Johns Hopkins University Press, 2008).

19. Bernardine Dohrn, "Declaration of a State of War, The Berkeley Tribe," July 31, 1970, quoted in Tom Parker and Nick Sitter, "The Four Horsemen of Terrorism: It's Not Waves, It's Strains," *Terrorism and Political Violence* 28, no. 2 (2016): 200.

20. This definition combines elements of those proposed by Hoffman, Schmid, and Wilkinson. See Bruce Hoffman, *Inside Terrorism*, rev. and exp. ed. (New York: Columbia University Press, 2006); Alex P. Schmid, *The Routledge Handbook of Terrorism Research* (London: Routledge, 2011); and Paul Wilkinson, *Terrorism Versus Democracy: The Liberal State Response*, 3rd ed. (London: Routledge, 2006).

21. See, for example, Daniel Byman, *Deadly Connections: States that Sponsor Terrorism* (Cambridge: Cambridge University Press, 2005); and Daniel Byman, Peter Chalk, Bruce Hoffman, William Rosenau, and David Brannan, *Trends in Outside Support for Insurgent Movements* (Santa Monica, CA: RAND, 2001).

22. For an overview of the literature, see Eric Price, "Selected Literature on Terrorism and Organized Crime," *Perspectives on Terrorism* 4, no. 6 (2010).

23. Brian J. Phillips, "Terrorist Group Cooperation and Longevity," *International Studies Quarterly* 58, no. 2 (June 2014); Benjamin Acosta and Steven J. Childs, "Illuminating the Global Suicide-Attack Network," *Studies in Conflict & Terrorism* 36, no. 1 (2013); Victor Asal and R. Karl Rethemeyer, "The Nature of the Beast: Terrorist Organizational Characteristics and Organizational Lethality," *Journal of Politics* 70, no. 2 (2008); and

Michael C. Horowitz and Philip B. K. Potter, "Allying to Kill: Terrorist Intergroup Cooperation and the Consequences for Lethality," *Journal of Conflict Resolution* 58, no. 2 (2014).

24. Michael C. Horowitz, "Nonstate Actors and the Diffusion of Innovation: The Case of Suicide Terrorism," *International Organization* 64, no. 1 (January 2010); Victor Asal, Gary A. Ackerman, and R. Karl Rethemeyer, "Connections Can Be Toxic: Terrorist Organizational Factors and the Pursuit of CBRN Weapons," *Studies in Conflict & Terrorism* 35, no. 3 (2012).

25. Bond, "Power," 2.

26. See for example Charles Lister, *The Syrian Jihad: Al Qaeda, the Islamic State, and the Evolution of an Insurgency* (New York: Oxford University Press, 2015), 83–116; and Jennifer Cafarella, "Jabhat Al-Nusra in Syria: An Islamic Emirate for Al-Qaeda," Middle East Security Report 25, Institute for the Study of War, December 2014.

27. "Augenzeugenbericht aus Sirt: IS Errichtet Terrorherrschaft in Libyen," *Spiegel Online*, May 18, 2016.

28. Byman, "ISIS Goes Global."

29. Kim Cragin, Peter Chalk, Sara A. Daly, and Brian A. Jackson, *Sharing the Dragon's Teeth: Terrorist Groups and the Exchange of New Technologies* (Santa Monica, CA: RAND, 2007), 3.

30. James R. Clapper, "Statement for the Record: Worldwide Threat Assessment of the US Intelligence Community," House Permanent Select Committee on Intelligence, February 25, 2016.

31. William Braniff, "Testimony Before the United States House Armed Services Committee Hearing on the State of Al Qaeda, Its Affiliates, and Associated Groups: View From Outside Experts," Washington, DC: United States House of Representatives, February 4, 2014, 2.

32. Braniff, "Testimony," 2.

33. Clapper, "Statement," 4.

34. Clapper, "Statement," 5.

35. Clapper, "Statement," 5.

36. Clapper, "Statement," 5.

37. Clapper, "Statement," 5.

38. Clapper, "Statement," 5.

39. Clapper, "Statement," 5.

40. Clapper, "Statement," 6.

1. THE PUZZLE OF TERRORIST COOPERATION

1. Jacob N. Shapiro, *The Terrorist's Dilemma: Managing Violent Covert Organizations* (Princeton: Princeton University Press, 2013).

2. Shapiro, *Terrorist's Dilemma*, 8.

3. Ely Karmon, *Coalitions Between Terrorist Organizations: Revolutionaries, Nationalists and Islamists* (Leiden: Martinus Nijhoff, 2005), 307.

4. Karmon argues that this explains why terrorist groups have few compunctions reneging on agreements. Karmon, *Coalitions*, 307.

5. On the risks of cooperation, see also Kent Layne Oots, *A Political Organization Approach to Transnational Terrorism* (New York: Greenwood Press, 1986), 41; and Tricia L. Bacon, "Strange Bedfellows or Brothers-In-Arms: Why Terrorist Groups Ally" (PhD dissertation, Georgetown University, 2013), 4–10.

6. Shapiro, *Terrorist's Dilemma*, 26–62; 82–100.

7. Quoted in David C. Rapoport, "The International World as Some Terrorists Have Seen It: A Look at a Century of Memoirs," in *Inside Terrorist Organizations*, ed. David C. Rapoport (London: Frank Cass, 2001), 45.

8. See Alan Cullison, "Inside Al-Qaeda's Hard Drive," *Atlantic Monthly* 294 (2004).

9. Phil Williams, "Cooperation Among Criminal Organizations," in *Transnational Organized Crime and International Security: Business as Usual*, ed. Mats Berdal and Monica Serrano (Boulder, CO: Lynne Rienner, 2002), 70. See also Refik Culpan, *Global Business Alliances: Theory and Practice* (Westport, CT: Quorum Books, 2002).

10. Max Abrahms, "Does Terrorism Really Work? Evolution in the Conventional Wisdom Since 9/11," *Defence and Peace Economics* 22, no. 6 (2011).

11. These two goals are often mutually reinforcing: Enhanced capacity can help promote ideological agendas, while widespread ideological influence can promote mobilization efforts, and hence survivability.

12. Martha Crenshaw, "An Organizational Approach to the Analysis of Political Terrorism," *Orbis* 29, no. 3 (1985).

13. In international relations theory, threat perception has long been considered a key motivation for alliance formation between state actors. See especially Stephen M. Walt, *The Origins of Alliances* (Ithaca, NY: Cornell University Press, 1990). Karmon adopts this existing body of literature in his work and applies it to terrorist groups.

14. Karmon, *Coalitions*.

15. Syed Saleem Shahzad, *Inside Al-Qaeda and the Taliban: Beyond bin Laden and 9/11* (New York: Palgrave McMillan, 2011), 9.

16. For a systematic study of divisions in the global jihad movement, for example, see Assaf Moghadam and Brian Fishman, *Fault Lines in Global Jihad: Organizational, Strategic, and Ideological Fissures* (London: Routledge, 2011).

17. Karmon, *Coalitions*, 25; and Brian A Jackson, John C. Baker, Kim Cragin, John Parachini, Horacio R. Trujillo, and Peter Chalk, *Aptitude for Destruction: Organizational Learning in Terrorist Groups and Its Implications for Combating Terrorism* (Santa Monica, CA: RAND, 2005).

18. "Amal Driving Hezbollah from West Beirut; 25 Killed," *Los Angeles Times*, November 27, 1988.

19. See, for example, "New Video Message from the Islamic State: Message to the Muslims in Somalia—Wilāyat al-Furāt," May 21, 2015, jihadology.net.

20. Crenshaw, "Organizational Approach."

21. Bruce Hoffman, *Inside Terrorism*, rev. and exp. ed. (New York: Columbia University Press, 2006), 76.

22. Brian J Phillips, "Terrorist Group Cooperation and Longevity," *International Studies Quarterly* 58, no. 2 (2014).

23. Phillips, "Terrorist Group Cooperation," 2. Resource aggregation explains cooperation of nonterrorist groups as well. Firms, for examples, may use cooperative strategies to cut costs, shorten production time, share risks, and, broadly speaking, achieve goals that they could not realize on their own. See Bo Feng, Zhi-Ping Fan, and Jian Ma, "A Method for Partner Selection of Codevelopment Alliances Using Individual and Collaborative Utilities," *International Journal of Production Economics* 124, no. 1 (2010). For cooperation in other contexts, see also Michael C. Horowitz and Philip B.K. Potter, "Allying to Kill: Terrorist Intergroup Cooperation and the Consequences for Lethality," *Journal of Conflict Resolution* 58 no. 2 (2014): 201–3; and Wim Wiewel and Albert Hunter, "The Interorganizational Network as a Resource: A Comparative Case Study on Organizational Genesis," *Administrative Science Quarterly* 30, no. 4 (1985). The favorable impact that cooperation can have on mobilization efforts is known to apply not only to terrorist groups. Sociologists have noted a similar positive impact of cooperation on the mobilization efforts of broader social movements as well. As Klandermans and Oegema argue, the more a social movement's "reach-out networks are woven into other organizations, the more people are reached by mobilization attempts." Bert Klandermans and Dirk Oegema, "Potentials, Networks, Motivations, and Barriers: Steps Towards Participation in Social Movements," *American Sociological Review* 52, no. 4 (1987): 520.

24. Peter Bergen, Bruce Hoffman, and Katherine Tiedemann, "Assessing the Jihadist Terrorist Threat to America and American Interests," *Studies in Conflict & Terrorism* 34, no. 2 (2011): 73.

25. From the perspective of the militant groups, the desire to survive may not always be distinguishable from the desire to thrive.

26. Some of the following challenges are described at greater length in Jackson et al., *Aptitude for Destruction*, 17–26. For the importance of resources as a cause for cooperation among rebel groups, see Afshon Ostovar and Will McCants, "The Rebel Alliance: Why Syria's Armed Opposition Has Failed to Unify" (Washington, DC: Center for Naval Analysis, 2013), 7.

27. Christopher Dobson, *Black September: Its Short, Violent History* (New York: Macmillan, 1974), 74–75.

28. Camille Tawil argues that it was Western counterterrorism pressures that rallied many jihadist groups behind bin Laden, even if they did not entirely agree with his agenda. See Camille Tawil, *Brothers in Arms: The Story of Al-Qa'ida and the Arab Jihadists* (London: Saqi 2010), 11.

29. Jackson et al., *Aptitude for Destruction*, 9. On terrorist learning, see also James Forest, *Teaching Terror: Strategic and Tactical Learning in the Terrorist World* (London: Rowman & Littlefield, 2006); and Kim Cragin, Peter Chalk, Sara A. Daly, and Brian A. Jackson,

Sharing the Dragon's Teeth: Terrorist Groups and the Exchange of New Technologies (Santa Monica, CA: RAND, 2007).

30. Jackson et al., *Aptitude for Destruction*, 11.

31. Jackson et al., *Aptitude for Destruction*, 11–12.

32. Jackson et al., *Aptitude for Destruction*, 14–15.

33. See, for example, Liz Sly, "The Hidden Hand Behind the Islamic State Militants? Saddam Hussein's," *Washington Post*, April 4, 2015.

34. Bard E. O'Neill, *Insurgency and Terrorism: From Revolution to Apocalypse* (Washington, DC: Potomac, 2005). Cooperation increases the effectiveness of groups that specialize in terrorism, as well as larger rebel and insurgent groups involved in civil wars. Seden Ackinaroglu, for example, shows that "credible" alliances between insurgent groups fighting an incumbent regime lower the chances of a government victory. By raising rebel effectiveness, they raise the overall chances of the rebels' victory. Seden Ackinaroglu, "Rebel Interdependences and Civil War Outcomes," *Journal of Conflict Resolution* 56, no. 5 (2012).

35. Z. Gad, "International Cooperation Among Terrorist Groups," in *On Terrorism and Combating Terrorism: Proceedings of an International Seminar, Tel Aviv, 1979*, ed. Ariel Merari (Frederick, MD: University Publications of America, 1985), 139.

36. Hoffman, *Inside Terrorism*, 79.

37. Cragin et.al., *Sharing the Dragon's Teeth*, 82.

38. Victor Asal and R. Karl Rethemeyer, "The Nature of the Beast: Organizational Structures and the Lethality of Terrorist Attacks," *Journal of Politics* 70, no. 2 (2008).

39. Daniel Byman, *A High Price: The Triumphs and Failures of Israeli Counterterrorism* (New York: Oxford University Press, 2011), 146.

40. Michael C. Horowitz, "Nonstate Actors and the Diffusion of Innovations: The Case of Suicide Terrorism," *International Organization* 64, no. 1 (2010); Michael C Horowitz, *The Diffusion of Military Power: Causes and Consequences for International Politics* (Princeton, NJ: Princeton University Press, 2010).

41. Horowitz, "Nonstate Actors," 34.

42. Horowitz, "Nonstate Actors," 34.

43. Quoted in Neil Ferguson, "Disengaging from Terrorism," in *The Psychology of Counter-Terrorism*, ed. Andrew Silke (London; New York: Routledge 2010), 114. For an additional discussion, see John P. Darby, "Borrowing and Lending in Peace Processes," in *Contemporary Peacemaking: Conflict, Violence and Peace Processes*, ed. John P. Darby and Roger MacGinty (New York: Macmillan, 2003).

44. Neil Ferguson, email communication with the author, July 8, 2014.

45. Sharing ideological affinity, a common goal, or a common enemy can also serve process goals.

46. Kanisha D. Bond, "Power, Identity, Credibility and Cooperation: Examining the Development of Cooperative Arrangements Among Violent Non-State Actors" (PhD dissertation, Pennsylvania State University, August 2010); Benjamin Acosta and Steven J. Childs, "Illuminating the Global Suicide-Attack Network," *Studies in Conflict & Terrorism* 36, no. 1 (2013).

47. Karmon, *Coalitions*, 49–50.

48. Xavier Raufer, "The Red Brigades: Farewell to Arms," *Studies in Conflict & Terrorism* 16, no. 4 (1993): 322.

49. Stefan H. Leader and Peter Probst, "The Earth Liberation Front and Environmental Terrorism," *Terrorism and Political Violence* 15, no. 4 (2003): 43. For a list of joint attacks by the ALF and ELF, see Southern Poverty Law Center, "Eco-Violence: The Record," *Intelligence Report* 107 (2002).

50. See, for example, the joint communiqués released by the Red Army Faction (RAF) and Action Direct (AD) following their official alliance in January 1985. Karmon, *Coalitions*, 157–72. See also Michael Gabbay, "Mapping the Factional Structure of the Sunni Insurgency in Iraq," *CTC Sentinel* 1, no. 4 (March 2008).

51. Combating Terrorism Center, "Al-Qaida's Five Aspects of Power," *CTC Sentinel* 2, no. 1 (January 2009).

52. Michel N. Barnett, "Identity and Alliances in the Middle East," in *The Culture of National Security: Norms and Identity in World Politics*, ed. Peter J. Katzenstein (New York: Columbia University Press, 1996), 410.

53. Quoted in Jaideep Saikia and Ekaterina Stepanova, *Terrorism: Patterns of Internationalization* (New Delhi: SAGE Publications India, 2009), 6.

54. Karmon adds that shared anti-Semitic sentiment also facilitated cooperation between the European and Palestinian militant groups. Karmon, *Coalitions*, 299.

55. For a good summary of existing explanations of cooperation between states, see Bond, "Power," 12–19.

56. See, for example, Daniel Byman, "Unlikely Alliance: Iran's Secretive Relationship with Al-Qaeda," in *Iranian Sponsorship of Terrorism* (IHS Defense, Risk and Security Consulting, July 2012), 29. An example of an attack coordinated between Hizballah and Hamas is the 2004 attack on the Israeli port of Ashdod by two suicide bombers. Ze'ev Schiff, "Background: Hezbollah Had a Role in Ashdod Bombing," *Haaretz*, March 28, 2004.

57. Quoted in Karmon, *Coalitions*, 226.

58. "Hezbollah, Hamas Coordinating on the Ground: Official," *Daily Star*, July 12, 2014.

59. Fotini Christia, *Alliance Formation in Civil Wars* (Cambridge: Cambridge University Press, 2012); Assaf Moghadam and Brian Fishman, eds. *Fault Lines in Global Jihad: Organizational, Strategic, and Ideological Fissures* (London: Routledge, 2011).

60. Bacon, "Strange Bedfellows," 26.

61. Ray Takeyh and Nikolas Gvosdev, "Do Terrorist Networks Need a Home?" *Washington Quarterly* 25, no. 3 (2002).

62. Cragin et al., *Sharing the Dragon's Teeth*, 34.

63. Mohammed M. Hafez, *Suicide Bombers in Iraq: The Strategy and Ideology of Martyrdom* (US Institute of Peace Press, 2007), 173.

64. Christia, *Alliance Formation*; Ostovar and McCants, "The Rebel Alliance."

65. Peter L Bergen, *Holy War, Inc.: Inside the Secret World of Osama bin Laden* (New York: Simon and Schuster, 2002); Marc Sageman, *Understanding Terror Networks* (Philadelphia: University of Pennsylvania Press, 2004); Michael Scheuer, *Through Our Enemies'*

Eyes: Osama bin Laden, Radical Islam, and the Future of America, 2nd ed. (Washington, DC: Potomac Books, 2006); and Moghadam, *Globalization of Martyrdom*.

66. Eric Schmitt, "American Commander Details Al Qaeda's Strength in Mali," *New York Times*, December 3, 2012; Samuel L. Aronson, "AQIM's Threat to Western Interests in the Sahel," *CTC Sentinel* 7, no. 4 (2014).

67. Daniel Byman, *Deadly Connections: States That Sponsor Terrorism* (New York: Cambridge University Press, 2005), 164, 166.

68. U.S. Department of State, "Patterns of Global Terrorism: 1993" (Washington, DC: Department of State, April 1994).

69. Bruce O. Riedel, *The Search for Al Qaeda: Its Leadership, Ideology, and Future* (Washington, DC: Brookings Institution Press, 2010), 49.

70. Riedel, *Search for Al Qaeda*; see also Marc Sageman, *Leaderless Jihad: Terror Networks in the Twenty-First Century* (Philadelphia: University of Pennsylvania Press, 2008), 41–42. The relationship between Hizballah and Al Qaeda is one example of cooperation resulting from Sudanese sponsorship (see chapter 8).

71. Mohammed M Hafez, "Jihad After Iraq: Lessons from the Arab Afgans Phenomenon," *CTC Sentinel* 1, no. 4 (2008).

72. R. Davis, "Kilson Versus Marighela: The Debate Over Northern Ireland Terrorism," in *Ireland's Terrorist Dilemma*, ed. Yonah Alexander and Alan O'Day (Leiden: Martinus Nijhoff, 1986), 202; C. J. M. Drake, *Terrorists' Target Selection* (London: Macmillan, 1998), 76.

73. Nur Bilge Criss, "The Nature of PKK Terrorism in Turkey," *Studies in Conflict & Terrorism* 18, no. 1 (1995): 19.

74. O'Neill, *Insurgency and Terrorism*, 146.

75. Cragin et al., *Sharing the Dragon's Teeth*, 41–43.

76. Edgar O'Ballance, *Language of Violence: The Blood Politics of Terrorism* (San Rafael, CA: Presidio Press, 1979), 141–42.

77. Bacon, "Strange Bedfellows," 26.

78. Karmon, *Coalitions*, 160. For a detailed analysis of the RAF-AD alliance, see Karmon, *Coalitions*, 157–72.

79. Sageman, *Understanding Terror Networks*, 19.

80. Rogelio Alonso and Florencio Dominguez Iribarren, "The IRA and ETA: The International Connections of Ethno-Nationalist Terrorism in Europe," in *Terrorism: Patterns of Internationalization*, ed. Jaideep Saikia and Ekaterina Stepanova (New Delhi: SAGE Publications India, 2009).

81. Gad, "International Cooperation," 138.

82. Shanaka Jayasekara, "Tamil Tiger Links with Islamist Terrorist Groups," in *The Global Impact of Terrorism 2008—8th World Summit on Counter-Terrorism*, ed. Boaz Ganor and Eitan Azani (Herzliya, Israel: IDC Herzliya, Israel International Institute for Counter-Terrorism, 2010).

83. Cynthia Balana, "Tamil Rebels Sent Arms to Abus-Sri Lanka Exec," *Inquirer*, August 4, 2007.

84. Anthony David, "Proliferation of Stingers in Sri Lanka," *Jane's Intelligence Review*, September 1, 1998.

85. U.S. House of Representatives Committee on International Relations, "Summary of Investigation of IRA Links to Farc Narco-Terrorists in Colombia" (Washington, DC, 2002).

86. Karl Vick, "Al-Qaeda's Hand in Istanbul Plot," *Washington Post*, February 13, 2007.

87. Provision of safe haven or training can amount to operational cooperation if it directly abets terrorist operations.

88. Gad, "International Cooperation," 138.

89. Alonso and Iribarren, "The IRA and ETA," 7.

90. Gad, "International Cooperation," 138–39.

91. Kirsten E Schulze, "The Struggle for an Independent Aceh: The Ideology, Capacity, and Strategy of Gam," *Studies in Conflict & Terrorism* 26, no. 4 (2003): 253; Zachary Abuza, "The Moro Islamic Liberation Front at 20: State of the Revolution," *Studies in Conflict & Terrorism* 28, no. 6 (2005): 465.

92. Hizballah has reportedly also trained members of the IRA, PKK, ETA, Red Brigades, and Al Qaeda. Victor Asal, Brian Nussbaum, and D. William Harrington, "Terrorism as Transnational Advocacy: An Organizational and Tactical Examination," *Studies in Conflict & Terrorism* 30, no. 1 (2007): 26.

93. Jeffrey W Lewis, *The Business of Martyrdom: A History of Suicide Bombing* (Annapolis, MD: Naval Institute Press, 2012): 156.

94. Cited in Claire Sterling, *The Terror Network: The Secret War of International Terrorism* (New York: Henry Holt, 1981), 124.

95. Warren Strobel and Mark Hosenball, "Elite Iranian Guards Training Yemen's Houthis: U.S. Officials," Reuters, March 27, 2015.

96. Karmon, *Coalitions*, 49–50. Karmon's definition of operational cooperation is broader than the one used here. For example, Karmon classifies all joint training as operational cooperation, whereas I define operational cooperation more narrowly as cooperation in support of specific terrorist operations.

97. Leon O'Broin, *Revolutionary Underground: The Story of the Irish Republican Brotherhood, 1858–1924* (New York: Rowman and Littlefield, 1976); and Lindsay Clutterbuck, "Countering Irish Republican Terrorism in Britain: Its Origin as a Police Function," *Terrorism and Political Violence* 18, no. 1 (2006): 100–101.

98. Gad, "International Cooperation," 138.

99. Gad, "International Cooperation," 136.

100. Hoffman, *Inside Terrorism*, 77.

101. Rohan Gunaratna and Arabinda Acharya, *The Terrorist Threat from Thailand: Jihad or Quest for Justice?* (Washington, DC: Potomac Books, 2012), chap. 4.

102. Yoram Schweitzer and Sari Goldstein Ferber, *Al-Qaeda and the Internationalization of Suicide Terrorism*, Memorandum #78 (Tel Aviv, Israel: Tel Aviv University, Jaffee Center for Strategic Studies, 2005), 63–65.

103. Anne Stenersen, "Al Qaeda's Foot Soldiers: A Study of the Biographies of Foreign Fighters Killed in Afghanistan and Pakistan between 2002 and 2006," *Studies in Conflict & Terrorism* 34, no. 3 (2011): 178–79.

104. Bacon, "Strange Bedfellows," 12.

105. Bacon, "Strange Bedfellows," 756. Bacon mentions a fifth type of "transactional relationship," but does not discuss this type at length as it "does not qualify as an alliance." Bacon, "Strange Bedfellows," 755.

106. As mentioned above, while Bacon defines transactional relationships, she excludes them from in-depth discussion in her dissertation, as she does not regard them as alliances.

2. ACTOR SPECTRUM

1. Derek Layder, *Understanding Social Theory*, 2nd ed. (London: Sage, 2006).

2. Colin Wight, *Agents, Structures and International Relations: Politics as Ontology* (Cambridge: Cambridge University Press, 2006), 105.

3. Alexander Wendt, "The Agent-Structure Problem in International Relations Theory," *International Organization* 41, no. 3 (1987); David Dessler, "What's at Stake in the Agent-Structure Debate?" *International Organization* 43, no. 3 (1989); Walter Carlsnaes, "The Agent-Structure Problem in Foreign Policy Analysis," *International Studies Quarterly* 36, no. 3 (1992).

4. Compare Dessler, "What's at Stake," 443.

5. Dessler, "What's at Stake," 443.

6. Carlsnaes, "Agency-Structure Problem," 245–46.

7. Wendt, "Agent-Structure Problem," 365.

8. Wendt, "Agent-Structure Problem," 365. In his application of the agency-structure debate to international relations, Wendt is incorporating insights from structuration theory. On structuration and its relationship to the agency-structure debate, see especially Roy Bhaskar, *The Possibility of Naturalism: A Philosophical Critique of the Contemporary Human Sciences*, 2nd ed. (Brighton, UK: Harvester, 1979); Anthony Giddens, *The Constitution of Society: Outline of the Theory of Structuration* (Cambridge: Policy Press, 1984); and Margaret Archer, "Structuration versus Morphogenesis," in *Macro Sociological Theory*, ed. S.N. Eisenstadt and H. Helle (London: Sage, 1985).

9. Wendt, "Agent-Structure Problem," 361.

10. Kate O'Neill, Jörg Balsiger, and Stacy D. VanDeveer, "Actors, Norms, and Impact: Recent International Cooperation Theory and the Influence of the Agent-Structure Debate," *Annual Review of Political Science* 7 (2004): 152. See also Wendt, "Agent-Structure Problem," 361.

11. See for example, O'Neill, Balsiger, and VanDeveer, "Actors, Norms, and Impact," 168.

12. A notable exception to this rule is O'Neill, Balsiger, and VanDeveer, "Actors, Norms, and Impact."

13. Roxanne Lynn Doty, "Aporia: A Critical Exploration of the Agent-Structure Problematique in International Relations Theory," *European Journal of International Relations* 3, no. 3 (1997).

14. See, for example, Wendt, "Agent-Structure Problem"; and Wight, *Agents*, 104, 206.

15. Wendt, "Agent-Structure Problem," 359.

16. Sharon Hays, "Structure and Agency and the Sticky Problem of Culture," *Sociological Theory* 12, no. 1 (1994), 64.

17. Roy Bhaskar, *Dialectic: The Pulse of Freedom* (London: Verso, 1993); cited in Wight, *Agents*, 212. Clearly, the predominant application of agency to states is also the outcome of the dominance of the realist paradigm in international relations throughout the second half of the twentieth century.

18. O'Neill, Balsiger, and VanDeveer, "Actors, Norms, and Impact," 158-59.

19. Wendt, "Agent-Structure Problem," 359.

20. The growing importance of nonstate actors has been a key aspect of the "new wars" literature that emerged in the 1990s, as well as of the globalization literature, among others. See, for example, Mary Kaldor, *New and Old Wars* (Cambridge: Polity, 2012); James Rosenau, "Governance in the Twenty-First Century," *Global Governance* 1 (1995); Martin van Creveld, *The Transformation of War* (New York: Macmillan, 1991); Herfried Münkler, *New Wars* (Malden, MA: Polity, 2004); David Held, Anthony McGrew, David Goldblatt, and Jonathan Perraton, *Global Transformations: Politics, Economics and Culture* (Stanford, CA: Stanford University Press, 1999); and Bas Arts, "Non-State Actors in Global Governance: Three Faces of Power" (Bonn, Germany: Max Planck Institute, 2003/2004). For a critique of the new wars debate, see Edward Newman, "The 'New Wars' Debate: A Historical Perspective Is Needed," *Security Dialogue* 35, no. 2 (June 2004)

21. O'Neill, Balsiger, and VanDeveer, "Actors, Norms, and Impact," 170.

22. On the central role of ideology in terrorism, see C. J. M. Drake, "The Role of Ideology in Terrorists' Target Selection," *Terrorism and Political Violence* 10, no. 2 (1998). For a discussion of jihadism as an ideology, see Assaf Moghadam, "The Salafi Jihad as a Religious Ideology," *CTC Sentinel* 1, no. 3 (2008). On the link between ideology and action, see Mohammed M. Hafez, "Martyrdom Mythology in Iraq: How Jihadists Frame Suicide Terrorism in Videos and Biographies," *Terrorism and Political Violence* 19, no. 1 (2007); and David A. Snow and Robert C. Byrd, "Ideology, Framing Processes, and Islamic Terrorist Movements," *Mobilization: An International Journal* 12, no. 2 (2007).

23. James J. F. Forest, *Teaching Terror: Strategic and Tactical Learning in the Terrorist World* (Lanham: Rowman & Littlefield, 2006), 1.

24. Forest, *Teaching Terror*; Brian Jackson, John C. Baker, Kim Cragin, John Parachini, Horacio R. Trujillo, and Peter Chalk, *Aptitude for Destruction: Volume 1: Organizational Learning in Terrorist Groups and Its Implications for Combating Terrorism* (Santa Monica, CA: RAND, 2005); and Brian Jackson, John C. Baker, Kim Cragin, John Parachini, Horacio R. Trujillo, and Peter Chalk, *Aptitude for Destruction: Volume 2: Case Studies of Organizational Learning in Five Terrorist Groups* (Santa Monica, CA: RAND, 2005). On terrorist innovation, see Adam Dolnik, *Understanding Terrorist Innovation* (London: Routledge, 2007); and Assaf Moghadam, "How Al Qaeda Innovates," *Security Studies* 22, no. 3 (2013).

25. Martha Crenshaw, "Theories of Terrorism: Instrumental and Organizational Approaches," in *Inside Terrorist Organizations*, 2nd ed., ed. David C. Rapoport (London: Frank Cass, 2001), 14.

26. Martha Crenshaw, "The Logic of Terrorism: Terrorist Behavior as a Product of Strategic Choice," in *Origins of Terrorism: Psychologies, Ideologies, Theologies, States of Mind*, ed. Walter Reich (Washington, DC: Woodrow Wilson Center, 1998), 8.

27. "Extra-normal violence" is violence that "violates the norms regulating disputes, protests, and dissent." Paul Wilkinson, *Terrorism Versus Democracy: The Liberal State Response*, 3rd ed. (London: Routledge, 2011), 4.

28. Note, for example, the U.S. response to the attacks of 9/11. The tendency to provoke a harsh target response by using extra-normal violence was particularly well displayed in February 2015, when the "Islamic State" released a twenty-two-minute video showing a captured Jordanian pilot, Mouath al-Kasaesbeh, being burned alive in a cage. In response, less than twelve hours of the release of the video, Jordanian authorities executed two imprisoned terrorists with ties to ISIS, and King Abdullah pledged to wage a "relentless war" against ISIS. Ian Black, "Jordan's King Abdullah Vows 'Relentless' War Against ISIS," *Guardian*, February 4, 2015.

29. On the strategic success or failure of terrorist groups, see especially Max Abrahms, "Why Terrorism Does Not Work," *International Security* 31, no. 2 (Fall 2006); Max Abrahms, "The Political Effectiveness of Terrorism Revisited," *Comparative Political Studies* 45 (2012); and Peter Krause, "The Political Effectiveness of Non-State Violence: A Two-Level Framework to Transform a Deceptive Debate," *Security Studies* 22, no. 2 (2013).

30. See, for instance, Ely Karmon, *Coalitions Between Terrorist Organizations: Revolutionaries, Nationalists and Islamists* (Leiden: Martinus Nijhoff, 2005); Michael C. Horowitz and Philip B. K. Potter, "Allying to Kill: Terrorist Intergroup Cooperation and the Consequences for Lethality," *Journal of Conflict Resolution* 58 no. 2 (2014); Navin A. Bapat and Kanisha D. Bond, "Alliances Between Militant Groups," *British Journal of Political Science* 42, no. 4 (October 2012); Tricia L. Bacon, "Strange Bedfellows or Brothers-In-Arms: Why Terrorist Groups Ally" (PhD dissertation, Georgetown University, 2013); and Brian J Phillips, "Terrorist Group Cooperation and Longevity," *International Studies Quarterly* 58, no. 2 (2014).

31. See, for example, Thomas X. Hammes, *The Sling and the Stone: On War in the 21st Century* (St. Paul, MN: Zenith Press, 2004); Bas Arts, "Non-State Actors"; and Newman, "'New Wars' Debate."

32. See, for example, Daniel Byman, *Deadly Connections: States that Sponsor Terrorism* (New York: Cambridge University Press, 2005).

33. This is not to suggest that these three actors are the only agents of terrorism. Some might argue that social movements, for example, may function as terrorist agents. The present division of actors does not seek to be comprehensive in nature, but rather illustrative. Its main purpose is to give credence to the idea that an exclusive focus on terrorist organizations as the unit of analysis is misguided. Subsequent scholarship may well identify additional types of terrorist agents.

34. Martha Crenshaw, *Explaining Terrorism: Causes, Processes and Consequences* (London: Routledge, 2011), 69.

35. See, for example, Richard Barrett, "The Islamic State," (New York: Soufan Group, November 2014); and "The Islamic State's Organizational Structure One Year In," *Al-Monitor*, July 2, 2015.

36. Daniel Milton and Muhammad al-`Ubaydi, "Pledging Bay`a: A Benefit or Burden to the Islamic State?" *CTC Sentinel* 8, no. 3 (March 2015).

37. Charles Lister, "Islamic State Senior Leadership: Who's Who," Brookings Institution, http://www.brookings.edu/~/media/Research/Files/Reports/2014/11/profiling-islamic-state-lister/en_whos_who.pdf?la=en.

38. Will McCants, "The Believer," Brookings Essay (Washington, DC: Brookings Institution, September 1, 2015).

39. The following passages incorporate elements from Assaf Moghadam, Ronit Berger, and Polina Beliakova, "Say Terrorist, Think Insurgent: Labeling and Analyzing Contemporary Terrorist Actors," *Perspectives on Terrorism* 8, no. 5 (2014).

40. Alex P. Schmid and Albert I. Jongman, *Political Terrorism. A Research Guide to Concepts, Theories, Databases and Literature* (Amsterdam: Transaction, 1988).

41. See James Khalil, "Know Your Enemy: On the Futility of Distinguishing Between Terrorists and Insurgents," *Studies in Conflict & Terrorism* 36, no. 5 (2013). For a traditional description of terrorist groups, see Martha Crenshaw, "An Organizational Approach to the Analysis of Political Terrorism," *Orbis* 29 (1985). See also Bruce Hoffman, *Inside Terrorism*, exp. and rev. ed. (New York: Columbia University Press, 2006), chap. 1.

42. Hoffman, *Inside Terrorism*, 35.

43. For classic texts on guerrilla warfare, see Mao Tse-tung, *On Guerrilla Warfare*, trans. Samuel B. Griffith II (Urbana: University of Illinois Press, 2000); Ernesto "Che" Guevara, *Guerrilla Warfare* (Lincoln: University of Nebraska Press, 1998); and Robert Taber, *The War of the Flea* (Washington, DC: Potomac Books, 2002).

44. For a comparison of terrorism and guerrilla strategies, see Bard E. O'Neill, *Insurgency and Terrorism: From Revolution to Apocalypse*, 2nd ed. (Washington, DC: Potomac Books, 2005); Walter Laqueur, *Guerrilla Warfare: A Historical and Critical Study* (New Brunswick, NJ: Transaction, 1998); Max Boot, *Invisible Armies: An Epic History of Guerrilla Warfare from Ancient Times to the Present* (New York: Norton, 2013); and Ariel Merari, "Terrorism as a Strategy of Insurgency," *Terrorism and Political Violence* 5, no. 4 (1993).

45. Robert H. Scales and Douglas Ollivant, "Terrorist Armies Fight Smarter and Deadlier than Ever," *Washington Post*, August 1, 2014.

46. Scales and Ollivant, "Terrorist Armies."

47. Scales and Ollivant, "Terrorist Armies."

48. The study was conducted based on organizations listed in the Global Terrorism Database at START/University of Maryland, one of the most prominent and widely used databases on terrorism. Moghadam, Berger, and Beliakova, "Say Terrorist, Think Insurgent."

49. Government targets are associated with both terrorism and guerrilla tactics.

50. Merari, "Terrorism as a Strategy of Insurgency."

51. James R. Clapper, "Statement for the Record: Worldwide Threat Assessment of the US Intelligence Community" (Washington, DC: House Permanent Select Committee on Intelligence, February 25, 2016), 5.

52. Miles Kahler, "Networked Politics: Agency, Power and Governance," in *Networked Politics: Agency, Power and Governance*, ed. Miles Kahler (Ithaca, NY: Cornell University Press, 2009), 2.

53. Among the main weaknesses of networks, and of networked organizations, is their greater potential for internal strife. Donatella Della Porta and Mario Diani, *Social Movements: An Introduction*, 2nd ed. (Malden, MA: Blackwell, 2006): 161; Assaf Moghadam and Brian Fishman, eds., *Fault Lines in Global Jihad: Organizational, Strategic, and Ideological Fissures* (London: Routledge, 2011).

54. Michele Zanini and Sean J. A. Edwards, "The Networking of Terror in the Information Age," in *Networks and Netwars*, ed. John Arquilla and David Ronfeldt (Santa Monica, CA: RAND, 2001), 31. On the benefits of networks for international criminal groups, see Phil Williams, "Transnational Criminal Networks," in *Networks and Netwars*.

55. Della Porta and Diani, *Social Movements*; Arquilla and Ronfeldt, "The Advent of Netwar (Revisited)," in *Networks and Netwars*, ed. John Arquilla and David Ronfeldt (Santa Monica, CA: RAND, 2001), 6.

56. Jessica Stern, *Terror in the Name of God: Why Religious Militants Kill* (New York: Ecco, 2003); Marc Sageman, *Understanding Terror Networks* (Philadelphia: University of Pennsylvania Press, 2004); Marc Sageman, *Leaderless Jihad: Terror Networks in the Twenty-First Century* (Philadelphia: University of Pennsylvania Press, 2008); Arie Perliger and Ami Pedahzur, "Social Network Analysis in the Study of Terrorism and Political Violence," *PS: Political Science and Politics* 44, no. 1 (2011).

57. Matthew Levitt, "Untangling the Terror Web: Identifying and Counteracting the Phenomenon of Crossover Between Terrorist Groups," *SAIS Review of International Affairs* 24, no. 1 (2004), 34.

58. Sageman, "The Next Generation of Terror," *Foreign Policy*, October 8, 2009; Sageman, *Leaderless Jihad*.

59. Bruce Hoffman, "The Myth of Grass-Roots Terrorism: Why Al Qaeda Still Matters," *Foreign Affairs*, May/June 2008.

60. This is a common definition of networks. See, for example, Kahler, "Networked Politics," 5; and Williams "Transnational Criminal Networks," 66.

61. Williams, "Transnational Criminal Networks," 64–65.

62. As Keck and Sikkink write, "Part of what is so elusive about networks is how they seem to embody elements of agent and structure simultaneously." Margaret E. Keck and Kathryn Sikkink, *Activists Beyond Borders: Advocacy Networks in International Politics* (Ithaca, NY: Cornell University Press, 1998), 5. See also Kahler, "Networked Politics," 5–6. Hafner-Burton, Kahler, and Montgomery, for example, rely on a structural definition of networks and view them primarily as "sets of relations that form structures, which in turn may constrain and enable agents." Emilie Hafner-Burton, Miles Kahler, and

Alexander H. Montgomery, "Network Analysis for International Relations," *International Organization* 63, no. 3 (July 2009): 559–60.

63. In no way do I suggest that formal networks, terrorist or otherwise, do not exist. But my main concern in this book lies with informal networks.

64. See, for example, Renate Mayntz, "Organizational Forms of Terrorism: Hierarchy, Network, or a Type Sui Generis?" MPIfG Discussion Paper 04/4 (Munich: Max-Planck-Institut für Gesellschaftsforschung, 2004), 8–12.

65. Ami Pedahzur and Arie Perliger, "The Changing Nature of Suicide Attacks: A Social Network Perspective," *Social Forces* 84, no. 4 (2006): 1988.

66. Raviv Drucker and Ofer Shelah, *Bumerang* (Jerusalem: Keter, 2005); cited in Pedahzur and Perliger, "Changing Nature." For another study that examines networks within organizations, see Sarah Elizabeth Parkinson, "Organizing Rebellion: Rethinking High-Risk Mobilization and Social Networks in War," *American Political Science Review* 107, no. 3 (2013).

67. Sageman, *Leaderless Jihad*, 85–86.

68. Ineke Roex, "The Rise of Public *Dawa* Networks in the Netherlands: Behind Bars, Sharia4Holland, and Streetdawah," in *Sharia4: Straddling Political Activism and Jihad in the West*, ed. Lorenzo Vidino (Dubai: Al Mesbar Studies and Research Centre, 2015), 6.

69. Roex, "Rise of Public *Dawa* Networks," 7.

70. Peter L. Bergen, *The Osama bin Laden I Know: An Oral History of al-Qaeda's Leader* (New York: Free Press, 2006), 76–84.

71. Charles Lister, *The Syrian Jihad: Al-Qaeda, the Islamic State and the Evolution of an Insurgency* (New York: Oxford University Press, 2015), 58.

72. Steve Ressler, "Social Network Analysis as an Approach to Combat Terrorism: Past, Present and Future Research," *Homeland Security Affairs* 2 (July 2008), 2.

73. Williams, "Transnational Criminal Networks," 71.

74. Jose Antonio Gutierrez, as quoted in Angel Rabasa and Cheryl Benard, *Eurojihad: Patterns of Islamist Radicalization and Terrorism in Europe* (New York: Cambridge University Press, 2015), 128.

75. "Violent Jihad in the Netherlands: Current Trends in the Islamist Terrorist Threat," General Intelligence and Security Service (AIVD) Report, March 2006, 13.

76. Francesc Badia, "Small-World Networks, Violence, and Global Distress," in *Terrorism, Security, and the Power of Informal Networks*, ed. David Martin Jones, Ann Lane, and Paul Schulte (Cheltenham: Edward Elgar, 2010), 236; Sageman, *Understanding Terror Networks*, 142.

77. On the LTTE, see for example Celia W. Dugger, "Sri Lankan Rebels Said to Be Recruiting Children," *New York Times*, October 12, 2001; on the RUF, see for example Macartan Humphreys and Jeremy M. Weinstein, "Who Fights? The Determinants of Participation in Civil War," *American Journal of Political Science* 52, no. 2 (April 2008), 436–55.

78. See, for example, Assaf Moghadam, "Failure and Disengagement in the Red Army Faction," *Studies in Conflict & Terrorism* 35, no. 2 (February 2012); and "Islamic State Executed Nearly 2,000 People in Six Months: Monitor," Reuters, December 28, 2014.

79. Donatella della Porta, "Recruitment Processes in Clandestine Political Organizations: Italian Left-Wing Terrorism," in *Terrorism in Context*, ed. Martha Crenshaw (University Park: Pennsylvania State University Press, 1995); and Sageman, *Understanding Terror Networks*.

80. "Violent Jihad in the Netherlands," 13.

81. Alexander Evans, Presentation at the Workshop on "Competition vs. Cooperation in the Global Jihad," ICT's 14th Annual World Summit on Counter-Terrorism, International Institute for Counter-Terrorism (ICT), IDC Herzliya, September 11, 2014, http://www.ict.org.il/Article/1280/Competition-vs-Cooperation-in-Global-Jihad.

82. Alexander Evans, "The Utility of Informal Networks to Policy-Makers," in David Martin Jones, Ann Lane, and Paul Schulte, eds., *Terrorism, Security and the Power of Informal Networks* (Cheltenham, UK: Edward Elgar, 2010), 15; and Badia, "Small-World Networks."

83. Sageman, *Understanding Terror Networks*, 152–57.

84. Pedahzur and Perliger, "Changing Nature," 1990.

85. Rabasa and Benard, *Eurojihad*, 124.

86. Fernando Reinares, "The Madrid Bombings and Global Jihadism," *Survival* 52, no. 2 (April–May 2010).

87. Rabasa and Benard, *Eurojihad*, 124.

88. Sageman, *Leaderless Jihad*, 141.

89. Pedahzur and Perliger, "Changing Nature."

90. "The Transformation of Jihadism in the Netherlands: Swarm Dynamics and New Strength," General Intelligence and Security Service (AIVD), The Hague, Netherlands, September 2014, 22.

91. "Transformation of Jihadism in the Netherlands," 22–23.

92. On bin Laden as an innovative leader, see Moghadam, "How Al Qaeda Innovates," 478–80. On George Habash, see Yoram Schweitzer, "The Case of the PFLP and Its Offshoots," in *Terrorist Innovations in Weapons of Mass Effect: Preconditions, Causes, and Predictive Indicators*, ed. Maria J. Rasmussen and Mohammed M. Hafez, Workshop Report, Defense Threat Reduction Agency (DTRA) Advanced Systems and Concepts Office, Report Number ASCO 2010-019, Washington, DC, August 2010.

93. On Abu Nidal, see, for example, Walter Laqueur, *The Age of Terrorism* (Boston: Little Brown, 1987), 286–88; and Patrick Seale, *Abu Nidal, A Gun for Hire* (London: Hutchinson, 1992).

94. In his excellent study of European jihadist groups, Petter Nesser refers to terrorist entrepreneurs, but views them largely as cell leaders. Although his description has some parallels to my definition (e.g., Nesser highlights the role of charisma), I tend to view entrepreneurs as independently minded and highly charismatic terrorist innovators. Petter Nesser, *Islamist Terrorism in Europe: A History* (Oxford: Oxford University Press, 2015), 13–14.

95. Sherzod Abdukadirov, "Terrorism: The Dark Side of Social Entrepreneurship," *Studies in Conflict and Terrorism* 33, no. 7 (2010): 604.

96. Compare the definition of activists in Pamela E. Oliver and Gerald Marwell, "Mobilizing Technologies for Collective Action," in *Frontiers in Social Movement Theory*, ed. Aldon D. Morris and Carol McClurg Mueller (New Haven, CT: Yale University Press, 1992), 252.

97. For this categorization of innovation, see Martha Crenshaw, "Innovation: Decision Points in the Trajectory of Terrorism," in *Terrorist Innovations in Weapons of Mass Effect: Preconditions, Causes, and Predictive Indicators*, ed. Maria J. Rasmussen and Mohammed M. Hafez, Workshop Report, Defense Threat Reduction Agency (DTRA) Advanced Systems and Concepts Office, Report Number ASCO 2010-019, Washington, DC, August 2010.

98. National Commission on Terrorist Attacks Upon the United States, *The 9/11 Commission Report*, 1st ed. (New York: Norton, 2004), 154.

99. KSM even boasted of his personal involvement in acts of terrorism, including his responsibility for personally beheading *Wall Street Journal* reporter Daniel Pearl. It is highly plausible that KSM personally killed Pearl. See Asra Q. Nomani, "This is Danny Pearl's Final Story," *Washingtonian*, January 24, 2014.

100. Although the Internet and social media platform, which have truly revolutionized terrorism, have somewhat obviated the need for physical encounters to establish ties, physical encounters continue to be critical for planning and executing terrorist attacks.

101. Williams, "Transnational Criminal Networks," 77.

102. Mark Granovetter, "The Strength of Weak Ties," *American Journal of Sociology* 78, no. 6 (1973).

103. Mark Granovetter, "The Strength of Weak Ties: A Network Theory Revisited," *Sociological Theory* 1 (1983): 202, 220; Sageman, *Understanding Terror Networks*, 169; Williams, *Transnational Criminal Organizations*, 73.

104. Arquilla and Ronfeldt, "Advent of Netwar," 6.

105. Arquilla and Ronfeldt, "Advent of Netwar," 12.

3. SHIFTING ENVIRONMENT

1. Martha Crenshaw, "Thoughts on Relating Terrorism to Historical Contexts," in *Terrorism in Context*, ed. Martha Crenshaw (University Park: Pennsylvania State University Press, 2001); Alexander Wendt, "The Agent-Structure Problem in International Relations Theory," *International Organization* 41, no. 3 (1987).

2. David Dessler, "What's at Stake in the Agent-Structure Debate?" *International Organization* 43, no. 3 (1989); and Sharon Hays, "Structure and Agency and the Sticky Problem of Culture," *Sociological Theory* 12, no. 1 (1994).

3. Theorists have offered several general conceptualizations of agency and structure. See Douglas Porpora, "Four Concepts of Social Structure," *Journal for the Theory of Social Behavior* 19, no. 2 (1989). For a more recent overview, see Colin Wight, *Agents, Structures and International Relations: Politics as Ontology* (Cambridge: Cambridge University

Press, 2006): 121–76. The idea of structure as "rules and resources" is influenced strongly by the work of Anthony Giddens. Among those adopting a rules and resources approach are Dessler, in "What's at Stake"; Nicholas Greenwood Onuf, in *World of Our Making: Rules and Rule in Social Theory and International Relations* (Columbia: University of South Carolina Press, 1989); and Alexander Wendt, in "Bridging the Theory/Meta-Theory Gap in International Relations," *Review of International Studies* 17, no. 4 (1991).

4. Dessler, "What's at Stake," 453.
5. Wight, *Agents*, 142.
6. Wendt, "Agent-Structure Problem."
7. Wight, *Agents*, 142.
8. Wight, *Agents*, 147.
9. On the growing importance of identity issues in the post–Cold War security environment, see also Peter J. Katzenstein, Introduction, in *The Culture of National Security: Norms and Identity in World Politics*, ed. Peter J. Katzenstein (New York: Columbia University Press, 1996).
10. Alexander Wendt and Daniel Friedheim, "Hierarchy Under Anarchy: Informal Empire and the East German State," *International Organization* 49, no. 4 (1995): 691.
11. Wendt and Friedheim, "Hierarchy Under Anarchy."
12. The truly Islamic nature of the causes advanced by jihadists is disputed among Muslims and non-Muslims. For a recent example of the debate, see, for example, Graeme Wood, "What Isis Really Wants," *Atlantic*, March 2015; and Mehdi Hasan, "How Islamic Is the Islamic State? Not at All," *New Republic*, March 12, 2015.
13. Assaf Moghadam, "The Salafi Jihad as a Religious Ideology," *CTC Sentinel* 1, no. 3 (February 2008). I have since come to prefer the term "jihadi" over "Salafi-jihadi" because not all members of the global jihad are, strictly speaking, Salafis. See, for example, Brynjar Lia, "Jihadists Divided Between Strategists and Doctrinarians," in *Fault Lines in Global Jihad: Organizational, Strategy and Ideological Fissures*, ed. Assaf Moghadam and Brian Fishman (London: Routledge, 2011).
14. Moghadam and Fishman, eds., *Fault Lines*; Fawaz Gerges, *The Far Enemy: Why Jihad Went Global* (Cambridge: Cambridge University Press, 2005).
15. For more extensive discussions of global jihad, see Gilles Kepel, *Jihad: The Trail of Political Islam* (Cambridge, MA: Harvard University Press, 2003); Olivier Roy, *Globalized Islam: The Search for a New Ummah* (New York: Columbia University Press, 2004); Quintan Wiktorowicz, "Anatomy of the Salafi Movement," *Studies in Conflict & Terrorism* 29, no. 3 (2006); Assaf Moghadam, *The Globalization of Martyrdom: Al Qaeda, Salafi Jihad, and the Diffusion of Suicide Attacks* (Baltimore, MD: Johns Hopkins University Press, 2008); and Nelly Lahoud, *The Jihadis' Path to Self-Destruction* (New York: Columbia University Press, 2010).
16. On jihad, see especially Reuven Firestone, *Jihad: The Origin of Holy War in Islam* (New York: Oxford University Press, 1999); Rudolph Peters, *Jihad in Classical and Modern Islam: A Reader*, 2nd ed. (Princeton, NJ: Markus Wiener, 2005); and David Cook, *Understanding Jihad* (Oakland: University of California Press, 2005).

17. Reuven Paz, "Global Jihad and WMD: Between Martyrdom and Mass Destruction," *Current Trends in Islamist Ideology* 2 (September 2005).

18. For more on this, see Roy, *Globalized Islam*, and Farhad Khosrokhavar, *Suicide Bombers: Allah's New Martyrs*, transl. David Macey (London: Pluto, 2002).

19. Arie W. Kruglanski, Xiaoyan Chen, Mark Dechesne, Shira Fishman, and Edward Orehek, "Fully Committed: Suicide Bombers' Motivation and the Quest for Personal Significance," *Political Psychology* 30, no. 3 (June 2009); and Zach Goldberg, "A Jihadi's Search for Meaning" (master's thesis, Interdisciplinary Center Herzliya, Israel, 2014).

20. Cook, *Understanding Jihad*, 141–42. See also Mohammed Hafez, "*Takfir* and Violence against Muslims," in *Fault Lines in Global Jihad: Organizational, Strategic and Ideological Fissures*, ed. Assaf Moghadam and Brian Fishman (London: Routledge, 2011).

21. Sidney Tarrow, *The New Transnational Activism* (New York: Cambridge University Press, 2005): 59–76.

22. Moghadam, "Salafi Jihad."

23. See, for example, Ayman Al-Zawahiri, *Knights Under the Prophet's Banner*, serialized in *Al-Sharq al-Awsat*, 2001.

24. Assaf Moghadam and Brian Fishman, "Introduction: Jihadi 'Endogenous' Problems," in *Fault Lines in Global Jihad: Organizational, Strategic and Ideological Fissures*, ed. Assaf Moghadam and Brian Fishman (London: Routledge, 2011), 10.

25. National Commission on Terrorist Attacks upon the United States, *The 9/11 Commission Report*, 1st ed. (New York: Norton, 2004), 165. Henceforth cited as *9/11 Commission Report*.

26. Lorenzo Vidino, "Wrong Assumptions: Integration, Responsibility, and Counterterrorism in France," *War on the Rocks*, January 22, 2015.

27. Vidino, "Wrong Assumptions."

28. David Held, Anthony McGrew, David Goldblatt, and Jonathan Perraton, *Global Transformations: Politics, Economics and Culture* (Stanford: Stanford University Press, 1999), 2. This is a shorter definition on which Held et al. later expand. The full definition appears in footnote 33 below.

29. The phrase "dark side of globalization" is commonly credited to former U.S. President Bill Clinton, who used it in several speeches in 1995, although not necessarily in the context of terrorism. See, for example, William Jefferson Clinton, "Remarks to the White House Conference on Trade and Investment in Ireland," May 25, 1995, in *Public Papers of the Presidents of the United States: Administration of William J. Clinton*, Book 1 (Washington, DC: United States Government Printing Office, 1996), 751. See also Jorge Heine and Ramesh Takur, eds., *The Dark Side of Globalization* (New York: United Nations University Press, 2011).

30. Held et al., *Global Transformations*, 2.

31. Held et al., *Global Transformations*, 2.

32. Bruce Hoffman, *Inside Terrorism*, exp. and rev. ed. (New York: Columbia University Press, 2006), 2.

33. Held et al., who have written what many consider the definitive account of globalization, define globalization more fully as "a process (or set of processes) which embodies a

transformation in the spatial organization of social relations and transactions—assessed in terms of their extensity, intensity, velocity and impact—generating transcontinental or interregional flows and networks of activity, interaction, and the exercise of power" (Held et al., *Global Transformations*, 16). This definition of globalization, according to the DHL Global Connectedness Index 2014, is "probably the most widely cited." See Pankaj Ghemawat and Steven A. Altman, "DHL Global Connectedness Index 2014: Analyzing Global Flows and Their Power to Increase Prosperity" (Bonn, Germany: Deutsche Post DHL, October 2014), 13.

34. On the benefits of globalization for transnational activism, see especially Margaret E. Keck and Kathryn Sikkink, *Activists Beyond Borders: Advocacy Networks in International Politics* (Ithaca, NY: Cornell University Press, 1998); and Tarrow, *New Transnational Activism*. On the impact of these links on political violence, see Richard Devetak and Christopher W. Hughes, eds., *The Globalization of Political Violence: Globalization's Shadow* (London: Routledge, 2008).

35. See, for example, Gabriel Weimann, *Terror on the Internet: The New Arena, The New Challenges* (Washington, DC: United States Institute of Peace Press, 2006); Brigitte L. Nacos, *Mass-Mediated Terrorism: The Central Role of the Media in Terrorism and Counterterrorism*, 2nd ed. (Lanham, MD: Rowman & Littlefield, 2007); Richard Clarke and Robert K. Knake, *Cyber War: The Next Threat to National Security and What to Do About It* (New York: Ecco/Harper Collins, 2010); Philip Seib and Dana M. Janbek, *Global Terrorism and New Media: The Post-Al Qaeda Generation* (New York: Routledge, 2011); Ghaffar Hussein and Erin Marie Saltman, *Jihad Trending: A Comprehensive Analysis of Online Extremism and How to Counter It* (London: Quilliam, 2014); and Gabriel Weimann, *Terrorism in Cyberspace: The Next Generation* (Washington, DC: Woodrow Wilson Center Press, 2015).

36. David C. Benson, "Why the Internet Is Not Increasing Terrorism," *Security Studies* 23, no. 2 (2014).

37. Ronald L. Jepperson, Alexander Wendt, and Peter J. Katzenstein, "Norms, Identity, and Culture in National Security," in *The Culture of National Security: Norms and Identity in World Politics*, ed. Peter J. Katzenstein (New York: Columbia University Press, 1996), 41.

38. Katzenstein, Introduction, 22.

39. George Michael, *Lone Wolf Terror and the Rise of Leaderless Resistance* (Nashville, TN: Vanderbilt University Press, 2012): 5.

40. Peter L. Bergen, *The Osama bin Laden I Know: An Oral History of al Qaeda's Leader* (New York: Free Press, 2006), 302.

41. Michele Zanini and Sean J. A. Edwards, "The Networking of Terror in the Information Age," in *Networks and Netwars: The Future of Terror, Crime, and Militancy*, ed. John Arquilla and David Ronfeldt (Santa Monica, CA: RAND, 2001), 35–36.

42. Zanini and Edwards, "Networking of Terror," 35–36.

43. Benson, "Why the Internet Is Not Increasing Terrorism."

44. Jytte Klausen, "Tweeting the Jihad: Social Media Networks of Western Foreign Fighters in Syria and Iraq," *Studies in Conflict & Terrorism* 38, no. 1 (2015): 20.

45. Klausen, "Tweeting the Jihad," 20.

46. This benefit applies also to criminal organizations. See Phil Williams, "Transnational Criminal Networks," in *Networks and Netwars: The Future of Terror, Crime, and Militancy*, ed. John Arquilla and David Ronfeldt (Santa Monica, CA: RAND, 2001), 78.

47. Zanini and Edwards, "Networking of Terror," 37.

48. Steve Coll and Susan B. Glasser, "Terrorists Turn to the Web as Base of Operations," *Washington Post*, August 7, 2005.

49. I thank Danit Gal for this insight.

50. Matthew Levitt, "Untangling the Terror Web: Identifying and Counteracting the Phenomenon of Crossover Between Terrorist Groups," *SAIS Review of International Affairs* 24, no. 1 (2004): 35.

51. Levitt, "Untangling," 37.

52. Levitt, "Untangling," 41.

53. Levitt, "Untangling."

54. Marc Sageman, *Understanding Terror Networks* (Philadelphia: University of Pennsylvania Press, 2004): 159.

55. J. M. Berger, *Jihad Joe: Americans Who Go to War in the Name of Islam* (Washington, DC: Potomac Books, 2011), 177.

56. Marc Sageman, *Leaderless Jihad: Terror Networks in the Twenty-First Century* (Philadelphia: University of Pennsylvania Press, 2008), 110.

57. Klausen, "Tweeting the Jihad," 2.

58. Joseph A. Carter, Shiraz Maher, and Peter R. Neumann, "#Greenbirds: Measuring Importance and Influence in Syrian Foreign Fighter Networks," International Centre for the Study of Radicalisation (London, April 2014).

59. Carter, Maher, and Neumann, "#Greenbirds," 17.

60. Carter, Maher, and Neumann, "#Greenbirds," 29.

61. Hussain and Saltman, *Jihad Trending*, 53, 47.

62. I am grateful to Danit Gal for research support on the impact of the Internet on terrorist cooperation.

63. Thomas Hegghammer, "Interpersonal Trust on Jihadi Internet Forums," in *Fight, Flight, Mimic: Identity Signaling in Armed Conflicts*, ed. Diego Gambetta (forthcoming); currently available at http://hegghammer.com/_files/Interpersonal_trust.pdf/.

64. Cole Bunzel, "Al-Qaeda Advises the Syrian Revolution: Shumukh al-Islam's 'Comprehensive Strategy' for Syria," *Jihadica*, February 25, 2013.

65. "Al-Qaeda Seeks to Unite Islamic Front Ahead of US Airstrikes in Syria," RT.com, September 16, 2014.

66. "English-language Jihadi Forum Publishes Eulogy for Anwar Al-Awlaki, Samir Khan; Online Jihadi Calls for 'Vengeance Raid' on American Websites," *MEMRI Special Dispatch* no. 4197, October 11, 2011.

67. See, for example, Liam Collins, "The Abbottabad Documents: Bin Ladin's Security Measures," *CTC Sentinel* 5, no. 5 (May 2012).

68. Nadya Labi, "Jihad 2.0," *Atlantic*, July/August 2006.

69. Hussain and Saltman, *Jihad Trending*, 53.

70. Juha Saarinen, "Guest Post: The History of Jihadism in Finland and an Early Assessment of Finnish Foreign Fighters in Syria," *Jihadology*, November 21, 2013.

71. Berger, *Jihad Joe*, 178.

72. 304th Military Intelligence Battalion OSINT Team, "Sample Overview: al Qaida-Like Mobile Discussions & Potential Creative Use," October 16, 2008, http://fas.org/irp/eprint/mobile.pdf.

73. Michael Martinzez, "Cyberwar: CyberCaliphate Targets U.S. Military Spouses; Anonymous Hits ISI," *CNN*, February 11, 2015.

74. See, for example, Nima Elbagir, Paul Cruickshank, and Mohammed Tawfeeq, "Boko Haram Purportedly Pledges Allegiance to ISIS," *CNN*, March 9, 2015; and Rukmini Callimachi and Andrew Higgins, "Video Shows a Paris Gunman Declaring His Loyalty to the Islamic State," *New York Times*, January 12, 2015.

75. Department of Homeland Security, "Terrorist Use of Social Networking: Facebook Case Study," December 5, 2010, https://publicintelligence.net/ufouoles-dhs-terrorist-use-of-social-networking-facebook-case-study/.

76. S. Benjamin, "An In-Depth Look at One of the Facebook/Twitter Networks of French-Speaking Jihadis Fighting in Syria: Glorifying Jihad in Syria, Condemning 'Heretical' France," *MEMRI Cyber & Jihad Lab*, February 17, 2014; and Ewen MacAskill and Leila Haddou, "The Facebook Jihadis Seeking Action in Syria," *Guardian*, April 15, 2014.

77. In addition, the links often include the banner of the forum publishing the post as an additional seal of authentication to sustain online trust among jihadis. See Hegghammer, "Interpersonal Trust," fn. 58.

78. Paul Cruickshank and Tim Lister, "Al-Shabaab Breaks New Ground with Complex Nairobi Attack," *CNN*, September 23, 2013.

79. Nico Prucha and Ali Fisher, "Tweeting for the Caliphate: Twitter as the New Frontier for Jihadist Propaganda," *CTC Sentinel* 6, no. 6 (June 2013).

80. The tweet was available at https://twitter.com/JbhatALnusra/status/32190435003113 0624, but is no longer active.

81. Thomas Joscelyn, "Islamic Front and Al Nusrah Front Promote 'Liberation' of Border Crossing," *Long War Journal*, August 29, 2014.

82. Doug Gross, "Leak: Government Spies Snooped in 'Warcraft,' Other Games," *CNN*, December 10, 2013.

83. Office of the Director of National Intelligence, "3D Cyberspace Spillover: Where Virtual Worlds Get Real," December 30, 2013, http://fas.org/irp/eprint/virtual.pdf.

84. Carlo M. Rossotto, Siou Chew Kuek, and Cecilia Paradi-Guilford Rossotto, "New Frontiers and Opportunities in Work," *ICT Policy Notes 3* (June 2013).

85. Sam Rkaina, "Call of Duty Video Game Used to Recruit Jihadists, British Father of Radicalized Fighters Claims," *Mirror* (UK), August 25, 2014.

86. Terrence McCoy, "The Islamic State's 'Call of Duty' Allure," *Washington Post*, October 28, 2014.

87. Philip M. Seib and Dana M. Janbek, *Global Terrorism and the New Media: The Post-Al Qaeda Generation* (London: Routledge, 2011): 34.

88. For detailed discussions on the impact of the Internet in building a jihadi identity, see, for example, Roy, *Globalized Islam*; Khosrokhavar, *Allah's New Martyrs*; Moghadam, *Globalization of Martyrdom*; and Hussein and Saltman, *Jihad Trending*. The following discussion incorporates material from Moghadam, *Globalization of Martyrdom*.

89. Moghadam, *Globalization of Martyrdom*, 121.

90. Michael Radu, "London 7/7 and Its Impact," *Foreign Policy Research Institute e-Notes 6*, July 2005.

91. For a more detailed description, see Moghadam, *Globalization of Martyrdom*, chap. 2.

92. *Dabiq* 9, no. 3 (July/August 2014).

93. Sageman, *Understanding Terror Networks*, 161.

94. Eli Lake and Josh Rogin, "Exclusive: U.S. Intercepted Al Qaeda's 'Legion of Doom' Conference Call," *Daily Beast*, August 7, 2013.

95. Caitlin Dewey, "Inside the Battle for Ask.fm, the Site Where Islamic State Recruited Three American Teens," *Washington Post*, December 12, 2014.

96. Sageman, *Leaderless Jihad*, 114.

97. In fact, one might well argue that the Internet, which has been treated as a "medium" in the preceding discussion, is a tool that creates opportunities for cooperation. This only underlines the fact that the conceptual divisions among causes, mediums, and opportunities are hardly definitive and that there is a very large overlap among all the structural factors discussed in this chapter, as well as among agential elements covered in the previous chapter.

98. Paul Wilkinson, *Terrorism Versus Democracy: The Liberal State Response*, 3rd ed. (London: Routledge, 2011): 10.

99. Alexander B. Downes, *Targeting Civilians in War* (Ithaca, NY: Cornell University Press, 2008); Max Boot, *Invisible Armies: An Epic History of Guerrilla Warfare from Ancient Times to the Present* (New York: Norton, 2013); Stathis N. Kalyvas, *The Logic of Violence in Civil Wars* (Cambridge: Cambridge University Press, 2006); Stathis N. Kalyvas, "The Paradox of Terrorism in Civil Wars," *Journal of Ethics* 8 (2004).

100. Downes, *Targeting Civilians in War*.

101. For details, see the Armed Conflict Dataset of the Uppsala Conflict Data Program (UCDP), http://www.pcr.uu.se, and the Peace Research Institute Oslo (PRIO), http://www.prio.org. For a recent discussion of UCDP/PRIO conflict data, see Lotta Themnér and Peter Wallensteen, "Armed Conflict, 1946–2013," *Journal of Peace Research* 51, no. 4 (2014).

102. Michael G. Findley and Joseph K. Young, "Terrorism and Civil War: A Spatial and Temporal Approach to a Conceptual Problem," *Perspectives on Politics* 10, no. 2 (June 2012); Ariel Merari, "Terrorism as a Strategy of Insurgency," *Terrorism and Political Violence* 5, no. 4 (1993); and Assaf Moghadam, Ronit Berger, and Polina Beliakova, "Say Terrorist, Think Insurgent: Labeling and Analyzing Contemporary Terrorist Actors," *Perspectives on Terrorism* 8, no. 5 (2014). This section incorporates elements from the latter.

103. Findley and Young, "Terrorism and Civil War," 286.

104. See, for example, Seth G. Jones and Patrick B. Johnston, "The Future of Insurgency," *Studies in Conflict & Terrorism* 36, no. 1 (January 2013).

105. James D. Fearon and David D. Laitin, "Ethnicity, Insurgency, and Civil War," *American Political Science Review* 97, no. 1 (February 2003).

106. See, for example, Nicholas Sambanis, "What Is a Civil War? Conceptual and Empirical Complexities of an Operational Definition," *Journal of Conflict Resolution* 48, no. 6 (2004): 829–30. I present a condensed version of Sambanis's definition.

107. United States Department of the Army, *The US Army/Marine Corps Counterinsurgency Field Manual*, US Army Field Manual No. 3-24/Marine Corps Warfighting Publication No. 3-33.5 (Chicago: University of Chicago Press, 2007), 2.

108. David Martin Jones and M. L. R. Smith, "Whose Hearts and Whose Minds? The Curious Case of Global Counter-Insurgency," *Journal of Strategic Studies* 33, no. 1 (2010); David Kilcullen, "Counter-Insurgency Redux," *Survival* 48, no. 4 (Winter 2006–2007); David J. Kilcullen, "Countering Global Insurgency," *Journal of Strategic Studies* 28, no. 4 (2005).

109. Ann Hironaka, *Neverending Wars: The International Community, Weak States, and the Perpetuation of Civil War* (Cambridge, MA: Harvard University Press, 2005); Michael W. Doyle and Nicholas Sambanis, *Making War and Building Peace: United Nations Peace Operations* (Princeton, NJ: Princeton University Press, 2006); Seth G. Jones, "The Rise of Afghanistan's Insurgency: State Failure and Jihad," *International Security* 32, no. 4 (Spring 2008).

110. This is the definition used by the World Bank. The traditions and practices include "the process by which governments are selected, monitored and replaced; the capacity of the government to effectively formulate and implement sound policies; and the respect of citizens and the state for the institutions that govern economic and social interactions among them." See "Worldwide Governance Indicators," World Bank, http://info.worldbank.org/governance/wgi/index.aspx#home.

111. See also David Galula, *Counter-Insurgency Warfare: Theory and Practice* (New York: Praeger, 2006); Bard O'Neill, *Insurgency and Terrorism: From Revolution to Apocalypse*, 2nd ed. (Washington, DC: Potomac Books, 2005); and Mao Tse-tung, *On Guerrilla Warfare*, transl. Samuel B. Griffith II (Urbana: University of Illinois Press, 2000).

112. Moghadam, Berger, and Beliakova, "Say Terrorist"; Eitan Azani, "The Hybrid Terrorist Organization: Hezbollah as a Case Study," *Studies in Conflict & Terrorism* 36, no. 11 (2013); and Benedetta Berti, *Armed Political Organizations: From Conflict to Integration* (Baltimore, MD: Johns Hopkins University Press, 2013).

113. Fotini Christia, *Alliance Formation in Civil Wars* (Cambridge: Cambridge University Press, 2012), 3.

114. Christia, *Alliance Formation*; Paul Staniland, *Networks of Rebellion: Explaining Insurgent Cohesion and Collapse* (Ithaca, NY: Cornell University Press, 2014); Kristin M. Bakke, Kathleen Gallagher Cunningham, and Lee J.M. Seymour, "A Plague of Initials: Fragmentation, Cohesion, and Infighting in Civil Wars," *Perspectives on Politics* 10, no. 2 (June 2012).

115. Erik Melander, "Organized Violence in the World 2015: An Assessment by the Uppsala Conflict Data Program," UCDP Paper No. 9 (Uppsala: Uppsala Conflict Data Program, 2016), 1.

116. Dexter Filkins, "Profusion of Rebel Groups Helps Them Survive in Iraq," *New York Times*, December 5, 2005.
117. Wladimir van Wilgenburg, "The Rise of Jaysh al-Fateh in Northern Syria," *Terrorism Monitor* 13, 12 (June 12, 2015); Charles Lister, *The Syrian Jihad: Al-Qaeda, the Islamic State and the Evolution of an Insurgency* (Oxford: Oxford University Press, 2015): 339–50.
118. Alexander Evans, Presentation at the workshop on "Competition vs. Cooperation in the Global Jihad," 14th Annual World Summit on Counter-Terrorism, International Institute for Counter-Terrorism (ICT), IDC Herzliya, September 11, 2014, http://www.ict.org.il/Article/1280/Competition-vs-Cooperation-in-Global-Jihad.
119. Petter Nesser, *Islamist Terrorism in Europe: A History* (Oxford: Oxford University Press), 23.

4. CONTEMPORARY TERRORIST COOPERATION

1. Ely Karmon, *Coalitions Between Terrorist Organizations: Revolutionaries, Nationalists and Islamists* (Leiden: Martinus Nijhoff, 2005), 48.
2. Tricia L. Bacon, "Strange Bedfellows or Brothers-In-Arms: Why Terrorist Groups Ally" (PhD dissertation, Georgetown University, 2013), 756.
3. The discussion of the "domains" of cooperation is not absent, but is subsumed within the discussion of the quality of the cooperation.
4. Raymond Bonner, "Plot Echoes One Planned by 9/11 Mastermind in '94," *New York Times*, August 10, 2006; Assaf Moghadam, "How Al Qaeda Innovates," *Security Studies* 22, no. 3 (2013).
5. Moghadam, "How Al Qaeda Innovates"; National Commission on Terrorist Attacks Upon the United States, *The 9/11 Commission Report*, 1st ed. (New York: Norton, 2004). Henceforth cited as *9/11 Commission Report*.
6. Mary Anne Weaver, "The Short, Violent Life of Abu Musab al-Zarqawi," *Atlantic*, July/August 2006.
7. Bacon, "Strange Bedfellows," 12.
8. See also Phil Williams, "Transnational Criminal Networks," in *Networks and Netwars*, ed. John Arquilla and David Ronfeldt (Santa Monica, CA: RAND, 2001).
9. Benjamin Acosta and Steven J. Childs, "Illuminating the Global Suicide-Attack Network," *Studies in Conflict & Terrorism* 36, no. 1 (2013): 68.
10. Bacon refers to these as "pooled relationships." Bacon, "Strange Bedfellows," 753–54.
11. Daniel Byman, "Buddies or Burdens? Understanding the Al Qaeda Relationship with Its Affiliate Organizations," *Security Studies* 23, no. 3 (2014): 442.
12. Byman, "Buddies or Burdens?"
13. Steven Brooke, "Jihadist Strategic Debates before 9/11," *Studies in Conflict & Terrorism* 31, no. 3 (2008): 205–7.
14. Matthew Levitt, *Hezbollah: The Global Footprint of Lebanon's Party of God* (Washington, DC: Georgetown University Press, 2013), 11. See also Nicholas Blanford, *Warriors of*

God: Inside Hezbollah's Thirty-Year Struggle Against Israel (New York: Random House, 2011), 46–48.

15. This also characterizes strategic partnerships between criminal organizations. See Patrick Clawson and Rensselaer W. Lee, *The Andean Cocaine Industry* (Basingstoke: Macmillan, 1996), quoted in Williams, "Cooperation among Criminal Organizations," 72–73.

16. "Cooperation among Criminal Organizations," 69. See also Peter J. Buckley, *Cooperative Forms of Transnational Corporation Activity* (London: Routledge 1994).

17. See Karmon, *Coalitions*, 167–72.

18. For a description of some of the earlier coalitions formed during the Syrian civil war, see Aron Lund, "The Non-State Militant Landscape in Syria," *CTC Sentinel* 6, no. 8 (August 2013).

19. Mohammed M. Hafez, *Suicide Bombers in Iraq: The Strategy and Ideology of Martyrdom* (Washington, DC: US Institute of Peace Press, 2007), 52–54. A more recent example of a tactical cooperation is the Punjabi Taliban. See Hassan Abbas, "Defining the Punjabi Taliban Network," *CTC Sentinel* 2, no. 4 (April 2009).

20. Transactional relationships are not limited to terrorist cooperation. Phil Williams, for example, describes similar relationships among cooperating international criminal organizations in "Cooperation among Criminal Organizations." See also Clawson and Lee, *Andean Cocaine Industry*.

21. See also Michael N. Barnett, "Identity and Alliances in the Middle East," in the *Culture of National Security: Norms and Identity in World Politics*, ed. Peter J. Katzenstein (New York: Columbia University Press, 1996).

22. Michael Kenney argues that illegal entities such as terrorist and criminal organizations have several commonalities. They need to be adaptive to rapidly changing circumstances "as their survival is usually dependent on that," and to have low enforcement costs, fewer coordination challenges, and smaller or simpler task environments. Michael Kenney, *From Pablo to Osama: Trafficking and Terrorist Networks, Government Bureaucracies, and Competitive Adaptation* (University Park: Pennsylvania State University Press, 2007), 7.

23. Kenney, *From Pablo to Osama*, 73.

24. Kenney, *From Pablo to Osama*, 75.

25. Compare Kenney, *From Pablo to Osama*, 70, 74–75.

26. Karmon, *Coalitions*, 108.

27. Hamas has traditionally had ideological differences with global jihadist groups. See Reuven Paz, "Jihadists and Nationalist Islamists: Al-Qa'ida and Hamas," in *Fault Lines in Global Jihad: Organizational, Strategic and Ideological Fissures*, ed. Assaf Moghadam and Brian Fishman (London: Routledge, 2011).

28. Ehud Yaari, "Hamas and the Islamic State: Growing Cooperation in the Sinai," *PolicyWatch* 2533, Washington Institute for Near East Policy, December 15, 2015; "Hamas Has Close Ties to IS Affiliates in Sinai, Say Israel, Egypt," *Times of Israel*, July 2, 2015.

29. On this point, see also Clint Watts, "What is the Future of Al Qaeda and the Islamic State?," *Marcaz: Middle East Politics & Policy*, Brookings Institution, January 28, 2016.

5. PRE-9/11 COOPERATION IN THE GLOBAL JIHAD

1. Jeff Goodwin and James M. Jasper, eds., *The Social Movements Reader: Cases and Concepts*, 3rd ed. (Malden, MA: Wiley-Blackwell, 2015): 3. For excellent introductions to social movements, see also Donatella Della Porta and Mario Diani, *Social Movements: An Introduction*, 2nd ed. (Malden, MA: Blackwell, 2006); and David Snow, Sarah Soule, and Hanspeter Kriesi, eds., *The Blackwell Companion to Social Movements* (Malden, MA: Blackwell, 2007).

2. See, for example, Gretel Kauffman, "FBI Director: Why ISIS Is a Bigger Threat to the US than Al Qaeda," *Christian Science Monitor*, July 23, 2015.

3. For an estimate of the relative strengths of the two camps and a list of actual and suspected members of them, see Clint Watts, "One Year Later, ISIS Overtakes Al Qaeda: What's Next?," *Geopoliticus: The FPRI Blog*, April 6, 2015. See also J. M. Berger, "Chart: Al Qaeda Fractures, ISIS Gains," Intelwire.com, April 8, 2015.

4. Fawaz Gerges, *The Far Enemy: Why Jihad Went Global* (Cambridge: Cambridge University Press, 2005); Lawrence Wright, *The Looming Tower: Al-Qaeda and the Road to 9/11* (New York: Vintage, 2006); and Assaf Moghadam, *The Globalization of Martyrdom: Al Qaeda, Salafi Jihad, and the Diffusion of Suicide Attacks* (Baltimore, MD: Johns Hopkins University Press, 2008), 129–33.

5. This introduction incorporates the definition of the global jihad movement provided in Bill Braniff and Assaf Moghadam, "Towards Global Jihadism: Al-Qaeda's Strategic, Ideological and Structural Adaptations Since 9/11," *Perspectives on Terrorism* 5, no. 2 (2011).

6. Eric Schmitt and David D. Kirkpatrick, "Islamic State Sprouting Limbs Beyond Its Base," *New York Times*, February 14, 2015. For example, the Nigerian group Boko Haram has sworn fealty to the Islamic State, and the Islamic State has formally accepted that oath, which makes Boko Haram an affiliate of the Islamic State. In this book, however, most references to affiliates are to those of Al Qaeda because researchers are more familiar with them.

7. Aaron Y. Zelin, "The Islamic State's Model," *Monkey Cage, Washington Post*, January 28, 2015.

8. Inclusion of the name "Al Qaeda" by a group does not necessarily imply formal affiliation by a group. For formal affiliation, the adoption of the Al Qaeda name has to be authorized by Al Qaeda. As to Jabhat al-Nusra, the group does at times refer to itself as Al Qaeda.

9. William McCants, "The Polarizing Effect of Islamic State Aggression on the Global Jihadist Movement," *CTC Sentinel* 9, no. 7 (July 2016).

10. This is evident in a famous letter sent by Zawahiri to Zarqawi, in which Al Qaeda reprimanded Al Qaeda in Iraq for brutal tactics that alienated many Muslims. The letter is available at the website of the Federation of American Scientists, http://fas.org/irp/news/2005/10/letter_in_english.pdf.

11. Vahid Brown and Don Rassler, *Fountainhead of Jihad: The Haqqani Nexus, 1973–2012* (New York: Columbia University Press, 2013).

12. Compare Bruce Hoffman and Fernando Reinares, *The Evolution of the Global Terrorist Threat: From 9/11 to Osama bin Laden's Death* (New York: Columbia University Press, 2014), 622–24.

13. Assaf Moghadam and Brian Fishman, "Introduction: Jihadi 'Endogenous' Problems," in *Fault Lines in Global Jihad: Organizational, Strategic and Ideological Fissures*, ed. Assaf Moghadam and Brian Fishman (London: Routledge, 2011).

14. Gerges, *Far Enemy*; Moghadam and Fishman, *Fault Lines in Global Jihad*; Barak Mendelsohn, *The Al-Qaeda Franchise: The Expansion of al-Qaeda and Its Consequences* (New York: Oxford University Press, 2016).

15. The literature on Al Qaeda and the global jihad movement is vast. For a useful resource, see the five-volume compilation by Paul Cruickshank. Paul Cruickshank, ed., *Al Qaeda* (London: Routledge, 2013). For a more recent general overview, see Daniel Byman, *Al Qaeda, the Islamic State, and the Global Jihadist Movement: What Everyone Needs to Know* (Oxford: Oxford University Press, 2015).

16. Thomas Hegghammer, *Jihad in Saudi Arabia: Violence and Pan-Islamism since 1979* (New York: Cambridge University Press, 2010): 39.

17. The idea to establish an Arab-led organization to support the Afghan jihad was proposed by Abu al-Walid al-Masri and some of his associates. See Mustafa Hamid and Leah Farrall, *The Arabs at War in Afghanistan* (London: Hurst, 2015), 65–87.

18. Peter L. Bergen, *The Osama bin Laden I Know: An Oral History of al Qaeda's Leader* (New York: Free Press, 2006), 50.

19. Brown and Rassler, *Fountainhead of Jihad*, 75.

20. Bergen, *The Osama bin Laden I Know*, 49–73.

21. On the Lion's Den and the battle of Jaji, see Hamid and Farrall, *Arabs at War*, 89–105.

22. Vahid Brown, "Classical and Global Jihad: Al-Qa'ida's Franchising Frustrations," in *Fault Lines in Global Jihad: Organizational, Strategic and Ideological Fissures*, ed. Assaf Moghadam and Brian Fishman (London: Routledge, 2011), 90.

23. Hegghammer, *Jihad in Saudi Arabia*, 7–8; Brown, "Classical and Global Jihad," 88–89.

24. Brown, "Classical and Global Jihad," 92.

25. For an overview of Al Qaeda's goals and strategy, including the role of the caliphate, see Moghadam, *Globalization of Martyrdom*, 62–78.

26. Document # AFGP-2002-600048, http://www.ctc.usma.edu.

27. Document # AFGP-2002-000078, http://www.ctc.usma.edu.

28. Document # AFGP-2002-000078.

29. Document # AFGP-2002-000078.

30. Document # AFGP-2002-000078.

31. Nelly Lahoud, *Beware of Imitators: Al-Qa'ida Through the Lens of Its Confidential Secretary*, (West Point, NY: Combating Terrorism Center, June 4, 2012), 36, 38–40.

32. Peter L. Bergen and Paul Cruickshank, "Revisiting the Early Al Qaeda: An Updated Account of Its Formative Years," *Studies in Conflict & Terrorism* 35, no. 1 (2012).

33. For more on Ali Muhammad, see J. M. Berger, *Jihad Joe: Americans Who Go to War in the Name of Islam* (Washington, DC: Potomac Books, 2011), 17–32. See also Lahoud, *Beware of Imitators*, 48.

34. Document # AFGP-2002-600048.

35. Lahoud, *Beware of Imitators*, 48–49.

36. Lahoud, *Beware of Imitators*, 49.

37. Bergen and Cruickshank, "Revisiting," 14.

38. Quoted in Bergen, *The Osama bin Laden I Know*, 109.

39. Brown, "Classical and Global Jihad," 94–95.

40. Vahid Brown, "Cracks in the Foundation: Leadership Schisms in al-Qa'ida 1989–2006," Combating Terrorism Center at West Point, NY, January 2, 2007, 10.

41. Brown and Rassler, *Fountainhead of Jihad*, 95.

42. Peter L. Bergen, *Holy War, Inc.: Inside the Secret World of Osama bin Laden* (New York: Touchstone, 2002), 87.

43. Michael Kenney, *From Pablo to Osama: Trafficking and Terrorist Networks, Government Bureaucracies, and Competitive Adaptation* (University Park: Pennsylvania State University Press, 2007), 140–43.

44. *United States v. Usama bin Laden*, February 2, 2001, 221–23.

45. Bergen and Cruickshank, "Revisiting," 17.

46. On Al Qaeda's relations with the Armed Islamic Group, see for example Jonathan Schanzer, *Al-Qaeda's Armies, Middle East Affiliate Groups and the Next Generation of Terror* (New York: Specialist, 2005), 103–5.

47. Marc Sageman, *Understanding Terror Networks* (Philadelphia: University of Pennsylvania Press, 2004), 41.

48. National Commission on Terrorist Attacks Upon the United States, *The 9/11 Commission Report*, 1st ed. (New York: Norton, 2004), 61, 240–41. Henceforth cited as *9/11 Commission Report*.

49. Anonymous [Michael Scheuer], *Through Our Enemies' Eyes: Osama bin Laden, Radical Islam, and the Future of America* (Washington, DC: Brassey's, 2003), 137–41.

50. *9/11 Commission Report*, 58.

51. Joseph Felter, J. Vahid Brown, Jacob N. Shapiro, and Clinton Watts, eds., "Al-Qa'ida's (Mis)Adventures in the Horn of Africa," Combating Terrorism Center at West Point, July 2, 2007, 5.

52. Felter et al., "Al-Qa'ida's (Mis)Adventures."

53. Felter et al., "Al-Qa'ida's (Mis)Adventures," 39.

54. *9/11 Commission Report*, 60; see also Mark Bowden, *Black Hawk Down: A Story of Modern War* (New York: Atlantic Monthly, 1999).

55. *United States v. Usama bin Laden*, February 28, 2001, 1652.

56. One such office was opened in Baku, Azerbaijan. Bergen and Cruickshank, "Revisiting," 18.

57. According to the 1991 census, Bosnian Muslims (Bosniaks) accounted for approximately 43.5 percent of the population of Bosnia, Serbs 31.2 percent, and Croats 17.4 percent.

58. Brown, "Classical and Global Jihad," 93–94.

59. Berger, *Jihad Joe*, 95.

60. Lahoud, *Beware of Imitators*, 22, 80; Leah Farrall, "How Al Qaeda Works," *Foreign Affairs*, March/April 2011.

61. A copy of the declaration can be accessed at the website of PBS. See "Bin Laden's Fatwa," August 23,1996, http://www.pbs.org/newshour/updates/military-july-dec96-fatwa _1996/.

62. Brown and Rassler, *Fountainhead of Jihad*, 113–15.

63. Hegghammer, *Jihad in Saudi Arabia*, 110.

64. Hegghammer, *Jihad in Saudi Arabia*, 111.

65. Anonymous [Scheuer], *Through Our Enemies' Eyes*, 55–57. See also Yoram Schweitzer and Aviv Oreg, "Al Qaeda's Odyssey to the Global Jihad," Memorandum No. 134, Institute for National Security Studies (INSS), Tel Aviv University, March 2014, 25.

66. Moghadam, *Globalization of Martyrdom*, 70–72.

67. *9/11 Commission Report*, 170–71.

68. In the summer of 1997, for example, Al Qaeda and the Haqqani Network supported the Taliban's siege of Mazari-Sharif. Brown and Rassler, *Fountainhead of Jihad*, 107. For a broader discussion of the military support provided to the Taliban, see Anonymous [Scheuer], *Through Our Enemies' Eyes*, 156–60. On Al Qaeda providing training on suicide attacks, see Bryan Glyn Williams, "Return of the Arabs: Al-Qa'ida's Current Military Role in the Afghan Insurgency," *CTC Sentinel* 1, no. 3 (February 2008).

69. See, for example, Brynjar Lia, "Abu Mus'Ab Al-Suri's Critique of Hard Line Salafists in the Jihadist Current," *CTC Sentinel*, 1, no. 1 (December 2007).

70. Peter L. Bergen, *Manhunt: The Ten-Year Search for bin Laden from 9/11 to Abbottabad* (New York: Broadway, 2012), 55.

71. *9/11 Commission Report*, 66.

72. *9/11 Commission Report*, 67; Lahoud, *Beware of Imitators*, 32.

73. Hegghammer, *Jihad in Saudi Arabia*, 109.

74. Thomas Hegghammer, "Global Jihadism After the Iraq War," *Middle East Journal* 60, no. 1 (Winter 2006), 14.

75. *9/11 Commission Report*, 66–67.

76. Marc Sageman, *Leaderless Jihad: Terror Networks in the Twenty-First Century* (Philadelphia: University of Pennsylvania Press, 2008), 45.

77. C. J. Chivers and David Rhode, "Turning Out Guerrillas and Terrorists to Wage a Holy War," *New York Times*, March 18, 2002.

78. On ties with groups in Algeria, Egypt, Lebanon, and Yemen in particular, see Schanzer, *Al-Qaeda's Armies*.

79. *9/11 Commission Report*, 67.

80. Moghadam, *Globalization of Martyrdom*, 127. Despite Al Qaeda's official name change, I will continue to refer to the group as Al Qaeda because it is under this name that the group is universally known. On Al Qaeda's merger with the EIJ and the change of names, see, for example, Reuven Paz, "Qa'idat Al-Jihad: Moving Forward or Backward? The Algerian GSPC Joins Al Qaeda," *PRISM Occasional Papers* 4, no. 5 (September 2006).

81. Schweitzer and Oreg, "Al Qaeda's Odyssey," 28.

82. Gerges, *The Far Enemy*.

83. Brown, "Classical and Global Jihad," 102.
84. Farrall, "How al Qaeda Works," and Brown, "Classical and Global Jihad," 103-4.
85. Assaf Moghadam, "How Al Qaeda Innovates," *Security Studies* 22, no. 3 (2013).
86. Bruce Hoffman, "Rethinking Terrorism and Counterterrorism Since 9/11," *Studies in Conflict and Terrorism* 25, no. 5 (September–October 2002): 309.
87. Sageman, *Leaderless Jihad*, 45.
88. Schweitzer and Oreg, "Al Qaeda's Odyssey," 31.
89. Two high-ranking LIFG members, Abu Yahya al-Libi and Abu Layth al-Libi, joined Al Qaeda in 2006, but according to the LIFG, they did so as individuals. Andrew Lebovich and Aaron Y. Zelin, "Assessing Al-Qa'ida's Presence in the New Libya," *CTC Sentinel* 5, no. 3 (March 2012).
90. Farrall, "How Al Qaeda Works."

6. POST-9/11 COOPERATION IN THE GLOBAL JIHAD

1. This section expands upon Bill Braniff and Assaf Moghadam, "Towards Global Jihad-ism: Al-Qaeda's Strategic, Ideological and Structural Adaptations since 9/11," *Perspectives on Terrorism* 5, no. 2 (May 2011).
2. On the London bombings, see Bruce Hoffman, "The 7 July 2005 London Bombings," in *The Evolution of the Global Terrorist Threat: From 9/11 to Osama bin Laden's Death*, ed. Bruce Hoffman and Fernando Reinares (New York: Columbia University Press, 2014). On Zazi and other plots centrally directed by Al Qaeda, see Raffaello Pantucci, "Manchester, New York, and Oslo: Three Centrally Directed Al-Qaida Plots," *CTC Sentinel* 3, no. 8 (August 2010).
3. Bruce Hoffman and Fernando Reinares, Conclusion, in *Evolution of the Global Terrorist Threat*, 628.
4. Stewart Bell, "Leadership and the Toronto 18," in *Evolution of the Global Terrorist Threat*.
5. See Paul Cruickshank, "The 2006 Airline Plot," in *Evolution of the Global Terrorist Threat*.
6. Mitchell B. Silber, "Al-Qa'ida's Center of Gravity in a Post–bin Ladin World," *CTC Sentinel* 4, nos. 11–12 (November 2011).
7. Brynjar Lia, *Architect of Global Jihad: The Life of Al-Qaida Strategist Abu Mus'ab al-Suri* (New York: Columbia University Press, 2008), 7.
8. Abu Musab al-Suri, *Global Islamic Resistance Call*, trans. Brynjar Lia, in Brynjar Lia, *Architect of Global Jihad: The Life of Al-Qaida Strategist Abu Mus'ab al-Suri* (New York: Columbia University Press, 2008), 366.
9. Suri, *Global Islamic Resistance Call*, 366.
10. Suri, *Global Islamic Resistance Call*, 396.
11. Daveed Gartenstein-Ross, "Large-Scale Arrests in Saudi Arabia Illustrate Threat to the Oil Supply," *Long War Journal*, March 24, 2010.
12. Brynjar Lia and Thomas Hegghammer, "Jihadi Strategic Studies: The Alleged Al Qaida Policy Study Preceding the Madrid Bombings," *Studies in Conflict & Terrorism*

27, no. 5 (September/October 2004). On jihadi strategic studies, see also Mark E. Stout, Jessica M. Huckabey, and John R. Schindler, *Terrorist Perspectives Project: Strategic and Operational Views of Al Qaida and Associated Movements* (Annapolis, MD: Naval Institute Press, 2008); and Dima Adamsky, "Jihadi Operational Art: The Coming Wave of Jihadi Strategic Studies," *Studies in Conflict & Terrorism* 33, no. 1 (January 2010).

13. The growing importance of media operations is reflected in Ayman al-Zawahiri's famous statement to Abu Musab al-Zarqawi that "we are in a battle, and . . . more than half of this battle is taking place in the battlefield of the media." "Letter from al-Zawahiri to Al-Zarqawi," released on October 11, 2005, by the U.S. Director for National Intelligence, http://fas.org/irp/news/2005/10/letter_in_english.pdf.

14. Releases in As-Sahab, Al Qaeda's media production company, jumped from 6 in 2002 to 11 in 2003, 13 in 2004, 16 in 2005, 58 in 2006, and peaked in 2007 with 97 releases. The number of media releases dropped to 49 releases in 2008 and picked up slightly to reach 79 in 2009, but seemed to drop again in 2010. See Peter Bergen and Katherine Tiedemann, "The Almanac of Al Qaeda," *Foreign Policy*, May/June 2010.

15. "Fight on Champions of Somalia" is a meme used frequently in As-Sahab's propaganda to demonstrate support for al-Shabaab, which offered it organizational *bayah* to Al Qaeda in March of 2009.

16. Usamah bin Ladin, "The Way to Save the Earth," *Inspire* 1 (Summer 2010); Benjamin Haas and Daniel McGrory, "Al-Qa'ida Seeking to Recruit African-American Muslims," *CTC Sentinel* 1, no. 8 (July 2008). Abu Dujana al-Khorosani was an elite pen on *al-Hesbah* and an independent blogger before conducting the December 2009 suicide attack at Forward Operating Base Chapman in Khost, Afghanistan.

17. Braniff and Moghadam, "Towards Global Jihadism."

18. In another example, the Islamic Jihad Union, which was associated with Al Qaeda, provided training to a German cell of jihadists known as the Sauerland bombers, who plotted to attack numerous targets in Germany before they were apprehended in September 2007.

19. Examples include the proliferation of suicide attacks against Western and U.N. targets in Pakistan, the February 2008 attack against the Israeli embassy in Nouakchott, Mauritania, carried out by militants trained in AQIM camps, the July 2008 attacks against the Danish embassy in Pakistan, the September 2008 attacks on the U.S. embassy in Yemen, and the September 2008 coordinated suicide attacks in Somaliland and Puntland, which included an attack on the local compound of the United Nations Development Program.

20. Assaf Moghadam, "Shifting Trends in Suicide Attacks," *CTC Sentinel* 2, no. 1 (January 2009); Assaf Moghadam, *The Globalization of Martyrdom: Al Qaeda, Salafi Jihad, and the Diffusion of Suicide Attacks* (Baltimore, MD: Johns Hopkins University Press, 2008); and Yoram Schweitzer, "Al Qaeda and Suicide Terrorism: Vision and Reality," *Military and Strategic Affairs* 2, no. 2, Institute for National Security Studies (INSS) (October 2010). See also Jean-Pierre Filiu, "The Local and Global Jihad of Al Qa'ida in the Islamic Maghrib," *Middle East Journal* 63, no. 2 (Spring 2009): 213–26; and Lianne

Kennedy-Boudali, "Al-Qa'ida in the Islamic Maghreb: Evaluating the Results of the al-Qa'ida Merger," Occasional Paper (West Point, NY: Combating Terrorism Center at West Point, September 2009).

21. Anonymous [Michael Scheuer], *Imperial Hubris: Why the West Is Losing the War on Terror* (Washington, DC: Brassey's, 2004): 64–65. See also David Rhode and James Risen, "A Hostile Land Foils the Quest for Bin Laden, *New York Times*, December 13, 2004.

22. See Sebastian Rotella, "Terrorism Suspects Traced to Iran," *Los Angeles Times*, August 1, 2004; Richard A. Clarke, Glenn P. Aga, Roger W. Cressey, Stephen E. Flynn, Blake W. Mobley, Eric Rosenbach, Steven Simon, William F. Wechsler, and Lee S. Wolosky, *Defeating the Jihadists: A Blueprint for Action* (New York: Century Foundation, 2004), 14.

23. The group's leader, Mullah Krekar, who was acquainted with bin Laden since 1988, had reportedly received hundreds of thousands of dollars from bin Laden to establish training camps in northern Iraq. Jonathan Schanzer, *Al-Qaeda's Armies, Middle East Affiliate Groups and the Next Generation of Terror* (New York: Specialist, 2005): 132–36.

24. Thomas Hegghammer, "Global Jihadism After the Iraq War," *Middle East Journal* 60, no. 1 (Winter 2006): 31.

25. Thomas Hegghammer, "The Ideological Hybridization of Jihadi Groups," *Current Trends in Islamist Ideology* 9 (November 2009).

26. Leah Farrall, "How Al Qaeda Works," *Foreign Affairs*, March/April 2011, 132.

27. Farrall, "How Al Qaeda Works," 134.

28. Farrall, "How Al Qaeda Works," 134.

29. Farrall, "How al Qaeda Works," 135.

30. Daniel Byman, "Buddies or Burdens? Understanding Al Qaeda's Relationship with Its Affiliate Organizations," *Security Studies* 23, no. 3 (2014); and Barak Mendelsohn, *The Al-Qaeda Franchise: The Expansion of al-Qaeda and Its Consequences* (New York: Oxford University Press, 2016).

31. For a useful overview of the benefits and drawbacks of affiliation, see Byman, "Buddies or Burdens?"; and Mendelsohn, *Al-Qaeda Franchise*.

32. Jacob N. Shapiro, *The Terrorist's Dilemma: Managing Violent Covert Organizations* (Princeton, NJ: Princeton University Press, 2013); Mendelsohn, *Al-Qaeda Franchise*; and Byman, "Buddies or Burdens?"

33. For example, it rejected offers by the Lebanese Fatah al-Islam and the Gaza-based Jaesh al-Islam to join Al Qaeda.

34. Vahid Brown, "Classical and Global Jihad: Al-Qa'ida's Franchising Frustrations," in *Fault Lines in Global Jihad: Organizational, Strategic, and Ideological Fissures*, ed. Assaf Moghadam and Brian Fishman (London: Routledge, 2011), 90, 103–4.

35. Byman, "Buddies or Burdens?," 462.

36. Byman, "Buddies or Burdens?," 463.

37. On this last point, see Mendelsohn, *Al-Qaeda Franchise*, 118.

38. According to Lahoud et al., the Abbottabad documents reveal that AQI's attacks on Sunnis were a major reason why AQ viewed AQI as a liability. Nelly Lahoud, Stuart Caudill, Liam Collins, Gabriel Koehler-Derrick, Don Rassler, and Mohammed

al-Ubaydi, "Letters from Abbottabad: Bin Ladin Sidelined?," Combating Terrorism Center at West Point, NY, May 3, 2012, 22.

39. See SOCOM-2012-0000004 and SOCOM-2012-0000011, www.ctc.usma.edu. See also Lahoud et al., "Letters from Abbottabad," 23; and Nelly Lahoud, *Beware of Imitators: Al-Qa'ida Through the Lens of Its Confidential Secretary*, (West Point, NY: Combating Terrorism Center, June 4, 2012), 76.

40. For a good background discussion, see Camille Tawil, *Brothers in Arms: The Story of Al-Qa'ida and the Arab Jihadists* (London: Saqi, 2010), 67–88.

41. Anneli Botha, "The 2007 Suicide Attacks in Algiers," in *Evolution of the Global Terrorist Threat*, 520. The GIA had some ties with Osama bin Laden, but bin Laden severed these ties around 1996 due to the GIA's indiscriminate use of violence in Algeria. See, for example, Brown, "Classical and Global Jihad," 99. For a profile of the GSPC, see Lianne Kennedy Boudali, "The GSPC: Newest Franchise in al-Qa'ida's Global Jihad," Combating Terrorism Center, April 2007.

42. On the reasons for the merger, see Mendelsohn, *Al-Qaeda Franchise*, chap. 7.

43. Moghadam, *Globalization of Martyrdom*, 159–63.

44. Craig Whitlock, "Al-Qaeda's Far-Reaching New Partner," *Washington Post*, October 5, 2006.

45. Janusz Biene, Daniel Kaiser, and Holger Marcks, "Explosive Affairs: Transnational Cooperation and the Escalation of Violent Dissidence," Paper Presented at the 56th Annual Convention of the International Studies Association (ISA), New Orleans, LA, February 19, 2015.

46. Kathryn Haahr, "GSPC Joins Al-Qaeda and France Becomes Top Enemy," *Terrorism Focus* 3, no. 37 (September 26, 2006).

47. Pascale Combelles Siegel, "AQIM Renews Its Threats Against France," *Terrorism Focus* 4, no. 26 (August 7, 2007).

48. Andrew Black, "AQIM Employs Martyrdom Operations in Algeria," *Terrorism Focus* 4, no. 29 (September 18, 2007).

49. The affiliation between the GSPC and Al Qaeda has frequently been described as a merger, including by the groups themselves, but the cooperation does not amount to a merger in the way it has been defined in this book.

50. Some authors, including Mendelsohn and Farrall, refer to the Al Qaeda–GSPC alliance in 2006 as a merger. I prefer the term "strategic alliance," because the quality of the cooperative ties between the two groups did not amount to the level of a merger as defined in this book. For example, it is evident, including from information seized in the Abbottabad compound that ACQ and AQIM did not have unified command and control. AQIM, for that matter, did not even have unified command and control with regard to itself. In addition, Al Qaeda operatives are not present in AQIM's leadership (unlike in AQAP, for example). See Yoram Schweitzer and Aviv Oreg, "Al Qaeda's Odyssey to the Global Jihad," Memorandum No. 134, Institute for National Security Studies (INSS), Tel Aviv University, March 2014, 42.

51. Botha, "2007 Suicide Attacks in Algiers," 522.

52. Souad Mekhennet, Michael Moss, Eric Schmitt, Elaine Sciolino, and Margot Williams, "A Threat Renewed: Ragtag Insurgency Gains a Lifeline from Al Qaeda," *New York Times*, July 1, 2008.

53. William Braniff, "The State of Al-Qaeda, Its Affiliates, and Associated Groups: View from Outside Experts," House Armed Services Committee, February 4, 2014, 8.

54. Byman, "Buddies or Burdens?," 451.

55. Schweitzer and Oreg, "Al Qaeda's Odyssey," 42.

56. Byman, "Buddies or Burdens?," 460.

57. Lahoud et al., "Letters from Abbottabad," 2–3, 38.

58. For background on jihadism in Somalia, see Joseph Felter, J. Vahid Brown, Jacob N. Shapiro, and Clinton Watts, eds., "Al-Qa'ida's (Mis)Adventures in East Africa," Combating Terrorism Center at West Point, NY, July 2, 2007; Lahoud, *Beware of Imitators*; and Stig Jarle Hansen, *Al-Shabaab in Somalia: The History and Ideology of a Militant Islamist Group, 2005–2012* (London: Hurst, 2013).

59. Lahoud, *Beware of Imitators*, 21.

60. Hansen, *Al-Shabaab in Somalia*, 20.

61. Hansen, *Al-shabaab in Somalia*, 20.

62. Matthew J. Thomas, "Exposing and Exploiting Weaknesses in the Merger of Al-Qaeda and Al-Shabaab," *Small Wars & Insurgencies* 24, no. 3 (2013): 414.

63. Robin Simcox, "Al-Qaeda's Global Footprint: An Assessment of al-Qaeda's Strength Today" (London: Henry Jackson Society, 2013), 22.

64. Lahoud, *Beware of Imitators*, 83–4.

65. Schweitzer and Oreg, "Al Qaeda's Odyssey," 43.

66. Schweitzer and Oreg, "Al Qaeda's Odyssey," 43.

67. Schweitzer and Oreg, "Al Qaeda's Odyssey," 43–44.

68. Lahoud, *Beware of Imitators*, 95.

69. Mendelsohn, *Al-Qaeda Franchise*, 143.

70. Mendelsohn, *Al-Qaeda Franchise*, 148–49.

71. For a discussion of some of these ties, see Simcox, "Al-Qaeda's Global Footprint."

72. Vahid Brown and Don Rassler, *Fountainhead of Jihad: The Haqqani Nexus, 1973–2012* (New York: Columbia University Press, 2013), 59–82.

73. Brown and Rassler, *Fountainhead*, 130–31, 141–46.

74. Brown and Rassler, *Fountainhead*, 187–89, 196–97, 206, 211.

75. Lahoud et.al., "Letters from Abbottabad," 37.

76. Kathleen Hennessey and Richard A. Serrano, "Pakistani Taliban Behind Times Square Bombing Attempt, White House Says," *Los Angeles Times*, May 10, 2010.

77. Seth Jones, "Al Qaeda Terrorism in Afghanistan," in *Evolution of the Global Terrorist Threat*, 379.

78. See Don Rassler, "Al-Qa'ida's Pakistan Strategy," *CTC Sentinel* 2, no. 6 (June 2009).

79. Muhammad al-Obaidi, Nassir Abdullah, and Scott Helfstein, "Deadly Vanguards: A Study of al-Qa'ida's Violence Against Muslims," Occasional Paper, Combating Terrorism Center, December 2009.

80. Jason Burke, "Bin Laden Wanted to Change al-Qaida's Bloodied Name," *Guardian*, June 24, 2011.
81. See, for example, Christopher Swift, "Arc of Convergence: AQAP, Ansar al-Shari'a and the Struggle for Yemen," *CTC Sentinel* 5, no. 6 (June 2012).
82. Lahoud et al., "Letters from Abbottabad." Bruce Hoffman, in contrast, argues that bin Laden did maintain a measure of control, as evidenced in his refusal to accept al-Shabaab's bayah. Bruce Hoffman, "Al Qaeda's Uncertain Future," *Studies in Conflict & Terrorism* 36, no. 8 (2013): 640.
83. Philipp Mudd, "Are Jihadist Groups Shifting Their Focus from the Far Enemy?" *CTC Sentinel* 5, no. 5 (May 2012).
84. J. M. Berger, "War on Error," *Foreign Policy*, February 5, 2014; Assaf Moghadam, Ronit Berger, and Polina Beliakova, "Say Terrorist, Think Insurgent: Labeling and Analyzing Contemporary Terrorist Actors," *Perspectives on Terrorism* 8, no. 5 (2014).
85. Clint Watts, "Al Qaeda Loses Touch: ISIS and the Future of Terrorism," *Foreign Affairs*, February 4, 2015; Hoffman, "Al Qaeda's Uncertain Future," 643.
86. Tricia Bacon, "Alliance Hubs: Focal Points in the International Terrorist Landscape," *Perspectives on Terrorism* 8, no. 4 (2014); and Stephen Tankel, "Not Another Al Qaeda Article," *War on the Rocks*, August 6, 2013. For an example of cooperation between Al Qaeda affiliates, specifically between Al-Shabaab and Al Qaeda in the Arabian Peninsula, see the indictment of Ahmed Abdulkadir Warsame, *United States v. Ahmed Abdulkadir Warsame*, https://www.nytimes.com/packages/pdf/world/Warsame_Indictment.pdf. I thank J.M. Berger for pointing out this example to me.
87. Jacob Zenn, "Cooperation or Competition: Boko Haram and Ansaru After the Mali Intervention," *CTC Sentinel* 6, no. 3 (March 2013).
88. Anne Wolf, "Tunisia: Signs of Domestic Radicalization," *CTC Sentinel* 6, no. 1 (January 2013).
89. Jacob Zenn, "Boko Haram's International Connections," *CTC Sentinel* 6 no. 1 (January 2013).
90. David Smith, "Africa's Islamist Militants 'Co-ordinate Efforts in Threat to Continent's Security,'" *Guardian*, June 26, 2012. See also Laurent Prieur, "Boko Haram Got Al Qaeda Bomb Training, Niger Says," Reuters, January 25, 2012.
91. "Mali–Al Qaeda's Sahara Playbook," Associated Press, July 27, 2015.
92. Some have suggested that it was Zawahiri who requested Abu Bakr to dispatch a delegation to Syria, but this question is not settled to date. See Rania Abouzeid, "The Jihad Next Door: The Syrian Roots of Iraq's Newest Civil War," *Politico*, June 23, 2014. For the more conventional account that credits the Islamic State of Iraq, and not Al Qaeda Central, with the establishment of Jabhat al-Nusra, see Charles Lister, *The Syrian Jihad: Al-Qaeda, the Islamic State, and the Evolution of an Insurgency* (Oxford; New York: Oxford University Press, 2015), 55–56.
93. Lister, *The Syrian Jihad*, 55–60.
94. Lister, *The Syrian Jihad*, 58.
95. Shiv Malik, Ali Younes, Spencer Ackerman, and Mustafa Khalili, "How Isis Crippled Al-Qaida," *Guardian*, June 10, 2015.

96. Lister, *The Syrian Jihad*, 124–25.

97. William McCants, "How Zawahiri Lost al Qaeda: Global Jihad Turns on Itself," *Foreign Affairs*, November 9, 2013.

98. Christoph Reuter, "The Terror Strategist: Secret Files Reveal the Structure of Islamic State," *Spiegel Online*, April 18, 2015.

99. Anurag Chandran, "Al Qaeda in the Indian Subcontinent: Almost Forgotten," *AEI Critical Threats*, September 3, 2015.

100. Richard Barrett, "The Islamic State Goes Global," *CTC Sentinel* 8, no. 11 (2015).

101. Abu Muhammad al-Adnani, "Indeed Your Lord Is Ever Watchful," blog post, September 22, 2014, https://pietervanostaeyen.wordpress.com/2014/09/25/abu-muhammad-al-adnani-ash-shami-indeed-your-lord-is-ever-watchful/.

102. Thomas Hegghammer and Peter Nesser, "Assessing the Islamic State's Commitment to Attacking the West," *Perspectives on Terrorism* 9, no. 4 (2015).

103. Jean-Charles Brisard, "The Paris Attacks and the Evolving Islamic State Threat to France," *CTC Sentinel* 8, no. 11 (2015).

104. Wladimir van Wilgenburg, "The Rise of Jaysh al-Fateh in Northern Syria," *Terrorism Monitor* 13, no. 12 (2015).

105. Maria Abi-Habib, "Al Qaeda Emissary in Syria Killed by Rival Islamist Rebels," *Wall Street Journal*, February 23, 2014.

106. Jeffrey White and Andrew J. Tabler, "The ISIS Battle for Yarmouk Camp: Troubling Implications," *PolicyWatch* 2407, Washington Institute for Near East Policy, April 10, 2015.

107. Jamie Dettmer, "In Video, Coulibaly Says He Coordinated with Hebdo Shooters," *Daily Beast*, January 11, 2015.

108. Scott Bronstein, Drew Griffin, and Deborah Feyerick, "For Paris Attackers, Terror Ties Ran Deep," *CNN*, January 13, 2015.

109. On this point, see also Lorenzo Vidino, "Wrong Assumptions: Integration, Responsibility, and Counterterrorism in France," *War on the Rocks*, January 22, 2015.

110. Jennifer Cafarella, "Jabhat al-Nusra in Syria: An Islamic Emirate for Al-Qaeda," Middle East Security Report No. 25, Institute for the Study of War, December 2014, 15.

111. Cafarella, "Jabhat al-Nusra in Syria," 15.

112. Cafarella, "Jabhat al-Nusra in Syria," 16.

113. Cafarella, "Jabhat al-Nusra in Syria," 17.

114. Lina Khatib, "The Islamic State's Strategy: Lasting and Expanding," Carnegie Endowment for International Peace, June 29, 2015.

115. Bridget Moreng and Daveed Gartenstein-Ross, "Al Qaeda is Beating the Islamic State: Get Ready for the Clash of Caliphates," *Politico*, April 14. 2015.

7. HIGH-END COOPERATION

1. The second-generation AQAP is also regarded as an official branch of Al Qaeda by some scholars. Nevertheless, it is clear that the two entities do not act in unison. Also, as Farrall has argued, AQAP has regional autonomy. Their relations, therefore, do not

meet the criteria of a merged entity as described in this book. Leah Farrall, "How Al Qaeda Works," *Foreign Affairs*, March/April 2011, 132–33.

2. For an overview of jihadism in Yemen in the 1990s, see Gregory D. Johnsen, *The Last Refuge: Yemen, Al-Qaeda, and the Battle for Arabia* (London: Oneworld, 2013); and Gabriel Koehler-Derrick, ed., "A False Foundation? AQAP, Tribes and Ungoverned Spaces in Yemen," Combating Terrorism Center at West Point, September 2011.

3. "Yemen: The Campaign Against Global Jihad—Situation Report and Directions of Development," *Jihadi Websites Monitoring Group (JWMG) Report*, October 2010, 16–17.

4. Thomas Hegghammer, "The 2003 Riyadh and 2008 Sanaa Bombings," in *The Evolution of the Global Terrorist Threat: From 9/11 to Osama bin Laden's Death*, ed. Bruce Hoffman and Fernando Reinares (New York: Columbia University Press, 2014), 539.

5. Hegghammer, "2003 Riyadh," 542.

6. Thomas Hegghammer, "The Failure of Jihad in Saudi Arabia," *Occasional Paper Series*, Combating Terrorism Center at West Point, February 25, 2010, 13. For more on the Ayeri network, see Thomas Hegghammer, *Jihad in Saudi Arabia: Violence and Pan-Islamism since 1979* (New York: Cambridge University Press, 2010), 118–27.

7. Barak Mendelsohn, *The Al-Qaeda Franchise: The Expansion of al-Qaeda and Its Consequences* (New York: Oxford University Press, 2016), 110.

8. On this point, see especially Farrall, "How Al Qaeda Works."

9. Hegghammer, "Failure of Jihad," 14.

10. Hegghammer, "2003 Riyadh," 555.

11. Johnsen, *Last Refuge*, 208–9.

12. Hegghammer, "2003 Riyadh," 555.

13. Gregory D. Johnsen, "Assessing the Strength of Al-Qa'ida in Yemen," *CTC Sentinel* 1, no. 10 (September 2008).

14. For more on the attacks, see Hegghammer, "2003 Riyadh."

15. "Al Qaeda in Yemen," Mapping Militant Organizations, Stanford University, http://web.stanford.edu/group/mappingmilitants/cgi-bin/groups/view/23?highlight=AQAP.

16. "Yemen: The Campaign Against Global Jihad."

17. For more on the 2009 merger, see Johnsen, *Last Refuge*, 235–50.

18. "Yemen: The Campaign Against Global Jihad."

19. The bomber was the brother of chief AQAP bomb-maker, Ibrahim al-Asiri.

20. Natasha Mozgovaya, "Chicago Synagogues Targeted in Yemen-Based Plot," *Haaretz*, October 31, 2010.

21. Christopher Swift, "Arc of Convergence: AQAP, Ansar al-Shari'a and the Struggle for Yemen," *CTC Sentinel* 5, no. 6 (June 2012).

22. Hugh Naylor, "Quietly, al-Qaeda Offshoots Expand in Yemen and Syria," *Washington Post*, June 4, 2015.

23. Paul Cruickshank, "Bin Laden Documents: Competing Vision of Al Qaeda's Top Two," *CNN Security Clearance*, May 7, 2012

24. See for example, *Inspire* 11 (2013): 13–17.

25. The series has been published in *Inspire* magazine. For the first part of the series, see *Inspire* 11 (Spring 2013): 27–28.

26. SOCOM-2012-0000016-HT, 1, https://www.ctc.usma.edu/posts/letters-from-abbottabad -bin-ladin-sidelined.

27. SOCOM-2012-0000016-HT, 3.

28. SOCOM-2012-0000016-HT, 6.

29. SOCOM-2012-0000016-HT, 10.

30. SOCOM-2012-0000019-HT, 20, https://www.ctc.usma.edu/posts/letters-from-abbot tabad-bin-ladin-sidelined.

31. For discussions of jihadist failures, see, for example, Fawaz Gerges, *The Far Enemy: Why Jihad Went Global* (Cambridge: Cambridge University Press, 2005); and Assaf Moghadam and Brian Fishman, *Fault Lines in Global Jihad: Organizational, Strategic, and Ideological Fissures* (London: Routledge, 2011).

32. SOCOM-2012-0000019-HT, 19.

33. SOCOM-2012-0000016-HT, 2.

34. SOCOM-2012-0000016-HT, 3.

35. Gabriel Koehler-Derrick, "The Abbottabad Documents: Bin Ladin's Cautious Strategy in Yemen," *CTC Sentinel* 5, no. 5 (May 2012).

36. SOCOM-2012-0000016-HT, 5.

37. SOCOM-2012-0000019-HT, 32.

38. SOCOM-2012-0000019-HT, 32.

39. SOCOM-2012-0000019-HT, 32.

40. SOCOM-2012-0000003, 2, https://www.ctc.usma.edu/posts/letters-from-abbottabad -bin-ladin-sidelined.

41. William McCants, *The ISIS Apocalypse: The History, Strategy, and Doomsday Vision of the Islamic State* (New York: St. Martin's, 2015), 55–56.

42. For an English version of Al Qaeda guidelines issued by Ayman al-Zawahiri in 2013, see Ayman al-Zawahiri, "General Guidelines for Jihad (As-Sahab Media, 2013)," http:// tinyurl.com/okz7fx5.

43. Thomas Joscelyn, "Osama bin Laden's Files: Al Qaeda's Deputy General Manager in Yemen," *Long War Journal*, March 1, 2015.

44. Joscelyn, "Osama bin Laden's Files."

45. Thomas Joscelyn, "Analysis: Why AQAP Quickly Denied Any Connection to Mosque Attacks," *Long War Journal*, March 20, 2015.

46. Thomas Joscelyn, "Analysis."

47. Thomas Joscelyn, "Analysis."

48. Cited in McCants, *The ISIS Apocalypse*, 61.

49. "Al Qaeda Apologizes for Yemeni Hospital Attack," *Al-Jazeera America*, December 22, 2013.

50. "Al Qaeda Apologizes."

51. For a description of responsibilities of the general manager of Al Qaeda, see SOCOM-2012-0000019-HT.

52. Joscelyn, "Osama bin Laden's Files."

53. Usama bin Ladin, "The Way to Save the Earth," *Inspire* 1 (Summer 1431/2010): 8; and Dr. Ayman al-Zawahiri, "Message to the People of Yemen," *Inspire* 1 (Summer 1431/2010): 11.

54. Thomas Joscelyn, "AQAP Praises Ayman al Zawahiri, Defends Jihadist Scholars Against 'Slander,'" *Long War Journal*, July 8, 2014.

55. "Letter from the Editor," *Inspire* 3 (November 1431/2010): 3.

56. "Letter from the Editor," 3.

57. Thomas Joscelyn, "New AQAP Leader Renews Allegiance to the 'Beloved Father,' Ayman al Zawahiri," *The Long War Journal*, July 9, 2015.

58. "Al-Qaeda Leader Al-Zawahiri Rejects ISIS Caliphate, Predicts Imminent 'Islamic Spring,'" *MEMRI JTTM*, September 9, 2015.

59. Thomas Joscelyn, "Al Qaeda Leader Praises Charlie Hebdo Massacre in New Message," *Long War Journal*, December 2, 2015.

60. Cited in Thomas Joscelyn, "Communications with Ayman al Zawahiri Highlighted in 'Nasr City Cell' Case," *Long War Journal*, February 10, 2013.

61. Clint Watts, "Al-Qaeda Plots, NSA Intercepts and the Era of Terrorism Competition," *Geopoliticus: The FPRI Blog*, August 2013.

62. "Al-Qaida Papers: The Yemen Letters," Associated Press, August 9, 2013.

63. Cited in Joscelyn, "Communications."

64. "Yemen: The Campaign Against Global Jihad," 60.

65. U.S. Senate Select Committee on Intelligence, "Review of the Terrorist Attacks on U.S. Facilities in Benghazi, Libya, September 11–12, 2012, Together with Additional Views," January 15, 2014, 40–41.

66. Eric Schmitt and Mark Mazzetti, "Qaeda Leader's Edict to Yemen Affiliate Is Said to Prompt Alert," *New York Times*, August 5, 2013.

67. Ibrahim ibn Hassan al-Asiri, "Charlie Hebdo: Military Analysis," *Inspire* 14 (Summer 1436/2015): 40.

68. Al-Asiri, "Charlie Hebdo," 41.

69. "Letter from the Editor," 2.

70. "From Here We Begin . . . And at al-Aqsa We Meet: Addresses of the Commanders of Al-Qaeda in the Arabian Peninsula," *Minbar al-Tawhid w'al Jihad*, translated at https://azelin.files.wordpress.com/2010/08/aqap-from-here-we-begin-and-at-al-aqsa-we-meet.pdf.

71. "From Here We Begin," 1.

72. "From Here We Begin," 2.

73. "From Here We Begin," 3.

74. "From Here We Begin," 5.

75. Quoted in McCants, *ISIS Apocalypse*, 52.

76. Quoted in McCants, *ISIS Apocalypse*, 52.

77. SOCOM-2012-0000017-HT, 1, https://www.ctc.usma.edu/posts/letters-from-abbottabad-bin-ladin-sidelined.

78. SOCOM-2012-0000017-HT, 4.

79. SOCOM-2012-0000017-HT, 4.

80. SOCOM-2012-0000017-HT, 5.

81. "Yemen: The Campaign Against Global Jihad," 6.

82. Quoted in McCants, *ISIS Apocalypse*, 52–53.

83. Quoted in McCants, *ISIS Apocalypse*, 53.

84. Tricia L. Bacon, "Strange Bedfellows or Brothers-In-Arms: Why Terrorist Groups Ally" (PhD Dissertation, Georgetown University, November 2013): 60.

85. Bacon, "Strange Bedfellows," 57.

86. Bacon, "Strange Bedfellows," 57.

87. Bacon, "Strange Bedfellows," 60–63.

88. Hegghammer, *Jihad in Saudi Arabia*, 118–22.

89. Johnsen, *Last Refuge*, 57.

90. Schmitt and Mazzetti, "Qaeda Leader's Edict."

91. Johnsen, *Last Refuge*, 57.

92. Johnsen, *Last Refuge*, 58.

93. *Sada al-Malahim* 8:36, cited in Barak Barfi, "Yemen on the Brink? The Resurgence of al Qaeda in Yemen," *Counterterrorism Strategy Initiative Policy Paper*, New America Foundation, January 2010, 3.

94. Robin Simcox, "Al-Qaeda's Global Footprint: An Assessment of al-Qaeda's Strength Today," Henry Jackson Society, London, 2013, 16.

95. Joscelyn "Osama bin Laden's Files."

96. Barfi, "Yemen on the Brink?," 2–3; and Murad Batal al-Shishani, "Ibrahim al-Rubaish: New Religious Ideologue of al-Qaeda in Saudi Arabia Calls for Revival of Assassination Tactic," *Terrorism Monitor* 7, no. 36 (November 2009).

97. McCants, *ISIS Apocalypse*, 68.

98. Aaron Zelin, "The Islamic State's Model," *Monkey Cage*, Washington Post, January 28, 2015.

99. McCants, *ISIS Apocalypse*, 68.

100. McCants, *ISIS Apocalypse*, 68.

8. LOW-END COOPERATION

1. Nelly Lahoud et al., "Letters from Abbottabad: Bin Ladin Sidelined?," Combating Terrorism Center at West Point, May 3, 2012, 42.

2. Former Al Qaeda member L'Houssaine Kherchtou, for example, denied the possibility of cooperation between Al Qaeda and Iran. See United States District Court, Southern District of New York, *USA v. Usama bin Ladin*, S(7) 98 Cr. 1023, February 26, 2001, 1385. For references to the Iran–Al Qaeda connection as an "alliance," see for example, Jay Solomon, "US Sees Iranian, Al Qaeda Alliance," *Wall Street Journal*, July 29, 2011.

3. National Commission on Terrorist Attacks Upon the United States, *The 9/11 Commission Report*, 1st ed. (New York: Norton, 2004), 241. Henceforth cited as *9/11 Commission Report*.

4. Lawrence Wright, *The Looming Tower: Al-Qaeda and the Road to 9/11* (New York: Vintage, 2006), 56.

5. Ali Alfoneh, "Iran's Suicide Brigades: Terrorism Resurgent," *Middle East Quarterly* 14, no. 1 (Winter 2007).

6. Wright, *Looming Tower*, 197.

7. "Affidavit of Dr. Ronen Bergman," United States District Court, Southern District of New York, Civil Action No. 03 MDL 1570 (GBD), April 8, 2010, 15.

8. *9/11 Commisssion Report*, 61.

9. *9/11 Commission Report*, 61.

10. *9/11 Commission Report*, 61.

11. *9/11 Commission Report*, 68.

12. Marc A. Thiessen, "Iran Responsible for 1998 U.S. Embassy Bombings," *Washington Post*, December 8, 2011.

13. Peter L. Bergen, *The Osama bin Laden I Know: An Oral History of al Qaeda's Leader* (New York: Free Press, 2006), 143.

14. Wright, *Looming Tower*, 211.

15. According to Wright, "Most of al-Qaeda's relationship with Iran came through Zawahiri." Wright, *Looming Tower*, 197.

16. Wright, *Looming Tower*, 193–94, 197.

17. James Risen, "Bin Laden Sought Iran as an Ally, U.S. Intelligence Documents Say," *New York Times*, December 31, 2001.

18. *9/11 Commission Report*, 240.

19. Risen, "Bin Laden Sought Iran."

20. *9/11 Commission Report*, 240.

21. Spencer S. Hsu, "U.S. Judge Finds Iran Liable in 2000 Attack on USS *Cole*," *Washington Post*, April 1, 2015.

22. *9/11 Commission Report*, 240.

23. Fuad Husayn, *Zarqawi . . . The Second Generation of Al-Qaeda*, part 8, trans. Foreign Broadcast Information Service, *Al-Quds al-Arabi*, May 2005.

24. Thomas Joscelyn, "Analysis: Al Qaeda's Interim Emir and Iran," *Long War Journal*, May 18, 2011.

25. Bergen, *Osama bin Laden I Know*, 354.

26. Bergen, *Osama bin Laden I Know*, 354. A senior IRGC member who defected, Hamid Zakiri, gave an interview for Al-Sharq al-Awsat in 2003 in which he seemed to confirm al-Adel's statement that the relationship between Al Qaeda was not with the Iranian government per se, but with the intelligence branch of the IRGC. *Al-Sharq al-Awsat*, February 18, 2003. Cited in Paul Hastert, "Al Qaeda and Iran: Friends or Foes, or Somewhere in Between?" *Studies in Conflict & Terrorism* 30, no. 4 (2007): 332.

27. *9/11 Commission Report*, 241.

28. According to a court filing in a federal lawsuit in Manhattan in May 2011, for instance, two defectors from Iran's intelligence services testified that Iranian officials had "foreknowledge of the 9/11 attacks." One of them even claimed that Iran was involved in

planning the attacks. The testimony was filed under seal, which made it hard to assess the allegations. The lawyers claimed in the court filing that Mughniyeh traveled to Saudi Arabia in 2000 to help prepare the 9/11 attacks. Benjamin Weiser and Scott Shane, "Court Filings Assert Iran had Link to 9/11 Attacks," *New York Times*, May 19, 2011.

29. *9/11 Commission Report*, 240.

30. *9/11 Commission Report*, 241.

31. Bergen, *Osama bin Laden I Know*, 353–54.

32. "Statement by Sulayman Abu Ghayth to the Federal Bureau of Investigation," March 1, 2013, Document number 415-A-NY-307616, 7, http://kronosadvisory.com/Kronos_US_v _Sulaiman_Abu_Ghayth_Statement.1.pdf; Brynjar Lia, *Architect of Global Jihad: The Life of Al-Qaida Strategist Abu Mus'ab al-Suri* (New York: Columbia University Press, 2008), 326; Mark Hosenball, "The Iran Connection," *Newsweek* 141, no. 9 (March 2003): 36.

33. Seth G. Jones, "Al Qaeda in Iran," *Foreign Affairs*, January 29, 2012. This is also confirmed by Sulayman Abu Ghayth. See "Statement by Sulayman Abu Ghayth," 7.

34. Jones, "Al Qaeda in Iran." The large number cited by Jones exceeds the number of formal Al Qaeda members. One can therefore assume that most of the "several hundreds" of people cited by Jones were not formal Al Qaeda members, but jihadists who had trained in Al Qaeda training camps in Afghanistan at the time of the U.S. invasion following 9/11.

35. One Al Qaeda member, Abu Abd al-Rahman Anas al-Subayi, later described the Iranian "deportations" of many jihadists as a "betrayal." He also said that the Iranians photographed and took fingerprints of those jihadists they deported. Letter by Abu abd al-Rahman Anas al-Subayi, October 13, 2010, Office of the Director of National Intelligence (DNI), "Bin Laden's Bookshelf," http://www.dni.gov/files/documents/ubl/english /Letter%20dtd%2013%20Oct%202010.pdf.

36. Peter L. Bergen, *Manhunt: The Ten-Year Search for Bin Laden from 9/11 to Abbottabad* (New York: Broadway, 2012), 159–60; Eric Schmitt and Thom Shanker, *Counterstrike: The Untold Story of America's Secret Campaign Against Al Qaeda* (New York: Times Books, 2011), 32. See also John Mintz, "Saudi Says Iran Drags Feet Returning Al Qaeda Leaders," *Washington Post*, August 12, 2003; and Douglas Farah and Dana Priest, "Bin Laden Son Plays Key Role in Al Qaeda," *Washington Post*, October 14, 2003.

37. Michael S. Smith II, "The Al-Qa'ida-Qods Force Nexus: Scratching the Surface of a 'Known Unknown,'" Kronos Advisory LLC, USA, April 29, 2011.

38. "President Delivers State of the Union Address," White House, http://georgewbush -whitehouse.archives.gov/news/releases/2002/01/20020129-11.html.

39. "Letter by Abu abd al-Rahman Anas al-Subayi." This is confirmed by Sulayman abu Ghayth. See "Statement by Sulayman Abu Ghayth."

40. " Letter by Abu abd al-Rahman Anas al-Subayi."

41. "Letter by Abu abd al-Rahman Anas al-Subayi."

42. Adam Zagorin and Joe Klein, "9/11 Commission Finds Ties Between al Qaeda and Iran," *Time*, July 16, 2004.

43. Jones, "Al Qaeda in Iran."

44. Matthew Levitt and Michael Jacobson, "The Iran–al-Qaeda Conundrum," *PolicyWatch* 1461, Washington Institute for Near East Policy, January 23, 2009; and Thomas Joscelyn, "Treasury Targets Iran's 'Secret Deal' with al Qaeda," *Long War Journal*, July 28, 2011.

45. Joscelyn, "Treasury Targets."

46. Daniel Byman, "Unlikely Alliance: Iran's Secretive Relationship with Al-Qaeda," *IHS Defense, Risk and Security Consulting*, July 2012, 31.

47. Pollack, *Persian Puzzle*, 358; Douglas Jehl and Eric Schmitt, "Havens: U.S. Suggests a Qaeda Cell in Iran Directed Saudi Bombings,' *New York Times*, May 21, 2003; Hastert, "Al Qaeda and Iran," 333–34; Byman, "Unlikely Alliance," 31.

48. The United States reportedly declined the offer. Pollack, *Persian Puzzle*, 360–61.

49. Farah and Priest, "Bin Laden Son."

50. Pollack, *Persian Puzzle*, 358.

51. Some of those who underwent harsh treatment include members of the bin Laden family. See Sarah el Deeb, "Bin Laden's Son Asks Iran to Free His Siblings," *Huffington Post*, March 15, 2010. The veracity of these claims is disputed, however.

52. "Letter by Abu abd al-Rahman Anas al-Subayi."

53. "Letter by Abu abd al-Rahman Anas al-Subayi"; see also "Statement by Sulayman Abu Ghayth." Al-Subayi's account of the experience of Al Qaeda members in Iran at times contradicts Abu Ghayth's account as far as dates and places of the detention are concerned. This may suggest that there were several facilities in Iran in which Al Qaeda members were detained. At present, there is insufficient information to settle this question.

54. Jones, "Al Qaeda in Iran."

55. "Letter by Abu abd al-Rahman Anas al-Subayi."

56. Levitt and Jacobson, "Iran–al-Qaeda Conundrum."

57. Byman, "Unlikely Alliance," 31. See also Guido W. Steinberg, *German Jihad: On the Internationalization of Islamist Terrorism* (New York: Columbia University Press), 56.

58. "Iran as Al-Qaida Base," *Investor's Business Daily*, March 19, 2010.

59. "Iran Frees bin Laden Son - German Newspaper," Reuters, August 2, 2006.

60. Chris Heffelfinger, "Saad bin Laden: The Key to Iranian–al-Qaeda Détente?" *Terrorism Focus* 3, no. 31 (August 8, 2006).

61. Bruce Riedel, "The Mysterious Relationship Between Al-Qa'ida and Iran," *CTC Sentinel* 3, no. 7 (July 2010); "Iran Eases Grip on Al Qaeda," Associated Press, May 13, 2010.

62. Jones, "Al Qaeda in Iran."

63. SOCOM-2012-0000012, 1, https://www.ctc.usma.edu/posts/letters-from-abbottabad -bin-ladin-sidelined. These included Abd al-Muhayman al-Misri, Salim al-Misri, Abu Suhayb al-Makki, Al-Zubayr al-Maghribi, and their families. For details on these individuals, see Lahoud et al., "Letters from Abbottabad," 43–44, fn. 186.

64. SOCOM-2012-0000019, 42–43, https://www.ctc.usma.edu/posts/letters-from-abbot tabad-bin-ladin-sidelined.

65. Lahoud et al., "Letters from Abbottabad," 45–46.

66. Yassin Musharbash, "A Top Terrorist Returns to Al Qaeda Fold," *Spiegel Online*, October 25, 2010.

67. Bruce Riedel, "The Al Qaeda–Iran Connection," *Daily Beast*, May 29, 2011.

68. "Top al-Qaeda Ranks Keep Footholds in Iran," *USA Today*, July 9, 2011.

69. SOCOM-2012-0000012, 2–4.

70. Rukmini Callimachi and Eric Schmitt, "Iran Released Top Members of Al Qaeda in a Trade," *New York Times*, September 17, 2015. The other Al Qaeda members reportedly released were Abu Kheyr al-Mazri, Abul Qassam, Sari Shibab, and Abu Muhammad al-Mizri.

71. Lahoud et al., "Letters from Abbottabad," 4, 42–47.

72. The other Al Qaeda operatives named were Umid Muhammadi, Salim Hasan Khalifa Rashid al Kuwari, Abdallah Ghanim Mafuz Muslim al Khawar, and Ali Hasan Ali al-Ajmi. Helene Cooper, "Treasury Accuses Iran of Aiding Al Qaeda," *New York Times*, July 28, 2011; Solomon, "U.S. Sees Iranian, al Qaeda Alliance"; Matthew Lee and Bradley Klapper, "Iran Accused of Al-Qaeda 'Secret Deal' by U.S. Officials," *Huffington Post*, July 28, 2011.

73. U.S. Department of the Treasury, "Treasury Further Exposes Al-Qa'ida's Iran-based Network," October 18, 2012.

74. U. S. Department of State, "Rewards for Justice—al-Qaeda Reward Offer," October 18, 2012.

75. U. S. Department of State, "Rewards for Justice."

76. U. S. Department of State, "Rewards for Justice."

77. Sam Kiley, "Fears Iran Is Helping Al Qaeda Plot Atrocity," *Sky News*, February 15, 2012.

78. " Letter to Karim," Office of the Director of National Intelligence, "Bin Laden's Bookshelf," 1, http://www.dni.gov/files/documents/ubl2016/english/Letter%20to%20Karim.pdf.

79. "Letter dtd 5 April 2011," Office of the Director of National Intelligence, "Bin Laden's Bookshelf," 4, http://www.dni.gov/files/documents/ubl/english/Letter%20dtd%205%20April%202011.pdf.

80. "Letter dtd 5 April 2011," 5.

81. For more on this plot, see Steinberg, *German Jihad*; and Yassin Musharbash, "'Euro Plot': Al-Qaida Said to Be Planning European Hostage-Takings," *Spiegel Online*, October 27, 2010.

82. Benjamin Weinthal and Thomas Joscelyn, "Al Qaeda's Network in Iran," *Weekly Standard*, April 2, 2012.

83. Ian Austen, "Two Are Accused in Canada of Plotting Train Derailment," *New York Times*, April 22, 2013.

84. U.S. Department of the Treasury, "Treasury Designates Iranian Ministry of Intelligence and Security for Human Rights Abuses and Support for Terrorism," February 16, 2012.

85. Thomas Joscelyn, "Doomed Diplomacy: There's No Way Iran Will Ever Help Fight Al Qaeda," *Weekly Standard* 20, no. 24 (March 2, 2015).

86. According to an IRGC defector interviewed in *Al Sharq al-Awsat*, the ties between the EIJ and Iran date back to the late 1980s, following the assassination of Egyptian President Sadat. For a translation of the interview, see "Top Iranian Defector on Iran's Collaboration with Iraq, North Korea, Al-Qa'ida, and Hizbullah," *MEMRI Special Dispatch* No. 473, February 21, 2003.

87. Affidavit of Patrick L. Clawson, United States District Court, Southern District of New York, Civil Action No. 03 MDL 1570 (GBD), June 25, 2010, 17.

88. Affidavit of Daniel L. Byman, United States District Court, Southern District of New York, Civil Action No. 03 MDL 1570 (GBD), June 8, 2010, 10.

89. Quoted in Daniel L. Byman, "The Odd Couple," *Foreign Policy*, February 21, 2012.

90. On Iranian support for Hamas, see for example Bureau of Counterterrorism, U.S. Department of State, *Country Reports on Terrorism 2014* (Washington, DC: U.S. State Department, 2015), chap. 3; and Matthew Levitt, *Hamas: Politics, Charity, and Terrorism in the Service of Jihad* (New Haven, CT: Yale University Press, 2006), 172–78.

91. Joscelyn, "Analysis: Al Qaeda's Interim Emir."

92. Dana Priest and Douglas Farah, "Terror Alliance Has U.S. Worried," *Washington Post*, June 30, 2002.

93. See also United States District Court, Southern District of New York, *Havlish v. Usama bin Laden et al.*, Civil Action No. 03 MDL 1570 (GBD), Findings of Fact and Conclusions of Law, 50.

94. Jarret Brachman, Brian Fishman, and Joseph Felter, "The Power of Truth: Questions for Ayman al-Zawahiri," Combating Terrorism Center at West Point, April 21, 2008, 16.

95. Byman, "Unlikely Alliance," 28.

96. Bruce Riedel, "Iran and Al Qaeda's Shadowy Relationship Could Firm Up This Spring," *Daily Beast*, February 17, 2012.

97. This section incorporates some passages from Assaf Moghadam, *The Globalization of Martyrdom: Al Qaeda, Salafi Jihad, and the Diffusion of Suicide Attacks* (Baltimore, MD: Johns Hopkins University Press, 2008).

98. Dexter Filkins, "U.S. Says Files Seek Qaeda Aid in Iraq Conflict," *New York Times*, February 9, 2004.

99. Filkins, "U.S. Says Files."

100. Quoted in Michael Scheuer, "Coalition Warfare, Part II: How Zarqawi Fits Into Bin Laden's World Front," *Terrorism Focus* 2, no. 8 (April 2005).

101. Toby Matthiesen, "The Islamic State Exploits Entrenched Anti-Shia Incitement," Carnegie Middle East Center, July 21, 2015.

102. "Audio Message by Abu Bakr al-Baghdadi—Even If the Disbelievers Despise Such," November 14, 2014, https://pietervanostaeyen.wordpress.com/2014/11/14/audio-message-by-abu-bakr-al-baghdadi-even-if-the-disbelievers-despise-such.

103. Matthiesen, "Islamic State Exploits."

104. "Houthis Gain Ground Against Yemen's al-Qaeda," *Al Jazeera*, November 15; Mohammed Ghobari, "IS Suicide Bomber Dressed as a Woman Kills 10 at Yemen Houthi Mosque," Reuters, September 24, 2015.

105. *9/11 Commission Report*, 61.

106. Bernard Haykel, interview with the author, Washington, DC, July 28, 2008.

107. Bernard Haykel, "Al-Qa'ida and Shiism," in *Fault Lines in Global Jihad: Organizational, Strategic, and Ideological Fissures*, ed. Assaf Moghadam and Brian Fishman (London: Routledge, 2011), 184.

108. Haykel, "Al-Qa'ida and Shiism," 186.

109. Haykel, "Al-Qa'ida and Shiism," 186.

110. "Affidavit of Daniel L. Byman," 10.

111. Pollack, *Persian Puzzle*, 359.

112. "Letter to Karim."

113. "Letter from al-Zawahiri to al-Zarqawi," http://fas.org/irp/news/2005/10/letter_in_english.pdf.

114. I am indebted to Dan Byman for this point. Daniel Byman, e-mail correspondence with the author, October 12, 2015.

115. SOCOM-2012-0000008, https://www.ctc.usma.edu/posts/letters-from-abbottabad-bin-ladin-sidelined.

116. SOCOM-2012-0000008, 3.

117. SOCOM-2012-0000008, 4.

118. "SOCOM-2012-0000019, 42.

119. "Letter dtd November 24 2010," Office of the Director of National Intelligence, "Bin Laden's Bookshelf," 2, http://www.dni.gov/files/documents/ubl/english/Letter%20dtd%20November%2024%202010.pdf.

120. "Letter to Wife," Office of the Director of National Intelligence, "Bin Laden's Bookshelf," http://www.dni.gov/files/documents/ubl2016/english/Letter%20to%20wife.pdf.

121. "Letter to Wife."

122. "SOCOM-2012-0000012, 4.

123. J. David Goodman, "Stop the Conspiracy Theories, Al Qaeda Tells Iranian Leader," *Lede' Blog, New York Times*, September 28, 2011.

124. Thomas Joscelyn, "DNI Clapper: 'Shotgun Marriage' Between Iran and Al Qaeda," *Weekly Standard Blog*, February 17, 2012.

9. NETWORKED COOPERATION

1. National Commission on Terrorist Attacks Upon the United States, *The 9/11 Commission Report*, 1st ed. (New York: Norton, 2004), 145. Henceforth cited as *9/11 Commission Report*.

2. *9/11 Commission Report*, 154.

3. For more on KSM's background, see *9/11 Commission Report*, 145–50; and Terry McDermott and Josh Meyer, *The Hunt for KSM: Inside the Pursuit and Takedown of the Real 9/11 Mastermind* (New York: Little Brown, 2012).

4. Asra Q. Nomani, "This Is Danny Pearl's Final Story," *Washingtonian*, January 23, 2014.

5. Simon Reeve, *The New Jackals: Ramzi Yousef, Osama bin Laden and the Future of Terrorism* (Boston: Northeastern University Press, 1999), 113–14.

6. According to Reeve, Youssef trained in camps near Peshawar in 1988. Reeve, *New Jackals*, 120. According to testimony Youssef gave to the FBI, he attended six months of training in various camps in Afghanistan in the second half of the 1990s. See Peter L. Bergen, *The Osama bin Laden I Know: An Oral History of al Qaeda's Leader* (New York: Free Press, 2006), 145. According to Rohan Gunaratna, Youssef was a graduate of the Al-Saddah training camp. Gunaratna also cited Youssef's childhood friend and co-conspirator Abdul Hakim Murad, who told investigators that Youssef underwent six months of training in Afghanistan in 1993. Rohan Gunaratna, "Al Qaeda's Lose and Learn Doctrine: The Trajectory from Oplan Bojinka to 9/11," in *Teaching Terror: Strategic and Tactical Learning in the Terrorist World*, ed. James J. F. Forest (Lanham, MD: Rowman & Littlefield, 2006), 173, 186 fn. 3.

7. Lawrence Wright, *The Looming Tower: Al-Qaeda and the Road to 9/11* (New York: Vintage, 2006), 202.

8. Wright, *Looming Tower*, 202.

9. Federal Bureau of Investigation (FBI), "Interview of Ramzi Ahmed Yousef," February 26, 1993. Quoted in Bergen, *Osama bin Laden I Know*, 145.

10. *9/11 Commission Report*, 147.

11. Gus Martin, ed., *The Sage Encyclopedia of Terrorism*, 2nd ed. (Thousand Oaks, CA: Sage, 2011), 391.

12. *9/11 Commission Report*, 147.

13. Reeve, *New Jackals*, 77.

14. Daniel Benjamin and Steven Simon, *The Age of Sacred Terror* (New York: Random House, 2002), 23.

15. "Terrorists Plotted to Blow Up 11 U.S. Jumbo Jets," *Los Angeles Times*, May 28, 1995.

16. Benjamin and Simon, *Age of Sacred Terror*, 22–23.

17. Benjamin and Simon, *Age of Sacred Terror*, 22–23.

18. Matthew Brzezinski, "Bust and Boom," *Washington Post*, December 30, 2001.

19. Benjamin and Simon, *Age of Sacred Terror*, 20.

20. Terry McDermott, "Early Scheme to Turn Jets Into Weapons," *Los Angeles Times*, June 24, 2002.

21. Brzezinski, "Bust and Boom."

22. Zachary Abuza, *Militant Islam in Southeast Asia: Crucible of Terror* (Boulder, CO: Lynne Rienner, 2003), 107.

23. Brzezinski, "Bust and Boom."

24. Bergen, *Osama bin Laden I Know*, 303; McDermott, "Early Scheme"; Assaf Moghadam, "How Al Qaeda Innovates," *Security Studies* 22, no. 3 (2013).

25. Abuza, *Militant Islam*, 101.

26. Abuza, *Militant Islam*, 104.

27. Raymond Bonner and Benjamin Weiser, "Echoes of Early Design to Use Chemicals to Blow Up Airliners," *New York Times*, August 11, 2006. Matthew Brzezinski, "Bust and Boom."

28. McDermott, "Early Scheme"; Bergen, *Osama bin Laden I Know*, 16.

29. Benjamin and Simon, *Age of Sacred Terror*, 25–26.

30. For additional details on the cooperative aspects of the planning of the 9/11 attacks, see Moghadam, "How Al Qaeda Innovates." The present case study incorporates sections of that article.

31. *9/11 Commission Report*, 154.

32. *9/11 Commission Report*, 149.

33. Moghadam, "How Al Qaeda Innovates."

34. Bruce Hoffman, "Rethinking Terrorism and Counterterrorism Since 9/11," *Studies in Conflict & Terrorism* 25, no. 5 (September/October 2002): 309.

35. *9/11 Commission Report*, 154.

36. Bergen, *Osama bin Laden I Know*, 303.

37. *9/11 Commission Report*, 251; Vahid Brown, "Cracks in the Foundation: Leadership Schisms in al-Qa'ida from 1989–2006," Combating Terrorism Center at West Point, NY, January 2, 2007; Camil Tawil, "The Other Face of Al-Qaeda," Quilliam Foundation, London, November 2010.

38. *9/11 Commission Report*, 235.

39. The quick selection of the candidates is not only due to Al Qaeda's ability to reach decisions quickly, but is also a result of bin Laden and Atef's likely realization that the initial team selected lacked the proper qualifications and skills. *9/11 Commission Report*, 166.

40. After swearing *bayah*, the future hijackers were sent to KSM to be trained and recorded for their martyrdom video. As Al Qaeda's head of the media committee, KSM also oversaw the shooting of these martyrdom videos. *9/11 Commission Report*, 235.

41. *9/11 Commission Report*, 154.

42. *9/11 Commission Report*, 154.

43. Khalid al-Hammadi, "The Inside Story of al-Qa'ida, Part 4," *Al-Quds al-Arabi*, March 22, 2005.

44. Wright, *Looming Tower*, 348. For a discussion of Al Qaeda's principle being akin to mission command, also known as Auftragstaktik, see Moghadam, "How Al Qaeda Innovates," 489-91.

45. *9/11 Commission Report*, 145.

46. *9/11 Commission Report*, 166.

47. *9/11 Commission Report*, 496, fn. 92.

48. *9/11 Commission Report*, 241. Ramzi Binalshibh was a member of the German cell and had been originally selected to pilot one of the 9/11 planes. After the U.S. government repeatedly rejected his attempts to obtain a visa, the 9/11 planners were forced to look for another fourth pilot and selected Hani Hanjour, a Saudi national with some flying experience. See *9/11 Commission Report*, 168, 225–26. Binalshibh described his role in the attacks as "simply a process of interconnecting various cells, establishing a line of contact between these cells and the General Command in Afghanistan as well as following up on work priorities of these cells until all phases of preparation are complete—up to the moment of execution." Quoted in Bergen, *Osama bin Laden I Know*, 303-4.

49. *9/11 Commission Report*, 157–58.

50. See, for example, *9/11 Commission Report*, 167, 245.

51. *9/11 Commission Report*, 148.

52. *9/11 Commission Report*, 149.

53. *9/11 Commission Report*, 149.

54. *9/11 Commission Report*, 150.

55. *9/11 Commission Report*, 154.

56. Nick Lowles and Joe Mulhall, "Gateway to Terror: Anjem Choudary and the al-Muhajiroun Network," HOPE Not Hate, London, 2014. As quoted in Andrew Anthony, "Anjem Choudary: The British Extremist Who Backs the Caliphate," *Guardian*, September 7, 2014.

57. Quintan Wiktorowicz, *Radical Islam Rising: Muslim Extremism in the West* (Lanham, MD: Rowman & Littlefield, 2005), 9.

58. Wiktorowicz, *Radical Islam Rising*, 9.

59. Wiktorowicz, *Radical Islam Rising*, 9.

60. Wiktorowicz, *Radical Islam Rising*, 10.

61. Wiktorowicz, *Radical Islam Rising*, 10.

62. Catherine Zara Raymond, "Al Muhajiroun and Islam4UK: The Group Behind the Ban," International Centre for the Study of Radicalization and Political Violence (ICSR), Kings College London, May 2010, 8.

63. Robin Simcox, Hannah Stuart, Houriya Ahmed, and Douglas Murray, "Islamist Terrorism: The British Connections," 2nd ed." (London: Henry Jackson Society, 2011), xii.

64. Joe Mulhall, "From Clowns to Contenders: The History and Development of al-Muhajiroun and its International Networks," in *Sharia4: Straddling Political Activism and Jihad in the West*, ed. Lorenzo Vidino (Dubai: Al Mesbar Studies and Research Centre, 2015), 20.

65. Joe Mulhall, "From Clowns to Contenders," 1.

66. For details on these plots and their connections to Al Muhajiroun, see Raffaello Pantucci, *We Love Death as You Love Life: Britain's Suburban Terrorists* (London: Hurst, 2015), 159–230.

67. Sandra Laville, Peter Walker, and Vikram Dodd, "Woolwich Attack Suspect Identified as Michael Adebolajo," *Guardian*, May 23, 2013.

68. Nico Hines, "Two Men Convicted of British Soldier Beheading," *Daily Beast*, December 19, 2013.

69. Jytte Klausen, Eliane Tschaen Barbieri, Aaron Reichlin Melnick, and Aaron Y. Zelin, "YouTube Jihadists: A Social Network Analysis of Al-Muhajiroun's Propaganda Campaign," *Perspectives on Terrorism* 6, no. 1 (March 2012).

70. Raymond, "Al Muhajiroun and Islam4UK," 12–13.

71. Raymond, "Al Muhajiroun and Islam4UK," 12–13.

72. Wiktorowicz, *Radical Islam Rising*, 120–21.

73. Wiktorowicz, *Radical Islam Rising*, 120.

74. Wiktorowicz, *Radical Islam Rising*, 120.

75. Wiktorowicz, *Radical Islam Rising*, 106-7; Mulhall, "From Clowns to Contenders," 11–12.
76. Mulhall, "From Clowns to Contenders," 11–12.
77. Mulhall, "From Clowns to Contenders," 8.
78. Klausen et al., "YouTube Jihadists," 39.
79. "Outrage as Muslim Extremists Hijack War Heroes' Town Wootton Bassett," *Daily Mail*, January 3, 2010.
80. "Muslim Cleric Anjem Choudary Admits Wootton Bassett March Is Publicity Stunt," *Telegraph*, January 4, 2010.
81. U.K. Home Office and James Brokenshire, MP, "Written Statement to Parliament: Alternative Names for Proscribed Organisation Al Muhajiroun," June 26, 2014.
82. Lorenzo Vidino, "Sharia4: From Confrontational Activism to Militancy," *Perspectives on Terrorism* 9, no. 2 (2015).
83. Pieter van Ostaeyen, "Belgian Fighters in Syria and Iraq—November 2014," *Jihadology*, November 22, 2014.
84. Elaine Sciolino and Souad Mekhennet, "Al Qaeda Warrior Uses Internet to Rally Women," *New York Times*, May 28, 2008; and Paul Cruickshank, "Love in the Time of Terror," *Marie Claire*, May 15, 2009.
85. Pieter van Ostaeyen, "Belgian Jihadists in Syria—5 September 2013," *Jihadology*, September 5, 2013.
86. Guy Van Vlierden, "How Belgium Became a Top Exporter of Jihad," *Terrorism Monitor* 13, no. 11 (May 29, 2015).
87. Matthew Dalton and Margaret Coker, "How Belgium Became a Jihadist Recruiting Hub," *Wall Street Journal*, September 28, 2014.
88. Ben Taub, "Journey to Jihad: Why Are Teen-Agers Joining ISIS?" *New Yorker*, June 1, 2015.
89. "UK Hate Preachers Linked to Fanatics," *Daily Mail*, January 8, 2016.
90. Taub, "Journey to Jihad."
91. Klausen et al., "YouTube Jihadists," 39.
92. Ristel Tchounand, "Sharia4UK menace la Belgique pour défendre Fouad Belkacem," *Yabiladi*, May 15, 2013.
93. Taub, "Journey to Jihad."
94. Pieter van Ostaeyen, "Sharia4Belgium," in *Sharia4: Straddling Political Activism and Jihad in the West*, ed. Lorenzo Vidino (Dubai: Al Mesbar Studies and Research Centre, 2015), 3.
95. Van Ostaeyen, "Sharia4Belgium," 4.
96. Melodie Bouchaud, "'Sharia4Belgium' Leader and Dozens of Other Militants Are Sentenced to Jail Time," *Vice News*, February 12, 2015.
97. Vidino, "Sharia4," 6.
98. Soeren Kern, "Let's Turn Belgium Into an Islamist State," Gatestone Institute, December 19, 2011.
99. Kern, "Let's Turn Belgium."

100. Bouchaud, "'Sharia4Belgium' Leader."

101. Van Vlierden, "How Belgium Became a Top Exporter of Jihad."

102. Bouchaud, "'Sharia4Belgium' Leader."

103. See, for example, Europol, "Europol TE-SAT 2014: EU Terrorism Situation and Trend Report," The Hague, Netherlands, 2014, 23; and Europol, "Europol TE-SAT 2015: EU Terrorism Situation and Trend Report," The Hague, Netherlands, 2015, 22.

104. Europol, "Europol TE-SAT 2015," 22.

105. Raffaello Pantucci, "Al-Muhajiroun's European Recruiting Pipeline," *CTC Sentinel* 8, no. 8 (August 2015): 24.

106. Vidino, "Sharia4," 10.

107. Peter Neumann cites 20,700 fighters overall, including up to 4,000 Western Europeans and 500 fighters from non-European Western nations. Peter R. Neumann, *Die Neuen Dschihadisten: IS, Europa und die Nächste Welle des Terrorismus* (Berlin: Econ, 2015), 109–11. The Central Intelligence Agency has similar estimates for this period, citing 20,000 foreign fighters overall, including at least 3,400 Westerners. Kristin Archick, Paul Belkin, Christopher M. Blanchard, Carla E. Humud, and Derek E. Mix, "European Fighters in Syria and Iraq: Assessments, Responses, and Issues for the United States," *Congressional Research Service Report 7-5700/R44003* (Washington, DC: Library of Congress, April 27, 2015), 1. Charles Lister, writing in April 2015, estimated that the total number of foreign fighters is likely closer to 30,000. Charles Lister, "Returning Foreign Fighters: Criminalization or Reintegration?" *Policy Briefing*, Brookings Institution, August 2015, 1.

108. Lister, "Returning Foreign Fighters," 1.

109. Neumann, *Die Neuen Dschihadisten*, 131.

110. For the former figure (11 percent), see Thomas Hegghammer, "Should I Stay or Should I Go? Explaining Variation in Jihadists' Choice Between Domestic and Foreign Fighting," *American Political Science Review* 107, no. 1 (February 2013); for the latter figure (26 percent), see Jytte Klausen and Adrienne Roach, "Western Jihadists in the Syrian and Iraqi Insurgencies," *Working Paper No. 4, The Western Jihadism Project*, August 2014, 40-44, cited in Neumann, *Die Neuen Dschihadisten*, 131–32.

111. Neumann, *Die Neuen Dschihadisten*, 111.

112. Anthony Faiola and Souad Mekhennet, "'He Is a Barbaric Man': The Belgian Who May Be Behind the Paris Attacks," *Washington Post*, November 16, 2015; "Des Djihadistes Belges d'une cellule de l'EI ont partagé leurs expériences sur Facebook," *MEMRI FR*, January 26, 2015; Jay Akbar, "Mastermind of Paris Terror Attacks Was Linked to at Least Six UK Hate Preachers Including 'Tottenham Ayatollah' Omar Bakri Muhammad," *Daily Mail*, November 22, 2015.

113. Raphael Satter and John-Thor Dahlburg, "Belgian Jihadi ID'd as Mastermind of Paris Attacks," *Associated Press*, November 16, 2015.

114. Pieter van Ostaeyen, "Belgian Fighters in Syria and Iraq—December 2015," https://pietervanostaeyen.com/2015/12/07/belgian-fighters-in-syria-and-iraq-december-2015.

115. Van Ostaeyen, "Belgian Fighters in Syria and Iraq—December 2015."

116. Van Ostaeyen, "Belgian Fighters in Syria and Iraq—December 2015."

117. Van Ostaeyen, "Belgian Fighters in Syria and Iraq—December 2015."

118. Pieter van Ostaeyen, "Update on the Belgians in Syria," *Jihadology*, May 7, 2014.

119. Quoted in Van Ostaeyen, "Sharia4Belgium," 13.

120. Little is known about this group. However, the group is clearly not to be confused with its most prominent namesake, the Mujahideen Shura Council (MSC), an umbrella group that included Al Qaeda in Iraq and existed throughout most of 2006. It is also different from a group known as Majlis Shura al-Mujahideen al-Sharqiya, founded in Deir az-Zour, in eastern Syria, in 2014. Florian Wätzel, e-mail communication with the author, February 19, 2016.

121. Van Vlierden, "How Belgium Became a Top Exporter of Jihad."

122. Dalton and Coker, "How Belgium Became a Jihadist-Recruiting Hub."

123. Dalton and Coker, "How Belgium Became a Jihadist-Recruiting Hub."

124. Taub, "Journey to Jihad."

125. "Sharia4Belgium: Enquête pour terrorisme," *Figaro*, July 17, 2012.

126. Taub, "Journey to Jihad."

127. Taub, "Journey to Jihad."

128. Quoted in Vidino, "Sharia4," 10.

129. Vidino, "Sharia4," 10.

130. Taub, "Journey to Jihad."

131. Dalton and Coker, "How Belgium Became a Jihadist-Recruiting Hub."

132. Taub, "Journey to Jihad."

133. Van Vlierden, "How Belgium Became a Top Exporter of Jihad."

134. Van Ostaeyen, "Sharia4Belgium," 12.

135. Pieter van Ostaeyen, "Belgian Jihadists in Syria," *Jihadology*, September 5, 2013.

136. Dalton and Coker, "How Belgium Became a Jihadist-Recruiting Hub."

137. Vidino, "Sharia4," 10.

138. Taub, "Journey to Jihad."

139. Pieter van Ostaeyen, "Belgian Fighters in Syria and Iraq—November 2014," *Jihadology*, November 22, 2014.

140. Dalton and Coker, "How Belgium Became a Jihadist-Recruiting Hub."

141. Europol, "Europol TE-SAT 2015," 22.

142. Central Intelligence and Security Service (AIVD), "The Transformation of Jihadism in the Netherlands: Swarm Dynamics and New Strength," The Hague, Netherlands, September 2014, 13.

143. Ineke Roex, "The Rise of Public *Dawa* Networks in the Netherlands: Behind Bars, Sharia4Holland, and Streetdawah," in *Sharia4: Straddling Political Activism and Jihad in the West*, ed. Lorenzo Vidino (Dubai: Al Mesbar Studies and Research Centre, 2015), 9.

144. Jytte Klausen, "Tweeting the Jihad: Social Media Networks of Western Foreign Fighters in Syria and Iraq," *Studies in Conflict & Terrorism* 38, no. 1 (2015): 19.

145. Raymond, "Al Muhajiroun and Islam4UK," 25.

146. Mulhall, "From Clowns to Contenders," 18.

147. Vidino, "Sharia4," 5.
148. For background information on these movements and additional examples, see R. Green, "Shari'a Movement Struggles to Globalize Campaign for Islamizing Western World," *MEMRI Inquiry & Analysis Series Report* No. 723, August 14, 2011; and Vidino, "Sharia4."
149. Vidino, "Sharia4," 6.
150. Vidino, "Sharia4," 6.
151. Mulhall, "From Clowns to Contenders," 19.
152. Klausen et al., "YouTube Jihadists," 36.
153. Klausen et al., "YouTube Jihadists."
154. Klausen et al., "YouTube Jihadists."
155. Mulhall, "From Clowns to Contenders," 19–20.
156. Klausen et al., "YouTube Jihadists," 43.
157. Europol, "Europol TE-SAT 2013: EU Terrorism Situation and Trend Report," The Hague, Netherlands, 2013, 18.
158. Europol, "Europol TE-SAT 2013," 18.
159. Green, "Shari'a Movement Struggles," 3–4.
160. Roex, "Rise of Public *Dawa* Networks," 9.
161. Vidino, "Sharia4," 2.
162. Vidino, "Sharia4," 2.
163. Central Intelligence and Security Service (AIVD), "Transformation of Jihadism," 12.
164. Vidino, "Sharia4," 4.
165. Vidino, "Sharia4," 5.
166. Kirstine Sinclair and Saad Ali Khan, "Current Islamist and Jihadi-Salafi Trends in Denmark: Hizb ut-Tahrir and Kaldet," in *Sharia4: Straddling Political Activism and Jihad in the West*, ed. Lorenzo Vidino (Dubai: Al Mesbar Studies and Research Centre, 2015), 11.
167. Sinclair and Khan, "Current Islamist and Jihadi-Salafi Trends," 12.
168. Green, "Shari'a Movement Struggles."
169. Green, "Shari'a Movement Struggles."
170. Neumann, *Die Neuen Dschihadisten*, 145.
171. Pantucci, "Al-Muhajiroun's European Recruiting Pipeline," 22.
172. Pantucci, "Al-Muhajiroun's European Recruiting Pipeline," 22; and Lorenzo Vidino, "Home-Grown Jihadism in Italy: Birth, Development and Radicalization Dynamics" (Milan: Istituto per gli Studi di Politica Internazionale, 2015), 60–68.
173. Mulhall, "From Clowns to Contenders," 18.
174. Sharia4Italy no longer exists. The only real member of the "group" is currently in Syria and presumed dead. See Lorenzo Vidino, "The Development of Home-Grown Jihadist Radicalisation in Italy," *Real Instituto Elcano*, Madrid, 2014.
175. Roex, "Rise of Public *Dawa* Networks," 6.
176. Green, "Shari'a Movement Struggles," 3–4.
177. Philippe Migaux, "Forsane Alizza: From Radical Demonstrations to the Preparation of Terrorist Action," in *Sharia4: Straddling Political Activism and Jihad in the West*, ed. Lorenzo Vidino (Dubai: Al Mesbar Studies and Research Centre, 2015), 4–5.

178. Klausen et al., "YouTube Jihadists," 39.

179. Klausen et al., "YouTube Jihadists," 39.

180. Klausen et al., "YouTube Jihadists," 39–40.

181. Klausen et al., "YouTube Jihadists," 4.

182. Neumann, *Die Neuen Dschihadisten*, 142.

183. "Sharia4America.com: Advocating an American 'Islamic State' and Shariah Law in the United States," *MEMRI Special Dispatch* No. 3782, April 24, 2011.

184. Taub, "Journey to Jihad."

185. Taub, "Journey to Jihad."

186. Klausen et al., "YouTube Jihadists," 43.

187. Roex, "Rise of Public *Dawa* Networks," 1.

CONCLUSION

1. Henry Johnson, "Mapped: The Islamic State Is Losing Its Territory—and Fast," *Foreign Policy*, March 16, 2016.

2. The question of how to address the use of the Internet and social media is a highly complex one that cannot be separated from broader ethical and legal concerns, nor can it be addressed at length here. For a useful discussion and sensible policy recommendations, see J. M. Berger and Jonathon Morgan, "The ISIS Twitter Census: Defining and Describing the Population of ISIS Supporters on Twitter," Brookings Project on U.S. Relations with the Islamic World, Analysis Paper No. 20, March 2015, 53–61.

3. See the recent results of state elections in Germany in March 2016, for example, where far-right parties have achieved significant successes by garnering up to 25 percent of the electoral vote. Alison Smale, "German State Elections Point to Vulnerability for Angela Merkel," *New York Times*, March 14, 2016.

4. Noémie Bisserbe, "Carlos the Jackal Faces New French Trial," *Wall Street Journal*, November 7, 2011.

5. Stephen Tankel, *Storming the World Stage: The Story of Lashkar-e Taiba* (New York: Oxford University Press, 2013).

6. Bruno Schirra, "The Most Dangerous Man in the World," *Cicero*, April 2005, as discussed in Thomas Joscelyn, "Iran's Proxy War Against America," Claremont Institute, September 2007, 62–63.

7. Paul Cruickshank, "The Inside Story of the Paris Attack," CNN, March 22, 2016.

8. Petter Nesser, *Islamist Terrorism in Europe: A History* (Oxford; New York: Oxford University Press, 2015), 8–9.

9. Matthew Levitt, "Untangling the Terror Web: Identifying and Counteracting the Phenomenon of Crossover Between Terrorist Groups," *SAIS Review of International Affairs* 24, no. 1 (2004).

10. An important exception to this is the project Mapping Militant Organizations led by Martha Crenshaw of Stanford University, http://web.stanford.edu/group/mapping militants/cgi-bin/.

BIBLIOGRAPHY

Abbas, Hassan. "Defining the Punjabi Taliban Network." *CTC Sentinel* 2, no. 4 (2009): 1–4.

Abdukadirov, Sherzod. "Terrorism: The Dark Side of Social Entrepreneurship." *Studies in Conflict & Terrorism* 33, no. 7 (2010): 603–17.

Abi-Habib, Maria. "Al Qaeda Emissary in Syria Killed by Rival Islamist Rebels." *Wall Street Journal*, February 23, 2014.

Abouzeid, Rania. "The Jihad Next Door: The Syrian Roots of Iraq's Newest Civil War." *Politico*, June 23, 2014.

Abrahms, Max. "Why Terrorism Does Not Work." *International Security* 31, no. 2 (2006): 42–78.

——. "Does Terrorism Really Work? Evolution in the Conventional Wisdom Since 9/11." *Defence and Peace Economics* 22, no. 6 (2011): 583–94.

——. "The Political Effectiveness of Terrorism Revisited." *Comparative Political Studies* 45, no. 3 (2012): 366–93.

Abuza, Zachary. *Militant Islam in Southeast Asia: Crucible of Terror*. Boulder, CO: Lynne Rienner, 2003.

——. "The Moro Islamic Liberation Front at 20: State of the Revolution." *Studies in Conflict & Terrorism* 28, no. 6 (2005): 453–79.

Acosta, Benjamin, and Steven J. Childs. "Illuminating the Global Suicide-Attack Network." *Studies in Conflict & Terrorism* 36, no. 1 (2013): 49–76.

Adamsky, Dima. "Jihadi Operational Art: The Coming Wave of Jihadi Strategic Studies." *Studies in Conflict & Terrorism* 33, no. 1 (2010): 1–19.

Adnani, Abu Muhammad al-. "Indeed Your Lord Is Ever Watchful." September 22, 2014. https://pietervanostaeyen.wordpress.com/2014/09/25/abu-muhammad-al-adnani-ash -shami-indeed-your-lord-is-ever-watchful/.

Affidavit of Daniel L. Byman. United States District Court, Southern District of New York, Civil Action No. 3 MDL 1570 GBD, June 8, 2010.

Affidavit of Dr. Ronen Bergman. United States District Court, Southern District of New York, Civil Action No. 3 MDL 1570 GBD, April 8, 2010.

Affidavit of Patrick L. Clawson. United States District Court, Southern District of New York, Civil Action No. 3 MDL 1570 GBD, June 25, 2010.

Akbar, Jay. "Mastermind of Paris Terror Attacks Was Linked to at Least Six UK Hate Preachers Including Tottenham Ayatollah' Omar Bakri Muhammad." *Daily Mail*, November 22, 2015.

Akcinaroglu, Seden. "Rebel Interdependencies and Civil War Outcomes." *Journal of Conflict Resolution* 56, no. 5 (2012): 879–903.

Alfoneh, Ali. "Iran's Suicide Brigades: Terrorism Resurgent." *Middle East Quarterly* 14, no. 1 (2007): 37–44.

Alonso, Rogelio, and Florencio Dominguez Iribarren. "The IRA and ETA: The International Connections of Ethno-Nationalist Terrorism in Europe." In *Terrorism: Patterns of Internationalization*, edited by Jaideep Saikia and Ekaterina Stepanova, 3–17. New Delhi: SAGE Publications India, 2009.

"Al Qaeda Apologizes for Yemeni Hospital Attack." Al-Jazeera America, December 22, 2013. http://america.aljazeera.com/articles/2013/12/22/al-qaeda-apologizesforyemenihospitalattack.html.

"Al Qaeda in Yemen." Mapping Militant Organizations. Stanford University. http://web.stanford.edu/group/mappingmilitants/cgi-bin/groups/view/23?highlight=AQAP.

"Al-Qaeda Leader Al-Zawahiri Rejects ISIS Caliphate, Predicts Imminent Islamic Spring." *MEMRI Jihad & Terrorism Threat Monito (JTTM)*, September 9, 2015. http://www.memrijttm.org/al-qaeda-leader-al-zawahiri-rejects-isis-caliphate-predicts-imminent-islamic-spring.html.

"Al-Qaeda Seeks to Unite Islamic Front Ahead of US Airstrikes in Syria." RT.com, September 16, 2014.

"Al-Qaida Papers: The Yemen Letters." Associated Press, August 9, 2013. http://hosted.ap.org/specials/interactives/_international/_pdfs/al-qaida-papers-how-to-run-a-state.pdf.

"Al-Qaida's Five Aspects of Power." *CTC Sentinel* 2, no. 1 (2009): 1–4.

"Amal Driving Hezbollah from West Beirut; 25 Killed." *Los Angeles Times*, November 27, 1988.

Anonymous [Michael Scheuer]. *Through Our Enemies' Eyes: Osama Bin Laden, Radical Islam, and the Future of America*. Washington, DC: Brassey's, 2003.

——. *Imperial Hubris: Why the West Is Losing the War on Terror*. Washington, DC: Brassey's, 2004.

Anthony, Andrew. "Anjem Choudary: The British Extremist Who Backs the Caliphate." *Guardian*, September 7, 2014.

Archer, Margaret. "Structuration Versus Morphogenesis." In *Macro Sociological Theory*, edited by S. N. Eisenstadt and H. Helle, 58–88. London: Sage, 1985.

Archick, Kristin, Paul Belkin, Christopher M. Blanchard, Carla E. Humud, and Derek E. Mix. "European Fighters in Syria and Iraq: Assessments, Responses, and Issues for the

United States." *Congressional Research Service Report 7-5700/R44003.* Washington, DC: Library of Congress, April 27, 2015.

Aronson, Samuel L. "AQIM's Threat to Western Interests in the Sahel." *CTC Sentinel* 7, no. 4 (2014): 6–10.

Arts, Bas. "Non-State Actors in Global Governance: Three Faces of Power." Max Planck Institute, 2003/2004.

Asal, Victor, Brian Nussbaum, and D. William Harrington. "Terrorism as Transnational Advocacy: An Organizational and Tactical Examination." *Studies in Conflict & Terrorism* 30, no. 1 (2007): 15–39.

Asal, Victor, and R. Karl Rethemeyer. "The Nature of the Beast: Organizational Structures and the Lethality of Terrorist Attacks." *Journal of Politics* 70, no. 2 (2008): 437–49.

Asal, Victor H., Gary A. Ackerman, and R. Karl Rethemeyer. "Connections Can Be Toxic: Terrorist Organizational Factors and the Pursuit of CBRN Weapons." *Studies in Conflict & Terrorism* 35, no. 3 (2012): 229–54.

"Audio Message by Abu Bakr al-Baghdadi—Even If the Disbelievers Despise Such." November 14, 2014. https://pietervanostaeyen.wordpress.com/2014/11/14/audio-message-by-abu-bakr-al-baghdadi-even-if-the-disbelievers-despise-such.

"Augenzeugenbericht aus Sirt: IS Errichtet Terrorherrschaft in Libyen." *Spiegel Online,* May 18, 2016. http://www.spiegel.de/politik/ausland/islamischer-staat-errichtet-terrorherrschaft-in-sirt-in-libyen-a-1092790.html.

Austen, Ian. "Two Are Accused in Canada of Plotting Train Derailment." *New York Times,* April 22, 2013.

Azani, Eitan. "The Hybrid Terrorist Organization: Hezbollah as a Case Study." *Studies in Conflict & Terrorism* 36, no. 11 (2013): 899–916.

Bacon, Tricia L. "Strange Bedfellows or Brothers-In-Arms: Why Terrorist Groups Ally." PhD Dissertation, Georgetown University, November 2013.

——. "Alliance Hubs: Focal Points in the International Terrorist Landscape." *Perspectives on Terrorism* 8, no. 4 (2014): 4–25.

Badia, Francesc. "Small-World Networks, Violence, and Global Distress." In *Terrorism, Security, and the Power of Informal Networks,* edited by David Martin Jones, Ann Lane, and Paul Schulte, 217–40. Cheltenham, UK: Edward Elgar, 2010.

Bakke, Kristin M., Kathleen Gallagher Cunningham, and Lee J. M. Seymour. "A Plague of Initials: Fragmentation, Cohesion, and Infighting in Civil Wars." *Perspectives on Politics* 10, no. 02 (2012): 265–83.

Balana, Cynthia. "Tamil Rebels Sent Arms to Abus-Sri Lanka Exec." *Inquirer,* August 4, 2007.

Bapat, Navin A., and Kanisha D. Bond. "Alliances Between Militant Groups." *British Journal of Political Science* 42, no. 04 (2012): 793–824.

Barfi, Barak. "Yemen on the Brink? The Resurgence of al Qaeda in Yemen." Counterterrorism Strategy Initiative Policy Paper. New America Foundation, 2010.

Barnett, Michael N. "Identity and Alliances in the Middle East." In *The Culture of National Security: Norms and Identity in World Politics,* edited by Peter J. Katzenstein, 400–450. New York: Columbia University Press, 1996.

Barrett, Richard. "The Islamic State." The Soufan Group, November 2014. http://soufangroup
.com/wp-content/uploads/2014/10/TSG-The-Islamic-State-Nov14.pdf.

———. "The Islamic State Goes Global." *CTC Sentinel* 8, no. 11 (2015): 1-4.

Benjamin, Daniel, and Steven Simon. *The Age of Sacred Terror.* New York: Random House, 2002.

Benjamin, S. "An In-Depth Look at One of the Facebook/Twitter Networks of French-Speaking Jihadis Fighting in Syria: Glorifying Jihad in Syria, Condemning Heretical France." *MEMRI Cyber & Jihad Lab,* February 17, 2014. http://cjlab.memri.org/lab-projects
/tracking-jihadi-terrorist-use-of-social-media/an-in-depth-look-at-one-of-the
-facebooktwitter-networks-of-french-speaking-jihadis-fighting-in-syria-glorifying-jihad
-in-syria-condemning-heretical-france/.

Benson, David C. "Why the Internet Is Not Increasing Terrorism." *Security Studies* 23, no. 2 (2014): 293–328.

Bergen, Peter, and Paul Cruickshank. "Revisiting the Early Al Qaeda: An Updated Account of Its Formative Years." *Studies in Conflict & Terrorism* 35, no. 1 (2012): 1–36.

Bergen, Peter, Bruce Hoffman, and Katherine Tiedemann. "Assessing the Jihadist Terrorist Threat to America and American interests." *Studies in Conflict & Terrorism* 34, no. 2 (2011): 65–101.

Bergen, Peter, and Katherine Tiedemann. "The Almanac of Al Qaeda." *Foreign Policy* 179 (2010): 68.

Bergen, Peter L. *Holy War, Inc.: Inside the Secret World of Osama bin Laden.* New York: Simon and Schuster, 2002.

———. *The Osama bin Laden I Know: An Oral History of al Qaeda's Leader.* New York: Free Press, 2006.

———. *Manhunt: The Ten-Year Search for Bin Laden from 9/11 to Abbottabad.* New York: Broadway, 2012.

Berger, J. M. *Jihad Joe: Americans Who Go to War in the Name of Islam.* Washington, DC: Potomac, 2011.

———. "War on Error." *Foreign Policy,* February 5, 2014.

———. "Chart: Al Qaeda Fractures, ISIS Gains." Intelwire.com, April 8, 2015. http://news
.intelwire.com/2015/04/chart-al-qaeda-fractures-isis-gains.html.

Berger, J. M., and Jonathon Morgan. "The ISIS Twitter Census: Defining and describing the Population of ISIS Supporters on Twitter." *Brookings Project on US Relations with the Islamic World* 3, no. 20 (2015): 1–66.

Berti, Benedetta. *Armed Political Organizations: From Conflict to Integration.* Baltimore, MD: Johns Hopkins University Press, 2013.

Bhaskar, Roy. *The Possibility of Naturalism: A Philosophical Critique of the Contemporary Human Sciences.* Brighton: Harvester, 1979.

Biene, Janusz, Daniel Kaiser, and Holger Marcks. "Explosive Affairs: Transnational Cooperation and the Escalation of Violent Dissidence." Paper Presented at the 56th Annual Convention of the International Studies Association, New Orleans, LA, February 19, 2015.

Bin Ladin, Usama. "The Way to Save the Earth." *Inspire* 1 (2010): 8–10.

Bin Laden's Fatwa, August 23, 1996. http://www.pbs.org/newshour/updates/military-july-dec96 -fatwa_1996/.

Bisserbe, Noémie. "Carlos the Jackal Faces New French Trial." *Wall Street Journal*, November 7, 2011.

Black, Andrew. "AQIM Employs Martyrdom Operations in Algeria." *Terrorism Focus* 4, no. 29 (2007). https://jamestown.org/brief/aqim-employs-martyrdom-operations-in-algeria/.

Black, Ian. "Jordan's King Abdullah Vows 'Relentless' War Against ISIS." *Guardian*, February 4, 2015.

Blanford, Nicholas. *Warriors of God: Inside Hezbollah's Thirty-Year Struggle Against Israel.* New York: Random House, 2011.

Bond, Kanisha D. "Power, Identity, Credibility and Cooperation: Examining the Development of Cooperative Arrangements Among Violent Non-State Actors." PhD dissertation, Pennsylvania State University, August 2010.

Bonner, Raymond. "Plot Echoes One Planned by 9/11 Mastermind in '94." *New York Times*, August 10, 2006.

Bonner, Raymond, and Benjamin Weiser. "Echoes of Early Design to Use Chemicals to Blow Up Airliners." *New York Times*, August 11, 2006.

Boot, Max. *Invisible Armies: An Epic History of Guerrilla Warfare from Ancient Times to the Present.* New York: Norton, 2013.

Botha, Anneli. "The 2007 Suicide Attacks in Algiers." In *The Evolution of the Global Terrorist Threat: From 9/11 to Osama bin Laden's Death*, edited by Bruce Hoffman and Fernando Reinares, 600–617. New York: Columbia University Press, 2014.

Bouchaud, Melodie. "'Sharia4Belgium' Leader and Dozens of Other Militants Are Sentenced to Jail Time." *Vice News*, February 12, 2015. https://news.vice.com/article/sharia4 belgium-leader-and-dozens-of-other-militants-are-sentenced-to-jail-time.

Bowden, Mark. *Black Hawk Down: A Story of Modern War.* New York: Atlantic Monthly, 1999.

Brachman, Jarret, Brian Fishman, and Joseph Felter, "The Power of Truth: Questions for Ayman al-Zawahiri." Combating Terrorism Center at West Point, April 21, 2008, 2–27.

Braniff, Bill, and Assaf Moghadam. "Towards Global Jihadism: Al-Qaeda's Strategic, Ideological and Structural Adaptations Since 9/11." *Perspectives on Terrorism* 5, no. 2 (2011): 1–14.

Braniff, William. "Testimony before the United States House Armed Services Committee Hearing on the State of Al Qaeda, Its Affiliates, and Associated Groups: View from Outside Experts." Washington, DC: United States House of Representatives, February 4, 2014. http://www.start.umd.edu/pubs/STARTCongressionalTestimony_StateofAQand Affiliates_WilliamBraniff.pdf.

Brisard, Jean-Charles. "The Paris Attacks and the Evolving Islamic State Threat to France." *CTC Sentinel* 8 (2015): 11.

Bronstein, Scott, Drew Griffin, and Deborah Feyerick. "For Paris Attackers, Terror Ties Ran Deep." CNN, January 13, 2015. http://edition.cnn.com/2015/01/12/europe/paris-terror -suspects-al-qaeda-ties/.

Brooke, Steven. "Jihadist Strategic Debates Before 9/11." *Studies in Conflict & Terrorism* 31, no. 3 (2008): 201–26.

Brown, Vahid. "Cracks in the Foundation: Leadership Schisms in al-Qa'ida from 1989–2006." *Combating Terrorism Center at West Point*, 2007.

——. "Classical and Global Jihad: Al-Qa'ida's Franchising Frustrations." In *Fault Lines in Global Jihad: Organizational, Strategic, and Ideological Fissures*, edited by Assaf Moghadam and Brian Fishman, 88–116. London: Routledge, 2011.

Brown, Vahid, and Don Rassler. *Fountainhead of Jihad: The Haqqani Nexus, 1973–2012*. New York: Columbia University Press, 2013.

Brzezinski, Matthew. "Bust and Boom." *Washington Post*, December 30, 2001.

Buckley, Peter J. *Cooperative Forms of Transnational Corporation Activity*. London: Routledge, 1994.

Bunzel, Cole. "Al-Qaeda Advises the Syrian Revolution: Shumukh al-Islam's Comprehensive Strategy for Syria." *Jihadica*, February 25, 2013. http://www.jihadica.com/al-qaeda-advises -the-syrian-revolution-shumukh-al-islams-%E2%80%9Ccomprehensive-strategy%E2 %80%9D-for-syria/.

Bureau of Counterterrorism, U.S. Department of State. *Country Reports on Terrorism 2014*. Washington, DC: U.S. State Department, 2015.

Burke, Jason. "Bin Laden Wanted to Change al-Qaida's Bloodied Name." *Guardian*, June 24, 2011.

Byman, Daniel. *Deadly Connections: States that Sponsor Terrorism*. Cambridge: Cambridge University Press, 2005.

——. *A High Price: The Triumphs and Failures of Israeli Counterterrorism*. New York: Oxford University Press, 2011.

——. "Unlikely Alliance: Iran's Secretive Relationship with Al-Qaeda." In *Iranian Sponsorship of Terrorism* (IHS Defense, Risk and Security Consulting, July 2012). https://www .brookings.edu/wp-content/uploads/2016/06/iran-al-qaeda-byman.pdf.

——. "Buddies or Burdens? Understanding the Al Qaeda Relationship with Its Affiliate Organizations." *Security Studies* 23, no. 3 (2014): 431–70.

——. *Al Qaeda, the Islamic State, and the Global Jihadist Movement: What Everyone Needs to Know*. Oxford: Oxford University Press, 2015.

——. "ISIS Goes Global." *Foreign Affairs*, March/April 2016.

Byman, Daniel, Peter Chalk, Bruce Hoffman, William Rosenau, and David Brannan. *Trends in Outside Support for Insurgent Movements*. Santa Monica, CA: RAND, 2001.

Cafarella, Jennifer. "Jabhat al-Nusra in Syria: An Islamic Emirate for Al-Qaeda." *Middle East Security Report*. Institute for the Study of War, December 2014. http://www.understanding war.org/report/jabhat-al-nusra-syria.

Callimachi, Rukmini, and Andrew Higgins. "Video Shows a Paris Gunman Declaring His Loyalty to the Islamic State." *New York Times*, January 12, 2015.

Callimachi, Rukmini, and Eric Schmitt. "Iran Released Top Members of Al Qaeda in a Trade." *New York Times*, September 17, 2015.

Carlsnaes, Walter. "The Agency-Structure Problem in Foreign Policy Analysis." *International Studies Quarterly* 36, no. 3 (1992): 245–70.

Carter, Joseph A., Shiraz Maher, and Peter R. Neumann. "#Greenbirds: Measuring Importance and Influence in Syrian Foreign Fighter Networks." International Centre for the Study of Radicalisation, April 2014, 1–36.

Central Intelligence and Security Service (AIVD), "The Transformation of Jihadism in the Netherlands: Swarm Dynamics and New Strength." The Hague, Netherlands, September 2014.

Chandran, Anurag. "Al Qaeda in the Indian Subcontinent: Almost Forgotten." *AEI Critical Threats*, September 3, 2015. http://www.criticalthreats.org/al-qaeda/chandran-al-qaeda-in -indian-subcontinent-backgrounder-september-3-2015.

Chivers, C. J., and David Rhode. "Turning Out Guerrillas and Terrorists to Wage a Holy War." *New York Times*, March 18, 2002.

Christia, Fotini. *Alliance Formation in Civil Wars*. Cambridge: Cambridge University Press, 2012.

Clapper, James R. "Statement for the Record: Worldwide Threat Assessment of the US Intelligence Community." House Permanent Select Committee on Intelligence, February 25, 2016. https://www.dni.gov/index.php/newsroom/testimonies/217-congressional-testi monies-2016/1324-statement-for-the-record-worldwide-threat-assessment-of-the-u-s -intelligence-community-hsci?tmpl=component&format=pdf.

Clarke, Richard, and Robert K. Knake. *Cyber War: The Next Threat to National Security and What To Do About It*. New York: Ecco/Harper Collins, 2010.

Clarke, Richard A., Glenn P. Aga, Roger W. Cressey, Stephen E. Flynn, Blake W. Mobley, Eric Rosenbach, Steven Simon, William F. Wechsler, and Lee S. Wolosky. *Defeating the Jihadists: A Blueprint for Action*. New York: Century Foundation, 2004.

Clinton, William Jefferson. "Remarks to the White House Conference on Trade and Investment in Ireland," May 25, 1995. In *Public Papers of the Presidents of the United States: Administration of William J. Clinton*, Book 1, 748–51. Washington, DC: United States Government Printing Office, 1996.

Clutterbuck, Lindsay. "Countering Irish Republican Terrorism in Britain: Its Origin as a Police Function." *Terrorism and Political Violence* 18, no. 1 (2006): 95–118.

Coll, Steve, and Susan B. Glasser. "Terrorists Turn to the Web as Base of Operations." *Washington Post*, August 7, 2005.

Collins, Liam. "The Abbottabad Documents: Bin Laden's Security Measures." *CTC Sentinel* 5, no. 5 (2012): 1–4.

Cook, David. *Understanding Jihad*. Oakland: University of California Press, 2005.

Cooper, Helene. "Treasury Accuses Iran of Aiding Al Qaeda." *New York Times*, July 28, 2011.

Cragin, Kim, Peter Chalk, Sara A. Daly, and Brian A. Jackson. *Sharing the Dragon's Teeth: Terrorist Groups and the Exchange of New Technologies*. Santa Monica, CA: RAND, 2007.

Crenshaw, Martha. "An Organizational Approach to the Analysis of Political Terrorism." *Orbis* 29, no 3 (1985): 465–89.

——. "The Logic of Terrorism: Terrorist Behavior as a Product of Strategic Choice." In *Origins of Terrorism: Psychologies, Ideologies, Theologies, States of Mind*, edited by Walter Reich, 7–24. Washington, DC: Woodrow Wilson Center, 1998.

———. "Theories of Terrorism: Instrumental and Organizational Approaches." In *Inside Terrorist Organizations*, 2nd ed., edited by David C. Rapoport, 13–31. London: Frank Cass, 2001.

———. "Thoughts on Relating Terrorism to Historical Contexts." In *Terrorism in Context*, edited by Martha Crenshaw, 3–24. University Park: Pennsylvania State University Press, 2001.

———. "Innovation: Decision Points in the Trajectory of Terrorism." In *Terrorist Innovations in Weapons of Mass Effect: Preconditions, Causes, and Predictive Indicators*, edited by Maria J. Rasmussen and Mohammed M. Hafez. Workshop Report, Defense Threat Reduction Agency DTRA Advanced Systems and Concepts Office, Report Number ASCO 2010-019, August 2010.

———. *Explaining Terrorism: Causes, Processes and Consequences*. London: Routledge, 2011.

Criss, Nur Bilge. "The Nature of PKK Terrorism in Turkey." *Studies in Conflict & Terrorism* 18, no. 1 (1995): 17–37.

Cruickshank, Paul. "Love in the Time of Terror." *Marie Claire*, May 15, 2009.

———. "Bin Laden Documents: Competing Vision of Al Qaeda's Top Two." CNN, May 7, 2012. http://security.blogs.cnn.com/2012/05/07/bin-laden-documents-the-sometimes-competing-vision-of-al-qaedas-top-two/.

———. "The 2006 Airline Plot." In *The Evolution of the Global Terrorist Threat: From 9/11 to Osama Bin Laden's Death*, edited by Bruce Hoffman and Fernando Reinares, 224–73. Columbia University Press, 2014.

———. "The Inside Story of the Paris Attack," CNN, March 22, 2016. http://edition.cnn.com/2016/03/21/europe/inside-paris-terror-attack/.

Cruickshank, Paul, ed. *Al Qaeda*. London: Routledge, 2013.

Cruickshank, Paul, and Tim Lister. "Al-Shabaab Breaks New Ground with Complex Nairobi Attack." CNN, September 23, 2013. http://edition.cnn.com/2013/09/22/world/meast/kenya-mall-al-shabaab-analysis/.

Cullison, Alan. "Inside Al-Qaeda's Hard Drive." *Atlantic Monthly* 294 (2004): 55–65.

Culpan, Refik. *Global Business Alliances: Theory and Practice*. Westport, CT: Quorum Books, 2002.

Dalton, Matthew, and Margaret Coker. "How Belgium Became a Jihadist Recruiting Hub." *Wall Street Journal*, September 28, 2014.

Dan Darling. "The Cicero Articles." *Long War Journal*, October 30, 2005. http://www.longwarjournal.org/archives/2005/10/the_cicero_arti.php.

Darby, John P. "Borrowing and Lending in Peace Processes." In *Contemporary Peacemaking: Conflict, Violence and Peace Processes*, edited by John P. Darby and Roger MacGinty, 339–51. New York: Macmillan, 2003.

David, Anthony. "Proliferation of Stingers in Sri Lanka." *Jane's Intelligence Review*, September 1, 1998.

Davis, R. "Kilson Versus Marighela: The Debate over Northern Ireland Terrorism." In *Ireland's Terrorist Dilemma*, edited by Yonah Alexander and Alan O'Day, 179–209. Leiden: Martinus Nijhoff, 1986.

Deeb, Sarah. "Bin Laden's Son Asks Iran to Free His Siblings." *Huffington Post*, March 15, 2010.

Della Porta, Donatella. "Recruitment Processes in Clandestine Political Organizations: Italian Left-Wing Terrorism." *International Social Movement Research* 1 (1988): 155–69.

Della Porta, Donatella, and Mario Diani. *Social Movements: An Introduction*, 2nd ed. Malden, MA: Blackwell, 2006.

Department of Homeland Security, "Terrorist Use of Social Networking: Facebook Case Study." December 5, 2010. https://publicintelligence.net/ufouoles-dhs-terrorist-use-of-social-networking-facebook-case-study/.

"Des Djihadistes Belges d'une Cellule de l'EI ont Partagé leurs Expériences sur Facebook." *MEMRI FR*, January 26, 2015. http://www.memri.fr/2015/01/26/cellule-terroriste-de-verviers-presence-sur-les-reseaux-sociaux-des-deux-membres-de-letat-islamique-tues-lors-du-raid-policier-belge/.

Dessler, David. "What's at Stake in the Agent-Structure Debate?" *International Organization* 43, no. 3 (1989): 441–73.

Dettmer, Jamie. "In Video, Coulibaly Says He Coordinated with Hebdo Shooters." *Daily Beast*, January 11, 2015. http://www.thedailybeast.com/articles/2015/01/11/in-video-coulibaly-says-he-coordinated-with-hebdo-shooters.html.

Devetak, Richard, and Christopher W. Hughes. *The Globalization of Political Violence: Globalization's Shadow*. London; New York: Routledge, 2008.

Dewey, Caitlin. "Inside the Battle for Ask.fm, the Site Where Islamic State Recruited Three American Teens." *Washington Post*, December 12, 2014.

Dobson, Christopher. *Black September: Its Short, Violent History*. New York: Macmillan, 1974.

Document # AFGP-2002-000078, undated. https://www.ctc.usma.edu/wp-content/uploads/2010/08/AFGP-2002-000078-Trans.pdf.

Document # AFGP-2002-600048, April 18, 2002. https://www.ctc.usma.edu//wp-content/uploads/2010/08/AFGP-2002-600048-Trans.pdf.

Dolnik, Adam. *Understanding Terrorist Innovation*. London: Routledge, 2007.

Doty, Roxanne Lynn. "Aporia: A Critical Exploration of the Agent-Structure Problematique in International Relations Theory." *European Journal of International Relations* 3, no. 3 (1997): 365–92.

Downes, Alexander B. *Targeting Civilians in War*. Ithaca, NY: Cornell University Press, 2008.

Doyle, Michael W., and Nicholas Sambanis. *Making War and Building Peace: United Nations Peace Operations*. Princeton, NJ: Princeton University Press, 2006.

Drake, Charles J. M. "The Role of Ideology in Terrorists' Target Selection." *Terrorism and Political Violence* 10, no. 2 (1998): 5–85.

——. *Terrorists' Target Selection*. London: Macmillan, 1998.

Dugger, Celia W. "Sri Lankan Rebels Said to Be Recruiting Children." *New York Times*, October 12, 2001.

Elbagir, Nima, Paul Cruickshank, and Mohammed Tawfeeq. "Boko Haram Purportedly Pledges Allegiance to ISIS." CNN, March 9, 2015. http://edition.cnn.com/2015/03/07/africa/nigeria-boko-haram-isis/.

Elman, Colin. "Explanatory Typologies in Qualitative Studies of International Politics." *International Organization* 59, no. 2 (2005): 293–326.

Emilie, M., and Miles Kahler Hafner-Burton. "Network Analysis for International Relations." *International Organization* 63, no. 3 (2009): 559–92.

"English-language Jihadi Forum Publishes Eulogy for Anwar Al-Awlaki, Samir Khan; Online Jihadi Calls for Vengeance Raid' on American Websites." *MEMRI Special Dispatch No. 4197*, October 11, 2011. http://www.memrijttm.org/english-language-jihadi-forum -publishes-eulogy-for-anwar-al-awlaki-samir-khan-online-jihadi-calls-for-vengeance -raid-on-american-websites.html.

Europol. "Europol TE-SAT 2013: EU Terrorism Situation and Trend Report." The Hague, Netherlands, 2013.

——. "Europol TE-SAT 2014: EU Terrorism Situation and Trend Report." The Hague, Netherlands, 2014.

——. "Europol TE-SAT 2015: EU Terrorism Situation and Trend Report." The Hague, Netherlands, 2015.

Evans, Alexander. "The Utility of Informal Networks to Policy-Makers." In *Terrorism, Security and the Power of Informal Networks*, edited by David Martin Jones, Ann Lane, and Paul Schulte, 13–27. Cheltenham, UK: Edward Elgar, 2010.

——. "Competition vs. Cooperation in the Global Jihad." Presentation at the 14th Annual World Summit on Counter-Terrorism, International Institute for Counter-Terrorism (ICT), Interdisciplinary Center Herzliya, Israel,September 11, 2014. http://www.ict.org.il /Article/1280/Competition-vs-Cooperation-in-Global-Jihad.

Faiola, Anthony, and Souad Mekhennet. "'He Is a Barbaric Man': The Belgian Who May Be Behind the Paris Attacks." *Washington Post*, November 16, 2015.

Farah, Douglas, and Dana Priest. "Bin Laden Son Plays Key Role in Al Qaeda." *Washington Post*, October 14, 2003.

Farrall, Leah. "How Al Qaeda Works." *Foreign Affairs*, March/April 2011.

Fearon, James D., and David D. Laitin. "Ethnicity, Insurgency, and Civil War." *American Political Science Review* 97, no. 1 (2003): 75–90.

Felter, Joseph J., Vahid Brown, Jacob N. Shapiro, and Clinton Watts, eds. "Al-Qa'ida's Misadventures in the Horn of Africa." Combating Terrorism Center at West Point, July 2, 2007.

Feng, Bo, Zhi-Ping Fan, and Jian Ma. "A Method for Partner Selection of Codevelopment Alliances Using Individual and Collaborative Utilities." *International Journal of Production Economics* 124, no. 1 (2010): 159–70.

Ferguson, Neil. "Disengaging from Terrorism." In *The Psychology of Counter-Terrorism*, edited by Andrew Silke, 111–22. London: Routledge, 2010.

Filiu, Jean-Pierre. "The Local and Global Jihad of al-Qa'ida in the Islamic Maghrib." *Middle East Journal* 63, no. 2 (2009): 213–26.

Findley, Michael G., and Joseph K. Young. "Terrorism and Civil War: A Spatial and Temporal Approach to a Conceptual Problem." *Perspectives on Politics* 10, no. 2 (2012): 285–305.

Firestone, Reuven. *Jihad: The Origin of Holy War in Islam*. New York: Oxford University Press, 1999.

Forest, James. *Teaching Terror: Strategic and Tactical Learning in the Terrorist World*. London: Rowman & Littlefield, 2006.

"From Here We Begin . . . And at al-Aqsa We Meet: Addresses of the Commanders of Al-Qaeda in the Arabian Peninsula." *Minbar al-Tawhid w'al Jihad*. https://azelin.files.wordpress.com/2010/08/aqap-from-here-we-begin-and-at-al-aqsa-we-meet.pdf.

Gabbay, Michael. "Mapping the Factional Structure of the Sunni Insurgency in Iraq." *CTC Sentinel* 1, no. 4 (2008): 10–12.

Gad, Z. "International Cooperation Among Terrorist Groups." In *On Terrorism and Combating Terrorism: Proceedings of an International Seminar, Tel Aviv, 1979*, edited by Ariel Merari, 135–44. Frederick, MD: University Publications of America, 1985.

Galula, David. *Counter-Insurgency Warfare: Theory and Practice*. New York: Praeger, 2006.

Gartenstein-Ross, Daveed. "Large-Scale Arrests in Saudi Arabia Illustrate Threat to the Oil Supply." *Long War Journal*, March 24, 2010. http://www.longwarjournal.org/archives/2010/03/largescale_arrests_i.php.

Gerges, Fawaz. *The Far Enemy: Why Jihad Went Global*. Cambridge: Cambridge University Press, 2005.

Ghemawat, Pankaj, and Steven A. Altman. *DHL Global Connectedness Index 2014: Analyzing Global Flows and Their Power to Increase Prosperity*. Bonn, Germany: Deutsche Post DHL, October 2014.

Ghobari, Mohammed. "IS Suicide Bomber Dressed as a Woman Kills 10 at Yemen Houthi Mosque." Reuters, September 24, 2015. http://www.reuters.com/article/us-yemen-security-idUSKCN0RO0EH20150924.

Giddens, Anthony. *The Constitution of Society: Outline of the Theory of Structuration*. Cambridge: Policy Press, 1984.

Goldberg, Zach. "A Jihadi's Search for Meaning." MA thesis, Interdisciplinary Center of Herzliya, Israel, 2014.

Goldman, Adam, and Matt Apuzzo. "Iran Eases Grip on Al Qaeda." Associated Press, May 13, 2010. http://www.ynetnews.com/articles/0,7340,L-3889011,00.html.

Goodman, J. David. "Stop the Conspiracy Theories, Al Qaeda Tells Iranian Leader." *Lede' Blog, New York Times*, September 28, 2011. http://thelede.blogs.nytimes.com/2011/09/28/stop-the-conspiracy-theories-al-qaeda-tells-iranian-leader/?_r=0.

Goodwin, Jeff, and James M. Jasper, eds. *The Social Movements Reader: Cases and Concepts*, 3rd ed. Malden, MA: Wiley-Blackwell, 2015.

Granovetter, Mark S. "The Strength of Weak Ties." *American Journal of Sociology* 78, no. 6 (1973): 1360–80.

——. "The Strength of Weak Ties: A Network Theory Revisited." *Sociological Theory* 1 (1983): 202–20.

Green, R. "Shari'a Movement Struggles to Globalize Campaign for Islamizing Western World." *MEMRI Inquiry & Analysis Series*, Report No. 723, August 14, 2011. http://www.memri.org/report/en/print5565.htm.

Gross, Doug. "Leak: Government Spies Snooped in 'Warcraft,' Other Games." CNN, December 10, 2013. http://edition.cnn.com/2013/12/09/tech/web/nsa-spying-video-games/.

Guevara, Ernesto Che. *Guerrilla Warfare*. Lincoln: University of Nebraska Press, 1998.

Gunaratna, Rohan. "Al Qaeda's Lose and Learn Doctrine: The Trajectory from Oplan Bojinka to 9/11." In *Teaching Terror: Strategic and Tactical Learning in the Terrorist World*, edited by James J. F. Forest, 171–88. Lanham, MD: Rowman & Littlefield, 2006.

Gunaratna, Rohan, and Arabinda Acharya. *The Terrorist Threat from Thailand: Jihad or Quest for Justice?* Washington, DC: Potomac, 2012.

Haahr, Kathryn. "GSPC Joins al-Qaeda and France Becomes Top Enemy." *Terrorism Focus* 3, no. 37 (2006): 4–6.

Haas, Benjamin, and Daniel McGrory. "Al-Qa'ida Seeking to Recruit African-American Muslims." *CTC Sentinel* 1, no. 8 (2008): 13–15.

Hafez, Mohammed M. "Martyrdom Mythology in Iraq: How Jihadists Frame Suicide Terrorism in Videos and Biographies." *Terrorism and Political Violence* 19, no. 1 (2007): 95–115.

——. *Suicide Bombers in Iraq: The Strategy and Ideology of Martyrdom*. Washington, DC: US Institute of Peace Press, 2007.

——. "Jihad After Iraq: Lessons from the Arab Afghans Phenomenon." *CTC Sentinel* 1, no. 4 (2008): 1–4.

——. "Takfir and Violence Against Muslims." In *Fault Lines in Global Jihad: Organizational, Strategic and Ideological Fissures*, edited by Assaf Moghadam and Brian Fishman, 25–46. London: Routledge, 2011.

"Hamas Has Close Ties to IS Affiliates in Sinai, Say Israel, Egypt." *Times of Israel*, July 2, 2015.

Hamid, Mustafa, and Leah Farrall. *The Arabs at War in Afghanistan*. London: Hurst, 2015.

Hammadi, Khalid al-. "The Inside Story of al-Qa'ida, Part 4." *Al-Quds al-Arabi*, March 22, 2005.

Hammes, Thomas X. *The Sling and the Stone: On War in the 21st Century*. St. Paul, MN: Zenith Press, 2004.

Hansen, Stig Jarle. *Al-Shabaab in Somalia: The History and Ideology of a Militant Islamist Group, 2005–2012*. London: Hurst, 2013.

Hasan, Mehdi. "How Islamic Is the Islamic State? Not at All." *New Republic*, March 12, 2015.

Hastert, Paul. "Al Qaeda and Iran: Friends or Foes, or Somewhere in Between?" *Studies in Conflict & Terrorism* 30, no. 4 (2007): 327–36.

Haykel, Bernard. Interview with the author. Washington, DC, July 28, 2008.

——. "Al-Qa'ida and Shiism." In *Fault Lines in Global Jihad: Organizational, Strategic, and Ideological Fissures*, edited by Assaf Moghadam and Brian Fishman, 184–202. London: Routledge, 2011.

Hays, Sharon. "Structure and Agency and the Sticky Problem of Culture." *Sociological Theory* 12 (1994): 57–72.

Heffelfinger, Chris. "Saad bin Laden: The Key to Iranian-al-Qaeda Détente?" *Terrorism Focus* 3, no. 31 (2006). https://jamestown.org/program/saad-bin-laden-the-key-to-iranian-al -qaeda-detente/.

Hegghammer, Thomas. "Global Jihadism After the Iraq War." *Middle East Journal* 60, no. 1 (2006): 11–32.

——. "The Ideological Hybridization of Jihadi Groups." *Current Trends in Islamist Ideology* 9 (2009): 26–45.

——. "The Failure of Jihad in Saudi Arabia." Occasional Paper Series, Combating Terrorism Center at West Point, February 2010.

——. *Jihad in Saudi Arabia: Violence and Pan-Islamism since 1979.* New York: Cambridge University Press, 2010.

——. "Should I Stay or Should I Go? Explaining Variation in Jihadists' Choice Between Domestic and Foreign Fighting." *American Political Science Review* 107, no. 1 (2013): 1–15.

——. "The 2003 Riyadh and 2008 Sanaa Bombings." In *The Evolution of the Global Terrorist Threat: From 9/11 to Osama bin Laden's Death*, edited by Bruce Hoffman and Fernando Reinares, 545–70. New York: Columbia University Press, 2014.

——. "Interpersonal Trust on Jihadi Internet Forums." In *Fight, Flight, Mimic: Identity Signaling in Armed Conflicts*, edited by Diego Gambetta [forthcoming]. http://hegghammer .com/_files/Interpersonal_trust.pdf.

Hegghammer, Thomas, and Petter Nesser. "Assessing the Islamic State's Commitment to Attacking the West."*Perspectives on Terrorism* 9, no. 4 (2015): 1–17.

Heine, Jorge, and Ramesh Takur, eds. *The Dark Side of Globalization.* New York: United Nations University Press, 2011.

Held, David, Anthony McGrew, David Goldblatt, and Jonathan Perraton. *Global Transformations: Politics, Economics and Culture.* Stanford, CA: Stanford University Press, 1999.

Hennessey, Kathleen, and Richard A. Serrano. "Pakistani Taliban Behind Times Square Bombing Attempt, White House Says." *Los Angeles Times*, May 10, 2010.

"Hezbollah, Hamas Coordinating on the Ground: Official." *Daily Star*, July 12, 2014.

Hines, Nico. "Two Men Convicted of British Soldier Beheading." *Daily Beast*, December 19, 2013. http://www.thedailybeast.com/articles/2013/12/19/two-men-convicted-of -british-soldier-beheading.html.

Hironaka, Ann. *Neverending Wars: The International Community, Weak States, and the Perpetuation of Civil War.* Cambridge, MA: Harvard University Press, 2009.

Hoffman, Bruce. "Rethinking Terrorism and Counterterrorism Since 9/11." *Studies in Conflict and Terrorism* 25, no. 5 (2002): 303–16.

——. *Inside Terrorism*, exp. and rev. ed. New York: Columbia University Press, 2006.

——. "The Myth of Grass-Roots Terrorism: Why Al Qaeda Still Matters." *Foreign Affairs*, May/June 2008.

——. "Al Qaeda's Uncertain Future." *Studies in Conflict & Terrorism* 36, no. 8 (2013): 635–53.

——. "The 7 July 2005 London Bombings." In *The Evolution of the Global Terrorist Threat: From 9/11 to Osama bin Laden's Death*, edited by Bruce Hoffman and Fernando Reinares, 192–223. New York: Columbia University Press, 2014.

Hoffman, Bruce, and Fernando Reinares, eds. *The Evolution of the Global Terrorist Threat: From 9/11 to Osama bin Laden's Death.* New York: Columbia University Press, 2014.

Horowitz, Michael C. *The Diffusion of Military Power: Causes and Consequences for International Politics.* Princeton, NJ: Princeton University Press, 2010.

——. "Nonstate Actors and the Diffusion of Innovations: The Case of Suicide Terrorism." *International Organization* 64, no. 1 (2010): 33–64.

Horowitz, Michael C., and Philip B. K. Potter. "Allying to Kill: Terrorist Intergroup Cooperation and the Consequences for Lethality." *Journal of Conflict Resolution* 58, no. 2 (2014): 199–225.

Hosenball, Mark. "The Iran Connection." *Newsweek* 141, no. 9 (2003): 36.

"Houthis Gain Ground Against Yemen's Al-Qaeda." Al Jazeera, November 15, 2014. http://www.aljazeera.com/news/middleeast/2014/11/houthis-gain-ground-against-yemen-al-qaeda-2014111414242880495.html.

Hsu, Spencer S. "U.S. Judge Finds Iran Liable in 2000 Attack on USS *Cole*." *Washington Post*, April 1, 2015.

Humphreys, Macartan, and Jeremy M. Weinstein. "Who Fights? The Determinants of Participation in Civil War." *American Journal of Political Science* 52, no. 2 (2008): 436–55.

Hussain, Ghaffar, and Erin Marie Saltman. *Jihad Trending: A Comprehensive Analysis of Online Extremism and How to Counter It*. London: Quilliam, 2014.

Hussein, Fou'ad. "Al-Zarqawi . . . : The Second Generation of Al Qaeda." *Al-Quds al-Arabi*, 2005.

Ibn Hassan, Ibrahim al-Asiri. "Charlie Hebdo: Military Analysis." *Inspire* 14, 1436 (2015): 38-48. https://azelin.files.wordpress.com/2015/09/inspire-magazine-14.pdf.

"Iran as Al-Qaida Base." *Investor's Business Daily*, March 19, 2010.

"Iran Frees bin Laden Son—German Newspaper." Reuters, August 2, 2006.

"Islamic State Executed Nearly 2,000 People in Six Months: Monitor." Reuters, December 28, 2014. http://www.reuters.com/article/us-mideast-crisis-casualties-idUSKBNoK6oEK20141228.

"The Islamic State's Organizational Structure One Year In." *Al-Monitor*, July 2, 2015. http://www.al-monitor.com/pulse/security/2015/07/islamic-state-caliphate-ministries-armies-syria-iraq.html.

Jackson, Brian, John C. Baker, Kim Cragin, John Parachini, Horacio R. Trujillo, and Peter Chalk. *Aptitude for Destruction: Volume I: Organizational Learning in Terrorist Groups and Its Implications for Combating Terrorism*. Santa Monica, CA: RAND, 2005.

——. *Aptitude for Destruction: Volume II: Case Studies of Organizational Learning in Five Terrorist Groups*. Santa Monica, CA: RAND, 2005.

Jayasekara, Shanaka. "Tamil Tiger Links with Islamist Terrorist Groups." In *The Global Impact of Terrorism 2008—8th World Summit on Counter-Terrorism*, edited by Boaz Ganor and Eitan Azani, 19–22. IDC Herzliya, Israel International Institute for Counter-Terrorism, 2010.

Jehl, Douglas, and Eric Schmitt. "Havens: U.S. Suggests a Qaeda Cell in Iran Directed Saudi Bombings." *New York Times*, May 21, 2003.

Jepperson, Ronald L., Alexander Wendt, and Peter J. Katzenstein. "Norms, Identity, and Culture in National Security." In *The Culture of National Security*, edited by Peter J. Katzenstein, 33–75. New York: Columbia University Press, 1996.

Johnsen, Gregory D. "Assessing the Strength of Al-Qa'ida in Yemen." *CTC Sentinel* 1, no. 10 (2008): 10–13.

——. *The Last Refuge: Yemen, Al-Qaeda, and the Battle for Arabia*. London: Oneworld, 2013.

Johnson, Henry. "Mapped: The Islamic State Is Losing Its Territory—and Fast." *Foreign Policy*, March 16, 2016.

Jones, David Martin, and M. L. R. Smith. "Whose Hearts and Whose Minds? The Curious Case of Global Counter-Insurgency." *Journal of Strategic Studies* 33, no. 1 (2010): 81–121.

Jones, Seth G. "The Rise of Afghanistan's Insurgency: State Failure and Jihad." *International Security* 32, no. 4 (2008): 7–40.

——. "Al Qaeda in Iran." *Foreign Affairs*, January 29, 2012.

——. "Al Qaeda Terrorism in Afghanistan." In *The Evolution of the Global Terrorist Threat: From 9/11 to Osama bin Laden's Death*, edited by Bruce Hoffman and Fernando Reinares, 375–99. New York: Columbia University Press, 2014.

Jones, Seth G., and Patrick B. Johnston. "The Future of Insurgency." *Studies in Conflict & Terrorism* 36, no. 1 (2013): 1–25.

Joscelyn, Thomas. "Iran's Proxy War Against America." National Security Studies. The Claremont Institute, September 2007.

——. "Analysis: Al Qaeda's Interim Emir and Iran." *Long War Journal*, May 18, 2011. http://www.longwarjournal.org/archives/2011/05/analysis_al_qaedas_i.php.

——. "Treasury Targets Iran's Secret Deal with al Qaeda." *Long War Journal*, July 28, 2011. http://www.longwarjournal.org/archives/2011/07/treasury_targets_ira_1.php.

——. "DNI Clapper: 'Shotgun Marriage' Between Iran and Al Qaeda." *Weekly Standard Blog*, February 17, 2012. http://www.weeklystandard.com/dni-clapper-shotgun-marriage-between-iran-and-al-qaeda/article/629992.

——. "Communications with Ayman al Zawahiri Highlighted in Nasr City Cell Case." *Long War Journal*, February 10, 2013. http://www.longwarjournal.org/archives/2013/02/communications_with.php.

——. "AQAP Praises Ayman al Zawahiri, Defends Jihadist Scholars Against 'Slander.'" *Long War Journal*, July 8, 2014. http://www.longwarjournal.org/archives/2014/07/aqap_praises_zawahir.php.

——. "Islamic Front and Al Nusrah Front Promote 'Liberation' of Border Crossing." *Long War Journal*, August 29, 2014. http://www.longwarjournal.org/archives/2014/08/islamic_front_and_al.php.

——. "Doomed Diplomacy: There's No Way Iran Will Ever Help Fight Al Qaeda." *Weekly Standard* 20, no. 24 (2015). http://www.weeklystandard.com/doomed-diplomacy/article/859655.

——. "Osama bin Laden's Files: Al Qaeda's Deputy General Manager in Yemen." *Long War Journal*, March 1, 2015. http://www.longwarjournal.org/archives/2015/03/osama-bin-ladens-files-al-qaedas-deputy-general-manager-in-yemen.php.

——. "Analysis: Why AQAP Quickly Denied Any Connection to Mosque Attacks." *Long War Journal*, March 20, 2015. http://www.longwarjournal.org/archives/2015/03/analysis-why-aqap-quickly-denied-any-connection-to-mosque-attacks.php.

——. "New AQAP Leader Renews Allegiance to the Beloved Father,' Ayman al Zawahiri." *Long War Journal*, July 9, 2015. http://www.longwarjournal.org/archives/2015/07/new-aqap-leader-renews-allegiance-to-the-beloved-father-ayman-al-zawahiri.php.

———. "Al Qaeda Leader Praises Charlie Hebdo Massacre in New Message." *Long War Journal*, December 2, 2015. http://www.longwarjournal.org/archives/2015/12/al-qaeda-leader -praises-charlie-hebdo-massacre-in-new-audio-message.php.

Kahler, Miles. "Networked Politics: Agency, Power and Governance." In *Networked Politics: Agency, Power and Governance*, edited by Miles Kahler, 1–22. Ithaca, NY: Cornell University Press, 2009.

Kaldor, Mary. *New and Old Wars*. Malden, MA: Polity, 2012.

Kalyvas, Stathis N. "The Paradox of Terrorism in Civil War." *Journal of Ethics* 8, no. 1 (2004): 97–138.

———. *The Logic of Violence in Civil Wars*. Cambridge: Cambridge University Press, 2006.

Karmon, Ely. *Coalitions Between Terrorist Organizations: Revolutionaries, Nationalists and Islamists*. Leiden: Martinus Nijhoff, 2005.

Katzenstein, Peter J. Introduction. In *The Culture of National Security: Norms and Identity in World Politics*, edited by Peter J. Katzenstein, 1–6. New York: Columbia University Press, 1996.

Katzenstein, Peter J., ed. *The Culture of National Security: Norms and Identity in World Politics*. New York: Columbia University Press, 1996.

Kauffman, Gretel. "FBI Director: Why ISIS Is a Bigger Threat to the US than Al Qaeda." *Christian Science Monitor*, July 23, 2015.

Keck, Margaret E., and Kathryn Sikkink. *Activists Beyond Borders: Advocacy Networks in International Politics*. Ithaca, NY: Cornell University Press, 1998.

Kennedy-Boudali, Lianne. "The GSPC: Newest Franchise in al-Qa'ida's Global Jihad." Combating Terrorism Center at West Point, NY, April 2007.

———. "Al-Qa'ida in the Islamic Maghreb: Evaluating the Results of the al-Qa'ida Merger." Combating Terrorism Center at West Point, NY, September 2009.

Kenney, Michael. *From Pablo to Osama: Trafficking and Terrorist Networks, Government Bureaucracies, and Competitive Adaptation*. University Park: Pennsylvania State University Press, 2007.

Kepel, Gilles. *Jihad: The Trail of Political Islam*. Cambridge, MA: Harvard University Press, 2003.

Kern, Soeren. "Let's Turn Belgium into an Islamist State." Gatestone Institute, December 19, 2011. https://www.gatestoneinstitute.org/2682/belgium-islamist-state.

Khalil, James. "Know Your Enemy: On the Futility of Distinguishing Between Terrorists and Insurgents." *Studies in Conflict & Terrorism* 36, no. 5 (2013): 419–30.

Khatib, Lina. "The Islamic State's Strategy: Lasting and Expanding." Carnegie Endowment for International Peace, June 29, 2015. http://carnegie-mec.org/2015/06/29/islamic-state-s -strategy-lasting-and-expanding-pub-60511.

Khosrokhavar, Farhad. *Suicide Bombers: Allah's New Martyrs*, translated by David Macey. London: Pluto, 2002.

Kilcullen, David J. "Countering Global Insurgency." *Journal of Strategic Studies* 28, no. 4 (2005): 597–617.

———. "Counter-Insurgency Redux." *Survival* 48, no. 4 (2006): 111–30.

Kiley, Sam. "Fears Iran Is Helping Al Qaeda Plot Atrocity." *Sky News*, February 15, 2012.

Klandermans, Bert, and Dirk Oegema. "Potentials, Networks, Motivations, and Barriers: Steps Toward Participation in Social Movements." *American Sociological Review* 52, no. 2 (1987): 519–31.

Klausen, Jytte. "Tweeting the Jihad: Social Media Networks of Western Foreign Fighters in Syria and Iraq." *Studies in Conflict & Terrorism* 38, no. 1 (2015): 1–22.

Klausen, Jytte, Eliane Tschaen Barbieri, Aaron Reichlin-Melnick, and Aaron Y. Zelin. "The YouTube Jihadists: A Social Network Analysis of Al-Muhajiroun's Propaganda Campaign." *Perspectives on Terrorism* 6, no. 1 (2012): 1–18.

Koehler-Derrick, Gabriel. "The Abbottabad Documents: Bin Ladin's Cautious Strategy in Yemen." *CTC Sentinel* 5, no. 5 (2012): 15–18.

Koehler-Derrick, Gabriel, ed. "A False Foundation? AQAP, Tribes and Ungoverned Spaces in Yemen." Combating Terrorism Center at West Point, NY, 2011.

Krause, Peter. "The Political Effectiveness of Non-State Violence: A Two-Level Framework to Transform a Deceptive Debate." *Security Studies* 22, no. 2 (2013): 259–94.

Kruglanski, Arie W., Xiaoyan Chen, Mark Dechesne, Shira Fishman, and Edward Orehek. "Fully Committed: Suicide Bombers' Motivation and the Quest for Personal Significance." *Political Psychology* 30, no. 3 (2009): 331–57.

Lahoud, Nelly. *The Jihadis' Path to Self-Destruction.* New York: Columbia University Press, 2010.

——. *Beware of Imitators: Al-Qa'ida Through the Lens of Its Confidential Secretary.* West Point, NY: Combating Terrorism Center, 2012.

Lahoud, Nelly, Stuart Caudill, Liam Collins, Gabriel Koehler-Derrick, Don Rassler, and Mohammed al-Ubaydi. "Letters from Abbottabad: Bin Ladin Sidelined?" Combating Terrorism Center at West Point, NY, May 3, 2012.

Lake, Eli, and Josh Rogin. "Exclusive: U.S. Intercepted Al Qaeda's 'Legion of Doom' Conference Call." *Daily Beast*, August 7, 2013. http://www.thedailybeast.com/articles/2013/08 /07/al-qaeda-conference-call-intercepted-by-u-s-officials-sparked-alerts.html.

Laqueur, Walter. *The Age of Terrorism.* Boston: Little Brown, 1987.

——. *Guerrilla Warfare: A Historical and Critical Study.* New Brunswick, NJ: Transaction, 1998.

Laville, Sandra, Peter Walker, and Vikram Dodd, "Woolwich Attack Suspect Identified as Michael Adebolajo." *Guardian*, May 23, 2013.

Layder, Derek. *Understanding Social Theory.* London: Sage, 2006.

Leader, Stefan H., and Peter Probst. "The Earth Liberation Front and Environmental Terrorism." *Terrorism and Political Violence* 15, no. 4 (2003): 37–58.

Lebovich, Andrew, and Aaron Y. Zelin. "Assessing Al-Qa'ida's Presence in the New Libya." *CTC Sentinel* 5, no. 3 (2012): 14–18.

Lee, Matthew, and Bradley Klapper. "Iran Accused of Al-Qaeda 'Secret Deal' by U.S. Officials." *Huffington Post*, July 28, 2011.

"Letter by Abu abd al-Rahman Anas al-Subayi," October 13, 2010. Office of the Director of National Intelligence, "Bin Laden's Bookshelf." http://www.dni.gov/files/documents/ubl /english/Letter%20dtd%2013%20Oct%202010.pdf.

"Letter dtd 5 April 2011." Office of the Director of National Intelligence, "Bin Laden's Bookshelf." http://www.dni.gov/files/documents/ubl/english/Letter%20dtd%205%20April%20 2011.pdf.

"Letter dtd November 24, 2010." Office of the Director of National Intelligence, "Bin Laden's Bookshelf." http://www.dni.gov/files/documents/ubl/english/Letter%20dtd%20November %2024%202010.pdf.

"Letter from al-Zawahiri to Al-Zarqawi." Released October 11, 2005, by the US Director for National Intelligence. http://fas.org/irp/news/2005/10/letter_in_english.pdf.

"Letter from the Editor." *Inspire* 3, 1431 (November 2010).

"Letter to Karim." Office of the Director of National Intelligence. http://www.dni.gov/files /documents/ubl2016/english/Letter%20to%20Karim.pdf.

"Letter to Wife." Office of the Director of National Intelligence. http://www.dni.gov/files /documents/ubl2016/english/Letter%20to%20wife.pdf.

Levitt, Matthew. "Untangling the Terror Web: Identifying and Counteracting the Phenomenon of Crossover between Terrorist Groups." *SAIS Review* 24, no. 1 (2004): 33–48.

——. *Hamas: Politics, Charity, and Terrorism in the Service of Jihad.* New Haven, CT: Yale University Press, 2006.

——. *Hezbollah: The Global Footprint of Lebanon's Party of God.* Washington, DC: Georgetown University Press, 2013.

Levitt, Matthew, and Michael Jacobson. "The Iran-al-Qaeda Conundrum." *PolicyWatch* 1461. Washington Institute for Near East Policy, January 23, 2009.

Lewis, Jeffrey W. *The Business of Martyrdom: A History of Suicide Bombing.* Annapolis, MD: Naval Institute Press, 2012.

Lia, Brynjar. "Abu Mus'Ab Al-Suri's Critique of Hard Line Salafists in the Jihadist Current." *CTC Sentinel* 1, no. 1 (2007): 1–4.

——. *Architect of Global Jihad: The Life of Al-Qaida Strategist Abu Mus'ab al-Suri.* New York: Columbia University Press, 2008.

——. "Jihadists Divided Between Strategists and Doctrinarians." In *Fault Lines in Global Jihad: Organizational, Strategy and Ideological Fissures*, edited by Assaf Moghadam and Brian Fishman, 69–87. London: Routledge, 2011.

Lia, Brynjar, and Thomas Hegghammer. "Jihadi Strategic Studies: The Alleged Al Qaida Policy Study Preceding the Madrid Bombings." *Studies in Conflict & Terrorism* 27, no. 5 (2004): 355–75.

Lister, Charles. "Islamic State Senior Leadership: Who's Who." N.d. Brookings Institution, n.d. http://www.brookings.edu/~/media/Research/Files/Reports/2014/11/profiling-islamic-state -lister/en_whos_who.pdf?la=en. Accessed February 10, 2016.

——. "Returning Foreign Fighters: Criminalization or Reintegration?" Policy Briefing, Brookings Institution, 2015. https://www.brookings.edu/wp-content/uploads/2016/06/En -Fighters-Web.pdf.

——. *The Syrian Jihad: Al Qaeda, the Islamic State, and the Evolution of an Insurgency.* New York: Oxford University Press, 2015.

Lund, Aron. "The Non-State Militant Landscape in Syria." *CTC Sentinel* 6, no. 8 (2013): 23–28.

MacAskill, Ewen, and Leila Haddou. "The Facebook Jihadis Seeking Action in Syria." *Guardian*, April 15, 2014.

"Mali—Al Qaeda's Sahara Playbook." Associated Press, July 27, 2015. http://hosted.ap.org /specials/interactives/_international/_pdfs/al-qaida-manifesto.pdf.

Malik, Shiv, Ali Younes, Spencer Ackerman, and Mustafa Khalili. "How Isis Crippled Al-Qaida." *Guardian*, June 10, 2015.

Martin, Gus, ed. *The Sage Encyclopedia of Terrorism*, 2nd ed. Thousand Oaks, CA: Sage, 2011.

Martinez, Michael. "Cyberwar: CyberCaliphate Targets U.S. Military Spouses; Anonymous Hits ISI." *CNN*, February 11, 2015. http://edition.cnn.com/2015/02/10/us/isis-cybercaliphate -attacks-cyber-battles/.

Matthiesen, Toby. "The Islamic State Exploits Entrenched Anti-Shia Incitement." Carnegie Middle East Center, July 21, 2015.

Mayntz, Renate. "Organizational Forms of Terrorism: Hierarchy, Network, or a Type Sui generis?" MPIfG Discussion Paper, No. 04/4, 2004. https://www.econstor.eu/bitstream /10419/19906/1/dp04-4.pdf.

McCants, Will. "The Believer." Brookings Institution, September 1, 2015. http://csweb.brookings .edu/content/research/essays/2015/thebeliever.html.

McCants, William. "How Zawahiri Lost al Qaeda: Global Jihad Turns on Itself." *Foreign Affairs*, November 9, 2013.

——. *The ISIS Apocalypse: The History, Strategy, and Doomsday Vision of the Islamic State*. New York: St. Martin's, 2015.

——. "The Polarizing Effect of Islamic State Aggression on the Global Jihadist Movement." *CTC Sentinel* 9, no. 7 (July 2016): 20–23.

McDermott, Terry. "Early Scheme to Turn Jets into Weapons." *Los Angeles Times*, June 24, 2002.

McDermott, Terry, and Josh Meyer. *The Hunt for KSM: Inside the Pursuit and Takedown of the Real 9/11 Mastermind*. New York: Little Brown, 2012.

Mekhennet, Souad, Michael Moss, Eric Schmitt, Elaine Sciolino, and Margot Williams. "A Threat Renewed: Ragtag Insurgency Gains a Lifeline from Al Qaeda." *New York Times*, July 1, 2008.

Mendelsohn, Barak. *The Al-Qaeda Franchise: The Expansion of al-Qaeda and Its Consequences*. New York: Oxford University Press, 2016.

Merari, Ariel. "Terrorism as a Strategy of Insurgency." *Terrorism and Political Violence* 5, no. 4 (1993): 213–51.

Michael, George. *Lone Wolf Terror and the Rise of Leaderless Resistance*. Nashville, TN: Vander-bilt University Press, 2012.

Migaux, Philippe. "Forsane Alizza: From Radical Demonstrations to the Preparation of Ter-rorist Action." In *Sharia4: Straddling Political Activism and Jihad in the West*, edited by Lorenzo Vidino, n.p. Dubai: Al Mesbar Studies and Research Centre, 2015.

Milton, Daniel, and Muhammad al-`Ubaydi. "Pledging Bay`a: A Benefit or Burden to the Islamic State?" *CTC Sentinel* 8, no. 3 (2015): 1–7.

Mintz, John. "Saudi Says Iran Drags Feet Returning Al Qaeda Leaders." *Washington Post*, August 12, 2003.

Moghadam, Assaf. *The Globalization of Martyrdom: Al Qaeda, Salafi Jihad, and the Diffusion of Suicide Attacks*. Baltimore, MD: Johns Hopkins University Press, 2008.

——. "The Salafi-Jihad as a Religious Ideology." *CTC Sentinel* 1, no. 3 (2008): 14–16.

——. "Shifting Trends in Suicide Attacks." *CTC Sentinel* 2, no. 1 (2009): 11–13.

——. "Failure and Disengagement in the Red Army Faction." *Studies in Conflict & Terrorism* 35, no. 2 (2012): 156–81.

——. "How al Qaeda Innovates." *Security Studies* 22, no. 3 (2013): 466–97.

Moghadam, Assaf, Ronit Berger, and Polina Beliakova. "Say Terrorist, Think Insurgent: Labeling and Analyzing Contemporary Terrorist Actors." *Perspectives on Terrorism* 8, no. 5 (2014): 1–16.

Moghadam, Assaf, and Brian Fishman, eds. *Fault Lines in Global Jihad: Organizational, Strategic, and Ideological Fissures*. London: Routledge, 2011.

Moreng, Bridget, and Daveed Gartenstein-Ross. "Al Qaeda Is Beating the Islamic State: Get Ready for the Clash of Caliphates." *Politico*, April 14, 2015. http://www.politico.com /magazine/story/2015/04/al-qaeda-is-beating-the-islamic-state-116954.

Mozgovaya, Natasha. "Chicago Synagogues Targeted in Yemen-Based Plot." *Haaretz*, October 31, 2010.

Mudd, Philip. "Are Jihadist Groups Shifting Their Focus from the Far Enemy?" *CTC Sentinel* 5, no. 5 (2012): 12–14.

Mulhall, Joe. "From Clowns to Contenders: The History and Development of al-Muhajiroun and its International Networks." In *Sharia4: Straddling Political Activism and Jihad in the West*, edited by Lorenzo Vidino, n.p. Dubai: Al Mesbar Studies and Research Centre, 2015.

Münkler, Herfried. *New Wars*. Malden, MA: Polity, 2004.

Musharbash, Yassin. *Die Neue al-Qaida: Innenansichten eines Lernenden Terrornetzwerks*. Cologne: Kiepenheuer & Witsch, 2006.

——. "Saif al-Adel Back in Waziristan: A Top Terrorist Returns to Al Qaeda Fold." *Spiegel Online*, October 25, 2010. http://www.spiegel.de/international/world/saif-al-adel-back-in -waziristan-a-top-terrorist-returns-to-al-qaida-fold-a-725181.html.

——. "'Euro Plot': Al-Qaida Said To Be Planning European Hostage-Takings." *Spiegel Online*, October 27, 2010. http://www.spiegel.de/international/europe/euro-plot-al-qaida -said-to-be-planning-european-hostage-takings-a-725618.html.

"Muslim Cleric Anjem Choudary Admits Wootton Bassett March Is Publicity Stunt." *Telegraph*, January 4, 2010.

Nacos, Brigitte L. *Mass-Mediated Terrorism: The Central Role of the Media in Terrorism and Counterterrorism*, 2nd. ed. Lanham, MD.: Rowman & Littlefield, 2007.

National Commission on Terrorist Attacks Upon the United States. *The 9/11 Commission Report*, 1st ed. New York: Norton, 2004

Naylor, Hugh. "Quietly, al-Qaeda Offshoots Expand in Yemen and Syria." *Washington Post*, June 4, 2015.

Nesser, Petter. *Islamist Terrorism in Europe: A History*. Oxford: Oxford University Press, 2015.

Neumann, Peter R. *Die Neuen Dschihadisten: IS, Europa und die Nächste Welle des Terrorismus.* Berlin: Econ, 2015.

Newman, Edward. "The 'New Wars' Debate: A Historical Perspective Is Needed." *Security Dialogue* 35, no. 2 (2004): 173–89.

"New Video Message from The Islamic State: Message to the Muslims in Somalia—Wilāyat al-Furāt." Jihadology.net, May 21, 2015. http://jihadology.net/2015/05/21/new-video-message-from-the-islamic-state-message-to-the-muslims-in-somalia-wilayat-al-furat/.

Nomani, Asra Q. "This Is Danny Pearl's Final Story." *Washingtonian*, January 24, 2014. https://www.washingtonian.com/projects/KSM/.

Obaidi, Muhammad al-, Nassir Abdullah, and Scott Helfstein. "Deadly Vanguards: A Study of al-Qa'ida's Violence Against Muslims." Occasional Paper, Combating Terrorism Center, December 2009.

O'Ballance, Edgar. *Language of Violence: The Blood Politics of Terrorism.* San Rafael, CA: Presidio Press, 1979.

O'Broin, Leon. *Revolutionary Underground: The Story of the Irish Republican Brotherhood, 1858–1924.* New York: Rowman & Littlefield, 1976.

Oliver, Pamela E., and Gerald Marwell. "Mobilizing Technologies for Collective Action." In *Frontiers in Social Movement Theory*, edited by Aldon D. Morris and Carol McClurg Mueller, 251–72. New Haven, CT: Yale University Press, 1992.

O'Neill, Bard E. *Insurgency and Terrorism: From Revolution to Apocalypse*, 2nd ed. Washington, DC: Potomac, 2005.

O'Neill, Kate, Jörg Balsiger, and Stacy D. VanDeveer. "Actors, Norms, and Impact: Recent International Cooperation Theory and the Influence of the Agent-Structure Debate." *Annual Review of Political Science* 7 (2004): 149–75.

Onuf, Nicholas Greenwood. *World of Our Making: Rules and Rule in Social Theory and International Relations.* Columbia: University of South Carolina Press, 1989.

Oots, Kent L. *A Political Organization Approach to Transnational Terrorism.* New York: Greenwood Press, 1986.

Ostovar, Afshin, and Will McCants. "The Rebel Alliance: Why Syria's Armed Opposition Has Failed to Unify." Washington, DC: Center for Naval Analysis, 2013.

"Outrage as Muslim Extremists Hijack War Heroes' Town Wootton Bassett." *Daily Mail*, January 3, 2010. http://www.dailymail.co.uk/news/article-1240044/Outrage-Muslim-extremists-hijack-war-heroes-town-Wootton-Bassett.html.

Pantucci, Raffaello. "Manchester, New York and Oslo: Three Centrally Directed Al Qaida Plots." *CTC Sentinel* 3, no. 8 (2010): 10–13.

——. "Al-Muhajiroun's European Recruiting Pipeline." *CTC Sentinel* 8, no. 8 (2015) 21–25.

——. *We Love Death as You Love Life: Britain's Suburban Terrorists.* London: Hurst, 2015.

Parker, Tom, and Nick Sitter. "The Four Horsemen of Terrorism: It's Not Waves, It's Strains." *Terrorism and Political Violence* (2015): 1–20.

Parkinson, Sarah Elizabeth. "Organizing Rebellion: Rethinking High-Risk Mobilization and Social Networks in War." *American Political Science Review* 107 (2013): 418–32.

Paz, Reuven. "Global Jihad and WMD: Between Martyrdom and Mass Destruction." *Current Trends in Islamist Ideology* 2 (2005): 74.

——. "Qa'idat Al-Jihad: Moving Forward or Backward? The Algerian GSPC Joins Al Qaeda." *PRISM Occasional Papers* 4, no. 5 (2006): n.p.

——. "Jihadists and Nationalist Islamists: Al-Qa'ida and Hamas." In *Fault Lines in Global Jihad: Organizational, Strategic and Ideological Fissures*, edited by Assaf Moghadam and Brian Fishman, 203–19. London; New York: Routledge, 2011.

Pedahzur, Ami, and Arie Perliger. "The Changing Nature of Suicide Attacks: A Social Network Perspective." *Social Forces* 84, no. 4 (2006): 1987–2008.

Perliger, Arie, and Ami Pedahzur. "Social Network Analysis in the Study of Terrorism and Political Violence." *PS: Political Science & Politics* 44, no. 1 (2011): 45–50.

Peters, Rudolph. *Jihad in Classical and Modern Islam: A Reader*, 2nd. ed. Princeton, NJ: Markus Wiener, 2005.

Phillips, Brian J. "Terrorist Group Cooperation and Longevity." *International Studies Quarterly* 58, no. 2 (2014): 336–47.

Pollack, Kenneth M. *The Persian Puzzle: The Conflict Between Iran and America*. New York: Random House, 2004.

Porpora, Douglas V. "Four Concepts of Social Structure." *Journal for the Theory of Social Behaviour* 19, no. 2 (1989): 195–211.

"President Delivers State of the Union Address." The White House, January 29, 2002. http://georgewbush-whitehouse.archives.gov/news/releases/2002/01/20020129-11.html.

Price, Eric. "Selected Literature on Terrorism and Organized Crime." *Perspectives on Terrorism* 4, no. 6 (2010): 1–11.

Priest, Dana, and Douglas Farah. "Terror Alliance Has U.S. Worried." *Washington Post*, June 30, 2002.

Prieur, Laurent. "Boko Haram Got Al Qaeda Bomb Training, Niger Says." Reuters, January 25, 2012. http://www.reuters.com/article/ozatp-sahara-bokoharam-qaeda-idAFJOE80OooK20120125.

Prucha, Nico, and Ali Fisher. "Tweeting for the Caliphate: Twitter as the New Frontier for Jihadist Propaganda." *CTC Sentinel* 6, no. 6 (2013): 19–23.

Rabasa, Angel, and Cheryl Benard. *Eurojihad: Patterns of Islamist Radicalization and Terrorism in Europe*. New York: Cambridge University Press, 2015.

Radu, Michael. "London 7/7 and Its Impact." *Foreign Policy Research Institute e-Notes*, July 2005.

Rapoport, David C. "The International World as Some Terrorists Have Seen It: A Look at a Century of Memoirs." In *Inside Terrorist Organizations*, edited by David C. Rapoport, 32–58. London: Frank Cass, 2001.

Rassler, Don. "Al-Qa'ida's Pakistan Strategy." *CTC Sentinel* 2, no. 6 (2009): 1–4.

Raufer, Xavier. "The Red Brigades: Farewell to Arms." *Studies in Conflict & Terrorism* 16, no. 4 (1993): 315–25.

Raymond, Catherine Zara. "Al Muhajiroun and Islam4UK: The Group Behind the Ban." International Centre for the Study of Radicalization and Political Violence ICSR, Kings College London, 2010.

Reeve, Simon. *The New Jackals: Ramzi Yousef, Osama bin Laden and the Future of Terrorism*. Boston: Northeastern University Press, 1999.

Reinares, Fernando. "The Madrid Bombings and Global Jihadism." *Survival* 52, no. 2 (2010): 83–104.

Ressler, Steve. "Social Network Analysis as an Approach to Combat Terrorism: Past, Present, and Future Research." *Homeland Security Affairs* 2, no. 2 (2006). https://www.hsaj.org /articles/171.

Reuter, Christoph. "The Terror Strategist: Secret Files Reveal the Structure of Islamic State." *Spiegel Online*, April 18, 2015. http://www.spiegel.de/international/world/islamic-state -files-show-structure-of-islamist-terror-group-a-1029274.html.

Rhode, David, and James Risen. "A Hostile Land Foils the Quest for Bin Laden." *New York Times*, December 13, 2004.

Riedel, Bruce. "The Mysterious Relationship Between Al-Qaʿida and Iran." *CTC Sentinel* 3, no. 7 (2010): 1–4.

——. *The Search for Al Qaeda: Its Leadership, Ideology, and Future*. Washington, DC: Brookings Institution Press, 2010.

——. "The Al Qaeda-Iran Connection." *Daily Beast*, May 29, 2011. http://www.thedailybeast .com/articles/2011/05/29/al-qaedas-iran-connection-bin-ladens-successors-vie-for-power .html.

——. "Iran and Al Qaeda's Shadowy Relationship Could Firm Up This Spring." *Daily Beast*, February 17, 2012. http://www.thedailybeast.com/articles/2012/02/17/iran-and-al-qaeda-s -shadowy-relationship-could-firm-up-this-spring.html.

Risen, James. "Bin Laden Sought Iran as an Ally, U.S. Intelligence Documents Say." *New York Times*, December 31, 2001.

Roex, Ineke. "The Rise of Public Dawa Networks in the Netherlands: Behind Bars, Sharia-4Holland, and Streetdawah." In *Sharia4: Straddling Political Activism and Jihad in the West*, edited by Lorenzo Vidino, n.p. Dubai: Al Mesbar Studies and Research Centre, 2015.

Rosenau, James N. "Governance in the Twenty-First Century." *Global Governance* 1, no. 1 (1995): 13–43.

Rotella, Sebastian. "Terrorism Suspects Traced to Iran." *Los Angeles Times*, August 1, 2004.

Roy, Olivier. *Globalized Islam: The Search for a New Ummah*. New York: Columbia University Press, 2004.

Saarinen, Juha. "Guest Post: The History of Jihadism in Finland and an Early Assessment of Finnish Foreign Fighters in Syria." *Jihadology*, November 21, 2013. http://jihadology.net /2013/11/21/guest-post-the-history-of-jihadism-in-finland-and-an-early-assessment-of -finnish-foreign-fighters-in-syria/.

Sageman, Marc. *Understanding Terror Networks*. Philadelphia: University of Pennsylvania Press, 2004.

——. *Leaderless Jihad: Terror Networks in the Twenty-First Century*. Philadelphia: University of Pennsylvania Press, 2008.

——. "The Next Generation of Terror." *Foreign Policy*, October 8, 2009.

Saikia, Jaideep, and Ekaterina Stepanova, eds. *Terrorism: Patterns of Internationalization*. New Delhi: SAGE Publications India, 2009.

Sambanis, Nicholas. "What Is Civil War? Conceptual and Empirical Complexities of an Operational Definition." *Journal of Conflict Resolution* 48, no. 6 (2004): 814–58.

Satter, Raphael, and John-Thor Dahlburg. "Belgian Jihadi ID'd as Mastermind of Paris Attacks." Associated Press, November 16, 2015.

Scales, Robert H., and Douglas Ollivant. "Terrorist Armies Fight Smarter and Deadlier than Ever." *Washington Post*, August 1, 2014.

Schanzer, Jonathan. *Al-Qaeda's Armies, Middle East Affiliate Groups and the Next Generation of Terror.* New York: Specialist, 2005.

Scheuer, Michael. "Coalition Warfare, Part II: How Zarqawi Fits into Bin Laden's World Front." *Terrorism Focus* 2 (2005). https://jamestown.org/program/coalition-warfare-part-ii -how-zarqawi-fits-into-bin-ladens-world-front/.

——. *Through Our Enemies' Eyes: Osama Bin Laden, Radical Islam, and the Future of America*, 2nd ed. Washington, DC: Potomac, 2006.

Schiff, Ze'ev. "Background: Hezbollah Had a Role in Ashdod Bombing." *Haaretz*, March 28 2004.

Schirra, Bruno. "The Most Dangerous Man in the World." *Cicero*, April 2005.

Schmid, Alex P. *The Routledge Handbook of Terrorism Research.* London: Routledge, 2011.

Schmid, Alex P., and Albert I. Jongman. *Political Terrorism. A Research Guide to Concepts, Theories, Databases and Literature.* Amsterdam: Transaction Publishers, 1988.

Schmitt, Eric. "American Commander Details Al Qaeda's Strength in Mali." *New York Times*, December 3, 2012.

Schmitt, Eric, and David D. Kirkpatrick. "Islamic State Sprouting Limbs Beyond Its Base." *New York Times*, February 14, 2015.

Schmitt, Eric, and Mark Mazzetti. "Qaeda Leader's Edict to Yemen Affiliate Is Said to Prompt Alert." *New York Times*, August 5, 2013.

Schmitt, Eric, and Thom Shanker. *Counterstrike: The Untold Story of America's Secret Campaign Against Al Qaeda.* New York: Times Books, 2011.

Schulze, Kirsten E. "The Struggle for an Independent Aceh: The Ideology, Capacity, and Strategy of GAM." *Studies in Conflict and Terrorism* 26, no. 4 (2003): 241–71.

Schweitzer, Yoram. "The Case of the PFLP and its Offshoots." In *Terrorist Innovations in Weapons of Mass Effect: Preconditions, Causes, and Predictive Indicators*, edited by Rasmussen, Maria J. and Mohammed M. Hafez, 85–96. Workshop Report, Defense Threat Reduction Agency, Advanced Systems and Concepts Office, Report Number ASCO 2010-019, August 2010.

——. "Al Qaeda and Suicide Terrorism: Vision and Reality." *Military and Strategic Affairs* 2, no. 2 (2010). http://www.inss.org.il/uploadimages/Import/(FILE)1298360264.pdf.

Schweitzer, Yoram, and Sari Goldstein Ferber. *Al-Qaeda and the Internationalization of Suicide Terrorism.* Memorandum No. 78. Tel Aviv, Israel Tel Aviv University, Jaffee Center for Strategic Studies, 2005.

Schweitzer, Yoram, and Aviv Oreg. *Al Qaeda's Odyssey to the Global Jihad.* Memorandum No. 134, Institute for National Security Studies INSS, Tel Aviv University, 2014.

Sciolino, Elaine, and Souad Mekhennet. "Al Qaeda Warrior Uses Internet to Rally Women." *New York Times*, May 28, 2008.

Seale, Patrick. *Abu Nidal, A Gun for Hire.* London: Hutchinson, 1992.

Seib, Philip M., and Dana M. Janbek. *Global Terrorism and the New Media: The Post-Al Qaeda Generation.* London: Routledge, 2011.

Shahzad, Syed Saleem. *Inside Al-Qaeda and the Taliban: Beyond Bin Laden and 9/11.* New York: Palgrave McMillan, 2011.

Shapiro, Jacob N. *The Terrorist's Dilemma: Managing Violent Covert Organizations.* Princeton, NJ: Princeton University Press, 2013.

"Sharia4America.com: Advocating an American I'slamic State' and Shariah Law in the United States." *MEMRI Special Dispatch* No. 3782, April 24 2011. http://www.memri.org /report/en/0/0/0/0/0/810/5218.htm.

"Sharia4Belgium: Enquête pour terrorisme." *Figaro*, July 17, 2012.

Shishani, Murad Batal al-. "Ibrahim al-Rubaish: New Religious Ideologue of al-Qaeda in Saudi Arabia Calls for Revival of Assassination Tactic." *Terrorism Monitor* 7, no. 25 (2009): 3–4.

Siegel, Pascale Combelles. "AQIM Renews Its Threats Against France." *Terrorism Focus* 4, no. 26 (2007). https://jamestown.org/program/aqim-renews-its-threats-against-france/.

Silber, Mitchell D. "Al-Q'aida's Center of Gravity in a Post-Bin Ladin World." *CTC Sentinel* 4, nos. 11–12 (2011): 1–4.

Simcox, Robin. "Al-Qaeda's Global Footprint: An Assessment of al-Qaeda's Strength Today." London: Henry Jackson Society, 2013.

Simcox, Robin, Hannah Stuart, Houriya Ahmed, and Douglas Murray. "Islamist Terrorism: The British Connections," 2nd ed. London: Henry Jackson Society, 2011.

Sinclair, Kirstine, and Saad Ali Khan, "Current Islamist and Jihadi-Salafi Trends in Denmark: Hizb ut-Tahrir and Kaldet." In *Sharia4: Straddling Political Activism and Jihad in the West*, edited by Lorenzo Vidino, n.p. Dubai: Al Mesbar Studies and Research Centre, 2015.

Sly, Liz. "The Hidden Hand Behind the Islamic State Militants? Saddam Hussein's." *Washington Post*, April 4, 2015.

Smale, Alison. "German State Elections Point to Vulnerability for Angela Merkel." *New York Times*, March 14, 2016.

Smith, David. "Africa's Islamist Militants Co-ordinate Efforts in Threat to Continent's Security." *Guardian*, June 26, 2012.

Smith, Michael S. "The Al-Qa'ida-Qods Force Nexus: Scratching the Surface of a Known Unknown." Kronos Advisory LLC, USA, April 29, 2011. http://www.kronosadvisory.com /Kronos_AQ_QF_Nexus_REDACTED.pdf.

Snow, David, and Scott Byrd. "Ideology, Framing Processes, and Islamic Terrorist Movements." *Mobilization: An International Quarterly* 12, no. 2 (2007): 119–36.

Snow, David, Sarah Soule, and Hanspeter Kriesi, eds. *The Blackwell Companion to Social Movements.* Malden, MA: Blackwell, 2007.

SOCOM-2012-0000003. https://www.ctc.usma.edu/v2/wp-content/uploads/2012/05/SOCOM -2012-0000003-Trans.pdf. Accessed March 14, 2016.

SOCOM-2012-0000004. http://www.jihadica.com/wp-content/uploads/2012/05/SOCOM -2012-0000004-Trans.pdf. Accessed November 22, 2016.

SOCOM-2012-0000008. http://www.jihadica.com/wp-content/uploads/2012/05/SOCOM -2012-0000008-Trans.pdf. Accessed March 14, 2016.

SOCOM-2012-0000011, March 28, 2007. http://assets.nationaljournal.com/pdf/OBL9.pdf

SOCOM-2012-0000012, June 11, 2009. http://www.jihadica.com/wp-content/uploads/2012 /05/SOCOM-2012-0000012-Trans.pdf.

SOCOM-2012-0000016-HT. https://www.ctc.usma.edu/v2/wp-content/uploads/2013/10/Letter -to-Nasir-al-Wuhayshi-Translation.pdf. Accessed March 14, 2016.

SOCOM-2012-0000017-HT. https://www.ctc.usma.edu/v2/wp-content/uploads/2013/10/Letter -Regarding-Al-Qaida-Strategy-Translation.pdf. Accessed March 14, 2016.

SOCOM-2012-0000019-HT. http://www.jihadica.com/wp-content/uploads/2012/05/SOCOM -2012-0000019-Trans.pdf. Accessed November 22, 2016.

Solomon, Jay. "US Sees Iranian, Al Qaeda Alliance." *Wall Street Journal*, July 29, 2011.

Southern Poverty Law Center. "Eco-Violence: The Record." Intelligence Report 107, 2002. https://www.splcenter.org/fighting-hate/intelligence-report/2015/eco-violence-record.

"Spotlight on Global Jihad, September 2–October 8 2015." Meir Amit Intelligence and Terrorism Information Center, 2015.

Staniland, Paul. *Networks of Rebellion: Explaining Insurgent Cohesion and Collapse.* Ithaca, NY: Cornell University Press, 2014.

"Statement by Sulayman Abu Ghayth to the Federal Bureau of Investigation." Document no. 415-A-NY-307616. March 1, 2013. http://kronosadvisory.com/Kronos_US_v_Sulaiman _Abu_Ghayth_Statement.1.pdf.

Steinberg, Guido W. *German Jihad: On the Internationalization of Islamist Terrorism.* New York: Columbia University Press, 2013.

Stenersen, Anne. "Al Qaeda's Foot Soldiers: A Study of the Biographies of Foreign Fighters Killed in Afghanistan and Pakistan Between 2002 and 2006." *Studies in Conflict & Terrorism* 34, no. 3 (2011): 171–98.

Sterling, Claire. *The Terror Network: The Secret War of International Terrorism.* New York: Henry Holt, 1981.

Stern, Jessica. *Terror in the Name of God: Why Religious Militants Kill.* New York: Ecco, 2003.

Stout, Mark E., Jessica M. Huckabey, and John R. Schindler. *Terrorist Perspectives Project: Strategic and Operational Views of Al Qaida and Associated Movements.* Annapolis, MD: Naval Institute Press, 2008.

Strobel, Warren, and Mark Hosenball. "Elite Iranian Guards Training Yemen's Houthis: U.S. Officials." Reuters, March 27, 2015.

Suri, Abu Musab al-. "The Global Islamic Resistance Call." In *Architect of Global Jihad: The Life of Al-Qaida Strategist Abu Mus' ab al-Suri*, by Brynjar Lia. London: Hurst, 2007. 347–484.

Swift, Christopher. "Arc of Convergence: AQAP, Ansar al-Sharia and the Struggle for Yemen." *CTC Sentinel* 5, no. 6 (2012): 1–6.

Taber, Robert. *The War of the Flea.* Washington, DC: Potomac, 2002.

Takeyh, Ray, and Nikolas Gvosdev. "Do Terrorist Networks Need a Home?."*Washington Quarterly* 25, no. 3 (2002): 97–108.

Tankel, Stephen. "Not Another Al Qaeda Article." *War on the Rocks*, August 6, 2013. http://warontherocks.com/2013/08/not-another-al-qaeda-article/.

——. *Storming the World Stage: The Story of Lashkar-e-Taiba*. New York: Oxford University Press, 2013.

Tarrow, Sidney. *The New Transnational Activism*. New York: Cambridge University Press, 2005.

Taub, Ben. "Journey to Jihad: Why Are Teen-Agers Joining ISIS?" *New Yorker*, June 1, 2015.

Tawil, Camille. *Brothers in Arms: The Story of Al-Qa'ida and the Arab Jihadists*. London: Saqi, 2010.

——. "The Other Face of Al-Qaeda." London: Quilliam Foundation, November 2010.

Tchounand, Ristel. "Sharia4UK Menace la Belgique pour Défendre Fouad Belkacem." *Yabiladi*, May 15, 2013. http://www.yabiladi.com/articles/details/17360/sharia4uk-menace -belgique-pour-defendre.html.

"Terrorists Plotted to Blow Up 11 U.S. Jumbo Jets." *Los Angeles Times*, May 28, 1995.

Themnér, Lotta, and Peter Wallensteen. "Armed Conflicts, 1946–2013." *Journal of Peace Research* 51, no. 4 (2014): 541–54.

Thiessen, Marc A. "Iran Responsible for 1998 U.S. Embassy Bombings." *Washington Post*, December 8, 2011.

Thomas, Matthew J. "Exposing and Exploiting Weaknesses in the Merger of Al-Qaeda and Al-Shabaab." *Small Wars & Insurgencies* 24, no. 3 (2013): 413–35.

304th Military Intelligence Battalion OSINT Team. "Sample Overview: Al Qaida-Like Mobile Discussions & Potential Creative Uses." Supplement, OSINT Team newsletter, October 16, 2008. http://fas.org/irp/eprint/mobile.pdf.

"Top al-Qaeda Ranks Keep Footholds in Iran." *USA Today*, July 9 2011.

"Top Iranian Defector on Iran's Collaboration with Iraq, North Korea, Al-Qa'ida, and Hizbullah." *MEMRI Special Dispatch* No. 473, February 21, 2003. http://www.memri.org /report/en/print814.htm.

Tse-tung, Mao. *On Guerrilla Warfare*, translated by Samuel B. Griffith II. Urbana: University of Illinois Press, 2000.

"UK Hate Preachers Linked to Fanatics." *Daily Mail*, January 8, 2016.

UK Home Office and James Brokenshire, MP. "Written Statement to Parliament: Alternative Names for Proscribed Organisation Al Muhajiroun." June 26, 2014. https://www.gov.uk /government/speeches/alternative-names-for-proscribed-organisation-al-muhajiroun.

"*United States v. Ahmed Abdulkadir Warsame*." United States District Court, Southern District of New York, 11 Cr. https://www.nytimes.com/packages/pdf/world/Warsame_Indictment .pdf. Accessed November 22, 2016.

U.S. Department of the Army. *The US Army/Marine Corps Counterinsurgency field Manual: US Army Field Manual No. 3-24; Marine Corps Warfighting Publication No. 3-33.5*. Chicago: University of Chicago Press, 2007.

U.S. Department of State. "Patterns of Global Terrorism: 1993." Washington, DC: Department of State, April 1994.

——. "Rewards for Justice—al-Qaeda Reward Offer." October 18, 2012. http://www.state.gov /r/pa/prs/ps/2012/10/199299.htm.

U.S. Department of the Treasury. "Treasury Designates Iranian Ministry of Intelligence and Security for Human Rights Abuses and Support for Terrorism." February 16, 2012. https://www.treasury.gov/press-center/press-releases/Pages/tg1424.aspx.

——. "Treasury Further Exposes Al-Qa'ida's Iran-Based Network." October 18, 2012. https://www.treasury.gov/press-center/press-releases/Pages/tg1741.aspx.

U.S. House of Representatives Committee on International Relations. "Summary of Investigation of IRA Links to Farc Narco-Terrorists in Colombia." Washington, DC, April 24, 2001.

U.S. Senate Select Committee on Intelligence. "Review of the Terrorist Attacks on U.S. Facilities in Benghazi, Libya, September 11–12, 2012 Together with Additional Views." Washington, DC, January 15, 2014.

U.S. v. Bin Laden. 126 F. Supp. 2d 290 (S.D.N.Y. 2001).

Van Creveld, Martin. *The Transformation of War.* New York: Macmillan, 1991.

Van Ostaeyen, Pieter. "Belgian Jihadists in Syria." *Jihadology,* September 5, 2013. http://jihadology.net/2013/09/05/guest-post-belgian-jihadis-in-syria/.

——. "Update on the Belgians in Syria." *Jihadology,* May 7, 2014. http://jihadology.net/2014/05/07/the-clear-banner-update-on-the-belgians-in-syria/.

——. "Belgian Fighters in Syria and Iraq—November 2014." *Jihadology,* November 22, 2014. http://jihadology.net/2014/11/22/the-clear-banner-belgian-fighters-in-syria-and-iraq-november-2014/.

——. "Sharia4Belgium." In *Sharia4: Straddling Political Activism and Jihad in the West,* edited by Lorenzo Vidino, n.p. Dubai: Al Mesbar Studies and Research Centre, 2015.

——. "Belgian Fighters in Syria and Iraq—December 2015." https://pietervanostaeyen.com/2015/12/07/belgian-fighters-in-syria-and-iraq-december-2015.

Van Vlierden, Guy. "How Belgium Became a Top Exporter of Jihad." *Terrorism Monitor* 13, no. 11 (2015). https://jamestown.org/program/how-belgium-became-a-top-exporter-of-jihad/.

Van Wilgenburg, Wladimir. "The Rise of Jaysh al-Fateh in Northern Syria." *Terrorism Monitor* 13, no. 12 (2015). https://jamestown.org/program/the-rise-of-jaysh-al-fateh-in-northern-syria/.

Vick, Karl. "Al-Qaeda's Hand in Istanbul Plot." *Washington Post,* February 13, 2007.

Vidino, Lorenzo. "The Development of Home-grown Jihadist Radicalisation in Italy." Madrid: Real Instituto Elcano, 2014.

——. "Home-Grown Jihadism in Italy: Birth, Development and Radicalization Dynamics." Milan: Istituto per gli Studi di Politica Internazionale, 2015.

——. "Sharia4: From Confrontational Activism to Militancy." *Perspectives on Terrorism* 9, no. 2 (2015): 1–15.

——. "Wrong Assumptions: Integration, Responsibility, and Counterterrorism in France." *War on the Rocks,* January 22, 2015. http://warontherocks.com/2015/01/wrong-assumptions-integration-responsibility-and-counterterrorism-in-france/.

"Violent Jihad in the Netherlands: Current Trends in the Islamist Terrorist Threat." General Intelligence and Security Service (AIVD) Report, March 2006, 13.

Walt, Stephen M. *The Origins of Alliances*. Ithaca, NY: Cornell University Press, 1990.

Watts, Clint. "Al-Qaeda Plots, NSA Intercepts and the Era of Terrorism Competition." *Geopoliticus: The FPRI Blog*, August 2013. http://www.fpri.org/2013/08/al-qaeda-plots-nsa-intercepts-the-era-of-terrorism-competition/.

———. "Al Qaeda Loses Touch: ISIS and the Future of Terrorism." *Foreign Affairs*, February 4, 2015.

———. "One Year Later, ISIS Overtakes Al Qaeda: What's Next?" *Geopoliticus: The FPRI Blog*, April 6, 2015. http://www.fpri.org/2015/04/one-year-later-isis-overtakes-al-qaeda-whats-next/.

———. "What Is the Future of Al Qaeda and the Islamic State? Part II." *Markaz: Middle East Politics & Policy* (blog), Brookings Institution, January 28, 2016. https://www.brookings.edu/blog/markaz/2016/01/28/experts-weigh-in-part-2-what-is-the-future-of-al-qaida-and-the-islamic-state/.

Weaver, Mary Anne. "The Short, Violent Life of Abu Musab al-Zarqawi." *Atlantic*, July/August 2006.

Weimann, Gabriel. *Terror on the Internet: The New Arena, the New Challenges*. Washington, DC: United States Institute of Peace Press, 2006.

———. *Terrorism in Cyberspace: The Next Generation*. Washington, DC: Woodrow Wilson Center Press, 2015.

Weinthal, Benjamin, and Thomas Joscelyn. "Al Qaeda's Network in Iran." *Weekly Standard*, April 2, 2012. http://www.weeklystandard.com/al-qaedas-network-in-iran/article/634428.

Weiser, Benjamin, and Scott Shane. "Court Filings Assert Iran Had Link to 9/11 Attacks." *New York Times*, May 19, 2011.

Wendt, Alexander. "Bridging the Theory/Meta-Theory Gap in International Relations." *Review of International Studies* 17, no. 4 (1991): 383–92.

Wendt, Alexander, and Daniel Friedheim. "Hierarchy Under Anarchy: Informal Empire and the East German State." *International Organization* 49, no. 4 (1995): 689–721.

Wendt, Alexander E. "The Agent-Structure Problem in International Relations Theory." *International Organization* 41, no. 3 (1987): 335–70.

White, Jeffrey, and Andrew J. Tabler. "The ISIS Battle for Yarmouk Camp: Troubling Implications." *PolicyWatch* 2407. Washington Institute for Near East Policy, April 10, 2015.

Whitlock, Craig. "Al-Qaeda's Far-Reaching New Partner." *Washington Post*, October 5, 2006.

Wiewel, Wim, and Albert Hunter. "The Interorganizational Network as a Resource: A Comparative Case Study on Organizational Genesis." *Administrative Science Quarterly* (1985): 482–96.

Wight, Colin. *Agents, Structures and International Relations: Politics as Ontology*. Cambridge: Cambridge University Press, 2006.

Wiktorowicz, Quintan. *Radical Islam Rising: Muslim Extremism in the West*. Lanham, MD: Rowman & Littlefield, 2005.

———. "Anatomy of the Salafi Movement." *Studies in Conflict & Terrorism* 29, no. 3 (2006): 207–39.

Wilkinson, Paul. *Terrorism Versus Democracy: The Liberal State Response*, 3rd. ed. London: Routledge, 2011.

Williams, Brian Glyn. "The Return of the Arabs: Al Qai'da's Military Role in the Afghan Insurgency." *West Point's Combating Terrorism Center Sentinel* 1, no. 3 (2008): 22–25.

Williams, Phil. "Transnational Criminal Networks." In *Networks and Netwars*, edited by John Arquilla and David Ronfeldt. Santa Monica, CA: RAND, 2001.

——. "Cooperation Among Criminal Organizations." In *Transnational Organized Crime and International Security: Business as Usual*, edited by Mats Berdal and Monica Serrano, 67–82. Boulder, CO: Lynne Rienner, 2002.

Wolf, Anne. "Tunisia: Signs of Domestic Radicalization." *CTC Sentinel* 6, no. 1 (2013): 1–4.

Wood, Graeme. "What Isis Really Wants." *Atlantic*, March 2015.

"Worldwide Governance Indicators." World Bank, 2016. http://info.worldbank.org/governance/wgi/index.aspx#home.

Wright, Lawrence. *The Looming Tower: Al-Qaeda and the Road to 9/11*. New York: Vintage, 2006.

Yaari, Ehud. "Hamas and the Islamic State: Growing Cooperation in the Sinai." *PolicyWatch* 2533. Washington Institute for Near East Policy, December 15, 2015.

"Yemen: The Campaign Against Global Jihad—Situation Report and Directions of Development." Jihadi Websites Monitoring Group Report, October 2010. https://www.ict.org.il/Article.aspx?ID=161.

Zagorin, Adam, and Joe Klein. "9/11 Commission Finds Ties Between al Qaeda and Iran." *Time*, July 16, 2004.

Zanini, Michele, and Sean J. A. Edwards. "The Networking of Terror in the Information Age." In *Networks and Netwars*, edited by John Arquilla and David Ronfeldt, 29–60. Santa Monica, CA: RAND, 2001.

Zawahiri, Ayman al-. "Knights Under the Prophet's Banner." *Al-Sharq al-Awsat*, 2001.

——. "Message to the People of Yemen." *Inspire* 1 (2010). https://azelin.files.wordpress.com/2010/06/aqap-inspire-magazine-volume-1-uncorrupted.pdf.

——. "General Guidelines for Jihad." As-Sahab Media, 2013. https://azelin.files.wordpress.com/2013/09/dr-ayman-al-e1ba93awc481hirc4ab-22general-guidelines-for-the-work-of-a-jihc481dc4ab22-en.pdf.

Zelin, Aaron Y. "The Islamic State's Model." *Monkey Cage, Washington Post*, January 28, 2015. https://www.washingtonpost.com/news/monkey-cage/wp/2015/01/28/the-islamic-states-model/.

Zenn, Jacob. "Boko Haram's International Connections." *CTC Sentinel* 6, no. 1 (2013): 7–13.

——. "Cooperation or Competition: Boko Haram and Ansaru After the Mali Intervention." *CTC Sentinel* 6, no. 3 (2013): 1–8.

INDEX

Abaaoud, Abdelhamid, 247–48

Abboubi, Anas el-, 257

Abdeslam, Saleh, 242

Abdukadirov, Sherzod, 62

Abdulkhaleq, Adel Muhammad Mahmoud, 206

Abdullah, Fazul Muhammad (a.k.a. Fadil Haroun), 130, 157–58

Abdullah, King of Jordan, 290n28

Abdulmutallab, Omar Farouk, 175

Absi, Amr al- (a.k.a. Abu Asir), 250

Abu Nidal Organization (ANO), 22, 62

Abu Sayyaf Group (ASG), 34, 133, 136, 228

Abuza, Zachary, 228

Ackinaroglu, Seden, 284n34

Action Directe (AD), 22, 33–34, 111

Adebolajo, Michael, 238

Adebowale, Michael, 238

Adel, Sayf al-, 152, 201, 203, 204, 207, 211

affiliates (Al Qaeda), 124–25; al-Shabaab, 156–58; benefits to Al Qaeda from, 155; formal recognition of, 305n8; franchising model for, 148–58; GSPC, 154–56; ideological requirements for, 150; Jamaat

al-Tawhid w'al Jihad, 152–53; local agendas of, 162; post-9/11, 147

affiliates (Islamic State), 117, 125

Afghan Arab fighters, 202

Afghanistan, 30, 31, 127, 136–44, 202

African National Congress (ANC), 26

agents: diversity of, 64–66; human, in agent-structure debate, 44–45; identity of, 99, 101–4; networks as, 56; nonstate actors as, 46–48; principal-agent problems, 18; social movements as, 290n33; state actors as, 275–76

agent-structure model, 7, 44–48, 288n8

Ahlus Sunnah wal Jamaah, 239

Ahmadinejad, Mahmoud, 220

Ahmed, Bilal, 238

Ahrar al-Sham, 96

Air France hijacking, 19, 37

Ajmi, Ali Hasan Ali al-, 323n72

Alamoudi, Abdurahman Muahammad, 81

Al Aqsa International Foundation, 81

Alfi, Hasan al-, 199

Al-Ghurabaa, 239, 240

al-Ittihad al-Islami (AIAI), 134, 157

Al-Jihad, 108
alliance(s), 4, 162; of affiliates and associates,
163; Bacon's typology of, 38–40; as biased
term, 48; in civil wars and insurgencies,
95–96; definitions of, 104; of IS, 168; of
Islamic State in Libya, 10; reasons for
engaging in, 21–22; strategic, 3, 107
(*see also* high-end cooperation)
Al-Muhajiroun (AM), 235–39
al-Murabitun, 30
Al Qaeda, 1; affiliates of, 117, 124, 125, 133,
147–58; alliance between GSPC and, 39;
alliance with Jamaat al-Tawhid w'al
Jihad, 18; alliance with LeJ, 22; alliance
with Taliban, 138–39; al-Shabaab's
allegiance to, 23; associates of, 124–26,
150; collaboration with Khaled Sheikh
Muhammad, 103; competition between
IS and, 22, 126, 166–69; cooperation
between Hizballah and, 27; cooperation
between IS and, 166–67; in EIJ
discussion with Iran, 197–98; founding
period of (1984–1992), 128–32; funding
for, 81, 138; funding from, 35; goals of,
129–30; golden era of (Afghanistan,
1996–2001), 136–43; as inspiration for
global Islamic community, 137–38; JI
supported by, 37–38; joint operation with
TTP and HQN, 38; leadership of global
jihad movement and, 123–24; Madrid
train bombings and, 60; merger of EIJ
and, 19–20, 39, 108, 142; military
committee of, 129–30, 142; 9/11 attacks
planning, 229–34; online forum of,
83–84; pledges of allegiance to, 124–25;
post-9/11 changes in, 144–49; recruiting
by, 131; relationship of AQI and, 117;
reputation of, 161–162; safe haven in
Afghanistan for, 30; security committee
of, 141; strategic alliances of, 109, 133,
150; structure of, 56, 129–30, 141–42,
147–48, 204; Sudan years of (1992–1996),

132–36; suicide attacks of, 8, 25; Twitter
use by, 87; "World Islamic Front against
the Crusaders and the Jews," 34
Al Qaeda Central (AQC): affiliations
(generally), 151–52; affiliation with Jabhat
al-Nusra, 164; alliances with affiliates,
111; alliance with AQAP, 116; alliance
with AQI, 153, 177; break of ties with
ISIS, 27; death of bin Laden and, 161;
ideological affinity of affiliates and, 27;
informal partnership with HQN, 159;
relationship with EIJ, 117; safe havens
for, 12; upheavals in Middle East and, 161
Al Qaeda in Iraq (AQI): alliance with Al
Qaeda, 18, 177; AQC affiliation with, 153;
GSPC support for, 154–55; relationship
of Al Qaeda and, 117, 125
Al Qaeda in the Arabian Peninsula (AQAP;
Yemen-based), 315–16n1; as affiliate, 125;
background of, 171–73; lethality of, 11;
origin of, 174–75; strikes in the West by,
162; Twitter publicized by, 87
Al Qaeda in the Arabian Peninsula (QAP;
Saudi-based), 170, 172–75, 191
Al Qaeda in the Indian Subcontinent
(AQIS), 125, 166
Al Qaeda in the Islamic Maghreb (AQIM):
as affiliate, 125; alliance with AQC, 111;
Benghazi attack, 186; origin of, 154, 155;
other groups influenced/established by,
163; targets of, 155, 156; work with local
militants, 12
Al Qaeda in the Southern Arabian
Peninsula (AQSAP), 174
Al Qaeda on the Arabian Peninsula–Soldier's
Brigade of Yemen (AQAP-SBY), 174
al-Shabaab: alliance with AQC, 111, 156–58;
as Al Qaeda affiliate, 125, 156–58; benefits
of allegiance to Al Qaeda, 23; lethality
of, 11; Mogadishu occupation and, 146;
origins of, 157; pledge of allegiance to bin
Laden by, 124; Twitter use by, 87

al-wala wa'l-bara, 73

American Muslim Foundation, 81

Animal Liberation Front, 27

AnjemChoudary.com, 255

Annon, Adel, 228

Ansar al-Islam, 60, 149

Ansar al-Mujahideen English Forum
(AMEF), 83

Ansar al-Sharia, 161, 163, 186

Ansar al-Sunnah Group (ASG), 112

Ansar Bayt al-Maqdis (ABM), 115

Ansi, Nasser bin Ali al-, 181, 182, 192

Apostates, 72–74

Arab Spring, 180–81, 259

Ariana Airlines, 139

armed conflict: as opportunity for terrorist
cooperation, 93–96; prevalence of, 273

Armed Islamic Group (GIA), 31, 133, 136,
154, 312n41

Arnaout, Enaam, 135

Aroud, Malika El, 241

Arquilla, John, 66

Asal, Victor, 25

Asir, Abu (Amr al-Absi), 250

Asiri, Abdullah al-, 175

Asiri, Ibrahim al-, 187

Ask.fm, 92–93

Assad, Bashar, 257

As-Sahab, 310n14

associates: of Al Qaeda, 124–26, 150, 162;
defined, 125

Atef, Mohammed (a.k.a. Abu Hafs
al-Masri), 128, 134, 231–33

Atta, Muhammad, 231, 232

Attarzadeh-Nyaki, Heshmatollah, 207

Australian embassy bombing, Jakarta, 35

AVID, 251, 252

Awfi, Mohammed al-, 174

Awlaki, Anwar al-, 64, 84, 177, 180

Ayeri, Yusuf al-, 172, 173, 191

Ayro, Aden Hashi, 157

Azzam, Abdullah, 127–29

Baathist insurgents, collaboration of
Islamist insurgents and, 24

Bacon, Tricia, 8, 28–29, 33, 38–40, 98, 104,
162, 190

Baghdadi, Abu Bakr al-, 51, 164, 165, 216

Bahtiyti, Muhammad Raba al Sayid al,
204

Bakr, Haji (Samir al-Khlifawi), 165

Bakri Mohammed, Omar, 64, 236–39, 243,
249, 253, 259, 260

Bali bombings (2002), 35

Balsiger, Jörg, 46

Banjshiri, Abu Ubaidah al (Ali Amin
al-Rashidi), 128

Bank Al-Taqwa, 81

Banna, Hassan al-, 217

Barnard, Benno, 244

Barnett, Michael, 27

Bates, John D., 198–99

Battle of Jaji, 128

Battle of Yarmouk, 166

Bayazid, Loay, 135

Beghal, Djamel, 167

Behind Bars, 57, 251–52, 256, 260

Belgium, as jihadist hub, 242, 247–49

Beliakova, Polina, 53

Belkacem, Fouad (a.k.a. Abu Imran), 241,
243, 245, 249, 255, 260

benefits of cooperation. *See* reasons for
cooperation

Benevolence International Foundation
(BIF), 135

Benghazi embassy attack, 162, 185, 186

Benjamin, Daniel, 226

Benson, David, 79

Berger, Ronit, 53

Bergman, Ronen, 197

Bermuda Trading Company, 228

Bilal, Abu (Abd al-Rahim al-Nashiri), 172

Binalshibh, Ramzi, 231, 232, 327n48

bin Laden, Fatima, 207

bin Laden, Khalid, 207

bin Laden, Osama, 62; Abbottabad documents' portrayal of, 161–62, 178–79; abilities of, 137, 138; affiliation with al-Shabaab and, 156, 158; alliance with TTP and, 160; AQAP and, 171–73; AQAP-AQC alliance and, 178; AQAP leadership's obedience to, 180–81; AQAP's allegiance to, 177; Bojinka plot and, 228–29; Bosnia conflict and, 135; contacts with Shiite partners, 200; death of, 161; decision to collude with Iran and Hizballah, 199; Europlot and, 210; GIA ties with, 312n41; Ibn al-Khattab and, 135–36; infrastructure established in Afghanistan, 140; on Iran, 209–10; jihadists refusing to unite with, 141; KSM's pledge of allegiance to, 279n3; KSM's proposal of planes operation to, 229–30; leadership style of, 142, 230, 232; mistrust of Iran and, 219–20; Mughniyeh's meeting with, 198; Operation Hemorrhage plot and, 184; outsourcing by, 232; overtures to Zarqawi, 152–53; pre-Al Qaeda endeavors of (1984–1988), 127–28; relationship with AQAP leaders, 191–92; Riyadh bombings and, 173; war on United States declared by, 136–37; Wuhayshi's personal ties to, 191; Zarqawi and, 201

bin Laden, Saad, 203–6

Black September group, 37

Bojinka plot, 223–29

Boko Haram, 10–11, 19, 30, 87, 116, 163, 305n6

Bond, Kanisha, 9

Bosnia, 135–36

Braniff, Bill, 11

Brennan, John, 160

British Consulate attack, Turkey, 35

Brown, Vahid, 128, 129

Brussels Airport bombings, 242, 270, 276–77

Brussels Jewish Museum attack, 242, 248

Bush, George W., 203, 276

Byman, Daniel, 10, 108, 153, 215, 217

Cafarella, Jennifer, 167

caliphate, 129, 272

Call of Duty, 89

Carlos the Jackal, 34, 62, 275

Casablanca suicide bombing, 205

Castro, Fidel, 30

Cerantonio, Musa, 82

Charlie Hebdo attack, 167, 175, 181, 185, 187, 242

Chechnya, 135–36

Choudary, Anjem, 103; background of, 235–42; cooperation between Sharia4Belgium and, 235–45; facilitation of jihadists' movement by, 249–50; global Sharia4 movement and, 252–60; ideological and logistical role of, 259; as logistical hub, 260; on spreading his concept of Islam beyond Belgium, 253; vision of, 252–53

Chowdhury, Mohammed, 238

Christia, Fotini, 95–96

Christmas Bomb Plot, 238

Christmas Day plot, 186

CIA headquarters, planned suicide attack on, 227

CIA station attack, Khost, Afghanistan, 38

civil wars: defined, 94; environment for, 3; as opportunity for terrorist cooperation, 93–96; safe havens and, 29; tactical cooperation in, 112

Clan na Gael (CNG), 36

Clapper, James, 11–12, 53–54, 221

Clawson, Patrick, 211

Clinton, Bill, 297n29

cliques, in informal networks, 60

Coalitions Between Terrorist Organizations (Karmon), 21–22, 98

Combating Terrorism Center, West Point, 195, 208

communication: between ACQ and affiliates, 151; AQAP as AQC intermediary for, 185–86; increased ease and speed of, 48; in informal networks, 59; by IS, 168; proliferation of devices for, 76; protecting, 80; system-wide, 92–93; via Internet, 79 (*see also* Internet; social media)

Conlon, Ibrahim Siddiq, 260

Contreras, Rudolph, 200

Coulibaly, Amedi, 166–67

counterterrorism policy, 268–

Crenshaw, Martha, 4, 47, 50–51, 333n10

crime: AQIM involvement in, 156; networks' role in, 54–55

criminal groups/networks, 9; commonalities of terrorist groups and, 304n22; support structures of, 65; transactional relationships in, 114

Crusaders (Western, Christian nations), 72–74

Cyber Caliphate Army, 85

Dar-es-Salaam embassy bombing, 137

decision making: agency and, 47; centralization of, 232; in informal networks, 57

Degauque, Muriel, 241–42

Dessler, David, 69

Dib, Tofik, 244

Dohrn, Bernardine, 8

Droukdel, Abdelmalik (a.k.a. Abu Musab Abdul Wadud), 155, 156, 164, 182, 185

duration of cooperation: between Al Qaeda, Iran, and Hizballah, 212–13; between AQC and AQAP, 177; as factor in quality of relationship, 105; in high-end cooperation, 110, 177; in low-end cooperation, 110, 212–13

Earth Liberation Front, 27

economic jihad, 146

Edwards, Sean J. A., 79

Egyptian Islamic Group (EIG), 135, 140, 142, 197–99

Egyptian Islamic Jihad (EIJ), 4, 19, 35, 39, 108, 117, 135

Elman, Colin, 5, 6

Elouassaki, Houssien (a.k.a. Abu Fallujah), 250

"Encyclopedia of the Afghan Jihad," 133

English Defence League, 239

Entebbe, Uganda, plane hijacking, 19, 37

Europlot, 210

Europol terrorism report, 246, 255

Euskadi Ta Askatasuna (ETA), 25–26, 28, 34, 35

extra-normal violence, 47–48, 290n27, 290n28

Facebook, 86–87, 257

facilitators of cooperation, online, 77, 80–89; conventional forums, 83–85; unconventional forums, 85–89

Fadhli, Muhsin al-, 208–9

Fallujah, Abu (Houssien Elouassaki), 250

Farrall, Leah, 150

Fatah, 22, 25, 34, 37, 56, 115

Fatah al-Islam, 27

Fatah Revolutionary Council, terrorist entrepreneurs associated with, 62

Fearon, James, 94–95

Ferguson, Neil, 26

Fertilizer Bomb Plot, 238

Findley, Michael, 94

Firqat un-Naajiyah al-, 239

foreign fighters, 49, 85; Ask.fm use by, 92–93; attracted by conflict-ridden environments, 96; Facebook as sphere for, 86–87; moved through Iran, 210; number of, 330n107; Sharia4Belgium as facilitator of, 246–52; Western, to Syria and Iraq, 246–52

formal terrorist actors, 49–50. *See also* state sponsorship

Forsane Alizza, 257, 259

"For the Unity of West European Revolutionaries," 33–34

Fouda, Yousri, 79, 231

Free Aceh Movement (GAM), 35–36
funding: from Al Qaeda, 133, 135, 138, 142;
    for Bojinka plot, 228–29; logistical
    cooperation in, 35; for MAK, 127; moved
    through Iran, 210; for Nasr City Cell,
    185; for 9/11 attack, 230; platforms for, 81
fund raising, cooperation in, 24

Gamaa Islamiya, 108
gaming, online, 88–89
Gartenstein-Ross, Daveed, 168
German militants, 37, 247
Ghaith, Sulaiman Abu, 207
Ghamdi, Ahmed al-, 202
Ghayth, Sulayman abu, 204
Giddens, Anthony, 69–70
Global Islamic Resistance Call (Suri), 145–46
globalization, 48–49, 73, 75–76, 297–98n33
global jihad movement: affiliations in,
    124–26, 148–58; after Arab Spring,
    161–65; characteristics of, 123; hatred of
    Shiites in, 217; history of Al Qaeda and,
    124; independent cells/networks in, 126;
    independent supporters in, 126; internal
    strife within, 126–27; Iraq as focus of,
    149; post-Arab Spring, 164–65
Godane, Ahmed Abdi, 157
Goldblatt, David, 75–76
Golden Chain, 138
Granovetter, Mark, 65–66
Greenbelt Theater bombing, 225
guerrilla warfare, 51–52, 95

Habash, George, 62
Haddad, Wadie, 62
Hafez, Mohammed, 112
Ham, Carter, 163
Hamas, 25, 36, 53, 56, 81, 115
Hambali, 38
Hamdan, Osama, 28
Hamid, Mustafa (Abu al-Walid al-Masri),
    199–200, 204, 306n17

Hammami, Omar, 163
Hanjour, Hani, 327n48
Hansen, Stig, 157
Haqqani Network (HQN), 4, 38, 126, 132,
    138–39, 159
Harakat al-Mujahideen, 34
Harbi, Adel Radi Saqr al-Wahabi al-, 209
Harkat-ul-Jihad al-Islami (HUJI), 159
Haroun, Fadil (Fazul Muhammad
    Abdullah), 130, 157–58
Haudara (Ali Muhammad), 131, 197
Haykel, Bernard, 217
Hays, Sharon, 45–46
Hegghammer, Thomas, 83, 137, 139–40, 172
Hekmatyar, Gulbuddin, 203
Held, David, 75–76
high-end cooperation, 99, 170–94; with
    affiliates, 125; duration of cooperation
    and, 105; in holistic typology, 5;
    ideological affinity and, 106; interdepen-
    dence and, 106; subtypes of, 107, 110;
    trust level and, 106; variety of coopera-
    tive activities and, 106
hijackings, 19, 37
Hizballah: Al Qaeda training from, 25, 199;
    collaboration with ANO, 22; coopera-
    tion between Al Qaeda and, 27;
    cooperation between ETA and, 28; EIJ
    training with, 197; Houthi rebels trained
    by, 36; IRA collaboration with, 24;
    mergers resulting in, 108; PULO support
    for, 37; role in 9/11 attacks, 201–2;
    training provided by, 36; weaponry of, 53
Hizb-I Islami Gulbuddin, 159
Hizb ut-Tahrir (HT), 236
Hoffman, Bruce, 22, 52, 55, 76, 80, 142, 145,
    230
Hofstad Group, 60, 81
holistic typology, 5–7, 97–120; advantages of,
    263–68; benefits of, 99, 100; dynamic
    nature of, 116–18; extending, 275–76;
    identity of agents (stage 1) in, 99, 101–4;

incorporating state actors in, 275–76; qualitative strength of cooperative arrangements (stage 2) in, 99, 104–16
homegrown terrorists, 145
Horowitz, Michael, 25
Houthi rebels, 36
HSBC BANK attack, Istanbul, 35
Hussain, Ali Salah, 204
Hussein, Saddam, 131

Ibrahim, Munir, 228
identity: of agents (typology stage 1), 99, 101–4; within informal networks, 59–60; Internet in forging of, 77, 89–92; online, 86
ideological affinity: between Al Qaeda, Iran, and Hizballah, 215–19; between AQC and AQAP, 187–90; disrupting, 274; in high-end cooperation, 110, 187–90; in intergroup cooperation, 26; in low-end cooperation, 110, 215–19; quality of relationships and, 105, 106; trust reinforced by, 190
ideological alignment, 3, 26–27, 126, 217–19
ideological cooperation, 33–34; between Al Qaeda, Iran, and Hizballah, 214–15; between AQC and AQAP, 183–85; disrupting, 274; ease of information/idea exchange and, 65; in high-end cooperation case study, 183–85; in mergers, 108; in Sharia4movement, 258–59; in strategic alliances, 109; transactional cooperation vs., 116; in transactional relationships, 113
Imran, Abu (Fouad Belkacem), 241, 243, 245, 249, 255, 260
In Amenas gas facility attack, 162
informal actors, 42–44, 49; in holistic typology, 5; international presence of, 65; Internet and emergence of, 77; in networked cooperation, 97 (see also networked cooperation); terrorist cooperation and, 64–65; transnational

cooperation by, 65. See also informal networks; terrorist entrepreneurs
informal arrangements, 8
informal networks, 1–2, 54–61; Anjem Choudary and Sharia4Belgium case study, 235–45; cooperation between formal terrorist and/or insurgent organizations and, 246–52; cooperation between Sharia4Belgium, IS, and JN, 246–52; cooperation between terrorist entrepreneurs and, 235–45; decentralization of, 61; empowerment of, 48, 79; global Sharia4 movement case study, 252–60; in holistic typology, 5, 102; jihadist, 57; membership and organizational boundaries of, 59–60; in networked cooperation, 97 (see also networked cooperation); non-terrorist activities of, 57, 60; state cooperation with, 275; structure of, 57–59; in terrorist cooperation, 64–66
information exchange, 24, 48, 65, 80.
Inspire, 176, 177, 184, 187–88, 221
insurgencies: Al Qaeda's involvement in, 134; by AQAP, 175; by AQC affiliates/associates, 162; costs of ignoring, 273; defined, 94; environment for, 3; as opportunity for terrorist cooperation, 93–96
insurgent organizations, 53.
insurgents, 95
International Centre for the Study of Radicalisation (ICSR), 82
International Islamic Relief Organization (IIRO), 228–29
Internet, 75–93; as both medium and opportunity, 70; capacity for terrorist cooperation and, 77–80; constraining exploitation of, 272–73; conventional forums on, 83–85; dependency on, 258; as force multiplier, 64, 77; global Sharia4 movement and, 254; online facilitators/

Internet (*continued*)
platforms of cooperation, 80–89;
opportunities created by, 301n97; role of,
32, 43; unconventional forums on, 85–89;
virtual community of believers fostered
by, 89–91
Iran: advanced explosives training from,
209; Al Qaeda members' shelter in or
transit through, 202–3, 206; detention of
Al Qaeda members in, 205–8, 218; as
facilitation hub, 206, 208; jihadists
deported by, 321n35; move of Pakistani
jihadists to, 203; 9/11 attacks and, 201–2,
320–21n28; Taliban relations with, 200;
weapons/explosives supplied by, 199;
Zawahiri's secret visit to, 197
Iranian Revolutionary Guards Corps
(IRGC), 196, 218
Iraq, 112–13, 204, 215–16, 246–52
Iraqi, Abu Hajer al-, 199
Iraq War (2003), 149
Irish Republican Army (IRA), 24–26, 34–35
Irish Republican Brotherhood (IRB), 36
Islam, jihadi ideology and, 73, 74
Islambouli, Khalid, 197
Islamic Army in Iraq (IAI), 112
Islamic Army Shura, 134
Islamic Courts Union (ICU), 157
Islamic Dawah Association, 240
Islamic Emergency Defence, 241
Islamic Jihad Union (IJU), 159, 310n18
Islamic Movement of Uzbekistan (IMU), 132
Islamic Resistance Movement-1920
Revolution Brigades, 112–13
Islamic Revolution in Iran, 197
Islamic State (IS): affiliates of, 117, 125;
alliances of, 168; Belgian fighters in, 248,
249, 251; Boko Haram as affiliate of, 116,
305n6; communications by, 168;
competition between Al Qaeda and, 22,
117, 126, 166–69; cooperation between
Sharia4Belgium, JN, and, 103, 246–52;

cooperative arrangements of, 9–10;
formal affiliation with, 124–25; as formal
organization, 51; gaming used by, 89;
history/development of, 104; JN
cooperation with, 4, 9–10; leadership of
global jihad movement and, 123; media
use by, 11; members of, 59; Sanaa attacks
on mosques and, 181–82; Shia hatred by,
216; Twitter use by, 87; Western foreign
fighters joining, 247
Islamic State in Iraq (ISI), 10–11, 117, 153,
163, 164
Islamic State in Iraq and Greater Syria
(ISIS), 27, 117, 164–66
Islam4UK, 240, 253, 255, 259
Israel Defense Forces (IDF), 25
Israeli embassy bombing attempt,
Bangkok, 37

Jabhat al-Nusra (JN): alliance with AQC,
111, 164; as Al Qaeda affiliate, 125;
Belgian fighters with, 249, 250;
cooperation between Sharia4Belgium,
IS, and, 103, 246–52; founding of, 58; IS
cooperation with, 4, 9–10, 166–67; ISI
founding of, 163; in Jaysh al-Fatah, 96;
origins of, 164; Twitter use by, 87–88;
Western foreign fighters joining, 247
Jabhat Fath al-Sham (JFS), 167–68, 279n4.
See also Jabhat al-Nusra (JN)
Jamaat al-Tawheed, 253, 255, 258, 260
Jamaat al-Tawhid w'al Jihad, 18, 152–53
Jamaat Ansar al-Muslimin fi Bilad
al-Sudan, 163
Jamal, Abd al-Razzaq al-, 192
Japanese Red Army (JRA), 19, 23, 35, 37
Jarrah, Ziad, 231
Jaysh al-Fatah, 96, 166
Jaysh al-Islam, 219
Jaysh al-Sunna, 96
Jemaah Islamiyah (JI), 29, 32, 35–38, 115, 228
Jibril, Ahmad Musa, 82

jihad: classical and global models of, 149; as divinely ordained, 74; economic, 146; enemies of, 73–74; individual, 145–46; leaderless, 55; legitimate zones of, 128 (*see also* global jihad movement); meaning of, 72

jihadi ideology: appeal of, 72; as basis of identity, 60; as cause of terrorist cooperation, 71–75; Internet as force multiplier for, 64; promoted through Internet, 70; as recent dominant force, 72–75

jihadist preachers, 49, 81, 82

John Paul II, Pope, 225, 226

Johnsen, Gregory, 174, 191

Jones, Seth, 205

Joscelyn, Thomas, 183

Joulani, Abu Muhammad al-, 164–65

Juhani, Khalid al-, 172

Jund al-Aqsa, 96

Kahler, Miles, 54

Kaldet til Islam, 253, 256–57

Karim, Abdul Basit Mahmoud Abdul. *See* Youssef, Ramzi

Karmon, Ely, 21–22, 26, 33–40, 98, 287n96

Kasaesbeh, Mouath al-, 290n28

Kashef, Muhammad Jamal al-, 185

Kashmir suicide bombing, 238

Kasmi, Nabil, 249

Katzenstein, Peter, 77

Kenney, Michael, 304n22

Kenya embassy attack, 19, 198–99

Khalifa, Muhammed Jamal, 228, 229, 234

Khalifawi, Samir al- (Haji Bakr), 165

Khalil, Ezedin Abdel Azia (a.k.a. Yasin al-Suri), 208–10

Khalis, Younis, 138

Khamenei, Ayatollah, 211

Khan, Muhammad Siddique, 238

Khan, Samir, 84

Khatib, Lina, 168

Khattab, Ibn al-, 135–36

Khawar, Abdallah Ghanim Mafuz Muslim al, 323n72

Kherchtou, L'Houssaine, 319n2

Khorasan Group, 208

Khyam, Omar, 238

Klausen, Jytte, 80, 252, 254, 255, 259

Klein, Hans-Joachim, 19

Konsojaya, 228

Kouachi, Chérif, 167, 175

Kouachi, Saïd, 167, 175

Krekar, Mullah, 29, 311n23

Kurdish Liberation Army of the Workers and Peasants of Turkey (TIKKO), 32

Kurdistan Workers Party (PKK), 30, 32, 34

Kuwari, Salim Hasan Khalifa Rashid al, 323n72

Lahoud, Nelly, 131

Laitin, David, 94–95

Lashkar-e Jhangvi (LeJ), 22, 159

Lashkar-e Taibeh (LET), 35

"leaderless jihad," 55

learning: access to knowledge, 25; for adoption of innovations, 25; cooperation for, 24; as sign of agency, 47

Levitt, Matt, 55, 81, 108

Lewis, Jeffrey William, 36

Liberation Tigers of Tamil Eelam (LTTE), 34, 59

Libi, Abu Layth al-, 309n89

Libi, Abu Yahya al-, 189, 309n89

Libi, Ibn al-Shaykh al-, 141

Libya, 10, 136, 166

Libyan Islamic Fighting Group (LIFG), 133, 136

Lion's Den of Supporters, 58, 104, 128

Lister, Charles, 164–65

Lod Airport Massacre, 23

logistical cooperation, 34–36; between Al Qaeda, Iran, and Hizballah, 214; between AQC and AQAP, 185–86; in

logistical cooperation (*continued*)
high-end cooperation case study, 185–86;
in mergers, 108; in strategic alliances,
109; in transactional relationships, 113–15
London bombings (July 7, 2005), 145, 238
London School of Sharia, 241
low-end cooperation, 5, 99; by Al Qaeda,
137; duration of cooperation, 105; in
holistic typology, 5; ideological affinity
and, 106; interdependence and, 106;
subtypes of, 107, 110; trust level and, 106;
variety of cooperative activities and, 106
Lufthansa airliner hijacking, 19

Maalbeek metro station bombing, 242, 270,
276–77
McCants, Will, 181, 192
McGrew, Anthony, 75–76
Madrid train bombings, 60, 145
Majlis Shura al-Mujahideen (MSM), 249,
250
Majlis Shura al-Mujahideen al-Sharqiya,
331n120
Makanesi, Rami, 206
Maktab al-Khidamat (MAK), 127
Manila Air Plot. *See* Bojinka plot
Manji, Irshad, 244
Mapping Militant Organizations project,
333n10
Mari, Abu Hamza al-, 259
Marriott Hotel attacks, Jakarta, 35
Masri, Abu al-Khayr al-, 204
Masri, Abu al-Walid al- (Mustafa Hamid),
199–200, 204, 306n17
Masri, Abu Hafs al- (Mohammed Atef),
128, 134, 231–33
Masri, Abu Khabab al-, 141
Masri, Abu Muhammad al-, 204, 207
Massoud, Ahmed Shah, 241
Matthiesen, Toby, 216
Mauritani, Abu Hafs al-, 204, 207
Mauritani, Shaykh Yunis al-, 180

Mazari-Sharif siege, 308n68
Mendelsohn, Barak, 2, 158
Merah, Mohammed, 256
mercenary forces, 49
mergers, 4, 107–8, 110, 174, 274, 312n50.
See also high-end cooperation
Meziche, Maamen, 206
Michael, George, 77
Millatu Ibrahim, 257
Millennium Plot, 142
Ministry of Intelligence and Security
(MOIS, Iran), 196, 210, 218
mission command, 232
Moayad, Mohammed Ali Hasan al-, 81
Mogadishu occupation, 146, 157
Mohammad Jamal Network, 186
Mohammed, Ali, 199
Mohammed, Amein, 228
Mohammed, Khaled Sheikh (KSM), 38,
63–64, 79; Bojinka plot case study,
223–29; collaboration with Al Qaeda,
103; cooperation with Ramzi Youssef,
102–3; martyrdom videos shot by,
327n40; as 9/11 planner, 1–2; on operative
passing through Iran, 202; Daniel Pearl
beheading, 224, 295n99; "planes
operation" and, 142, 229–30; pledge of
allegiance to bin Laden, 279n3;
September 11, 2001 attacks, 229–34
Mombasa attacks, 158
Moreng, Bridget, 168
Moroccan Islamist Combatant Group
(GICM), 60, 145, 241
Moro Islamic Liberation Front (MILF), 29,
35, 133, 136
Movement for Oneness and Jihad in Africa
(MUJAO), 30
Mubarak, Hosni, 197
Mughniyeh, Imad, 197, 198
Muhammad, Ali (a.k.a. Haidara), 131, 197
Muhammad bin Nayef, Prince, 175
Muhammadi, Umid, 323n72

Mujahedeen al-Khalq, 205

Mujahideen Shura Council (MSC), 112, 331n120

Mujahidun on the Arabian Peninsula (MAP), 172

Mulhall, Joe, 237, 254, 257

Munich Olympics massacre, 37

Murad, Abdul Hakim, 226–28

Muritani, Younis al-, 210

Muslim Brotherhood, 217

Muslim Prisoners, 241

Muslims Against Crusades (MAC), 240, 255

Muslim Youth Center, 87

Nabahan, Sallah Ali, 157–58

Nairobi embassy bombing, 137, 198–99

Nashiri, Abd al-Rahim al- (a.k.a. Abu Bilal), 172

Nasr City Cell, 185, 186

National Organization of Cypriot Fighters (EOKA), 31–32

Need4Khilafah, 240

Nemmouche, Mehdi, 242, 248

Nesser, Petter, 96, 294n94

networked cooperation, 43–44, 222–60, 262; coexistence of organizational cooperation and, 97–98; defined, 97; in holistic typology, 5; importance of, 119; recent increase in, 97; "swarming" and, 66; trends accounting for rise of, 43–44; types of, 101–2

networks, 54–56; as agents, 56; as both agent and structure, 292n62; boundaries between organizations and, 56; defined, 55; informal (see informal networks); jihadist, 2, 57, 61, 271; of networks, 55, 56, 235; roles of, 55; Salafist (see Salafist networks); terrorist, 57

Neumann, Peter, 247

New York City car bombing, 160

New York City subway bombing, 145

Nidal, Abu, 62

Nikbakht, Nour Ahmad, 208

Northwest Airlines Flight 253 attack, 175

Nuri, Abdullah, 200

Okamoto, Kozo, 23

Ollivant, Douglas, 52–53

Omar, Mullah, 138, 160

Omar, Omar abu, 228–29

O'Neill, Kate, 46

operational cooperation, 36–38; between AQC and AQAP, 186–87; defined, 36, 287n96; in high-end cooperation case study, 186–87; in mergers, 108; by Sharia4 networks, 260; in strategic alliances, 109

Operation Hemorrhage, 184

Operation Protective Edge, 28

Oplan Bojinka. See Bojinka plot

Oreg, Aviv, 156, 158

organizational cooperation, 5, 97–98

outcome goals, 21, 26–29

Pakistan, 30, 202

Palestine Liberation Organization (PLO), 24, 115

Palestinian Islamic Jihad (PIJ), 25, 36

Pantucci, Raffaello, 246

Paris attacks, 166, 167, 175, 242, 248, 277

Patani United Liberation Organization (PULO), 37

Pearl, Daniel, 224, 295n99

Pedahzur, Ami, 56, 60

People's Liberation Army of Turkey (THKO), 32

Perliger, Arie, 56, 60

Perraton, Jonathan, 75–76

Petraeus, David, 206

Philippine Airlines Flight 434 bombing, 226

Phillips, Brian, 23

platforms of cooperation, online, 80–89

Pollack, Kenneth, 205, 217

Popular Front for the Liberation of Palestine (PFLP): El Al plane attack, 36–37; geographic proximity to THKO, 32; JRA assistance from, 37; Lod Airport Massacre, 23; logistical cooperation by, 34; RB-PLO cooperation and, 115; terrorist entrepreneurs associated with, 62; training of Turkish youth by, 36; transnational cooperation by, 22

Popular Front for the Liberation of Palestine–External Organization (PFLP-EO), 19, 39, 62

principal-agent problems, 18, 151

prisons, common experiences formed in, 31–32

privatization: of security, 49; of terrorism, 43–44

process goals, 20–26

Profetens Ummah, 253–54, 256, 257

Provisional Irish Republican Army (PIRA), 31–32

psychological aspects of cooperation, 22–23

Qaddhafi, Muammar, 30

Qaedat al-Jihad, 4, 108, 140

quality of relationships, 5, 6, 38–40; with affiliates, 125; duration of cooperation and, 105; ideological affinity and, 106 (*see also* ideological affinity); interdependence and, 105 (*see also* degree of interdependence); trust level between parties and, 105, 106 (*see also* trust); variety of cooperative activities and, 106. *See also* high-end cooperation; low-end cooperation

Quds Force, 203

Quetta Shura Taliban, 159

Qunaitra border passage, Syria, 88

Qutb, Sayyid, 217

radicalization: online facilitators of, 82; through Internet, 64; via chat rooms, 85

Rahman, Abu abd al- (Anas al-Subayie), 203, 205, 321n35

Rahman, Attiyah Abd al-, 179, 180, 207, 208, 219, 220

Rashidi, Ali Amin al- (a.k.a. Abu Ubaidah al Banjshiri), 128

Raymi, Qasim bin Mahdi al-, 173, 174, 182, 184, 191

reasons for cooperation, 20–29; "influence and succeed" (support of outcome goals), 26–29; "survive and thrive" (support of process goals), 21–26

Red Army Faction (Rote Armee Fraktion; RAF), 19, 22, 33–34, 111

Red Brigades (RB), 26–27, 115

Reid, Richard, 238

Reinares, Fernando, 145

Ressam, Ahmed, 142

Rethemeyer, R. Karl, 25

Revolutionäre Zellen (RZ), 19

Revolutionary Armed Forces of Colombia (FARC), 24, 34–35

Revolutionary People's Liberation Party/ Front (DHKP/C), 30

Revolutionary United Front (RUF), 59

Riedel, Bruce, 31

Rigby, Lee, 238

Riyadh compound bombing, 172, 173, 204

Robow, Mukhtar, 157

Roex, Ineke, 258

Ronfeldt, David, 66

Rubaysh, Ibrahim al-, 192

Sadat, Anwar, 197

safe havens, 12; for AQC from HQN, 159; for bin Laden in Afghanistan, 138; for Carlos the Jackal, 275; as facilitating factor, 29–30; in Iran, 202–3, 206, 209–10; as logistical cooperation, 35; set up by states, 30–31; in Sudan, 199

Sageman, Marc, 34, 55, 81, 92

Salafimedia.com, 254

Salafist Group for Call and Combat (GSPC), 19, 39, 154–56

Salafist networks, 2, 57–58, 235, 271

Salah al-Malahim e-magazine, 176

Sanaa, Yemen, 173, 174, 181, 182, 216

Saudi Arabia, Al Qaeda in, 172–73

Sauerland bombers, 310n18

Sayf al-Islam al-Misri, 135

Scales, Robert, 52–53

Scheuer, Michael, 148

Schmid, Alex, 51–52

Schweitzer, Yoram, 156, 158

Second Life, 88–89

September 11, 2001 attacks, 137; Al Qaeda's changes following, 144–48; AQAP's praise of, 184; case study of planning for, 229–34; cell participating in, 74–75; Iran's and Hizballah's role in, 201–2; low-end cooperation case study, 201–2; as networked cooperation, 103; planners of, 1–2; as transformative, 48

Shah, Wali Khan Amin, 225–26, 228

Shahzad, Faizal, 160

Shapiro, Jacob, 17, 18

Sharia4Australia, 255, 258

Sharia4Bangladesh, 254

Sharia4Belgium, 103, 235–52, 258

Sharia courts, 157

Sharia4Finland, 257

Sharia4France, 259

Sharia4Hind, 257

Sharia4Holland, 256, 258

Sharia4Indonesia, 258

Sharia4Italy, 257, 258

Sharia4 movement, 252–60

Sharia4 networks (generally), 60, 103, 235, 246, 271

Sharia4Pakistan, 257

Sharia Project, 240

Sharia4Spain, 246

Sharia4USA, 255, 260

Shehhi, Marwan al-, 231

Shibh, Ramzi bin-al-, 79, 202

Shihri, Muhammad al-, 172

Shihri, Said al-, 186, 188, 191–92

Shiri, Said Ali al-, 174

Shumukh al-Islam, Al-, 83–84

Siddiqui, Ahmad Wali, 206

Simon, Steven, 226

Singapore, planned attacks in, 37–38

social media, 85–88; constraining exploitation of, 272–73; dependency on, 258; expanding terrorists' reach through, 80; Facebook, 86–87, 257; as force multiplier, 64, 86; jihadis' employment of, 72; perceived presence on, 86; Sharia4 use of, 259, 260; terrorist cooperation facilitated by, 3; Twitter, 87–88, 252

Somalia, 134–36, 141, 146, 156–58

Soviet Union, 30, 127

state actors: agent-structure model applied to, 45–48; incorporated into holistic typology, 275–76; role of, 8–9; state cooperation with, 275

state sponsorship: as facilitating factor, 30–31; harboring of terrorists and, 35

Stevens, Christopher, 186

Straatdawah, 253

strategic alliances, 3, 107, 109–11, 274, 312n50. *See also* high-end cooperation

strategic cooperation, tactical cooperation vs., 112, 113

Street Dawah (network), 57–58, 251–52, 256

"street dawah," 240, 244

"strength of weak ties," 65–66

structuration theory, 288n8

structure, 69–71; agent-structure model, 44–48; of Al Qaeda, 129–30, 141–42, 147–48; defining, 69–70; dynamic nature of, 68; of global jihad movement, 164–65; of informal networks, 57–59; motivational/ideational aspects and, 69, 70; as rules and resources, 69, 70

Subayie, Anas al- (a.k.a. Abu abd al-Rahman), 203, 205, 321n35

Sudan, 31, 132–36, 199, 275

Sudanese National Islamic Front, 199

Suhail, Abu, 221

suicide attacks, 8; adopting innovation of, 25; by Al Qaeda, 148; by Al Qaeda affiliates, 150; joint operations, 38; planned, on CIA headquarters, 227

Sunni-Shia conflict, 215–17

Suri, Abu Musab al-, 141, 145–46

Suri, Yasin al- (Ezedin Abdel Azia Khalil), 208–10

"survive and thrive" (support of process goals), 20–26

swarming, 66

Syria: civil war in, 96, 112, 273; facilitating Western foreign fighters to, 246–52; JN/ JFS in, 167–68; Joulani in, 164–65; safe haven offered by, 31; Shiite coalition in, 215

tactical cooperation, 5, 107, 110–13, 219, 274

Tajik Nahda Party, 132

takfir, 31

Taliban: in Afghanistan, 138; alliance with Al Qaeda, 138–39, 159, 160; Al Qaeda's partnership with, 200; HQN cooperation with, 159; Iran's relations with, 200; lethality of, 10–11; siege of Mazari-Sharif, 308n68; Twitter use by, 87

Tanweer, Shehzad, 238

Tanzania embassy attack, 19, 198–99

Tarrow, Sidney, 73

Taub, Ben, 243

Tawhid w'al Jihad al-, 141, 149–50

technologies, 12; associated with globalization, 76; as facilitating factor, 32; jihadis' employment of, 73; miniaturization of, 76; to protect communication, 80. See also Internet; social media

Tehrik-e Taliban Pakistan (TTP), 10–11, 38, 147, 159, 160

terrorist cooperation, 17–41; accounting for qualitative strength of, 38–40; Al Qaeda and, 4; collaboration as form of, 2–3;

contemporary forms of, 3–4; defined, 8; disrupting, 273–74; environmental factors enabling, 12; existing typologies of, 33–41; facilitating factors for, 29–32; "high-end" vs. "low-end," 4; holistic typology of, 5–7; how groups cooperate, 33–38; impact of globalization on, 76; implications of diversity of terrorist actors for, 64–66; importance of, 9–12; informal networks and, 2–3; junior and senior partners in, 18–19; networked cooperation as, 4; 9/11 attack and, 1–2; organizational cooperation vs., 4; reasons for, 20–29; risks of, 17–19; shortcoming of work on, 40; tradeoff in, 17. See also specific topics

terrorist entrepreneurs, 2, 61–64, 294n94; Anjem Choudary and Sharia4Belgium case study, 235–45; Bojinka plot case study, 223–29; characteristics of, 63; cooperation between, 223–29; cooperation between informal networks and, 235–45; cooperation between terrorist organizations and, 229–34; defined, 63; empowered by Internet, 77–79; in holistic typology, 5, 102; in networked cooperation, 97 (see also networked cooperation); 9/11 attacks planning case study, 229–34; state cooperation with, 275; in terrorist cooperation, 64–66

Toronto, attack attempt in, 210

training: by Al Qaeda, 139; by Choudary, 243; for EIJ, 199; for EIJ by Iranians, 197; for FARC, 24; forms of, 35–36; by Hizballah, 25; by HQN, 159; by IRA, 24; from Iran, 197, 209; logistical cooperation in, 35–36; for 9/11 attack, 232–33; 9/11 Commission Report on, 198; PLO's charge for, 24; for Taliban, 138; of Youssef, 326n6

training camps: of Al Qaeda, 130–34, 139–40; differences among, 140; Lion's Den of Supporters, 128; of MSM, 250;

near Iran border, 201; as platform for cooperation, 80–81

transactional collaborations, 5, 107, 110–16, 274, 304n20

trust: between Al Qaeda, Iran, and Hizballah, 219–21; between AQC and AQAP, 190–92; between governments and local Muslim communities, 271; in high-end cooperation, 110, 190–92; in low-end cooperation, 110, 219–21; quality of relationship and, 105, 106; reinforcing, 190–91

Tupamaros, 8

Turabi, Hassan al-, 31, 199

Turkish insurgents, PFLP training for, 36

Twitter, 87–88, 252

typologies of terrorist cooperation: by Bacon, 38–40; existing, 33–41, 98; holistic, 5–7, 98–100 (see also holistic typology); ideological cooperation, 33–34; by Karmon, 33–38; logistical cooperation, 34–36; operational cooperation, 36–38

Ulster Volunteer Force (UVF), 25–26

Ultima Online, 88–89

umma, 72, 73, 91, 92, 188

"Underwear Bomber," 175, 186

United Nations, as AQIM target, 155

United States: AQAP's Operation Hemorrhage against, 184; AQAP targets in, 175; bin Laden's economic jihad plan for, 146; bin Laden's focus on, 178–79; competitive anti-Americanism, 220–21; counterterrorism campaign of, 161; as enemy of GSPC, 154; on transfer of Al Qaeda leaders from Iran, 204–5

U.S. commercial airliners, plot against. See Bojinka plot

U.S. embassy attack, Malaysia, 35

Uqba ibn Nafi Brigade, 163

USS Cole attack, 137, 172, 200

VanDeveer, Stacy, 46

van Gogh, Theo, 60

van Ostaeyen, Pieter, 241, 248

Van Vlierden, Guy, 245, 248

vehicle-borne improvised explosive devices (VBIEDs), 148

Verviers, Belgium, terrorist cell in, 248

Vidino, Lorenzo, 75, 246, 250, 254, 256

Viet Cong, 8

violence, 25–26, 47–48, 290n27, 290n28

Wadie Haddad Faction, 19

Wadud, Abu Musab Abdul (Abdelmalik Droukdel), 155, 156, 164, 182, 185

Walid, Abu al-, 135

Watts, Clint, 185

Weather Underground, 8

Weinrich, Johannes, 36–37

Wendt, Alexander, 44–45, 70

Westgate Mall attack, Nairobi, Kenya, 87, 162

Wight, Colin, 45, 70

Wiktorowicz, Quintan, 239

Wilayat al-Jazira al-Arabiyya, 236

Wilders, Geert, 244

Williams, Phil, 20, 55–56, 65, 109, 110, 114, 304n20

"World Islamic Front against the Crusaders and the Jews," 34, 142

World of Warcraft, 88–89

World Trade Center bombing (1993), 64, 223–25

Wuhayshi, Nasir al- (a.k.a. Abu Basir), 116; advice to Droukdel, 182, 185; in AQAP's first message, 188; as AQC's general manager, 176, 183, 185, 193; attacks in Sanaa and, 181; communications with Zawahiri, 186; correspondence with bin Laden, 178; death of, 184; on his successor, 180; personal ties to bin Laden, 191; prison escape by, 173; rebuilding of Al Qaeda Yemen network by, 173–74; tribute to Zawahiri, 184

Yemen, 179–80, 189–90, 200–201, 216

Young, Joseph, 94

Youssef, Ramzi (Abdul Basit Mahmoud Abdul Karim), 64, 102–3, 223–29, 326n6

YouTube, 254–55, 257, 259

Zakiri, Hamid, 320n26

Zanini, Michele, 79

Zarqawi, Abu Musal al-, 18, 29, 104, 141, 152–53, 201, 215–16, 218

Zawahiri, Ayman al-, 18, 83–84; affiliation with al-Shabaab, 156, 158; al-Ansi's allegiance to, 181, 182; on Al Qaeda captives in Iran, 218; Al Qaeda influenced by, 131; Al Qaeda-Iran link of, 199; al-Shabaab's pledge of allegiance and, 124; appeal to other activists by, 146–47; AQAP-AQC alliance and, 178; communi-cations with Wuhayshi, 186; consolidation of AQC-AQAP ties, 176; correspondence with Kashef, 185; electronic communica-tion by, 3; formation of ISIS and, 164–65; integration of AQC/AQAP personnel and, 182–83; integration of GSPC into Al Qaeda network and, 155, 156; on Iran-Al Qaeda collaboration, 211; lack of attack on Iran by Al Qaeda and, 214–15; leadership qualities of, 161; on the media, 310n13; praise of AQAP from, 184–85; promotion of Wuhayshi by, 183, 185, 193; Raymi's allegiance to, 184; secret visit to Iran, 197; Wuhayshi's tribute to, 184; on Yemen-based Al Qaeda, 174

Zionists, 72, 73–74

Zubaydah, Abu, 35, 141

Zubayr, Mukhtar Ali, 157

CPSIA information can be obtained
at www.ICGtesting.com
Printed in the USA
LVHW030010300719
625772LV00004B/4